Discover Thailand

Contents

Throu... highlig...

Don't Miss
A must-see – don't go home until you've ...

Local Knowledge
Local experts' top picks ...

Detour
Special places ...

If you like...
Lesser-known altern... world-famous attractions

...se icons ...p you ...ckly identify ...iews in the ...t and on ... map:

Sights

Eating

Drinking

Sleeping

Information

This edition written and researched by

China Williams,
Mark Beales, Tim Bewer, Celeste Brash,
Austin Bush, Alan Murphy, Brandon Presser

Chiang Mai

- Th Nimmanhaemin
- Temples
- Outdoor Activities
- Meditation & Retreats
- Doi Suthep
- Shopping
- Thai Cooking Courses

Chiang Rai & Northern Thailand

- Chiang Rai Province
- Pai
- Sukhothai
- Northern Thailand
- Mae Hong Son
- Small Town Thailand
- Golden Triangle

Bangkok

- Culinary Bangkok
- Chao Phraya River
- Ko Ratanakosin
- Thai Cooking Courses
- Spas & Massages
- Shopping
- Rooftop Bars

Bangkok Getaways

- Ayuthaya
- Khao Yai National Park
- Khmer Ruins
- Kanchanaburi
- Ko Samet
- Ko Chang
- Ko Kut

Ko Samui & the Gulf Coast

- Ko Samui
- Hua Hin
- Ko Pha-Ngan
- Diving Ko Tao
- Khao Sam Roi Yot
- Phetchaburi
- Ang Thong Marine National Park

Contents

Plan Your Trip

On the Road

Contents

On the Road

In Focus

Survival Guide

This Is Thailand

Thailand is blessed: it has the looks, the temperament and the personality to entice the world to its shores. It is exotic and mysterious yet approachable and inviting.

The tranquil southern coast massages away modern worries. The waters are clear, the diving is spectacular and the pace is reminiscent of an afternoon nap. Like the country as a whole, Thailand's famous islands and beaches specialise in having fun, from late-night beach parties to casual beachside dining. Clustered along the Andaman Coast are dramatic limestone mountains looking like prehistoric monuments.

Beyond the beach scene, Thailand's culture trail educates and enlightens visitors with intense displays of religious devotion and tangible fragments of historic eras. The hyperactive city of Bangkok, the centre of the Thai universe and the seat of religion and monarchy, boasts flamboyant and revered temples. Further north, the ancient capitals of Ayuthaya and Sukhothai are peppered with gravity-ravaged monuments and Buddha figures meditating serenely.

Northern Thailand crowns the country with lush mountains, historic cities and border intrigue. The gateway to the region, Chiang Mai has a well-preserved old city and university atmosphere. In higher altitudes, minority hill tribes preserve a cultural identity that defies modern borders. The interplay of border cultures and the daily alms route of orange-robed monks compel visitors to trundle through Chiang Rai and Mae Hong Son Provinces and absorb the landscape along switchback mountain roads.

In every corner of the kingdom, Thais concoct a flavourful feast from simple ingredients. Travelling from region to region becomes an edible buffet, sampling fresh coconut curries in southern Thailand, steamy bowls of noodles in Bangkok and hearty stews in Chiang Mai.

> “In every corner of the kingdom, Thais concoct a flavourful feast”

Buddhist monks, Wat Pho (p69), Bangkok

RICHARD I'ANSON/LONELY PLANET IMAGES ©

Thailand
MYANMAR (BURMA)
LAOS
VIETNAM
CAMBODIA
HANOI
VIENTIANE
YANGON (RANGOON)
BANGKOK
Gulf of Tonkin
Gulf of Martaban
Mekong River
Mae Sai
Chiang Saen
Chiang Khong
Tha Ton
Fang
Chiang Rai
Luang Prabang
Huay Kon
Pai
Mae Hong Son
Doi Inthanon (2565m)
Doi Inthanon National Park
Chiang Mai
Lamphun
Lampang
Nan
Vang Vieng
Mae Sariang
Kheuan Sirikit
Chiang Khan
Beung Kan
Nong Khai
Si Chiangmai
Den Chai
Kheuan Phumiphon
Utaradit
Loei
Nakhon Phanom
Tha Khaek
Sakhon Nakhon
Udon Thani
Phu Kradung National Park
Kheuan Ubon Ratana
Kheuan Lam Pao
Phu Phan National Park
Sukhothai
Tak
Phitsanulok
Lom Sak
Nam Nao National Park
Savannakhet
Myawadi
Lang San National Park
Mawlamyaing
Phichit
Phetchaburi
Khon Kaen
Kalasin
Mukdahan
Kamphaeng Phet
Kheuan Chulabhol
Roi Et
Nakhon Sawan
Amnat Charoen
Three Pagodas Pass
Kheuan Mae Wong
Chaiyaphum
Yasothon
Pha Taem National Park
Nakhon Ratchasima (Khorat)
Ubon Ratchathani
Si Saket
Mae Nam Chao Phraya
Chainat
Phimai
Buriram
Warin Chamrap
Chong Mek
Pakse
Sangkhlaburi
Si Nakharin Reservoir
Khao Laem Reservoir
Surin
Ang Thong
Saraburi
Khao Yai National Park
Prasat Phanom Rung
Suphanburi
Ayuthaya
Tavoy
Prachinburi
Kanchanaburi
Aranya Prathet
Angkor Wat
Ratchaburi
Chachoengsao
Chonburi
Tonlé Sap
Phetchaburi
Kaeng Krachan National Park
Cha-am
Sattahip
Rayong
Chanthaburi
Hua Hin
Ko Samet
Ko Chang
Trat
18° N
16° N
14° N
12° N
1
2
3
8
9
12
13
14
15
16
17
18
19

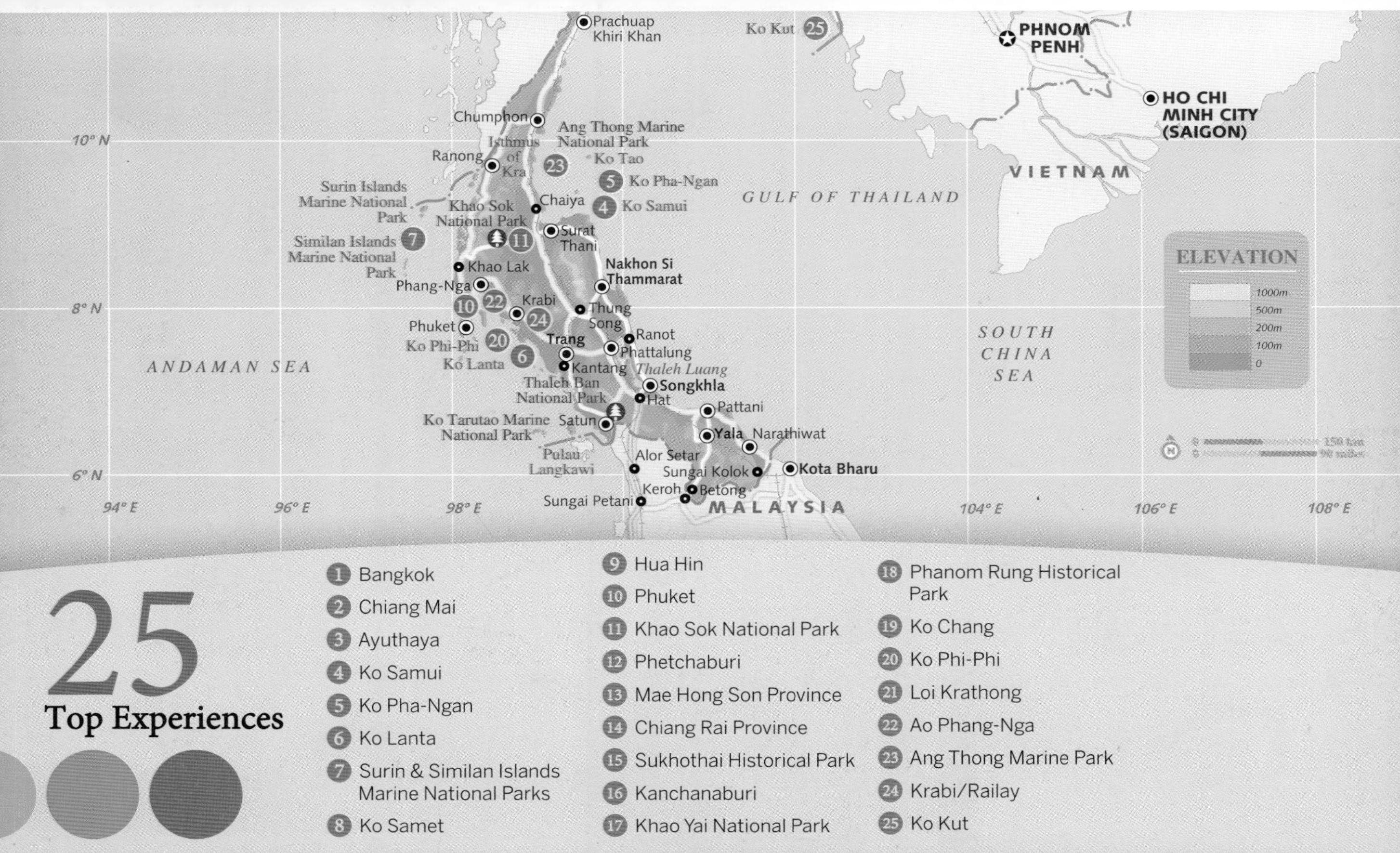

25 Top Experiences

1. Bangkok
2. Chiang Mai
3. Ayuthaya
4. Ko Samui
5. Ko Pha-Ngan
6. Ko Lanta
7. Surin & Similan Islands Marine National Parks
8. Ko Samet
9. Hua Hin
10. Phuket
11. Khao Sok National Park
12. Phetchaburi
13. Mae Hong Son Province
14. Chiang Rai Province
15. Sukhothai Historical Park
16. Kanchanaburi
17. Khao Yai National Park
18. Phanom Rung Historical Park
19. Ko Chang
20. Ko Phi-Phi
21. Loi Krathong
22. Ao Phang-Nga
23. Ang Thong Marine Park
24. Krabi/Railay
25. Ko Kut

25 Thailand's Top Experiences

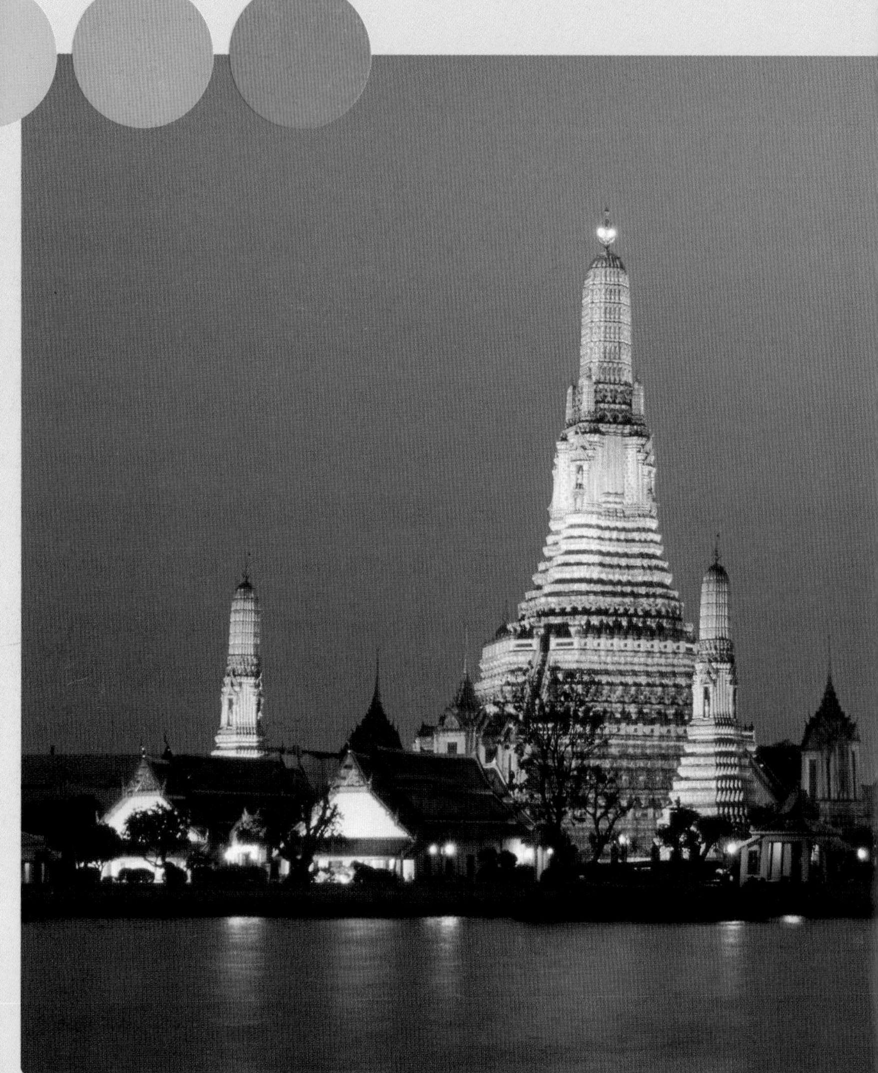

Bangkok

Food, shopping, fun, temples, palaces... What isn't available in Bangkok (p51)? Be prepared to adjust your itinerary if you've only given Bangkok the requisite day or two. The Bangkok of today is tidier and easier to navigate than ever before, and will pull you in with Chatuchak Weekend Market (p87), one of the world's biggest markets, happening bars, sublime eats and endless opportunities for urban exploration. Supplement your fun with more scholarly pursuits, such as a cooking or Thai massage course, and we're certain you'll see Bangkok as much more than just a transit point. Wat Arun (p65), Chao Phraya River

1

PAOLO CORDELLI/LONELY PLANET IMAGES ©

2

Chiang Mai

Chiang Mai (p131) looks respectfully up to mighty Doi Suthep. The old city, framed by a moat, is crammed with soaring temple peaks and quiet, twisting sois (lanes) best explored by bicycle. Stop for a temple 'monk chat', an intimate insight into those orange-robed figures you're always dodging on the streets. Browse the traditional handicrafts and, when the sun sinks over Doi Suthep, feast on some of the north's best Burmese cuisine. Wat Chiang Man (p147)

Ayuthaya

A once vibrant, glittering capital packed with hundreds of temples, today Ayuthaya (p104) only hints at its erstwhile glory. Cycle around the brick-and-stucco ruins, which form part of a Unesco World Heritage Site, and try to imagine how the city must have looked in its prime, when it greeted merchants from around the globe. On the outskirts of the city sit several more attractions, including an enormous handicraft centre, the most eclectic royal palace you'll ever see and a water theatre. Wat Chai Wattanaram (p107)

3

The Best... Beaches

KO PHA-NGAN
Master the art of hammock-hanging (p259).

KO SAMUI
Devote yourself to sandy beaches, seaside yoga and loads of people-watching (p250).

KO SAMET
Ditch the chaotic capital for a beach-island fling (p116).

PHUKET
Bulls-eye for high-energy international resort (p290).

HUA HIN
Mainland surf-and-turf destination for beach frolicking and Thai town surveying (p244).

KO PHI-PHI
Behold the prettiest tropical island you've ever seen (p311).

The Best... Diving & Snorkelling

SURIN & SIMILAN ISLANDS MARINE NATIONAL PARKS
Snorkel and dive the acclaimed reefs of these two marine preserves (p290 & p288).

KO TAO
Get dive certified on this reef-fringed island (p264).

KO LANTA
Fish big and small flock to Lanta's coral (p314).

KO CHANG
Coral-encrusted seamounts attract turtles and schools of fish (p121).

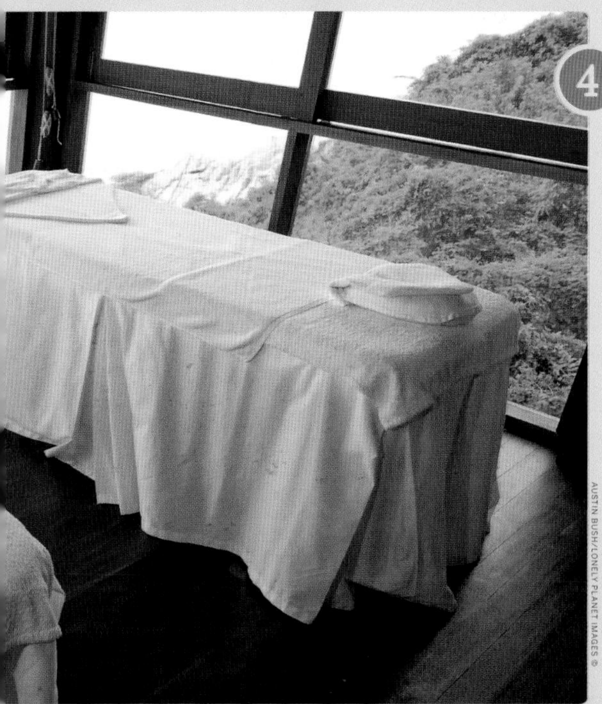

AUSTIN BUSH/LONELY PLANET IMAGES ©

4 Ko Samui

Eager to please, Ko Samui (p250) is a civilised beach-resort island for the vacationing masses, many of whom fly in and out having made hardly any contact with the local culture. Chaweng is a luxurious stretch of sand where sun-worshippers come to see and be seen; however, there are still sleepy spits reminiscent of Samui's old moniker, 'Coconut Island', and a few gentle coves for families. Samui also boasts great amenities and a thriving health scene with yoga, massage, detoxing and other yins to the island's partying yang.

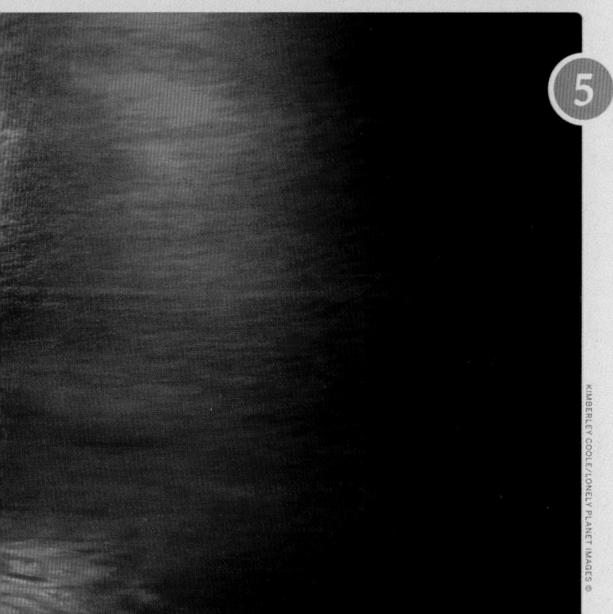

KIMBERLEY COOLE/LONELY PLANET IMAGES ©

5 Ko Pha-Ngan

Famous for its sloppy Full Moon parties, Ko Pha-Ngan (p259) has graduated from a sleepy bohemian island to a full-on attraction for migrating party-people. The beach shanties have been transformed into boutiques, meaning comfort seekers have an alternative to Ko Samui. And, on the northern and eastern coasts, the ascetic hammock-hangers can still escape enough of the modern life to feel like castaways. Just offshore is Sail Rock, one of the gulf's best dive sites.

Ko Lanta

6

Ko Lanta (p314) sports a mellow island vibe and a parade of peachy sand. Social butterflies alight on the northern beaches for a same-same but different party scene. Solitude seekers migrate southward to low-key beach huts and a sleepy village ambiance. Activities abound, from hiking through a landscape of limestone caves and crevices to diving in underwater hang-outs for sharks and rays. Hat Nui

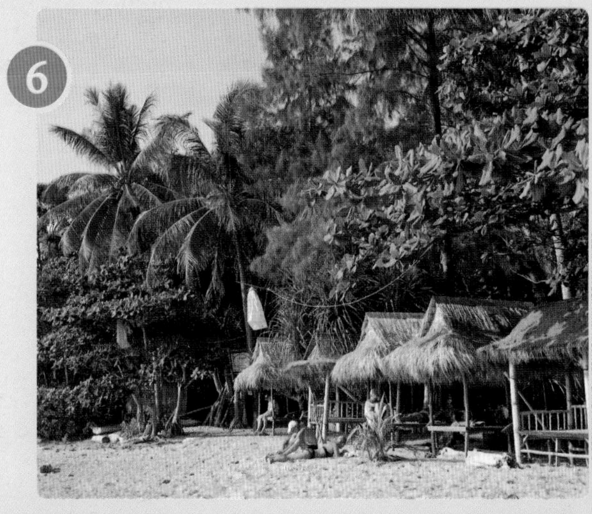

7

Surin & Similan Islands Marine National Parks

These world-renowned dive sites (p287 & p288) have anchored Thailand as a global diving destination. Live-aboard trips set out from Khao Lak, allowing for more time at the famous sites where you can meet the local manta rays and whale sharks. And there is the thrill of being far from land as the sun sinks into the sea and the night shows off its twinkling lights. The islands are an attraction in their own right, with jungle-filled interiors and smooth white beaches surrounded by decent coral reefs. School of fish, Similan Islands Marine National Park

Ko Samet

So close to Bangkok and, oh, so pretty, Ko Samet (p116) is a perfect beach when you are pinched for time. The jungle eclipses developments, the sand and sea are tropically proportioned and a wooded coastal trail skirts between rocky headlands and a string of beautiful coves. People-watch by day and party by night on the popular northern beaches or hideaway on the southern beaches for a well-earned nap. When your vacation is done, board the boat and be back in Bangkok by lunchtime.

8

The Best... Karst Scenery

RAILAY, KRABI PROVINCE
Defy gravity with a rock-climbing scramble up a limestone peak (p307).

AO PHANG-NGA
Paddle through a karst canyon into echo-chamber caves (p288).

ANG THONG
Discover this deep-ocean collection of limestone islands (p267).

KO PHI-PHI
Snorkel the underwater anchors of the Andaman's resident rock towers (p311).

Hua Hin

The king's choice, Hua Hin (p244) is a fine fit for city and sea creatures. The beaches are long and wide, the market meals are fantastic and there's even Thai culture (fancy meeting you here). Explore the quiet beaches south of the city for a more secluded feel, hike to the top of a headland shrine or master the sea and the wind with a kiteboard lesson. And, of course, feast like a Thai from morning to night.

The Best... Historic Sites

SUKHOTHAI
A meditative journey through an early Thai kingdom (p205).

AYUTHAYA
Tumbledown temples of a golden ancient capital (p104).

PHIMAI
The closest Khmer ruin to Bangkok for history buffs short on time (p125).

PHANOM RUNG
An ornate sanctuary of Khmer art (p116).

PHETCHABURI
A royal retreat crowned with a hilltop palace (p242).

9

GETIDEAKAW/DREAMSTIME ©

AUSTIN BUSH/LONELY PLANET IMAGES ©

10 Phuket

An international-strength beach resort, Phuket (p290) is an easy-peasy destination for all ages. You can fly in from Bangkok, cutting out the long land journey, and retreat into a five-star resort or arty boutique hotel for a trouble-free tropical vacation. There are slinky stretches of sand, hedonistic party pits and all the mod cons needed for 21st-century rest and recreation. Plus there are day trips to mangrove forests, monkey-rescue centres and a tonne of watersports, from diving to surfing (when the weather is right).

11 Khao Sok National Park

A deep, dark jungle hugs the midsection of southern Thailand. This ancient rainforest (p284) is filled with long sweaty hiking routes up dramatic limestone formations that offer postcard views. Just remember to wear leechproof gear to prevent an involuntary blood donation. Birds and bats call this forest home as does the rare *Rafflesia kerrii,* one of the stinkiest flowers on the planet. Reward your outdoor work with riverside camping and listen to the symphony of the jungle.

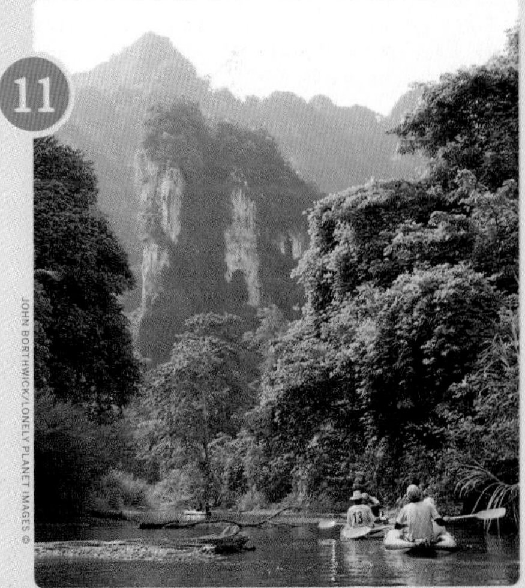

JOHN BORTHWICK/LONELY PLANET IMAGES ©

CHRIS MELLOR/LONELY PLANET IMAGES ©

12 Phetchaburi

A delightful mix of culture and nature combine in this provincial capital (p242), a close and quiet alternative to the hectic streets of Bangkok. Explore an antique hilltop palace, sacred cave shrines and bustling temples, then wander the old shophouse neighbourhood filled with do-it-yourself businesses run by Thai aunties and grannies. Buddha statues, Tham Khao Luang (p242)

VIVIANE PONTI/LONELY PLANET IMAGES ©

13 Mae Hong Son Province

Tucked in the country's northwest corner, this province (p216) has a lot in common with neighbouring Myanmar (Burma). In fact, with its remote location, mountains and unique culture and cuisine, Mae Hong Son can seem like an entirely different country. Exploration here can take the form of tramping through one of the province's many caves or doing a self-guided walk from Mae La-Na to Soppong. Prayers during Poy Sang Long, Mae Hong Son

Chiang Rai Province

The days of the Golden Triangle opium trade are over, but Chiang Rai (p190) still packs intrigue in the form of fresh-air fun such as trekking and self-guided exploration. It's also a great destination for a unique cultural experience, ranging from a visit to an Akha village to a stay at the Yunnanese-Chinese hamlet of Mae Salong. From the Mekong River to the mountains, Chiang Rai is arguably Thailand's most beautiful province and also functions as a convenient gateway to Myanmar (Burma), Laos and China. Wat Rong Khun (p196)

14

The Best... Temples

BANGKOK
Glittering temples protect the faith and attract the faithful (p64).

CHIANG MAI
Teak temples fill the atmospheric old quarter and a hilltop temple marks the guardian mountain (p144).

LAMPANG
Mini–Chiang Mai built by lumber barons, best visited by horse-drawn carriage (p187).

PHITSANULOK
Revered bronze Buddha conveniently located along the culture trail (p202).

The Best... Shopping

BANGKOK
From markets to malls, you can practically shop anywhere (p86).

CHIANG MAI
Handicraft centre specialising in homespun and chic (p165).

LAMPANG
Weekend bazaar monopolises historic shophouse district (p188).

CHIANG RAI
Night markets and weekend bazaar peddle hill-tribe and northern crafts (p195).

15

Sukhothai Historical Park

Step back in time approximately 800 years at Thailand's most impressive historical park (p206). Exploring the ruins by bicycle is the classic Thailand experience and is a leisurely way to wind through the park's crumbling temples, graceful Buddha statues and fish-filled ponds. Worthwhile museums and good-value accommodation round out the package. Despite its popularity, Sukhothai rarely feels crowded, but for something off the beaten track you could always head to nearby Si Satchanalai-Chaliang Historical Park (p212), where you might be the only one scaling an ancient stairway.

16 Kanchanaburi

Walks on the wild side are the main reason to visit Kanchanaburi (p110), where dragon-scaled limestone mountains gaze down upon dense jungle. Trek past silvery waterfalls and rushing rivers in search of elusive tigers and gibbons, then spend the night at a homestay organised through an ethnic group. Once you've explored this western province's war-time past – the infamous Death Railway Bridge (p111) is here – hold on tight to experience adventure activities, which include ziplining, kayaking and elephant rides. Death Railway Bridge

17 Khao Yai National Park

Here you'll find elephants, monkeys, gibbons, hornbills, pythons, bears, a million bats and a few wily tigers. Wildlife sightings, of course, are at the mercy of chance, but your odds are excellent at this vast Unesco World Heritage–listed reserve (p126) just a few hours outside Bangkok. And even if you don't meet many big animals, the orchids, birds and waterfalls guarantee a good day.

Phanom Rung Historical Park

Perched high atop an extinct volcano, the biggest and best Khmer ruin in Thailand (p128) is something special. As you amble along the promenade, up the stairs and over the *naga*-flanked bridges, the sense of anticipation builds. And when you enter the temple, completely restored and still rich with Hindu sculpture, you will experience a moment of timelessness. While Phanom Rung is not as awe-inspiring as Cambodia's Angkor Wat, the experience here is impressive and different enough that you should visit both. Phanom Rung temple

18

The Best... Jungle Trekking

KHAO YAI NATIONAL PARK
Monkeys, elephants, wilderness – just around the corner from Bangkok (p126).

KHAO SOK NATIONAL PARK
Trek and paddle through this southern tropical rainforest (p284).

KANCHANABURI
Elephant-riding, river-rafting and waterfall-spotting close to Bangkok (p110).

CHIANG RAI PROVINCE
Visit high-altitude hill-tribe villages for physical exertion and cultural immersion (p190).

MAE HONG SON PROVINCE
A remote, mountainous corner overlooking Myanmar (Burma; p216).

KO CHANG
Reward a sweaty hike with a sea view (p120).

Ko Chang

19

Steep mountains rise with military presence out of the blue seas of Thailand's far-eastern territorial waters. This jungle-clad island (p119) has a bustling resort atmosphere with plenty of party places, belying its distance from civilisation. It is an athletic island with a variety of adventure sports: diving, snorkelling, hiking and kayaking. In the evenings the tide recedes and the narrow beaches become wide swaths of rippled sand dotted with elegant spiral-shelled molluscs. The west coast is very busy but the east coast is barely developed. Lonely Beach (p120)

The Best... Thai Food

BANGKOK
A culinary superstar with noodles, haute cuisine and immigrant fare (p78).

CHIANG MAI
Learn how to chop and wok through a Thai menu (p153).

HUA HIN
Combine two great Thai specialities – seafood and night markets – into one (p246).

PHUKET
Sample southern fare, seafood and fusion (p295).

GLENN VAN DER KNIJFF/LONELY PLANET IMAGES ©

20 Ko Phi-Phi

Quite possibly the prettiest island in all of Thailand, Ko Phi-Phi (p311) has a gorgeous hourglass shape, blonde-sand beaches, scenic limestone cliffs and jewel-toned waters. A carless and carefree island where the parties go on all night and the sound systems serenade the stars, it is the island equivalent of a popular party girl. Its sister island Ko Phi-Phi Leh (p315) is an uninhabited park where snorkelling tours explore offshore coral reefs and interior lagoons. *The Beach* (2000), starring Leonardo DiCaprio, was filmed here. Ko Phi-Phi Leh seen from Long Beach

Loi Krathong Festival

21

Loi Krathong (p44) honours the goddess of the waters with floating offerings usually made of banana leaves folded into a circular shape and decorated with flowers and candles. Merit-makers gather at local waterways to set sail their illuminated boats on the full moon of the 12th lunar month (usually November). Sukhothai, Ayuthaya, Bangkok and Chiang Mai festivities have the most appeal for visitors. Buddhist monk holding a lantern, Loi Krathong, Chiang Mai

22

Ao Phang-Nga Marine National Park

An easy day trip from Phuket, Ao Phang-Nga (p288) is a scenic bay filled with karst islands and surrounded by mangrove forests. Everyone comes here on a boat tour – either long-tail or kayak – stopping at the islands and wandering around indentations in the craggy, weather-worn exterior. For a more serene communion with these peaks, head to Ko Yao (p289), a small fishing community with a front-row view of the bay.

Ang Thong Marine National Park

Accessible on a boat tour from Ko Samui, this collection of limestone mountain islands (p267) appears on the distant horizon like a lost city. Peach-coloured sand rings the hump-backed peaks and interior lagoons glow with an otherworldly blue. Kayaking, snorkelling and hiking tours on various islands give you a close-up of the pockmarked formations inhabited by barnacles and other tidal creatures. Development is limited to basic park infrastructure, preserving the wild and remote ambiance.

23

The Best... Elephant Encounters

CHIANG MAI
Sanctuaries provide refuge for overworked elephants (p152).

LAMPANG
Learn about the mahout tradition at an elephant education centre (p187).

AYUTHAYA
Visit the temple ruins like the kings of yore, astride a regally clad elephant (p104).

KANCHANABURI
Get a canopy view of the forest on an elephant ride (p110).

Railay, Krabi Province

You'd never know that you were still on the mainland when you wade from a long-tail boat to the shore of this limestone-studded peninsula (p307). Towering karst peaks hem in on all sides, creating the illusion of a sandy fortress. Rock climbers have transformed the onshore sea cliffs into vertical challenges, scrambling high enough for a view of the karst-filled bay. Kayakers and snorkellers take to the sea to explore low-tide caves and peak at the marine life sheltered by these gigantic anchor islands.

The Best... Scenic Journeys

MAE SA VALLEY
Climb from coconut palms to fir trees on this mountain loop from Chiang Mai (p169).

MAE HONG SON
Cascading mountain vistas are the reward of dizzying switchback roads (p216).

BANGKOK CANALS
Take a long-tail boat through the 'Venice of the East' (p88).

MAE SALONG
Ride up the ridge to this mountain-top village (p196).

24

25

Ko Kut

Bangkok Thais, visiting families and middle-aged couples move beyond busy Ko Chang to this semideveloped island (p124) for seclusion and scenery. There's no shopping, dining or nightlife, which suits everyone just fine. This island excels in layabout living: wake up, wander the beach, snack on tropical fruits, swim, nap under a coconut tree and wait for sunset. Active types scoot between the west coast beaches on a motorcycle, hike the jungle tracks to waterfalls and kayak through the mangroves filled with birdsong and insect symphonies.

Thailand's Top Itineraries

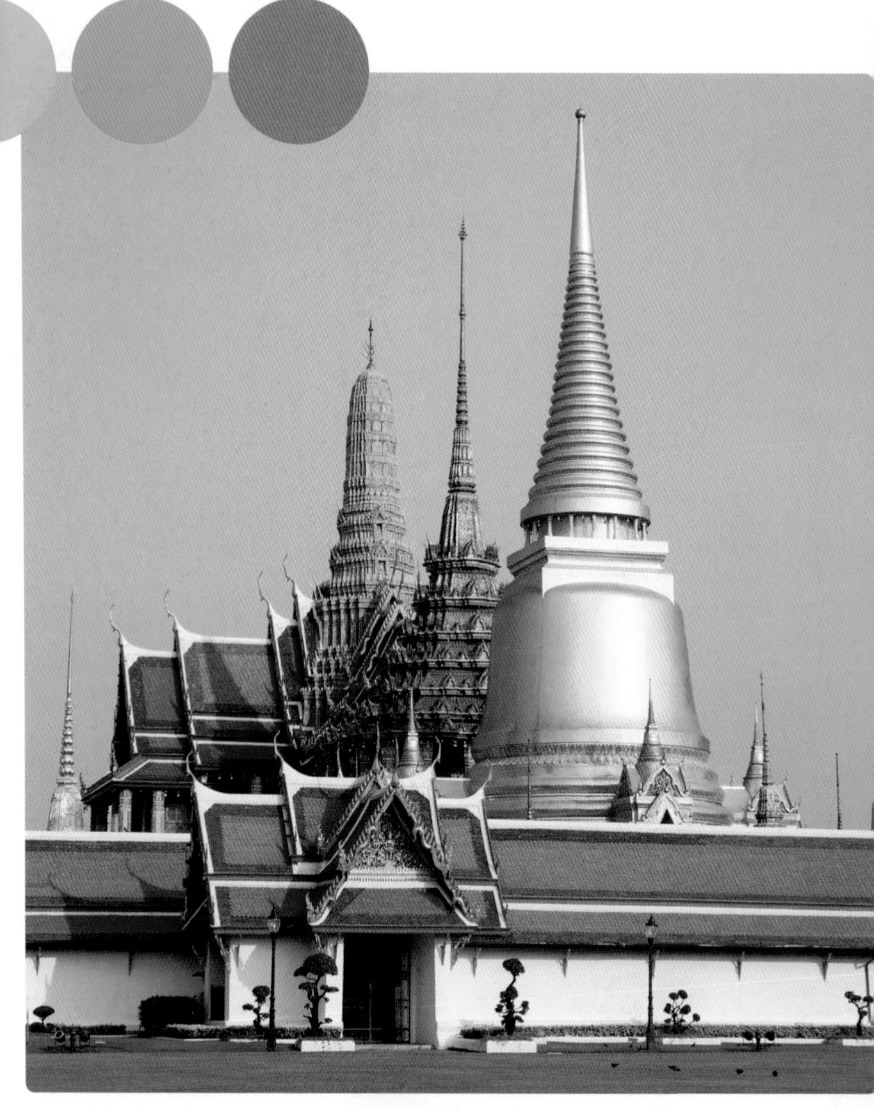

Bangkok to Chiang Mai Jet-Setters' Game Plan

5 DAYS

Thailand makes an easy 'pop-in' for anyone passing through the eastern half of the globe. Touch down in Bangkok, day-trip to Ayuthaya and jet to Chiang Mai.

1 Bangkok (p64)

Introduce yourself to one of Asia's most dynamic capital cities with a two-day crash course. Be dazzled by **Wat Phra Kaew**, get lost in the cluttered but peaceful temple grounds of **Wat Pho**, ride the **Chao Phraya Express** and drink to the stars from a **rooftop bar**. The next day, shop till you drop for *chotchke* at **MBK Center**, contemporary Asian decor at **Siam Center & Siam Discovery Center** and uberluxe treasures at **Siam Paragon**, then admire pretty stuff at **Jim Thompson House**. Stay out late at the rollicking **bars** and grab a noodle nightcap at **Soi 38 Night Market**.

BANGKOK ➜ AYUTHAYA

🚌 **1½ hours** by minibus from Bangkok's Victory Monument. 🚆 **Two hours** from Bangkok's Hualamphong station.

2 Ayuthaya (p104)

Balance out conspicuous consumption with culture in the ancient capital of **Ayuthaya**, an easy day trip from Bangkok. Hire a bicycle, an elephant taxi or a knowledgeable guide for a tour of the Unesco World Heritage–listed ruins, built when this powerful city-state was a stop on the Asian trade-winds route. Fill your camera with pictures and then take a bus back to Bangkok to beat rush hour.

BANGKOK ➜ CHIANG MAI

✈ **One hour** from Bangkok's Don Muang and Suvarnabhumi airports.

3 Chiang Mai (p131)

Fly to the laid-back university town of **Chiang Mai**. Explore the old quarter, filled with the distinctive temple architecture of northern Thailand. Slurp down a bowl of *kôw soy*, the north's signature noodle dish, and hang out at **Riverside Bar & Restaurant**. The next day, make a morning pilgrimage to the cool environs of **Doi Suthep** and its sacred hillside temple. If you're here on a weekend, visit the **Saturday Walking Street** or the **Sunday Walking Street**. To return home, save yourself a Bangkok backtrack by booking a direct flight onward from Chiang Mai.

Wat Phra Kaew (p74), Bangkok

Phuket to Ao Phang-Nga Beach Routine

Replace your work routine with a beach routine: wake up late, hang out at the beach, sup on seafood and sip sundowners. Then do minitrips to exotic landscapes and sleepy fishing islands to add a little adventure to your lazy beach days.

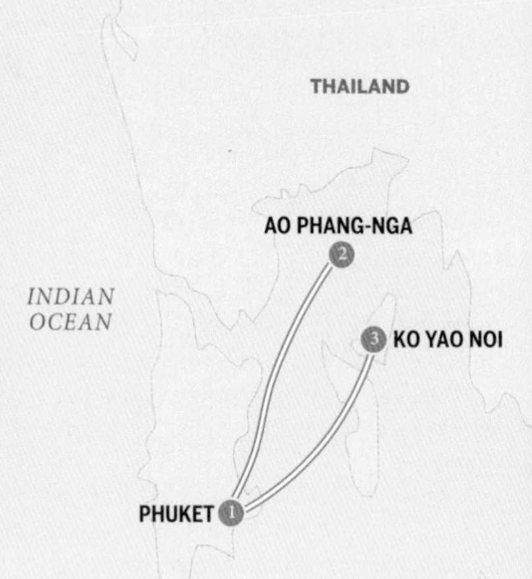

1 Phuket (p290)

Easily accessible from the mainland, Bangkok and even some international destinations, **Phuket** specialises in quick, comfortable beach retreats. Park yourself on the beaches of **Kata**, **Kamala** or **Surin** – three scenic bays with stylish resort hotels and international-style amenities. Soak up the sun and frolic in the sea for a few days and then devote an afternoon to exploring **Phuket Town**, reminiscent of Penang or other British colonial outposts, filled with grand but crumbling Sino-Portuguese architecture, bohemian cafes, flamboyant Chinese shrines and ancient apothecaries. In the evenings, sample **fusion fare** in a romantic setting, cruise the seedy party strip of **Patong** or find a down-home restaurant where the stir-fries are quick and tasty. When you tire of the beaches, there is a host of other entertainment: cooking classes, kiteboarding, spas and even animal attractions, such as **Phuket Aquarium** and **Phuket Gibbon Rehabilitation Centre**.

PHUKET → KO YAO NOI

20 minutes from Phuket's Tha Bano Rong.

2 Ko Yao Noi (p289)

Day-trip over to the Muslim fishing island of **Ko Yao Noi**, which garners a front-row view of **Ao Phang-Nga**, a turquoise bay cluttered with humpbacked karst mountains. The island feels a million miles away from the hustle and bustle of Phuket, without a tailor's shop in sight, and offers a cultural exploration of the Andaman's small-scale fishing communities. Bicycling, kayaking, rock-climbing and snorkelling tours can be arranged from Phuket or on the island to give those atrophied vacation muscles an overdue workout. Or you could just hire a motorbike and putter around. There's no traffic and the family-run guest houses have open-air restaurants for sitting and chatting.

PHUKET → AO PHANG-NGA

Two hours from Phuket to Phang-Nga Town.

Three hours long-tail or kayak tour.

3 Ao Phang-Nga (p288)

The other-worldly bay of **Ao Phang-Nga Marine National Park** is cradled between the mainland and the northeastern coast of Phuket. Limestone mountains stand stoically amid the water, having been eroded into Gaudi-like sculptures over millennia. Semi-submerged caves create rooms where bats slumber through daylight hours. Thick tangles of mangroves line the bay, criss-crossed by navigable canals. It is an exploration into a thriving natural landscape with stunning scenery to match. Parts of the bay are protected as a national park; crowds can be thick. Opt for an early-morning or late-evening tour to increase your likelihood of animal sightings instead of human sightings.

Ao Phang-Nga Marine National Park (p288)

10 DAYS

Ko Samui to Railay
Going Bi-Coastal

Soak up the sun and the tropical scenery by surveying the beaches and islands of Thailand's famed coasts. Flights from Bangkok to Ko Samui shorten the journey and minibuses burn rubber across the peninsula for travellers skipping between coasts.

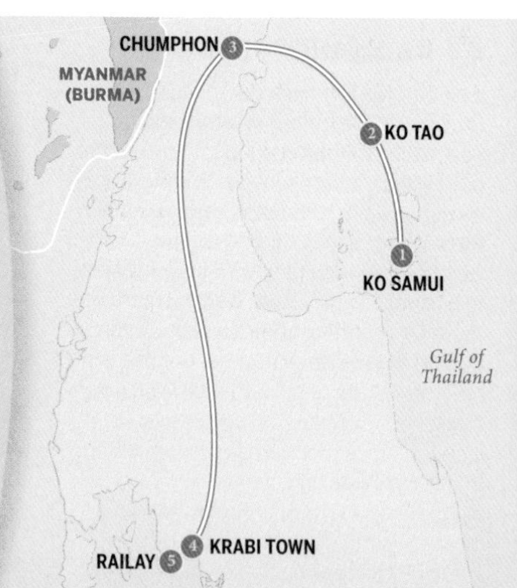

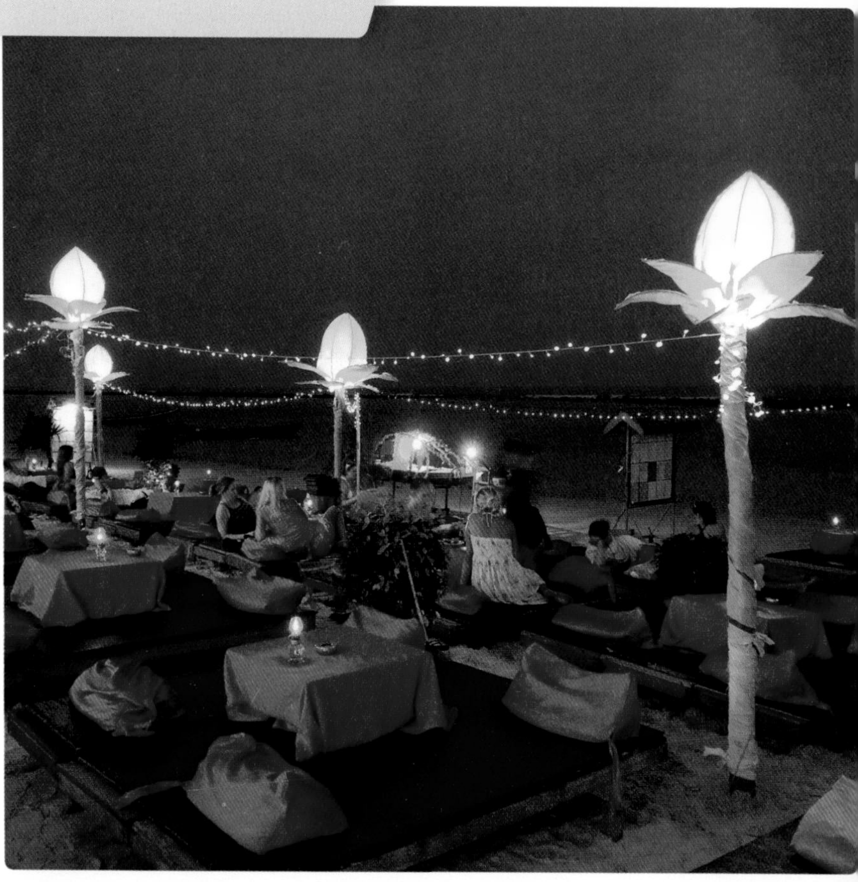

1 Ko Samui (p250)

Arrive in **Ko Samui** by air and make a beeline for **Chaweng**, Samui's stunning stretch of sand. Explore the quieter northern beaches, or snorkel and kayak around **Ang Thong Marine National Park**. Stressed-out professionals flock to Samui for a dose of health and wellness in addition to the usual beach treats of rest and recreation. Hire a motorcycle and cruise the southern part of the island past coconut groves and a few napping dogs.

KO SAMUI ➔ KO TAO

One to 2½ hours from Ko Samui's Na Thon, Mae Nam or Big Buddha piers.

2 Ko Tao (p264)

Once you've been tenderised on Ko Samui, head to **Ko Tao** for underwater-scouting missions. This little island competes with Thailand's more stunning beaches because of its many near-shore coral gardens and dive sites. Strap on your snorkelling gear and do an island swimming tour with the fish, or dive to greater depths to explore underwater landscapes.

KO TAO ➔ CHUMPHON

1½ to two hours from Ko Tao.

3 Chumphon (p249)

A ho-hum southern town, **Chumphon** is the mainland way-station for beach-bound transport, mainly to Ko Tao. Ferries trundle between Chumphon and the gulf islands, while buses and minivans vacuum up the sun-soaked faces bound for the opposite coast. You can get a minivan to just about anywhere; talk to the travel agents in town. Further south, **Surat Thani** is an alternative mainland jumping-off point and closer to Ko Samui.

CHUMPHON ➔ KRABI TOWN

Five to six hours by minibus from Chumphon.

4 Krabi Town (p307)

Krabi Town is a transit link for travellers sliding through to the offshore islands and beaches of the Andaman. Your long cross-peninsula journey will soon be rewarded with the Andaman's signature scenery, which is even prettier than the pretty gulf coast. While you're on the mainland, treat yourself to a night-market meal, a classic Thai experience.

KRABI TOWN ➔ RAILAY

45 minutes from Krabi's Khong Kha pier.

5 Railay (p309)

Stunning karst mountains jutting out of jewel-coloured seas define **Railay's** pinched bit of sand, known for its looks and its athletic abilities. Rock climbers scramble up the bearded limestone towers to survey the sea and the horizon. There are also sweaty jungle hikes, sea kayaking and cave exploring.

Ark Bar (p258), Ko Samui

Sukhothai to Mae Hong Son
Temples & Mountain Vistas

Follow the culture trail from the ancient capital of Sukhothai to the Lanna headquarters of Chiang Mai, then detour to Mae Hong Son Province, a close cousin to Burma. Travel on these mountain roads is slow, so plan on staying a while.

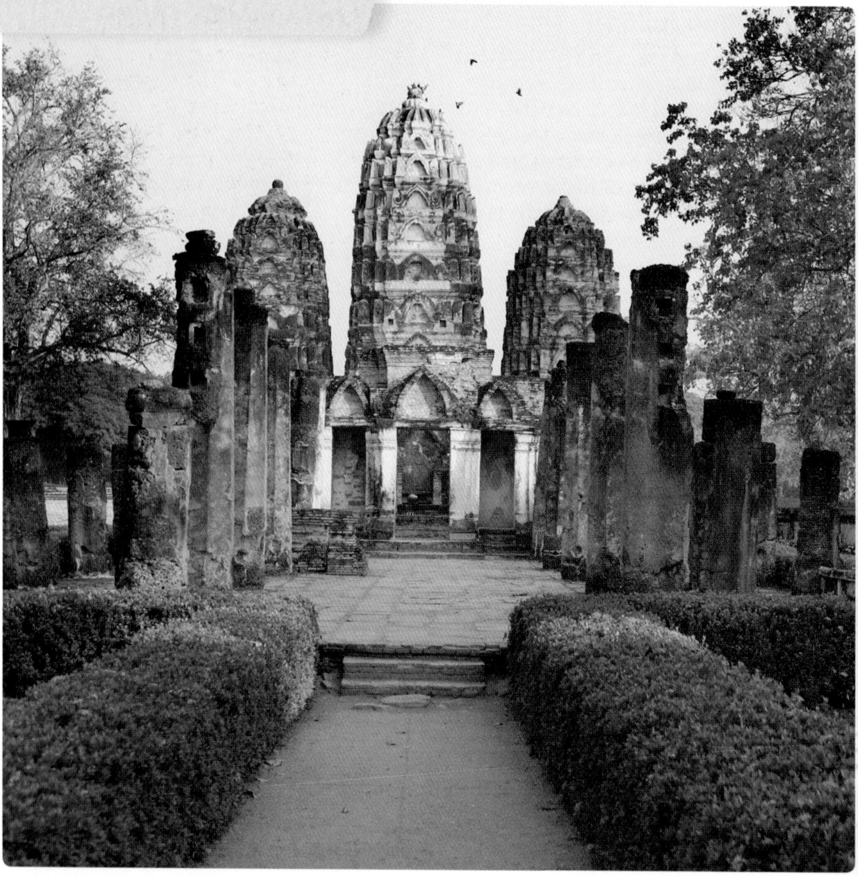

1 **Sukhothai** (p205)

The ruins of one of Thailand's first kingdoms reside in a peaceful parklike setting far enough from the modern city of **Sukhothai** to feel like a lost treasure. Hire a bicycle and spend the day among the eternally meditating Buddha figures and gravity-worn temples. For ruins among the countryside, do a day trip to **Si Satchanalai-Chaliang Historical Park**, where the surrounding rice paddies and dusty villages are part of the attraction. Sukhothai can be adequately explored in two days and the town is six to seven hours north of Bangkok by bus.

SUKHOTHAI ➔ CHIANG MAI

Six hours from Sukhothai's bus station.

2 **Chiang Mai** (p131)

The north's cultural capital, Chiang Mai can easily monopolise three days wandering around the old city, admiring temples and poking around the handicraft shops for gifts and souvenirs. Devote a day to exploring the surrounding countryside, navigated by curvy mountain roads and festooned with cool-weather flora and high-altitude villages. Spend an evening with the carefree university students along the fashionable avenue of Th Nimmanhaemin.

CHIANG MAI ➔ PAI

Three to four hours from Chiang Mai's Arcade bus terminal. **25 minutes** from Chiang Mai's airport.

3 **Pai** (p221)

From Chiang Mai, climb into the forested frontier that Thailand shares with Myanmar (Burma). Stop for a while in **Pai**, a mountain retreat for artists, backpackers and urban Thais. Pai does a little bit of everything: partying, mainly; trekking, some; and a lot of hanging out. Remember to bring some cool-weather clothes as the mountains get chilly after dark. Air travel is faster but you'll miss out on the twisty-turny mountain roads that make you feel like you earned the right to be in a Pai state of mind.

PAI ➔ MAE HONG SON

4½ hours from Pai's bus stop.

4 **Mae Hong Son** (p216)

The next stop on the northwest mountain circuit is this provincial capital that attracts cultural enthusiasts turned off by Pai's party scene. **Mae Hong Son** displays its Burmese heritage with distinctive temple architecture and signature market meals. It is also a gateway to remote jungle landscapes and offers a less popular trekking scene than Chiang Mai. There are daily flights back to Chiang Mai to speed up your return to the lowlands.

Wat Si Sawai (p207), Sukhothai

Phuket to Khao Sok National Park
Andaman Discovery

In two weeks, you can slide down the Andaman Coast and hit all the hot spots: party beaches, dive sites and scenic bays, going on and off the 'grid.' After all this island research, you'll be able to call yourself an expert in beachology.

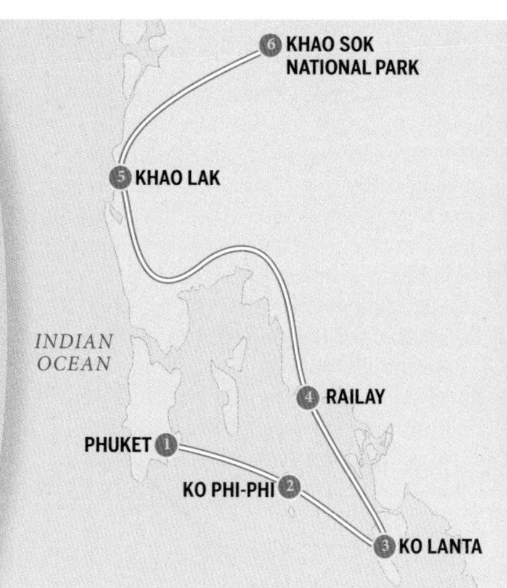

1 Phuket (p290)

An easy island to reach if transiting by air from Bangkok, Phuket dominates the comfort class for international beach retreats. Spend a day or two here downshifting into the island way of life and spa-ing away any travel and heat fatigue. Don't forget to explore **Ao Phang-Nga** for its unforgettable scenery, and spend a day touring Phuket Town for a historic perspective on this former port town.

PHUKET ➲ KO PHI-PHI

Two hours from Phuket's Tha Rasada.

2 Ko Phi-Phi (p311)

An island with perfect proportions, **Ko Phi-Phi** is decidedly less civilised than Phuket and a bit wilder (in the partying sense). But for quiet types, there are some secluded corners and close proximity to well-known dive sites to the south, snorkelling in Phi-Phi's uninhabited sister island and even rock climbing up vertical karst cliffs. After all these outings, reserve some night time stamina as this is a devout party beach.

KO PHI-PHI ➲ KO LANTA

1½ hours from Ko Phi-Phi.

3 Ko Lanta (p314)

If Phi-Phi is too popular for you, then defect to Ko Lanta, which is deliciously low-key though not as heart-achingly pretty. Lanta's personality charms its fans. It is closer to the famed Hin Daeng and Hin Muang dive sites, has an easygoing fishing village and goes to bed relatively early. Families typically opt for Lanta over rowdy Phi-Phi.

KO LANTA ➲ RAILAY

Two hours from Ko Lanta to Krabi Town.
45 minutes from Krabi Town to Railay.

4 Railay (p309)

Since you're in the neighbourhood, you might as well hop over to Railay's karst-studded bay for a big gulp of coastal scenery. If the view from the ground isn't good enough, you better strap on a harness so you can climb up the cliffs to find the horizon. A kayak trip skimming through the

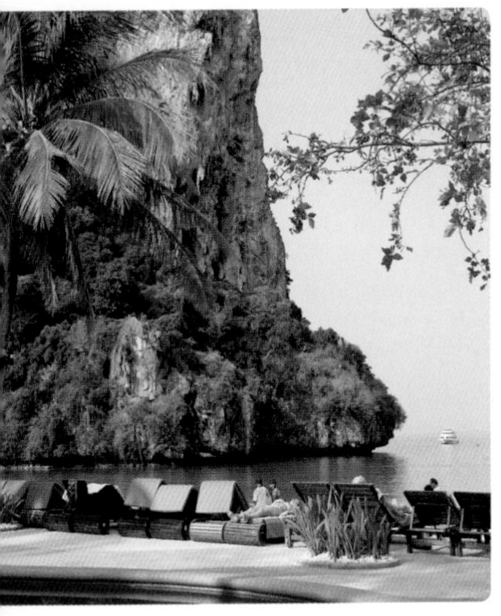

Hat Railay West (p310)
GLENN VAN DER KNIJFF/LONELY PLANET IMAGES ©

towers might offer a better perspective. Or better yet, a simple sunset cocktail might just do the trick.

RAILAY ➔ KHAO LAK

1½ hours from Railay to Phuket. **Two hours** from Phuket's bus station to Khao Lak.

5 Khao Lak (p285)

A mainland town on the Andaman Coast, **Khao Lak** is the most convenient gateway to the famous dive sites in the northern Andaman, including the **Surin Islands Marine National Park** and the **Similan Islands Marine National Park**. These two protected areas are renowned among globetrotting divers for their underwater geography and marine species. Dive companies arrange multiday live-aboard excursions that cut out the commute, giving you more chances to slip below the ocean's surface.

KHAO LAK ➔ KHAO SOK NATIONAL PARK

One hour from Khao Lak.

6 Khao Sok National Park (p284)

The southern rainforest refuge of **Khao Sok National Park** provides the perfect antidote to beach fatigue (if such a thing exists) as it sits midway between the gulf and the Andaman coasts. The park is filled with rugged limestone mountains criss-crossed by muddy trails and a dam-filled lake best explored by kayak. Your visit might coincide with the flowering of the giant *Rafflesia kerrii,* whose vegetal perfume mimics the smell of putrid flesh in order to attract carrion pollinators.

Thailand Month by Month

Top Events

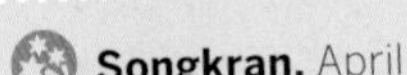

Songkran, April

Loi Krathong, November

Ubon Ratchathani's Khao Phansaa, July

Vegetarian Festival, October

Surin Elephant Round-up, November

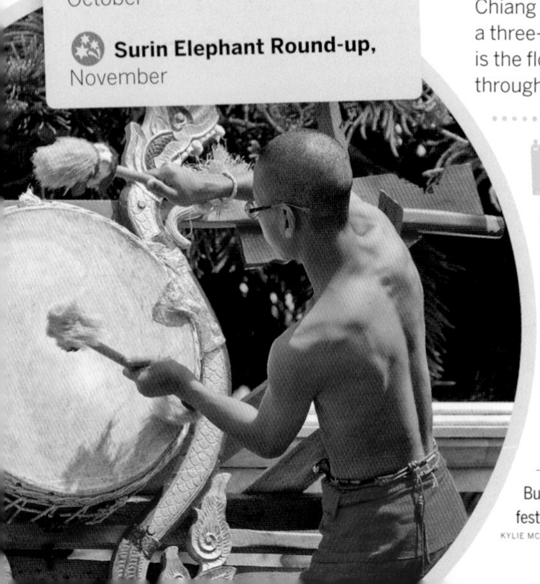

Buddhist monk drumming during Songkran festivities, Chiang Mai

KYLIE MCLAUGHLIN/LONELY PLANET IMAGES ©

January

The weather is cool and dry, ushering in the peak tourist season.

Chinese New Year

Thais with Chinese ancestry celebrate the Chinese lunar new year (dates vary) with a week of house-cleaning and fireworks. Phuket, Bangkok and Pattaya host citywide festivities, but Chinese New Year *(đrùd jeen)* is generally a family event.

February

Still in the high-season swing, snowbirds flock to Thailand for sun and fun.

Makha Bucha

One of three holy days marking important moments of Buddha's life, Makha Bucha *(mah·ká boo·chah)* falls on the full moon of the third lunar month and commemorates Buddha preaching to 1250 enlightened monks who came to hear him 'without prior summons'. It's a public holiday, mainly reserved for temple visits.

Flower Festival

Chiang Mai displays its floral beauty over a three-day period. The festival highlight is the flower-decorated floats that parade through town.

March

The hot, dry season approaches and the beaches start to empty out. The winds kick up, ushering in the kite-flying and kiteboarding season. This is also Thailand's semester break (bid term), and students head out on sightseeing trips.

 **Pattaya International Music Festival**

Pattaya showcases pop and rock bands from across Asia at this free music event, attracting bus loads of Bangkok university students.

 **Kite-Flying Festivals**

During the windy season, colourful kites battle it out over the skies of Sanam Luang in Bangkok and elsewhere in the country.

April

Hot, dry weather sweeps across the land and the tourist season is winding down, except for one last hurrah during Songkran. Make reservations well in advance, since the whole country is on the move for this holiday.

 **Songkran**

Thailand's traditional new year (12–14 April) starts out as a respectful affair then degenerates into a water war. Morning visits to the temple involve colourful processions of the sacred Buddha images, which are ceremoniously sprinkled with water. Later, Thais load up their water guns and head out to the streets for battle. Chiang Mai and Bangkok are the epicentres.

May

Leading up to the rainy season, festivals encourage plentiful rains and bountiful harvests. This is an under-appreciated shoulder season when prices are lower, there are fewer tourists, but it is still hot.

 **Royal Ploughing Ceremony**

This royal ceremony employs astrology and ancient Brahman rituals to kick off the rice-planting season. Sacred oxen are hitched to a wooden plough and part the ground of Sanam Luang in Bangkok.

 **Visakha Bucha**

The holy day of Visakha Bucha *(wí·săh·kà boo·chah)* falls on the 15th day of the waxing moon in the sixth lunar month and commemorates the date of the Buddha's birth, enlightenment and *parinibbana* (passing away). Activities are centred around the temple.

June

In some parts of the country, the rainy season is merely an afternoon shower, leaving the rest of the day for music and merriment.

 **Phi Ta Khon**

The Buddhist holy day of Bun Phra Wet is given a Carnival makeover in Dan Sai village in northeastern Thailand. Revellers disguise themselves in garish 'spirit' costumes and parade through the village streets wielding wooden phalluses and downing rice whisky.

July

With the start of the rainy season, the religious community and attendant festivals prepare for Buddhist Lent, a period of reflection and meditation.

 **Asarnha Bucha**

The full moon of the eighth lunar month commemorates Buddha's first sermon during Asarnha (also spelt Asalha) Bucha *(ah·săhn·hà boo·chah)*.

 **Khao Phansaa**

The day after Asarnha Bucha marks the beginning of Buddhist Lent (the first day of the waning moon in the eighth lunar month), the traditional time for men to enter the monkhood and when monks typically retreat inside the monastery for a period of study and meditation. In Ubon

Ratchathani, the traditional candle offerings have grown into elaborate sculptures that are shown off during the Candle Parade.

August

Overcast skies and daily showers mark the middle of the rainy season.

HM the Queen's Birthday

The Thai Queen's Birthday (12 August) is a public holiday and national Mother's Day. In Bangkok, the day is marked with cultural displays along Th Ratchadamnoen and Sanam Luang.

October

Religious preparations for the end of the rainy season and the end of Buddhist Lent begin. The monsoons are reaching the finish line (in most of the country).

Vegetarian Festival

A holiday from meat is taken for nine days (during the ninth lunar month) in adherence with Chinese Buddhist beliefs of mind and body purification. Cities with large Thai-Chinese populations, such as Bangkok, Hua Hin, Pattaya, Trang and Krabi, are festooned with yellow banners heralding vegetarian vendors, and merit-makers dressed in white shuffle off for meditation retreats.

Ork Phansaa

The end of the Buddhist lent (three lunar months after Khao Phansaa) is marked by the *gà·tĭn* ceremony, in which new robes are given to the monks by merit-makers. In Mae Hong Son, the end of Buddhist Lent is marked by the Shan-style Jong Para festival, in which miniature castles are paraded on poles to the temples. Localities near rivers and the ocean celebrate with traditional long-tail boat races. Nakhon Phanom's Illuminated Boat Festival electrifies an old-fashioned tradition.

King Chulalongkorn Day

Rama V is honoured on the anniversary of his death at the Royal Plaza in Dusit. Crowds of devotees come to make merit with incense and flower garlands. It's held on 23 October.

November

The cool, dry season has arrived, and if you get here early enough, you'll beat the tourist crowds.

Surin Elephant Round-Up

Held on the third weekend of November, Thailand's biggest elephant show celebrates this northeastern province's most famous residents. The event in Surin begins with a colourful elephant parade culminating in a fruit buffet for the pachyderms.

 Loi Krathong

Loi Krathong is celebrated on the first full moon of the 12th lunar month. The festival thanks the river goddess for providing life to the fields and forests and asks for forgiveness for the polluting ways of humans. Small handmade boats (called *kràthong* or *grà·tong*) are sent adrift in the country's waterways. The *grà·tong* are origami-like vessels made from banana leaves. They're decorated with flowers, and incense, candles and coins are placed in them. Loi Krathong is believed to have originated in Sukhothai, where it is celebrated today with much pomp. In Chiang Mai the festival is also called Yi Peng.

 Lopburi Monkey Festival

During the last week of November, the town's troublesome macaques get pampered with their very own banquet, while merit-makers watch merrily.

 December

The peak of the tourist season has returned with fair skies and a holiday mood.

 HM the King's Birthday

Honouring the king's birthday on 5 December, this public holiday hosts parades and merit-making events; it is also recognised as national Father's Day. Th Ratchadamnoen Klang in Bangkok is decorated with lights and regalia. Everyone wears pink shirts as pink is the colour associated with the monarchy.

 Chiang Mai Red Cross & Winter Fair

A 10-day festival that displays Chiang Mai's cultural heritage with a country-fair atmosphere; expect food (lots of it) and traditional performances.

Far Left: Vegetarian Festival, Phuket
Left: Loi Krathong, Chiang Mai

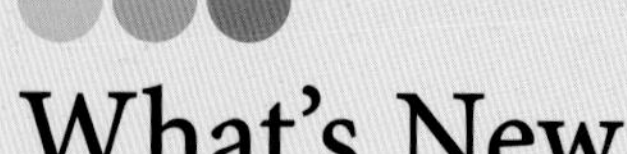

What's New

For this new edition of Discover Thailand, our authors have hunted down the fresh, the transformed, the hot and the happening. These are some of our favourites. For up-to-the-minute recommendations, see lonelyplanet.com/thailand.

1 **GET TO THE BEACH FASTER**
Recent transport routes have emerged directly from Thailand's Suvarnabhumi International Airport to the Eastern Seaboard beaches of Ko Samet and Ko Chang. That means you can bypass Bangkok and be beachside sooner.

2 **KITEBOARDING**
If all the watersports mated and had an offspring, it would be kiteboarding. Riders harness the wind and the waves at the kiteboarding hot spots of Hua Hin, Pranburi and Phuket.

3 **STYLISH SLEEP FOR ALL**
Bangkok has sprouted hip hostels, such as NapPark Hostel (☎ 0 2282 2324; www.nappark.com; 8 Th Tani; dm 550-750B; ❄@☎; river ferry Tha Phra Athit) and Lub*d (☎ 0 2634 7999; www.lubd.com; Th Pha Ram I; dm 550B; ❄@☎; BTS National Stadium), far removed from the functional dorms of yore.

4 **FLYING THROUGH THE CANOPY**
Why walk when you can fly through the forest on an elevated zipline? Ropes courses have proliferated wherever trees meet tourists in such places as Ko Tao, Sangkhlaburi, Pattaya and Pai.

5 **EXTREME DIVING**
Ko Tao is no longer just for beginners. Technical divers are now exploring underwater caves and even casting off their scuba gear for lung-stretching free dives.

6 **CLIFF-HANGING IN KRABI**
Everyone knows that Krabi is Thailand's rock-climbing capital, but did you know that free-climbing is the latest trend? Assaults on overhanging sea cliffs are done without ropes and the ocean is there to catch you.

7 **HIP CHIANG MAI**
Chiang Mai has its antique charms but Th Nimmanhaemin is a fountain of youth. Check out new restaurants such as Su Casa and the people-watching perch at At 9 Bar.

8 **ISAN FASHIONISTA**
More traditional than trendy, the northeast has graduated into the stylish world of boutique hotels with Khorat's V-One (☎ 0 4434 2444; www.v-onehotelkhorat.com; Th Chang Phuak; r incl breakfast 800-6750B; ❄@☎≋), Khao Yai's Hotel des Artists and Khon Kaen's Glacier Hotel (☎ 0 4333 4999; www.glacier-hotel.com; Soi Na Muang 25; s 1800-2100B d 2050-2350B; ❄@☎≋).

9 **RINGLEADERS: MUAY THAI WARRIORS**
Rather than packing on the pounds, train to be a lean, mean fighting machine at the new crop of *moo·ay tai* (muay Thai) training and fitness camps, such as Phuket's Promthep Muay Thai Camp (p293).

10 **RESORT BEACHES ON THE CHEAP**
Thailand's beaches have transformed quickly from bamboo huts to luxury villas. We can't turn back time, but we've got more budget options on big-spender beaches such as Ko Kut and Ko Chang.

Get Inspired

Books

- **Fieldwork** (Mischa Berlinski; 2008) A story about a fictional hill-tribe village in northern Thailand.
- **Sightseeing** (Rattawut Lapcharoensap; 2005) A collection of short stories, which provides a 'sightseeing' tour of Thai life.
- **The Beach** (Alex Garland; 1998) The ultimate beach read follows a backpacker's discovery of secluded island utopia.
- **Very Thai: Everyday Popular Culture** (Philip Cornwel-Smith; 2004) Bangkok-based writer Cornwel-Smith answers the ordinary whys and whats, from dashboard shrines to uniform obsessions.
- **Bizarre Thailand: Tales of Crime, Sex and Black Magic** (Jim Algie; 2010) Oddball places get their own guidebook.

Films

- **Fah Talai Jone** (Tears of the Black Tiger; 2000) Wisit Sasanatieng pays tribute to Thai action flicks and star-crossed lovers.
- **Agrarian Utopia** (2009) Director Uruphong Raksasad depicts the hardships of agricultural life in this film-fest darling.
- **Uncle Boonmee Who Can Recall His Past Lives** (2010) Winner of Cannes 2010 Palm d'Or award from director Apichatpong Weerasethakul.
- **Bangkok Traffic Love Story** (2009) A smart romantic comedy by director Adisorn Tresirikasem.

Music

- **That Song** (Modern Dog) Anthemic alt-rock.
- **Best** (Pumpuang Duangjan) The best from the late Thai country diva.
- **Boomerang** (Bird Thongchai) Beloved album from the king of Thai pop.
- **Romantic Comedy** (Apartment Khunpa) Post alt-rock's leading rockers.

Websites

- **Lonely Planet** (www.lonelyplanet.com) Country-specific information and Thorn Tree user-exchange.
- **Bangkok Post** (www.bangkokpost.com) English-language daily.
- **Agoda.com** (www.agoda.com) Discounted hotel bookings.
- **One Stop Thailand** (www.onestopthailand.com) One-stop travel site.

Short on time?

This list will give you instant insight into the country.

Read *Bangkok 8* (John Burdett) is the first and best in the Sonchai series, about a hardboiled Thai-Westener cop.

Watch *Ruang Rak Noi Nid Mahasan* (Last Life in the Universe; 2003), directed by Pen-Ek Ratanaruang, unfurls a dark tale of two lost souls.

Listen *Made in Thailand* (Carabao) is Thailand's classic classic-rock album.

Log On *Not the Nation* (www.notthenation.com) is a spoof Thai news website.

Long-tail boat, Ko Phi-Phi Leh (p315)

Need to Know

Currency
Thai baht (B)

Language
Thai

ATMs
Widespread and charge a 150B foreign-account fee.

Credit Cards
Visa and MasterCard accepted at most hotels and high-end restaurants but not at small family-owned businesses.

Visas
International air arrivals receive a 30-day visa.

Mobile Phones
Thailand is on a GSM network through inexpensive prepaid SIM cards. 3G is coming...soon.

Wi-Fi
Widespread and access is cheap.

Internet Access
Internet cafes common in tourist centres.

Driving
Easy to hire cars and motorcycles; drive on the left.

Tipping
In high-end hotels and restaurants; 10% gratuity, 7% tax.

When to Go

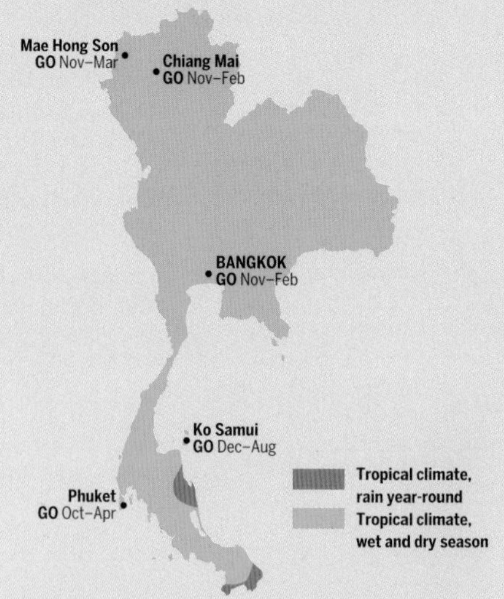

High Season (Nov–Mar)
- A cool, dry season follows the monsoons, meaning the landscape is lush and temperatures are comfortable.
- Western Christmas and New Year holidays bring crowds and inflated rates to the beaches.

Shoulder Season (Apr–Jun, Sept & Oct)
- Hot and dry (April to June) all over, but less so in the northern mountains.
- Tail-end of rainy season (September and October) is ideal for visiting the north and the Gulf Coast.

Low Season (Jul–Oct)
- Monsoon season can range from afternoon showers to multiday drenchers.
- Some islands shut down and boat service is limited during stormy weather.
- Be flexible with travel plans.

Advance Planning

- **One month before** Start shopping for airfares, planning an itinerary, booking accommodation for resort islands like Ko Samui and Phuket, and arranging Bangkok–Chiang Mai overnight train tickets.
- **One week before** Book your arrival hotel in Bangkok, Thai cooking course and dive trip. Start watching the web for Thailand news.
- **One day before** Confirm your flight, find a hearty book for your flight and bid adieu to ho-hum home life.

Your Daily Budget

Budget less than 1500B

- Basic guest house room 300–800B
- Excellent market and street-stall meals
- One or two evening drinks
- Get around town with public transport

Midrange 1500–3000B

- Flashpacker guest house or midrange hotel room 800–1500B
- Western-food lunches and seafood dinners
- Several evening beers
- Motorbike hire

Top End over 3000B

- Boutique hotel room 3000B
- Fine dining
- Private tours
- Car hire

Exchange Rates

Australia	A$1	32B
Canada	C$1	31B
Euro zone	€	44B
Japan	¥100	38B
New Zealand	NZ$1	25B
UK	£1	50B
USA	US$1	30B

For current exchange rates see www.xe.com.

What to Bring

- **Light wash-and-wear clothes** Laundry is cheap in Thailand, so pack light. You can buy most toiletries everywhere.
- **A pullover or jacket** For places that are over-air-conditioned and cool mountain mornings.
- **Slip-on shoes or sandals** For quick removal when entering temples.
- **Other handy items** A small torch, waterproof money/passport container (for swimming outings), earplugs and sunscreen (high SPF sunscreen is not widely available).

Arriving in Thailand

- **Suvarnabhumi International Airport**

Airport Rail Link Local service (30 minutes, 45B) to Phaya Thai station; express service (15 minutes, 150B) to Makkasan station.

Taxi Metered taxis 200B to 300B plus 50B airport surcharge and tolls; it's about an hour to the city, depending on traffic.

Getting Around

- **Air** Domestic routes from Bangkok are plentiful.
- **Bus** Intercity buses are convenient, affordable and comfortable; purchase tickets at bus stations to avoid unscrupulous agents.
- **Hired transport** Bangkok has metered taxis, elsewhere túk-túk (pronounced *đúk đúk*) and motorcycle taxis have negotiated fares; self-drive motorcycles and cars are easily rented.
- **Public transport** Bangkok has public buses, an elevated train system (BTS) and a subway (MRT). Most Thai cities have *sŏrng·tăa·ou* (converted pick-up trucks) that run fixed routes.
- **Train** Slow but scenic; popular for the overnight trip between Bangkok and Chiang Mai or the southern islands.

Accommodation

- **Guest houses** Thailand's most common option; some are simple rooms in a family's home, while others are small hotels for small budgets. They all tend to have a common lobby, a restaurant for socialising and tourist information.
- **Hotels** Hip and fashionable options abound in Bangkok, Chiang Mai and the resort islands, but the dour and impersonal Thai-Chinese hotels in the provinces often feel a little lonely.

Be Forewarned

- **Check travel advisories** Prior to your trip look for advisory warnings to Thailand on the website of your government's diplomatic mission abroad.
- **Health** Dengue fever is a concern throughout the country.
- **Dress** Cover up when visiting temples.
- **Public holidays** Domestic transport can be crowded or booked out during long holidays.
- **Rainy season** Some resorts close; boat service is limited.

Bangkok

Formerly the epitome of the steamy Asian metropolis, in recent years Bangkok has gone under the knife and emerged as a rejuvenated starlet. Her wrinkles haven't been totally erased, but you might not notice them in the expanding and efficient public transport system, air-conditioned megamalls and international-standard restaurants. A diverse expat community, a burgeoning art scene and a brand-new airport complete the new look, making even frequent visitors wonder what happened to the girl they once knew.

But don't take this to mean that there's no 'real' Bangkok left. The traditional framework that made this city unique is still very much alive and kicking, and can be found a short walk from any BTS station – or probably just around the corner from your hotel.

Along the way we're sure you'll find that the old personality and the new face culminate in one sexy broad.

What Phra Kaew (p74)

Traditional Thai dancers

Bangkok

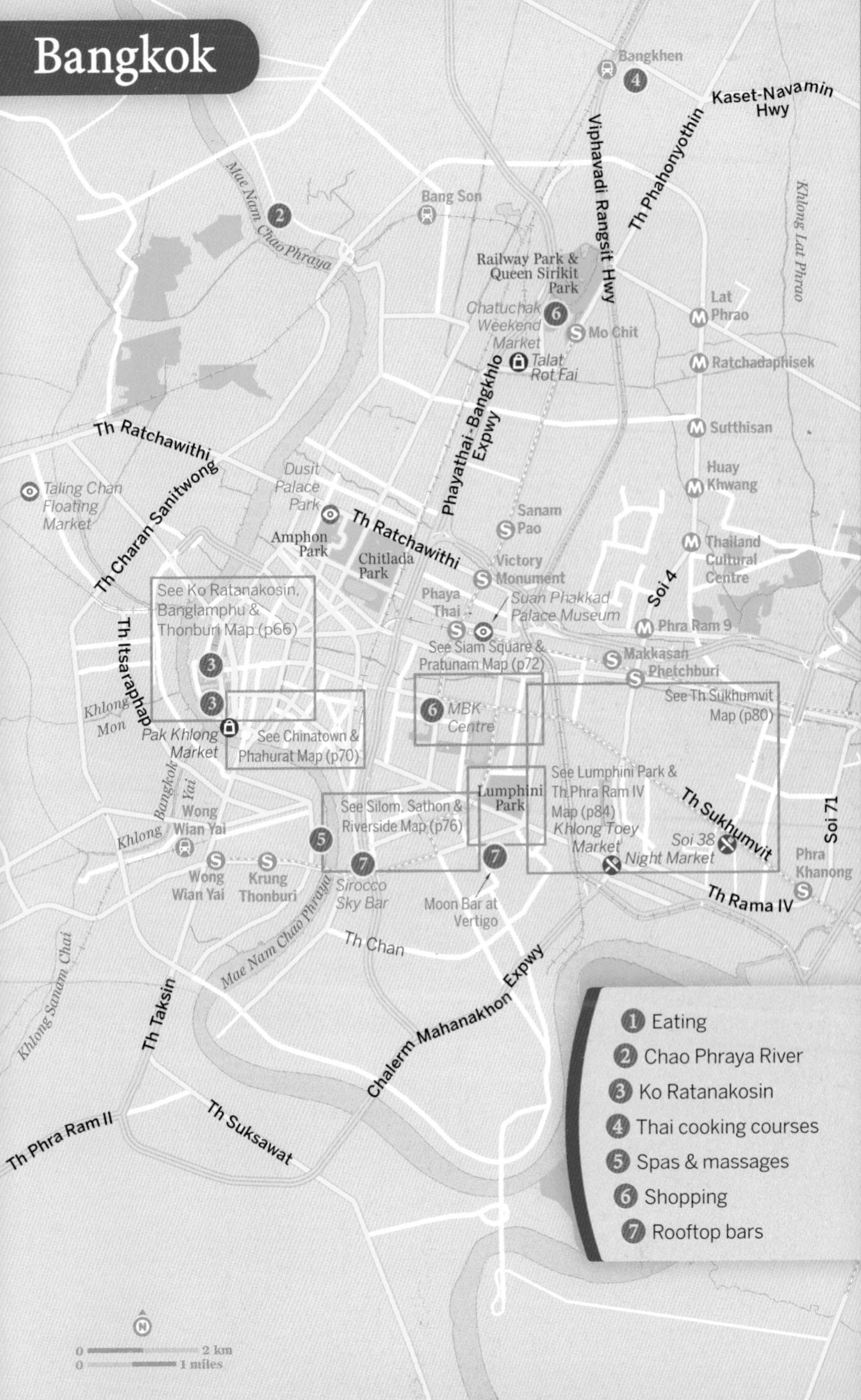

Bangkhen
Kaset-Navamin Hwy
Viphavadi Rangsit Hwy
Th Phahonyothin
Khlong Lat Phrao
Mae Nam Chao Phraya
Bang Son
Railway Park & Queen Sirikit Park
Chatuchak Weekend Market
Mo Chit
Lat Phrao
Talat Rot Fai
Ratchadaphisek
Phayathai-Bangkhlo Expwy
Sutthisan
Th Ratchawithi
Th Charan Sanitwong
Dusit Palace Park
Huay Khwang
Taling Chan Floating Market
Sanam Pao
Amphon Park
Th Ratchawithi
Chitlada Park
Thailand Cultural Centre
Victory Monument
Soi 4
Phaya Thai
Suan Phakkad Palace Museum
See Ko Ratanakosin, Banglamphu & Thonburi Map (p66)
Phra Ram 9
Th Itsaraphap
See Siam Square & Pratunam Map (p72)
Makkasan
Phetchburi
See Th Sukhumvit Map (p80)
Khlong Mon
MBK Centre
Pak Khlong Market
See Chinatown & Phahurat Map (p70)
See Lumphini Park & Th Phra Ram IV Map (p84)
Lumphini Park
Khlong Bangkok Yai
Th Sukhumvit
Soi 71
See Silom, Sathon & Riverside Map (p76)
Khlong Toey Market
Wong Wian Yai
Soi 38
Night Market
Phra Khanong
Wong Wian Yai
Krung Thonburi
Sirocco Sky Bar
Moon Bar at Vertigo
Th Rama IV
Th Chan
Mae Nam Chao Phraya
Khlong Sanam Chai
Chalerm Mahanakhon Expwy
Th Taksin
Th Phra Ram II
Th Suksawat
1 Eating
2 Chao Phraya River
3 Ko Ratanakosin
4 Thai cooking courses
5 Spas & massages
6 Shopping
7 Rooftop bars
0 2 km
0 1 miles

Bangkok's Highlights

1

Culinary Bangkok

Bangkok is just like Paris: all the good ingredients from across the region end up here. In terms of food, the city is very flavourful and acts as a 24-hour dining room, from market meals to haute cuisine. **Above:** Pak Khlong Market (p88); **Top Right:** Mee krob (crispy noodles); **Bottom Right:** Floating market

Need to Know

TOP TIP Thais use chopsticks to eat noodles but use a spoon to eat rice **AVOID** Restaurant Thai food can be overrated; street stalls are better **For further coverage, see p78**

Local Knowledge

Culinary Bangkok Don't Miss List

BY DUANGPORN (BO) SONGVISAVA,
CO-OWNER & CHEF, BO.LAN RESTAURANT

1 FRESH MARKETS

The best-stocked fresh market is Khlong Toey Market (p87). It is a wholesale market that supplies most of the city's restaurants, including my own. I often talk with the vendors to get the know-how of ingredients. Pak Khlong Market (p87) is great for its quality of products, always fresh and tempting me to buy.

2 FINE DINING

nahm (p83) is part of the new wave of upscale Thai restaurants – Western chefs resuscitating old-fashioned Thai dishes with high-end ingredients. Foreigners love it and Thais are hospitably intrigued. Bo.lan (p82) is another facet of the fine-dining scene: it is based on slow-food philosophy, promoting food biodiversity, cooking everything from scratch and safeguarding culinary heritage.

3 *GŎO·AY ĐĔE·O* (NOODLES)

Bangkok is *the* place for noodles. There are hundreds of places in Bangkok and everyone has their own recommendations. I like to go to **Rung Ruang** (Soi 26, Th Sukhumvit), which does noodle soups with pork and fish balls. There's also a little **no-name shop** (cnr Th Rama IV & Th Chua Pleang) under the expressway that does pork noodles. **Sia** (Th Rama IV; ⌚7pm-midnight Mon-Sat), opposite the BMW showroom, is a little duck-noodle shop that has flavourful broth and blood cake. I normally order wide noodles with broth and an extra bowl of braised duck wings.

4 NIGHT MARKETS

Night markets are everywhere in Bangkok and are a great way for tourists to explore culinary experiences. Centrally located ones include Soi 38 Night Market (p83), a popular late-night pit stop. **Talat Rot Fai** (Railway Market; p88) is a very cool place to shop and eat – all the indie kids are there.

Chao Phraya River

The Chao Phraya River (River of Kings) is the bloodline of the Thai people. It is used for trade and travel, for drinking and cooking. Branching off the river are small canals that support an old-fashioned way of life. **Below & Top Right:** Wat Arun (p65); **Bottom Right:** Long-tail boat decorated with flowers

Need to Know

TOP TIP Chao Phraya Express boats stop at popular riverside sites **DO AS THE THAIS** Visit a canal-side temple to release fish as offerings **For further coverage, see p88**.

Chao Phraya River Don't Miss List

BY PYLIN (JANE) SANGUANPIYAPAND, OWNER OF SEVEN HOTEL

1 LONG-TAIL BOAT RIDES

The long-tail boat ride through the Khlong Bangkok Noi (p88) is an unforgettable experience. There is a charming simplicity on these canals. Along the way, kids play in the water, granddads check out the scene from a humble wooden porch and monks clean the temple grounds. There are also *mâa káh* (vendors) selling all kinds of things from their boats, and housewives preparing dinner. I recommend this trip to all of my guests.

2 WAT ARUN

Wat Arun (Temple of Dawn; p65) sits directly on the river and is a very majestic site. It was founded after the fall of Ayuthaya as a sign that the country could be reborn. Though Wat Arun looks very good from the water, it is even better looking from land. Be sure to tour the grounds to discover that the imposing structure is covered with delicate pieces of porcelain mosaics.

3 DRINKS BY THE RIVER

Tourists can enjoy the river view from the Amorosa (p84), which overlooks some of Thailand's most famous riverside temples. It is a wonderful place to dream of a simple life and watch the evening show of boats zipping and lumbering along the river. There are often cool river breezes that are just as refreshing as an evening drink after a hot and humid day.

4 DINNER BESIDE THE RIVER

There are many restaurants beside the river, but my favourite is **Ban Klang Nam** (Soi 14, Th Phra Ram III, Bang Kho Laem), in the southern part of the city. It serves the best Thai seafood in my opinion. Call the head waiter Khun Chai (☎ 08 1581 5848) for a good table. The restaurant is far from the centre of town, so you should hire a taxi.

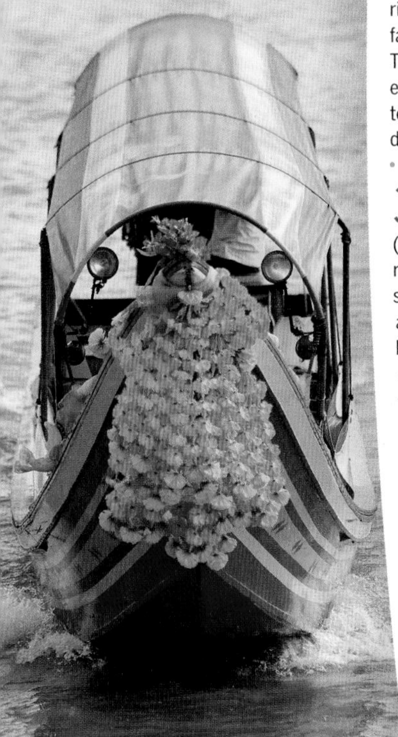

Explore Ko Ratanakosin

The country's most famous and sacred sites are in Ko Ratanakosin, the old royal district. Here you'll find Wat Phra Kaew (p74), a glittering and ornate temple that typifies Thai temple architecture and shelters the revered Emerald Buddha. More subdued Wat Pho (p69) is home to the gigantic reclining Buddha and is the national school for traditional Thai massage. There are other treasures worth exploring nearby. Wat Phra Kaew

3

4

Thai Cooking Courses

Learn to dice and stir-fry your way through many classic Thai dishes with a half-day cooking course. Bangkok's cooking schools, such as Baipai (p73), provide an excellent introduction to the cuisine (no more fumbling with a Thai menu), guided tours of markets and instructions for turning disparate ingredients into edible masterpieces. You also get to eat your handiwork and graduate with your very own recipe book – a souvenir that can do more than collect dust.

GREG ELMS/LONELY PLANET IMAGES ©

Get Pampered

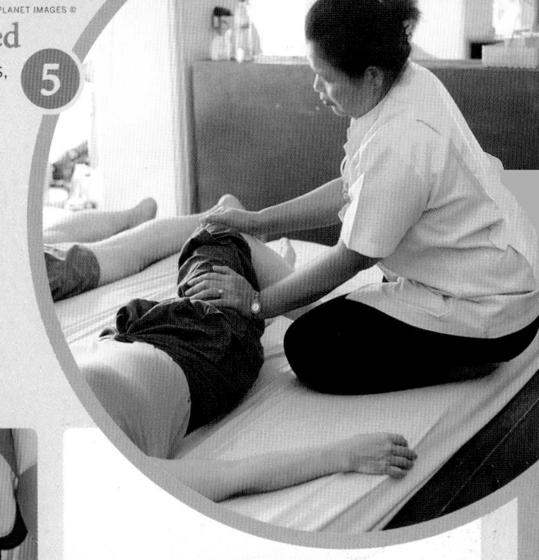

5

Bangkok excels in the pampering arts, with hundreds of massage parlours and spas. Stop into a corner shop for a foot massage or wind down the day with a traditional Thai massage, during which muscles are pinched and pulled into submission. Or dedicate a morning to a modern spa such as the Oriental Spa (p73), specialising in beauty and massage. Though it's a big chaotic city, you'll find you've never been more relaxed.

PETER UNGER/LONELY PLANET IMAGES ©

6

Shop-a-thon

Bangkok's malls and markets make their overseas counterparts look like country-bumpkin garage sales. Cut your teeth at MBK Centre (p86), an indoor mall that has all the energy of a streetside bazaar but without the heat. Then graduate to Chatuchak Weekend Market (p87), the mother of all markets that sells everything and the kitchen sink.

7

Rooftop Bars

Modern Bangkok is a manmade mountain range of skyscrapers, each reaching higher than the one before. Atop some of these towers are rooftop bars, including Sirocco Sky Bar (p79) and Moon Bar at Vertigo (pictured; p79), where evening and night-time tipplers drink from a heavenly eyrie accompanied by cool breezes and twinkling city lights. Bangkok's street-level cacophony is so far away from up here that it sounds almost melodic.

Bangkok's Best...

Museums & Historic Houses

- **National Museum** (p65) Get a crash course on Buddhist sculpture.
- **Jim Thompson House** (p87) Admire a homey collection of Asian art and architecture.
- **Suan Phakkad Palace Museum** (p65) Enjoy Old Siam art and architecture at this former farm.
- **Museum of Siam** (p65) Interact with Thai history at this hands-on museum.

Places to Wander

- **Chinatown** (p68) Ramble through a maze of old-world commerce.
- **Amulet Market** (p64) Pick your way through the vendors selling protective talismans.
- **Dusit Palace Park** (p71) Take a stroll through a pretty park filled with even prettier palaces.
- **Golden Mount** (p65) Climb to the top of this artificial hill for a bird's-eye view of old Bangkok.

Dining

- **nahm** (p83) High-end Thai for educated palettes.
- **MBK Food Court** (p78) Market meals in air-con comfort.
- **Krua Apsorn** (p78) A royal favourite for shellfish delicacies.
- **Bo.lan** (p82) Haute Thai cuisine.

Drinking & Clubbing

- **Center Khao San** (p85) Grab a front-row seat on Khao San's beer-slinging parade.
- **Brown Sugar** (p85) Settle in for good times and good tunes.
- **Iron Fairies** (p85) High-concept bar for Gothic imbibers.
- **WTF** (p85) Get cosy with cocktails at this art-house pub.

Left: nahm (p83)
e: Chinese New Year parade, Chinatown (p68)

Need to Know

ADVANCE PLANNING

- **One month before** Book accommodation.
- **One week before** Book your Thai cooking course.
- **One day before** Pack your hippest outfits.

RESOURCES

- **Bangkok Recorder** (www.bangkokrecorder.com) Find out who's playing where.
- **Bangkok Information Center** (www.bangkoktourist.com) City tourism office.
- **Tourism Authority of Thailand** (www.tourismthailand.org) Tourist information.

GETTING AROUND

- **Bus** From Siam Square to Chinatown (bus 73); Siam Square to Banglamphu (bus 15); frequent service.
- **MRT** Underground train (metro) from Sukhumvit and Silom to the train station; frequent service.
- **River ferry** Hop between riverside temples and neighbourhoods via frequent river ferry services.
- **BTS** Elevated skytrain from Sukhumvit, Siam Square, Silom and Chatuchak; frequent service.
- **Taxi** Plentiful and comfortable; insist on the meter.
- **Túk-túk** Cute but a rip-off.

BE FOREWARNED

- **Dress** Cover past your shoulders and knees in important temples.
- **Smoking** Banned indoors at bars and restaurants.
- **Street stalls** Don't set up on Monday.
- **Touts** Ignore friendly locals with touring/shopping advice.
- **Gems** Don't buy unset gems; it is an expensive con game (p86).
- **Tailor-made clothes** Set aside a week to get clothes tailored; most reliable tailors ask for two to five fittings.

Bangkok Walking Tour

Stroll between Bangkok's must-see attractions in the former royal district of Ko Ratanakosin. Start early to beat the heat and the crowds and dress modestly for entry to the temples.

WALK FACTS

- **Start** Wat Phra Kaew & Grand Palace
- **Finish** Sanam Luang
- **Distance** 5km
- **Duration** Four hours

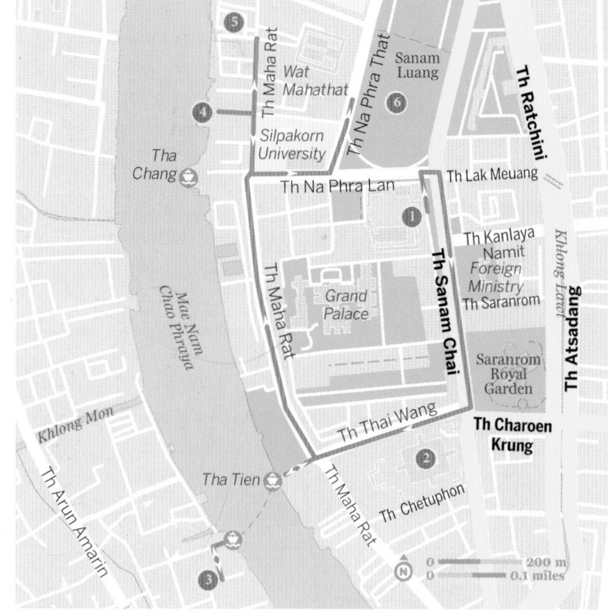

1 Wat Phra Kaew & Grand Palace

Architecturally flamboyant and domestically revered, this formerly cloistered royal complex now rules as the city's most famous attraction. It is best appreciated with a hired guide (available at the ticket kiosk) or an audio guide (200B for two hours), both of which will explain the ins and outs of Thai Buddhism and religious symbolism. Don't miss the temple's beautiful murals.

2 Wat Pho

Head to the temple with the most superlatives, including the giant reclining Buddha. This is a shady and subdued attraction with lots of quiet nooks and crannies. There are also on-site traditional Thai massage pavilions carrying on the temple's primary purpose as a repository for traditional healing. Where else can you tend to your soul and your soles?

3 Wat Arun

Catch the cross-river ferry from Tha Tien to this military-looking temple boasting a Khmer-style *chedi* (stupa). This temple served as the precursor to Bangkok after the fall of Ayuthaya. A closer look reveals that the granite-looking spire is really covered in ornate porcelain mosaics.

4 Trok Tha Wang

Return to the east bank and explore this narrow alleyway containing classic Bangkok architecture and riverside accoutrements, like many Asian port cities.

5 Amulet Market

Scoot north on Th Maha Rat and turn left into crowded Trok Mahathat to discover this cramped market where amulets are bought, sold and seriously inspected. Follow the alley all the way towards the river to appreciate how extensive the amulet trade is. As you continue north alongside the river, amulets are replaced by food vendors and amulet shoppers get crowded out by uniformed university students.

6 Sanam Luang

Exiting at Th Phra Chan, cross Th Maha Rat and continue east, passing even more traditional Thai medicine shops and amulet vendors until you reach the 'Royal Field'. The park is the site for the annual Ploughing Ceremony, in which the crown prince officially initiates the rice-growing season; a large kite competition is also held here during the kite-flying season (mid-February to April). The southern end of the park affords a photographic view of Wat Phra Kaew. Taxis and buses circle this shadeless expanse, offering a quick getaway for tuckered-out tourists.

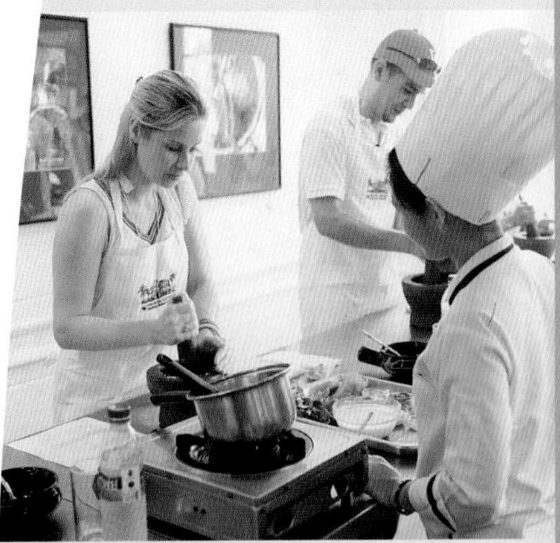

Bangkok In...

ONE DAY

Take the **Chao Phraya Express** (p88) to Tha Chang to explore the museums and temples of **Ko Ratanakosin**, followed by lunch in **Banglamphu**. Later, visit a **rooftop bar** (p84) for cocktails, followed by an upscale Thai dinner at **nahm** (p83).

TWO DAYS

Take the BTS to a **shopping mall** (p86), **Jim Thompson House** (p87), and wrap up the daylight hours with a **Thai massage** (p71). Then turn shopping into imbibing on **Th Khao San**.

THREE DAYS

Spend a day at **Chatuchak Weekend Market** (p87), enrol in a **cooking class** (p73), or jump aboard a long-tail boat to explore **Thonburi's canals** (p88).

FOUR DAYS

Escape Bangkok's chaos with a visit to **Dusit Palace Park** (p71). Splash out at one of **Sukhumvit's international restaurants** and then hang out with Bangkok's hipsters at **Iron Fairies** (p85) or **Fat Gut'z** (p85).

Thai cooking course

Discover Bangkok

At a Glance

Siam Square

History

The centre of government and culture in Thailand today, Bangkok was once a historical miracle during a time of turmoil. Following the fall of Ayuthaya in 1767, the kingdom fractured into competing forces, from which General Taksin emerged as a decisive unifier. He established his base in Thonburi, on the western bank of Mae Nam Chao Phraya (Chao Phraya River), a convenient location for sea trade from the Gulf of Thailand. He was later deposed by another important military general, Chao Phraya Chakri, who in 1782 moved the capital across the river to a more defensible location in anticipation of a Burmese attack.

Sights

Ko Ratanakosin, Banglamphu & Thonburi

เกาะรัตนโกสินทร์/บางลำพู/ธนบุรี

Welcome to Bangkok's birthplace. Within this area you'll find the glittering temples and palaces that most visitors associate with the city.

KO RATANAKOSIN

AMULET MARKET Market

(ตลาดพระเครื่องวัดมหาธาตุ; Map p66; Th Maha Rat; 7am-5pm; river ferry Tha Chang) This equal-parts bizarre and fascinating market claims both the footpaths along Th Maha Rat and Th Phra Chan, as well as a dense network of covered market stalls near Tha Phra Chan. The trade is based around small talismans carefully prized by collectors, monks, taxi drivers and people in dangerous professions. Potential buyers, often already sporting tens of amulets, can be seen bargaining and flipping through magazines dedicated to the amulets, some of which command astronomical prices.

NATIONAL MUSEUM Museum

(พิพิธภัณฑสถานแห่งชาติ; Map p66; 4 Th Na Phra That; admission 200B; 9am-3.30pm Wed-Sun; 32, 123, 503, river ferry Tha Chang) Often touted as Southeast Asia's biggest museum, the National Museum is home to an impressive collection of religious sculpture, best appreciated on one the museum's twice-weekly guided **tours** (**9.30am Wed & Thu**).

The **history wing** has made impressive bounds towards mainstream curatorial aesthetics with a succinct chronology of prehistoric, Sukhothai-, Ayuthaya- and Bangkok-era events and figures. In addition to the main exhibition halls, the **Buddhaisawan (Phutthaisawan) Chapel** includes some well-preserved original murals and one of the country's most revered Buddha images, Phra Phut Sihing. Legend says the image came from Sri Lanka, but art historians attribute it to 13th-century Sukhothai.

MUSEUM OF SIAM Museum

(สถาบันพิพิธภัณฑ์การเรียนรู้แห่งชาติ; Map p66; www.museumsiam.com; Th Maha Rat; admission 300B; 10am-6pm Tue-Sun; 32, 524, river ferry Tha Tien) This fun museum employs a variety of media to explore the origins and culture of the Thai people. Housed in a Rama III–era palace, the exhibits are superinteractive, well balanced and entertaining. Highlights include the informative and engaging narrated videos in each exhibition room, and an interactive Ayuthaya-era battle game.

BANGLAMPHU

GOLDEN MOUNT Buddhist Temple

(วัดสระเกศ (ภูเขาทอง); Map p66; Th Boriphat; admission 10B; 7.30am-5.30pm; 8, 37, 47, klorng taxi Tha Phan Fah) Even if you're wát-ed out, you should take a brisk walk to the Golden Mount. Like all worthy summits, the temple plays a good game of optical illusion, appearing closer than its real location. Serpentine steps wind through an artificial hill shaded by gnarled trees, some of which are signed in English, and past graves and pictures of wealthy benefactors. At the peak, you'll find a breezy 360-degree view of Bangkok's most photogenic side.

If you're coming from the eastern end of the city, the Golden Mount is a short walk from the *klorng* (canal) boats' western terminus at Tha Phan Fah.

Detour: Suan Phakkad Palace Museum

An overlooked treasure, Suan Phakkad (วังสวนผักกาด; 0 2245 4934; Th Sri Ayuthaya; admission 100B; 9am-4pm; BTS Phaya Thai) is a collection of eight traditional wooden Thai houses that was once the residence of Princess Chumbon of Nakhon Sawan and before that a lettuce farm – hence the name. Within the stilt buildings are displays of art, antiques and furnishings, and the landscaped grounds are a peaceful oasis complete with ducks, swans and a semi-enclosed garden.

THONBURI

WAT ARUN Buddhist Temple

(วัดอรุณฯ; Map p66; Th Arun Amarin; admission 50B; 8.30am-4.30pm; cross-river ferry from Tha Tien) Striking Wat Arun commands a martial pose as the third point in the holy trinity (along with Wat Phra Kaew and Wat Pho) of Bangkok's early history. After the fall of Ayuthaya, King Taksin ceremoniously clinched control here on the site of a local shrine (formerly known as Wat Jaeng) and established a royal palace and a temple to house the Emerald Buddha. The temple was renamed after the Indian god of dawn

Ko Ratanakosin, Banglamphu & Thonburi

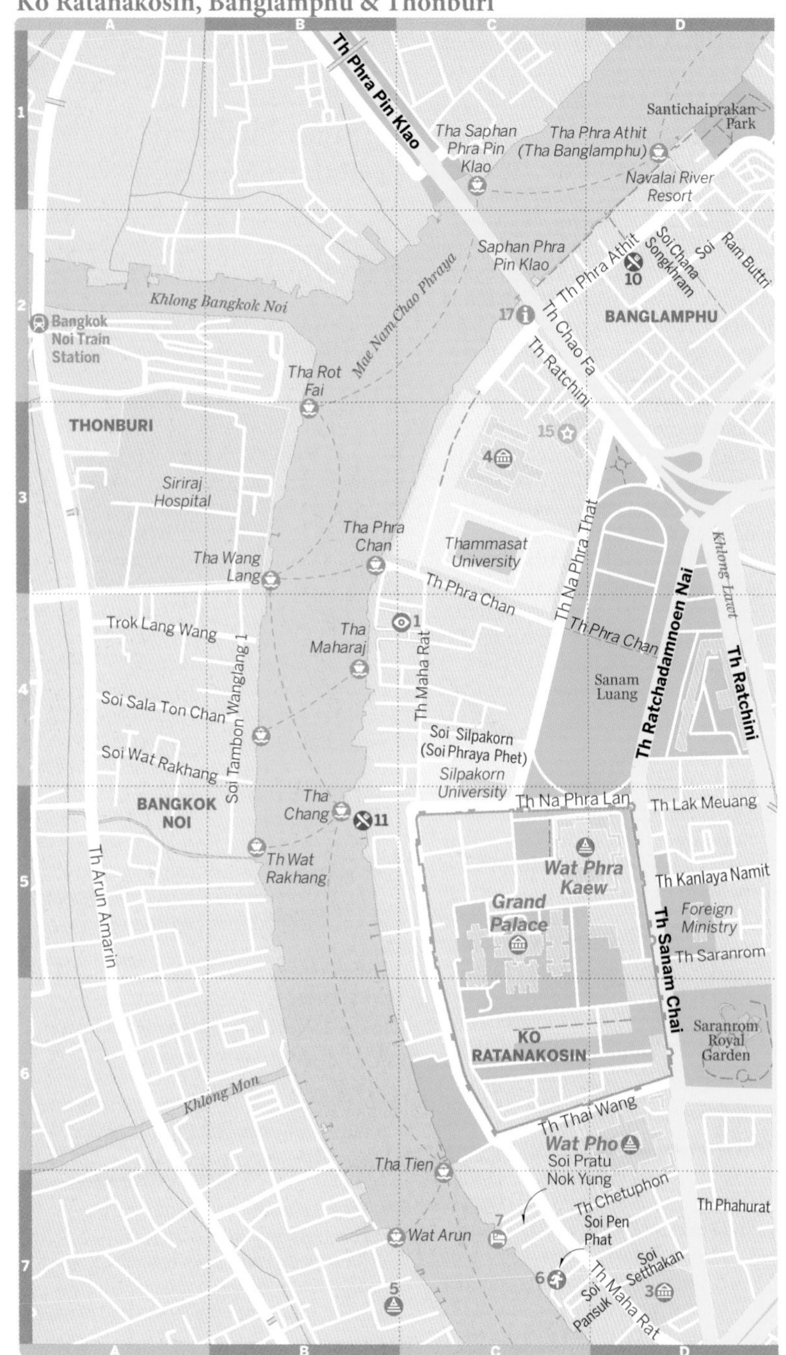

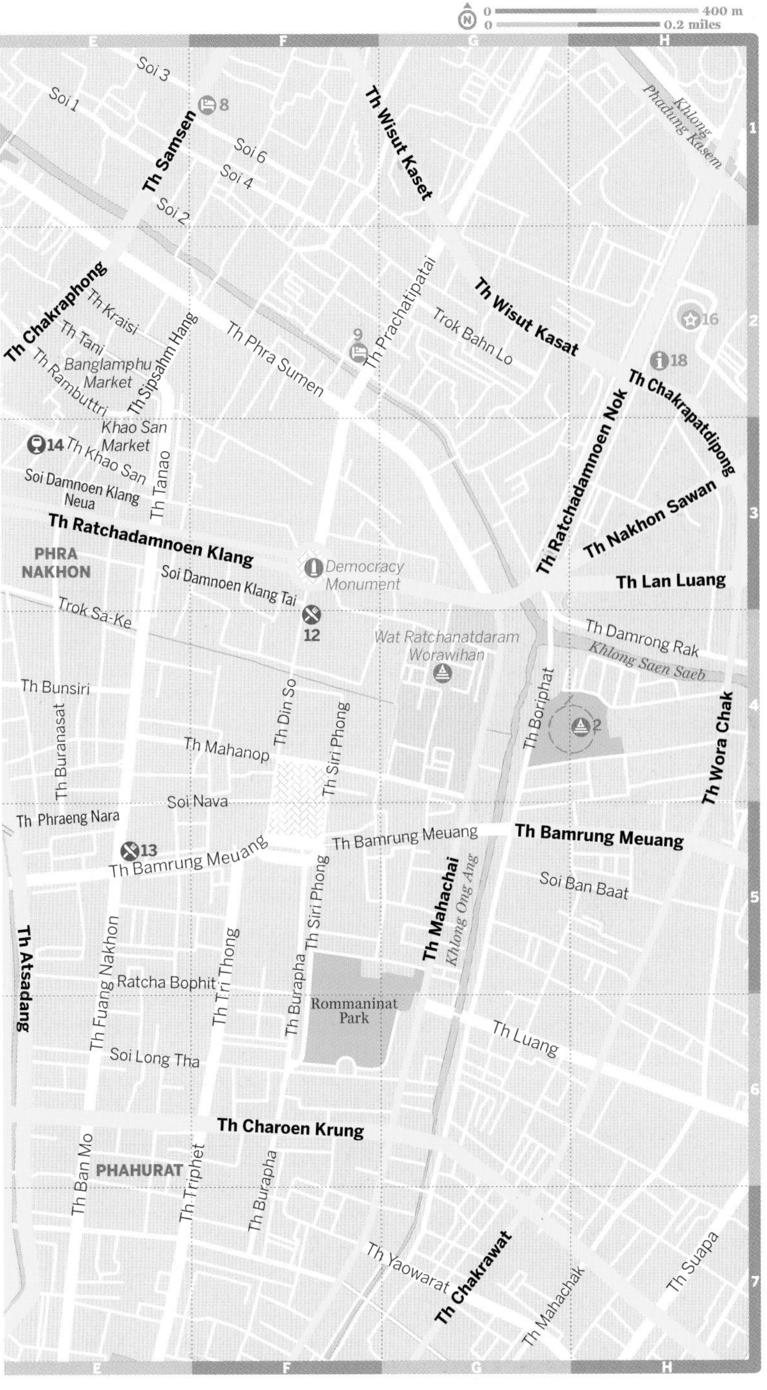

0 400 m
0 0.2 miles
Soi 3
Soi 1
8
Th Samsen
Soi 6
Soi 4
Soi 2
Th Wisut Kaset
Khlong Phadung Kasem
Th Chakraphong
Th Kraisi
Th Tani
Banglamphu Market
Th Rambuttri
Th Sipsahm Hang
Th Phra Sumen
9
Th Prachatipatai
Trok Bahn Lo
Th Wisut Kasat
16
18
Th Chakrapatdipong
Th Ratchadamnoen Nok
Khao San Market
14
Th Khao San
Th Tanao
Soi Damnoen Klang Neua
Th Ratchadamnoen Klang
PHRA NAKHON
Democracy Monument
Th Nakhon Sawan
Th Lan Luang
Soi Damnoen Klang Tai
Trok Sa-Ke
12
Wat Ratchanatdaram Worawihan
Th Damrong Rak
Khlong Saen Saeb
Th Bunsiri
Th Din So
Th Siri Phong
Th Boriphat
2
Th Wora Chak
Th Buranasat
Th Mahanop
Soi Nava
Th Phraeng Nara
13
Th Bamrung Meuang
Th Mahachai
Khlong Ong Ang
Soi Ban Baat
Th Atsadang
Th Fuang Nakhon
Ratcha Bophit
Th Tri Thong
Th Burapha
Rommaninat Park
Th Luang
Soi Long Tha
Th Charoen Krung
Th Ban Mo
PHAHURAT
Th Triphet
Th Yaowarat
Th Chakrawat
Th Mahachak
Th Suapa

Ko Ratanakosin, Banglamphu & Thonburi

Top Sights

	Grand Palace	C5
	Wat Pho	D6
	Wat Phra Kaew	C5

Sights

1	Amulet Market	C4
	Buddhaisawan (Phutthaisawan) Chapel	(see 4)
2	Golden Mount	H4
3	Museum of Siam	D7
4	National Museum	C3
5	Wat Arun	B7

Activities, Courses & Tours

6	Wat Pho Thai Traditional Medical and Massage School	C7

Sleeping

7	Arun Residence	C7
8	Baan Chantra	F1
9	Lamphu Tree House	F2

Eating

10	Hemlock	D2
11	Khunkung	B5
12	Krua Apsorn	F4
13	Poj Spa Kar	E5

Drinking

	Amorosa	(see 7)
14	Center Khao San	E3

Entertainment

15	National Theatre	C3
16	Ratchadamnoen Stadium	H2

Information

17	Bangkok Information Center	C2
18	Tourism Authority of Thailand	H2

(Aruna) and in honour of the literal and symbolic founding of a new Ayuthaya.

It wasn't until the capital and the Emerald Buddha were moved to Bangkok that Wat Arun received its most prominent characteristic: the 82m-high *prang* (Khmer-style tower). The tower's construction was started during the first half of the 19th century by Rama II and later completed by Rama III. Not apparent from a distance are the ornate floral mosaics made from broken, multihued Chinese porcelain, a common temple ornamentation in the early Ratanakosin period, when Chinese ships calling at the port of Bangkok discarded tonnes of old porcelain as ballast.

Cross-river ferries run over to Wat Arun every few minutes (3.50B per person) from Tha Tien.

Chinatown & Phahurat

เยาวราช (สำเพ็ง)/พาหุรัด

Bangkok's Chinatown (called Yaowarat after its main thoroughfare, Th Yaowarat) is the urban explorer's equivalent of the Amazon Basin.

The neighbourhood dates back to 1782 when Bangkok's Chinese population, many of them labourers hired to build the new capital, were moved here from today's Ko Ratanakosin area by the royal government. Relatively little has changed since then, and you can still catch conversations in various Chinese dialects, buy Chinese herbal cures or taste Chinese dishes not available elsewhere in Thailand.

At the western edge of Chinatown is a small but thriving Indian district, generally called Phahurat. Here, Indian-owned shops sell all kinds of fabric and clothes.

WAT TRAIMIT Buddhist Temple

(วัดไตรมิตร; Temple of the Golden Buddha; Map p70; cnr Th Yaowarat & Th Charoen Krung; admission 40B; 8am-5pm Tues-Sun; MRT Hua Lamphong, river ferry Tha Ratchawong) The attraction at Wat Traimit is undoubtedly the impressive 3m-tall, 5.5-tonne, solid-gold Buddha image, which gleams like, well, gold. Sculpted in the graceful Sukhothai style, the image was 'discovered' some 40 years ago beneath a stucco or plaster exterior, when it fell from a crane while being moved to a new building within the temple compound. It has been theorised that the covering was added to protect it from marauding hordes, either during the late Sukhothai period or later in the Ayuthaya period when the city was under

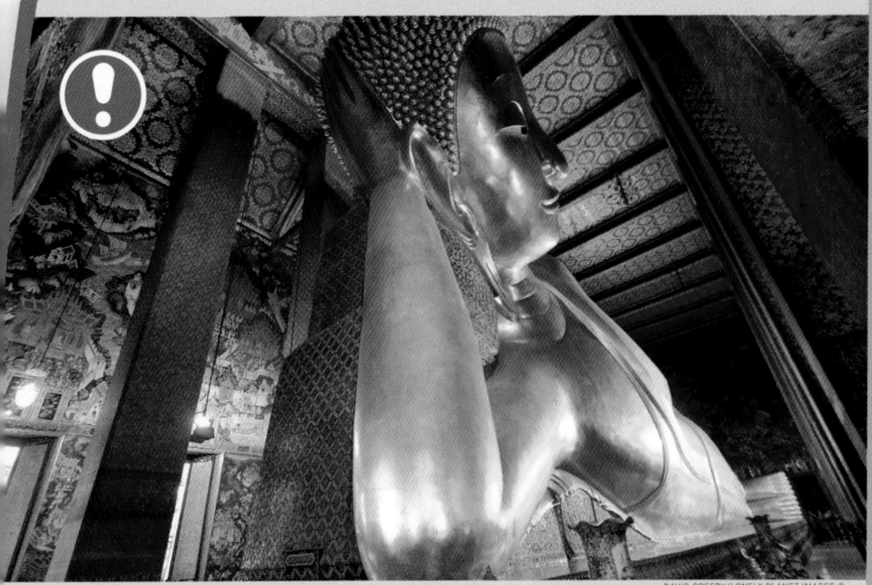

DAVID GREEDY/LONELY PLANET IMAGES ©

Don't Miss Wat Pho

You'll find (slightly) fewer tourists here than at Wat Phra Kaew, but Wat Pho is our personal favourite among Bangkok's biggest temples. In fact, the compound incorporates a host of superlatives: the largest reclining Buddha, the largest collection of Buddha images in Thailand and the country's earliest centre for public education.

Almost too big for its shelter, the genuinely impressive **Reclining Buddha**, 46m long and 15m high, illustrates the passing of the Buddha into nirvana (ie the Buddha's death). The figure is modelled out of plaster around a brick core and finished in gold leaf. Mother-of-pearl inlay ornaments the feet, displaying 108 different auspicious *lák·sà·nà* (characteristics of a Buddha).

Wat Pho is also the national headquarters for the teaching and preservation of traditional Thai medicine, including **Thai massage**, a mandate legislated by Rama III when the tradition was in danger of extinction. The famous massage school has two massage pavilions located within the temple area and additional rooms within the training facility outside the temple (p73).

THINGS YOU NEED TO KNOW

วัดโพธิ์ (วัดพระเชตุพน); Wat Phra Chetuphon; Map p66; Th Sanamchai; admission 50B; 8am-9pm; 508, 512, river ferry Tha Tien

siege by the Burmese. The temple itself is said to date from the early 13th century.

TALAT MAI Market

(ตลาดใหม่; Map p70; Soi 16/Trok Itsaranuphap, Th Yaowarat; 73, 159, 507, MRT Hua Lamphong, river ferry Tha Ratchawong) With nearly two centuries of commerce under its belt, 'New Market' is no longer an entirely accurate name for this market. Essentially it's a narrow covered alleyway between tall buildings, but even if you're not interested in food the hectic atmosphere and exotic

Chinatown & Phahurat

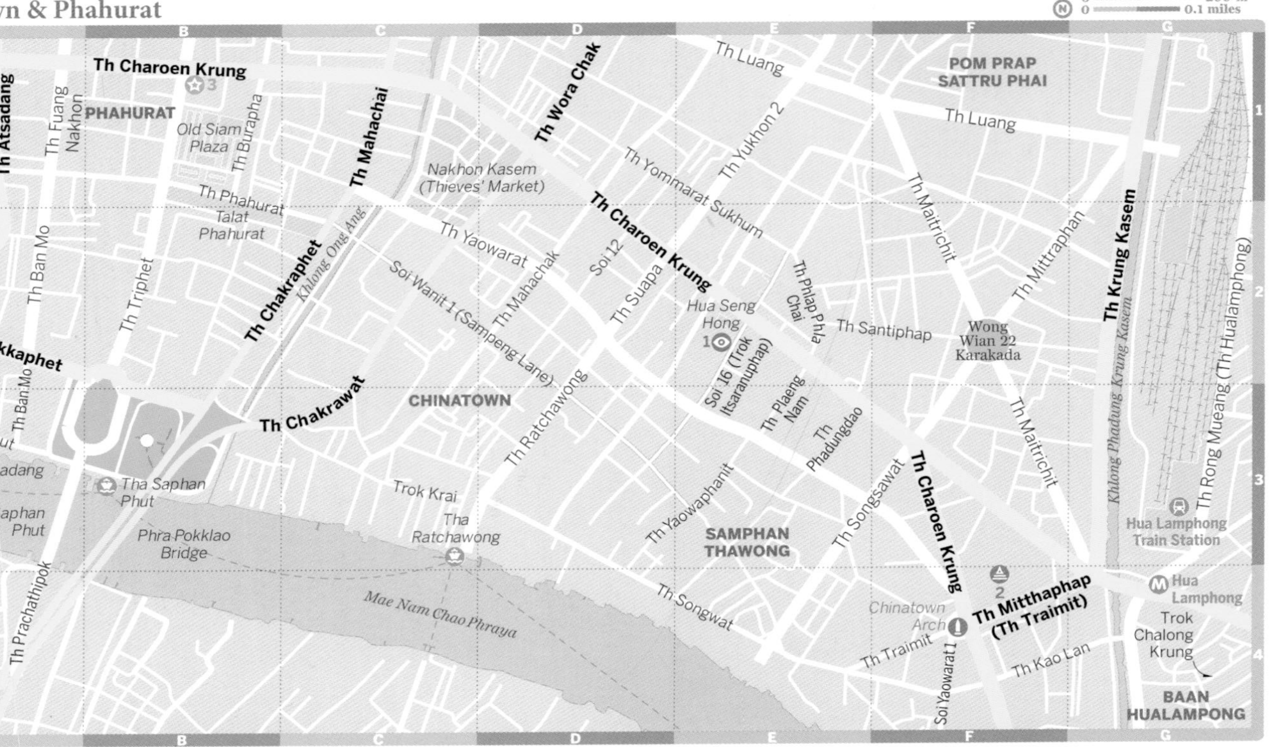

Chinatown & Phahurat

sights and smells culminate in something of a surreal sensory experience.

While much of the market centres on cooking ingredients, the section north of Th Charoen Krung (equivalent to Soi 21, Th Charoen Krung) is known for selling incense, paper effigies and ceremonial sweets – the essential elements of a traditional Chinese funeral.

Siam Square & Pratunam สยามสแควร์/ประตูน้ำ

ERAWAN SHRINE Brahmin Shrine

(ศาลพระพรหม; San Phra Phrom; Map p72; cnr Th Ratchadamri & Th Ploenchit; admission free; 6am-11pm; BTS Chit Lom) The Erawan Shrine was originally built in 1956 as something of a last-ditch effort to end a string of misfortunes that occurred during the construction of the hotel, at that time known as the Erawan Hotel.

Although the original Erawan Hotel was demolished in 1987, the shrine still exists, and today remains an important place of pilgrimage for Thais, particularly those in need of some material assistance.

Greater Bangkok

DUSIT PALACE PARK Royal Palace

(วังสวนดุสิต; bounded by Th Ratchawithi, Th U-Thong Nai & Th Ratchasima; adult/child 100/50B or free with Grand Palace ticket; 9.30am-4pm; 18, 28, 515) Following Rama V's first European tour in 1897 (he was the first Thai monarch to visit the continent), he returned home with visions of European castles and set about transforming these styles into a uniquely Thai expression: today's Dusit Palace Park. The royal palace, throne hall and minor palaces for extended family were all moved here from Ko Ratanakosin, the ancient royal court. Today the current King has yet another home and this complex now holds a house museum and other cultural collections.

Originally constructed on Ko Si Chang in 1868 and moved to the present site in 1910, **Vimanmaek Teak Mansion** contains 81 rooms, halls and anterooms, and is said to be the world's largest golden-teak building, apparently built without the use of a single nail. The mansion was the first permanent building on the Dusit Palace grounds, and served as Rama V's residence in the early 1900s. Compulsory tours (in English) leave every half-hour between 9.45am and 3.15pm, and last about an hour.

The smaller **Abhisek Dusit Throne Hall**, originally built as a throne hall for Rama V in 1904, is typical of the finer architecture of the era. Victorian-influenced gingerbread architecture and Moorish porticoes blend to create a striking and distinctly Thai exterior. The hall houses an excellent display of regional handiwork crafted by members of the Promotion of Supplementary Occupations & Related Techniques (Support) foundation, an organisation sponsored by Queen Sirikit.

Because this is royal property, visitors should wear long pants (no capri pants) or long skirts and shirts with sleeves.

Activities

TRADITIONAL THAI MASSAGE

A good massage is the birthright of every Bangkokian, and the joy of every visitor.

HEALTH LAND Spa, Massage

(www.healthlandspa.com; 2hr massage 450B) Ekamai (Map p80; 0 2392 2233; 96/1 Soi 10, Soi 63/Ekamai, Th Sukhumvit; 9am-11pm; BTS Ekkamai); Sathon (Map p76; 0 2637 8883; 120 Th Sathon Neua; 9am-11pm;

Siam Square & Pratunam

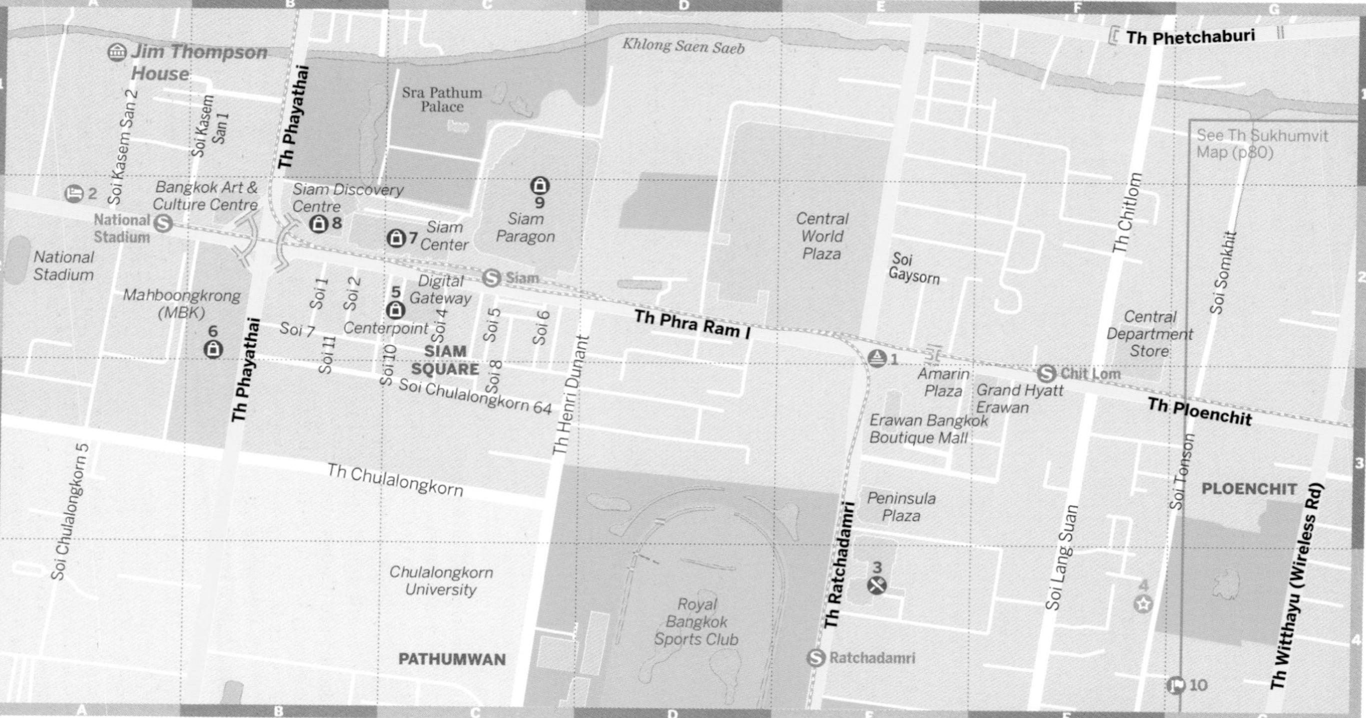

Siam Square & Pratunam

BTS Chong Nonsi); Sukhumvit **(Map p80; 0 2261 1110; 55/5 Soi 21/Asoke, Th Sukhumvit; 9am-midnight; BTS Asok, MRT Sukhumvit)** A winning formula of affordable prices, expert treatments and pleasant facilities has created a small empire of Health Land centres.

WAT PHO THAI TRADITIONAL MEDICAL & MASSAGE SCHOOL Massage
(Map p66; 0 2622 3550; Soi Penphat, Th Sanamchai; Thai massage per hr 220B; 8am-6pm; 123, 508, river ferry Tha Tien) The primary training ground for the masseuses who are deployed across the country; there are also massage pavilions inside the temple complex (see p69).

SPAS

ORIENTAL SPA Spa
(Map p76; 0 2659 9000; www.mandarinoriental.com/bangkok/spa; Oriental Hotel; spa packages from 2900B; 9am-10pm; hotel shuttle boat from Tha Sathon/Central Pier) Regarded as being among the premier spas in the world, the Oriental Spa also set the standard for Asian-style spa treatment.

SPA 1930 Spa
(Map p72; 0 2254 8606; www.spa1930.com; Soi Tonson, Th Ploenchit; spa treatments from 3800B; 9.30am-9.30pm; BTS Chit Lom) It rescues relaxers from the contrived spa ambience of New Age music and ingredients you'd rather experience at a dinner party. The menu is simple (face, body care and body massage) and all scrubs and massage oils are based on traditional Thai herbal remedies.

Courses

HELPING HANDS Cooking
(08 4901 8717; www.cookingwithpoo.com) This popular cookery course was started by a native of Khlong Toey's slums and is held in her neighbourhood. Courses, which must be booked in advance, span four dishes and include a visit to Khlong Toey Market and transportation to and from Emporium.

BAIPAI THAI COOKING SCHOOL Cooking
(0 2561 1404; www.baipai.com; 8/91 Soi 54, Th Ngam Wong Wan; lessons 1800B; 9.30am-1.30pm & 1.30-5.30pm Tue-Sat) Housed in an attractive suburban villa, and taught by a small army of staff, Baipai offers two daily lessons of four dishes each. Transportation is available.

Tours

If you would like a guide, recommended outfits include **Tour with Tong (0 81835 0240; www.tourwithtong.com; day tour from 1000B)**, whose team conduct tours in and around Bangkok, and **Thai Private Tour Guide (0 81860 9159; www.thaitourguide.com; day tour from 2000B)**, where Chob and Mee get good reviews.

PETER UNGER/LONELY PLANET IMAGES ©

Don't Miss Wat Phra Kaew & Grand Palace

Also known as the Temple of the Emerald Buddha, **Wat Phra Kaew** is the colloquial name of the vast, fairy-tale compound that also includes the former residence of the Thai monarch, the Grand Palace. Housed in a fantastically decorated *bòht* (temple) and guarded by pairs of *yaksha* (mythical giants), the **Emerald Buddha** is the temple's primary attraction. It sits atop an elevated altar, barely visible amid the gilded decorations. The diminutive figure is always cloaked in royal robes, one for each season (hot, cool and rainy). In a solemn ceremony, the king (or in recent years, the crown prince) changes the garments at the beginning of each season. Recently restored **Buddhist murals** line the interior walls of the *bòht,* and the **murals of the Ramakian** (the Thai version of the Indian epic the *Ramayana*) line the inside walls of the temple compound.

Except for an anteroom here and there, the buildings of the **Grand Palace** (Phra Borom Maharatchawong) are now put to use by the king only for certain ceremonial occasions, such as Coronation Day.

The largest of the palace buildings is the **Chakri Mahaprasat**, the Grand Palace Hall. Built in 1882 by British architects using Thai labour, the exterior is a peculiar blend of Italian Renaissance and traditional Thai architecture. It's a style often referred to as *fa·ràng sài chá·dah* (Westerner in a Thai crown) because each wing is topped by a *mon·dòp* – a heavily ornamented spire representing a Thai adaptation of the Hindu *mandapa* (shrine).

The admission fee for the complex includes entrance to Dusit Palace Park (p71), which includes Vimanmaek Teak Mansion and Abhisek Dusit Throne Hall.

THINGS YOU NEED TO KNOW

วัดพระแก้ว/พระบรมมหาราชวัง; Map p66; admission 350B; ⏲8.30am-3.30pm; 🚌 503, 508, river ferry Tha Chang

Sleeping

Ko Ratanakosin, Banglamphu & Thonburi

Ko Ratanakosin, the most touristed area of Bangkok, was until relatively recently utterly devoid of lodging options. But with the advent of the boutique-hotel craze, a few riverside shophouses are being transformed into charming tourists' nests.

Banglamphu, in particular the neighbourhood that includes the backpacker street of Th Khao San, is ground zero for budget accommodation in Bangkok.

In recent years many longstanding Banglamphu guest house owners have converted their former hovels into small hotels, leading to an abundance of new, good-value midrangers and posh backpacker hostels.

LAMPHU TREE HOUSE Boutique Hotel **$$**
(Map p66; ☎0 2282 0991; www.lamphutreehotel.com; 155 Wanchat Bridge, Th Prachatipatai; r incl breakfast 1500-2100B; ❄@📶🏊; 🚌56, 58, 516, klorng taxi Tha Phah Fah, river ferry Tha Phra Athit) Despite the name, this attractive midranger has its feet firmly on land and as such, represents brilliant value. Rooms are attractive and inviting, and the rooftop bar, pool, internet, restaurant and quiet canal-side location ensure that you may never feel the need to leave.

ARUN RESIDENCE Boutique Hotel **$$$**
(Map p66; ☎0 2221 9158; www.arunresidence.com; 36-38 Soi Pratu Nok Yung, Th Maha Rat; r 3500-3800B, ste 5500B; ❄@📶; 🚌123, 508, river ferry Tha Tien) Although strategically located across from Wat Arun, this multilevel wooden house on the river boasts much more than just brilliant views. The six rooms here manage to feel both homey and stylish, some being tall and loft-like, while others cojoin two rooms (the best is the top-floor suite with its own balcony).

Travels of the Emerald Buddha

The Emerald Buddha (Phra Kaew Morakot) holds a prominent position in Thai Buddhism in spite of its size (a mere 66cm) and original material (probably jasper quartz or nephrite jade rather than emerald). In fact, the Emerald Buddha was just another ordinary image, with no illustrious pedigree, until its monumental 'coming out' in 15th-century Chiang Rai. During a fall, the image revealed its luminescent interior, which had been covered with plaster (a common practice to safeguard valuable Buddhas from being stolen). After a few successful stints in various temples throughout northern Thailand, the image was stolen by Lao invaders in the mid-16th century and remained in that country for 200 years.

In 1778 Thailand's King Taksin waged war against Laos, retrieving the image and mounting it in Thonburi. Later, when the capital moved to Bangkok and General Chakri took the crown, the Emerald Buddha was honoured with one of the country's most magnificent monuments, Wat Phra Kaew.

BAAN CHANTRA Boutique Hotel **$$**
(Map p66; ☎0 2628 6988; www.baanchantra.com; 120 Th Samsen; r incl breakfast 2400-3500B; ❄@📶; 🚌32, 516, river ferry Tha Phra Athit) This beautiful converted house is without pretensions, preferring to be comfortable and roomy rather than fashionable and pinched. Many of the house's original teak details remain, and the deluxe room boasts a sunny patio.

Siam Square & Pratunam

For centrally located accommodation, there's really no better destination than the area surrounding Siam Square.

SIAM@SIAM Hotel $$$
(Map p72; ☎0 2217 3000; www.siamatsiam.com; 865 Th Phra Ram I; r incl breakfast 5000-7000B; ❄@🛜🏊; BTS National Stadium) The lobby of this new hotel is more amusement park than accommodation, but that's what makes it so much fun. A seemingly random mishmash of colours and materials result in a style one could only describe as 'junkyard' – but in a good way, of course.

Riverside

ORIENTAL HOTEL Luxury Hotel $$$
(Map p76; ☎0 2659 9000; www.mandarinoriental.com; 48 Soi 40/Oriental, Th Charoen Krung; r incl breakfast 12,800-14,800B, ste 24,000-141,000B; ❄@🛜🏊; hotel shuttle boat from Tha Sathon/Central Pier) For the true Bangkok experience, a stay at this grand old riverside hotel is a must. The majority of rooms are located in the modern and recently refurbished New Wing, but we prefer the old-world ambiance of the Garden and Authors' Wings.

Sukhumvit สุขุมวิท

ARIYASOMVILLA B&B $$$
(Map p80; ☎0 2254 880; www.ariyasom.com; 65 Soi 1, Th Sukhumvit; r incl breakfast 4250-9150B; ❄@🛜🏊; BTS Phloen Chit) Located at the end of Soi 1 behind a virtual wall of fragipani, this renovated 1940s-era villa is one of the worst-kept accommodation secrets in Bangkok. If you can score a reservation, you'll be privy to one of 24 spacious rooms, meticulously outfitted

Silom, Sathon & Riverside

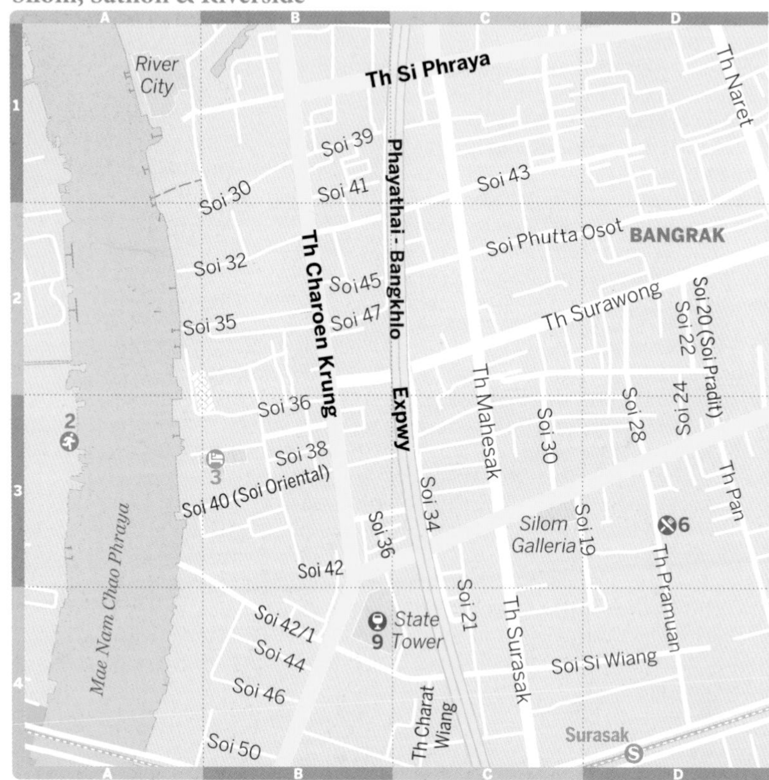

with thoughtful Thai design touches and beautiful antique furniture.

72 EKAMAI Boutique Hotel **$$**
(Map p80; ☎02 714 7327; www.72ekamai.com; 72 Soi 63/Ekamai, Th Sukhumvit; r 2100B, ste 2500-2850B; ❄@📶🏊; BTS Ekkamai) This fun, young-feeling, design-concscious hotel is a great choice. Reds, black and pop art prints define the look here, and perhaps we were mistaken, but on our visit, we swear the place smelled like candy. The junior suites are huge, and like all rooms, are well equipped and conveniently located.

NAPA PLACE B&B **$$**
(Map p80; ☎0 2661 5525; www.napaplace.com; 11/3 Yaek 2, Soi 36, Th Sukhumvit; r 2200-2400B, ste 3400B; ❄@📶; BTS Thong Lo) Seemingly hidden in the confines of a typical Bangkok urban compound is what must be the city's homiest accommodation. The 12 expansive rooms here have been decorated with dark woods from the family's former business and light brown cloths from the hands of Thai weavers.

SEVEN Boutique Hotel **$$$**
(Map p80; ☎0 2662 0951; www.sleepatseven.com; 3/15 Soi 31/Sawatdi, Th Sukhumvit; r incl breakfast 3290-5290B; ❄@📶; BTS Phrom Phong) This tiny hotel somehow manages to be chic and homey, stylish and comfortable, and Thai and international all at the same time. Each of the six rooms is decked out in a different colour that corresponds to Thai astrology, and thoughtful amenities abound.

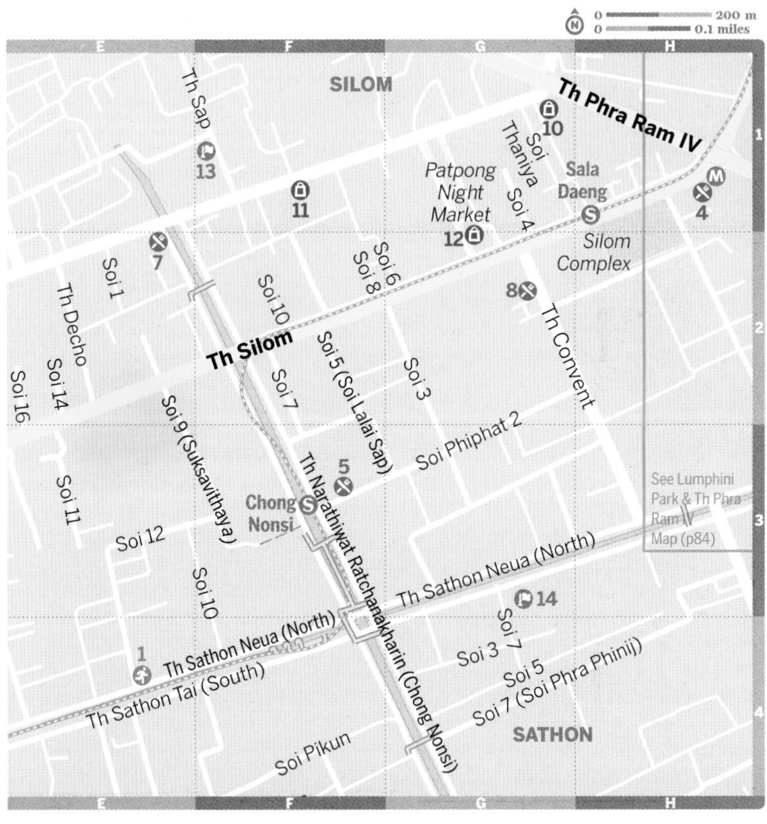

Silom, Sathon & Riverside

Activities, Courses & Tours
1 Health Land ... E4
2 Oriental Spa ... A3

Sleeping
3 Oriental Hotel ... B3

Eating
4 D'Sens ... H1
5 Foodie ... F3
6 Kalpapruek ... D3
Lord Jim's ... (see 3)
7 Somboon Seafood ... E2
8 Somtam Convent ... G2

Drinking
9 Sirocco Sky Bar ... B4

Shopping
10 Jim Thompson ... G1
11 Jim Thompson Factory Outlet ... F1
12 Patpong Night Market ... G2

Information
13 Russia Embassy ... F1
14 Singapore Embassy ... G3

Eating

The selection is enormous, with eating places in Bangkok ranging from wheeled carts that set up shop on a daily basis to chic dining rooms in five-star hotels. In our experience the tastiest eats are generally found somewhere in-between, at family-run shophouse restaurants serving a limited repertoire of dishes.

The influences are also vast, and you'll find everything from Chinese-Thai to Muslim-Thai, not to mention most regional domestic cuisines.

Ko Ratanakosin, Banglamphu & Thonburi

KRUA APSORN Thai $$

(Map p66; Th Din So; mains 70-320B; lunch & dinner Mon-Sat; ; 2, 25, 44, 511, klorng taxi to Tha Phan Fah) This homey dining room has served members of the Thai royal family and, back in 2006, was recognised as Bangkok's Best Restaurant by the *Bangkok Post*. Must-eat dishes include mussels fried with fresh herbs, the decadent crab fried in yellow chilli oil and the tortilla Española–like crab omelette.

POJ SPA KAR Thai $$

(Map p66; 443 Th Tanao; mains 100-200B; lunch & dinner; ; 2, 25, 44, 511, klorng taxi to Tha Phan Fah) Pronounced *pôht sà·pah kahn,* this is allegedly the oldest restaurant in Bangkok, and continues to maintain recipes handed down from a former palace cook. Be sure to order the simple but tasty lemongrass omelette or the deliciously sour/sweet *gaang sôm* (a traditional central Thai soup).

KHUNKUNG Thai $$

(Khun Kung Kitchen; Map p66; 77 Th Maha Rat; mains 75-280B; lunch & dinner; ; 25, 32, 503, 508, river ferry Tha Chang) The restaurant of the Royal Navy Association has one of the few coveted riverfront locations along this stretch of the Chao Phraya River. Locals come for the combination of riverfront views and cheap and tasty seafood-based eats. The entrance to the restaurant is near the ATM machines at Tha Chang.

HEMLOCK Thai $$

(Map p66; 56 Th Phra Athit; mains 60-220B; 4pm-midnight; ; 32, 33, 64, 82, river ferry Tha Phra Athit) Taking full advantage of its cosy shophouse setting, this white-tablecloth local is an excellent intro to Thai food. The vast menu has the usual suspects, but also includes some dishes you'd be hard pressed to find elsewhere, as well as a strong vegetarian section.

Siam Square & Pratunam

MBK FOOD COURT Thai $

(Map p72; 6th floor, MBK Center, cnr Th Phra Ram I & Th Phayathai; 10am-9pm; ; BTS National Stadium) The granddaddy of Bangkok food courts offers dozens of vendors selling dishes from virtually every corner of Thailand and beyond. It's a great introduction to Thai food, and standouts include an excellent vegetarian food stall (stall C8) and a very decent Isan food vendor (C22). To pay, you must first exchange your cash for a temporary credit card at one of several counters; your change is refunded at the same desk.

FOUR SEASONS HOTEL Brunch $$$

(Map p72; ☎ 0 2250 1000; 155 Th Ratchadamri; buffet 2750B; ⏰11.30am-3pm Sun; ❄; BTS Ratchadamri) Sunday brunch has become something of a Bangkok institution among resident foreigners, and virtually every large hotel in town puts together decadent buffets on every other day as well. The highly regarded restaurants at the Four Seasons Hotel set up steam tables for their decadent Sunday brunch buffet. Reservations are essential.Silom & Sathon

D'SENS French $$$

(Map p76; ☎ 0 2200 9000; 22nd fl, Dusit Thani, 946 Th Phra Ram IV; set menu 1850-3100B; ⏰11.30am-2.30pm & 6-10pm, 6-10pm Sat; ❄; BTS Sala Daeng, MRT Si Lom) Arguably Bangkok's best upscale *fa·ràng* (foreign) fine-dining restaurant, D'Sens is perched like an air traffic control tower atop the Dusit Thani hotel. A venture of French wonder-twins Laurent and Jacques Pourcel, creators of the Michelin-starred Le Jardin des Sens in Montpellier, France, the restaurant is handsome yet modern and the menu draws from the traditions of the south of France, relying mainly on high-quality French imports for its ingredients.

KALPAPRUEK Thai $$

(Map p76; 27 Th Pramuan; mains 80-120B; ⏰8am-6pm Mon-Sat, to 3pm Sun; ❄; BTS Surasak) This venerable Thai eatery has numerous branches and mall spin-offs around town, but we still like the quasi-concealed original branch. The diverse menu spans regional Thai specialties from just about every region, daily specials and, occasionally, seasonal treats.

SOMBOON SEAFOOD Chinese-Thai $$$

(Map p76; www.somboonseafood.com; 169/7-11 Th Surawong; mains 120-900B; ⏰dinner; ❄; BTS Chong Nonsi) Holy seafood factory: ascending the many staircases to a free table might make you nervous about the quality of so much quantity, but Somboon's famous crab curry will make you messy and full.

If You Like... Rooftop Bars

Bangkok is one of the few big cities in the world where nobody seems to mind if you set up the odd bar or restaurant on the top of a skyscraper. Note that reservations are recommended for the more restaurant-like of the following, and none allow shorts or sandals wearers.

1 **MOON BAR AT VERTIGO**
(Map p84; Banyan Tree Hotel, 21/100 Th Sathon Tai; ⏰5.30pm-1am; MRT Lumphini) Precariously perched on the top of 61 floors of skyscraper, Moon Bar offers a bird's-eye view of Bangkok. Things can get a bit crowded here come sunset, so be sure to show up a bit early to get the best seats.

2 **SIROCCO SKY BAR**
(Map p76; The Dome, 1055 Th Silom; ⏰6pm-1am; BTS Saphan Taksin) Descend the sweeping stairs like a Hollywood diva to the precipice bar of this rooftop restaurant that looks over the Mae Nam Chao Phraya.

3 **NEST**
(Map p80; ☎ 0 2255 0638; www.nestbangkok.com; 8th fl, Le Fenix Hotel, 33/33 Soi 11, Th Sukhumvit; ⏰5pm-2am; BTS Nana) Perched on the roof of the Le Fenix Hotel, Nest is a chic maze of cleverly concealed sofas and inviting daybeds. A DJ soundtrack and one of the most interesting pub grub menus in town bring things back down to ground level.

LORD JIM'S Brunch $$$

(Map p76; www.mandarinoriental.com; ☎ 0 2659 9000; 48 Soi Oriental/38, Th Charoen Krung; buffet 1480-1950B; ⏰noon-2.30pm Mon-Fri, 11.30am-3pm Sat, 11am-3pm Sun; ❄; river ferry Tha Oriental) Even if your not staying at the Oriental Hotel, you should save up for the riverside seafood buffet at Lord Jim's.

FOODIE Thai $$

(Map p76; Soi Phiphat 2; mains 80-150B; ⏰lunch & dinner; ❄; BTS Chong Nonsi) This airy, cafeteria-like restaurant boasts a menu of hard-to-find central- and southern-

Th Sukhumvit

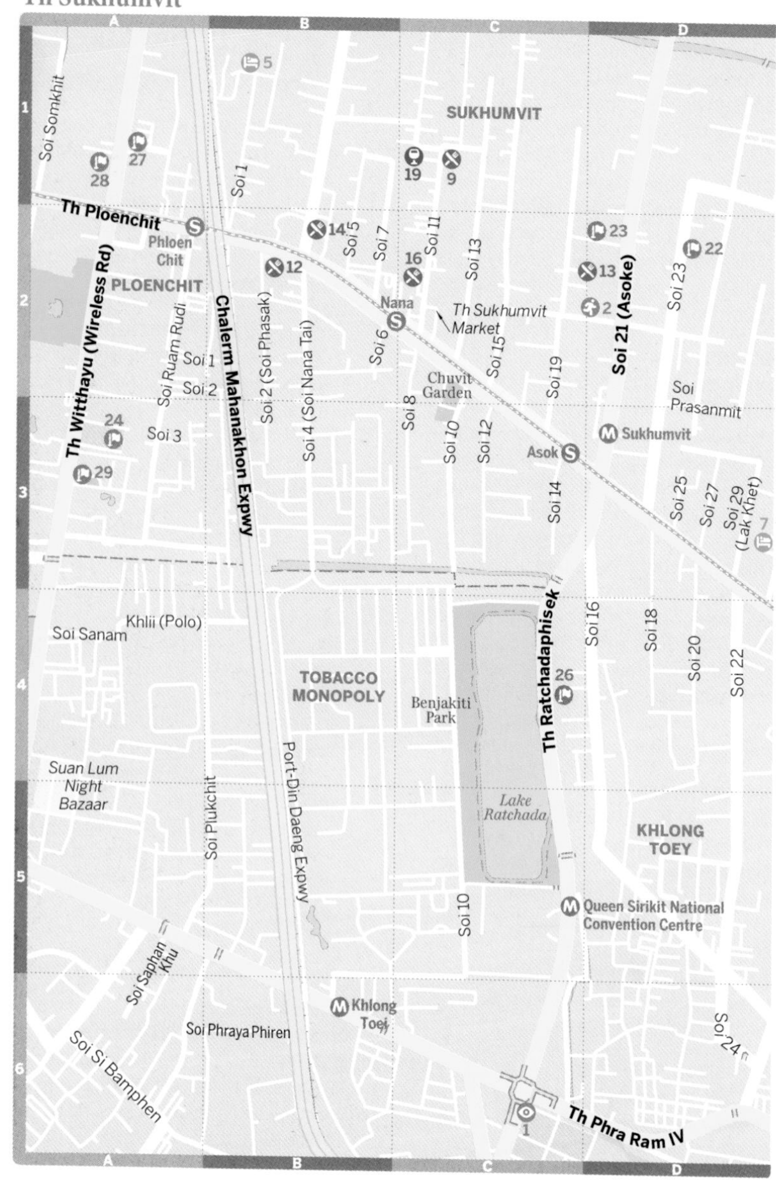

style Thai dishes. Highlights include the *yam sôm oh*, (a spicy/sour/sweet salad of pomelo) and the spicy *prík kǐng ɓlah dòok foo* (catfish fried in a curry paste until crispy).

SOMTAM CONVENT Thai $

(Map p76; 2/4-5 Th Convent; mains 20-120B; ⏲10.30am-9pm; BTS Sala Daeng, MRT Si Lom) Northeastern-style Thai food is usually relegated to less-than-hygienic stalls perched by the side of the road with no menu or

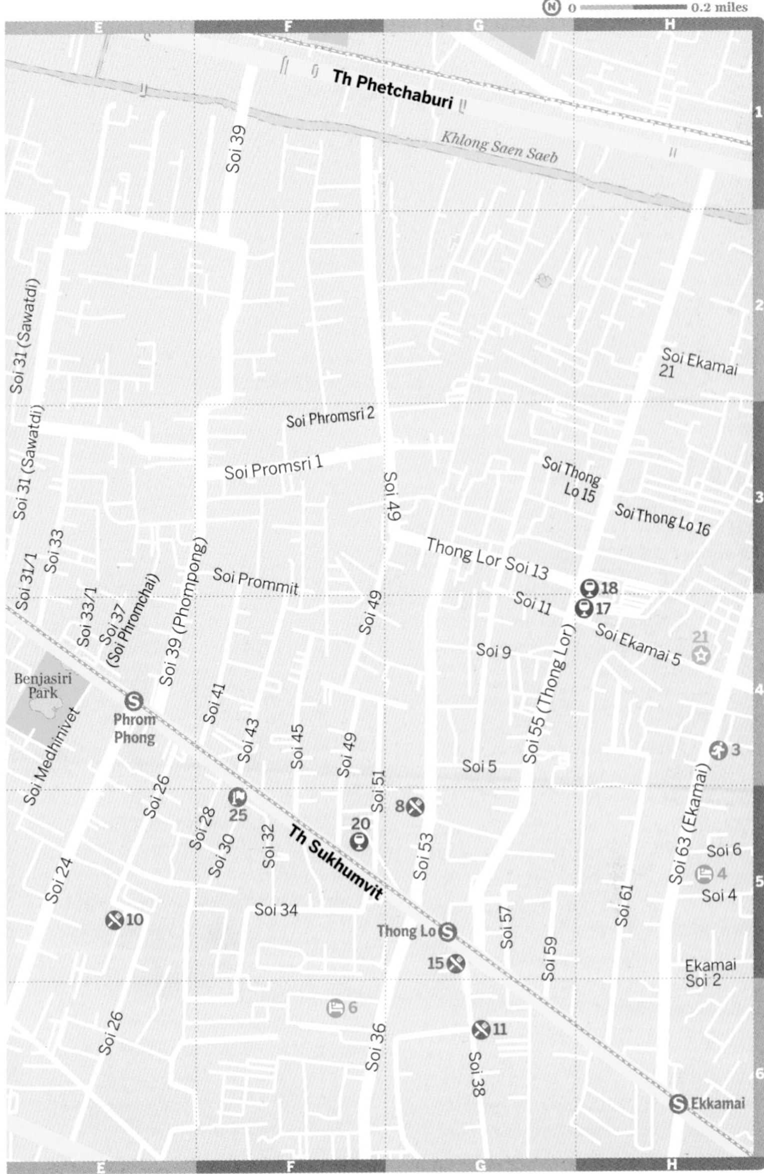

English-speaking staff in sight. A less intimidating introduction to the wonders of *lâhp* (a minced meat 'salad'), *sôm·đam* (papaya salad) and other Isan delights can be had at this popular restaurant.

KRUA AROY AROY Thai $

(Map p76; Th Pan; mains 30-70B; 8am-8.30pm, closed 2nd & 4th Sun of each month; BTS Surasak) It can be crowded and hot, but Krua 'Aroy-Aroy' (Delicious Kitchen) rarely fails to live up to its lofty name. Stop by for

Th Sukhumvit

Sights
1 Khlong Toey Market C6

Activities, Courses & Tours
2 Health Land D2
3 Health Land H4

Sleeping
4 72 Ekamai H5
5 AriyasomVilla B1
6 Napa Place F6
7 Seven D3

Eating
8 Bacco: Osteria da Sergio G5
9 Bed Supperclub C1
10 Bo.lan E5
11 Face G6
12 JW Marriott B2
13 Le Beaulieu D2
14 Nasir Al-Masri B2
15 Soi 38 Night Market G5
16 Tapas Café C2

Drinking
17 Fat Gut'z H4
18 Iron Fairies H3
19 Nest C1
20 WTF F5

Entertainment
21 Ekamai Soi 5 .... H4

Information
22 Indian Embassy D2
23 Israeli Embassy D2
24 New Zealand Embassy A3
25 Philippines Embassy F5
South African Embassy .... (see 24)
26 Spanish Embassy C4
27 Swiss Embassy A1
28 UK Embassy A1
29 US Embassy A3

some of Bangkok's richest curries, as well as a revolving menu of daily specials.

Sukhumvit

BO.LAN Thai **$$$**
(Map p80; 0 2260 2962; www.bolan.co.th; 42 Soi Rongnarong Phichai Songkhram, Soi 26, Th Sukhumvit; set meal 1500B; dinner Tue-Sun; BTS Phrom Phong) Bo and Dylan (Bo.lan, a play on words that also means 'ancient'), former chefs at London's Michelin-starred nahm, have provided Bangkok with a compelling reason to reconsider upscale Thai cuisine. The couple's scholarly approach to Thai cooking takes the form of seasonal set meals featuring dishes you're not likely to find elsewhere.

LE BEAULIEU French **$$$**
(Map p80; 0 2204 2004; www.le-beaulieu.com; 50 Soi 19, Th Sukhumvit; set lunch from 525B, dinner from 1950B; 11.30am-3pm & 6.30-11pm; ; BTS Asok, MRT Sukhumvit) This tiny service hotel–bound restaurant is considered by many residents to be Bangkok's best place for French cuisine. The menu ranges from the classic (steak tartare, bouillabaisse) to the modern (minute of scrambled eggs and fresh sea urchin), with dishes prepared using both unique imported ingredients and produce from Thailand's Royal Projects. Reservations recommended.

JW MARRIOTT Brunch **$$$**
(Map p80; 0 2656 7700; ground fl, JW Marriott Hotel, 4 Soi 2, Th Sukhumvit; buffet Sat 1285B, Sun 1885B; 11.30am-3pm Sat & Sun; ; BTS Nana) The award-winning buffet at US chain JW Marriott is likened to Thanksgiving all year-round, and generous options for free-flowing beer or wine are also available.

NASIR AL-MASRI Middle Eastern **$$$**
(Map p80; 4/6 Soi 3/1, Th Sukhumvit; mains 80-350B; 24hr; ; BTS Nana) One of several similar Middle Eastern restaurants on Soi 3/1, Nasir Al-Masri is easily recognisable by its genuinely impressive floor-to-ceiling stainless steel 'theme'. Middle Eastern food generally means meat, meat and more meat, but there are also several delicious vegie-based mezze.

BED SUPPERCLUB International **$$$**
(Map p80; 0 2651 3537; www.bedsupperclub.com; 26 Soi 11, Th Sukhumvit; mains 450-990B, set meals 790-1850B; 7.30-10pm Tue-Thu,

dinner 9pm Fri & Sat; ❄; BTS Nana) Within this sleek and futuristic setting – beds instead of tables and contemporary performances instead of mood music – the food stands up to the distractions with a changing menu described as 'modern eclectic cuisine'. Dining is à la carte except on Fridays and Saturdays when there's a four-course surprise menu served at 9pm sharp.

BACCO: OSTERIA DA SERGIO Italian $$$

(Map p80; www.bacco-bkk.com; 35/1 Soi 53, Th Sukhumvit; antipasti 100-1200B, mains 250-850B; lunch & dinner; ❄; BTS Thong Lo) The slightly cheesy interior of this osteria serves as something of a cover for one of Bangkok's better Italian menus.

TAPAS CAFÉ Spanish $$

(Map p80; 1/25 Soi 11, Th Sukhumvit; mains 75-750B; 11am-midnight; ❄; BTS Nana) If vibrant tapas, refreshing sangria and an open, airy atmosphere aren't reasons enough to eat here, consider that before 7pm dishes and drinks are buy-two, get-one-free.

FACE International $$$

(Map p80; 0 2713 6048; 29 Soi 38, Th Sukhumvit; mains 310-670B; lunch & dinner; ❄; BTS Thong Lo) This handsome dining complex is essentially three very good restaurants in one: Lan Na Thai does solid upscale Thai, Misaki focuses on the Japanese end of things, while Hazara dabbles in exotic-sounding 'North Indian frontier cuisine.'

SOI 38 NIGHT MARKET Thai-Chinese $

(Map p80; Soi 38, Th Sukhumvit; mains 30-60B; 8pm-3am; BTS Thong Lo) After a hard night of clubbing, this gathering of basic Thai-Chinese hawker stalls will look like a shimmering oasis. If you're going sober, stick to the knot of 'famous' vendors tucked into an alley on the right-hand side as you enter the street.

KHLONG TOEY MARKET Market

(Map p80; cnr Th Ratchadaphisek & Th Phra Ram IV; 5-10am; Metro Khlong Toei) One of the largest suppliers of fresh ingredients for the city's restaurants and street stalls.

Lumphini

NAHM Thai $$$

(Map p84; 0 2625 3333; Metropolitan Hotel, 27 Th Sathon Tai; set meal 1500B; dinner; ❄;

Chicken satay

RICHARD I'ANSON/LONELY PLANET IMAGES ©

Lumphini Park & Th Phra Ram IV

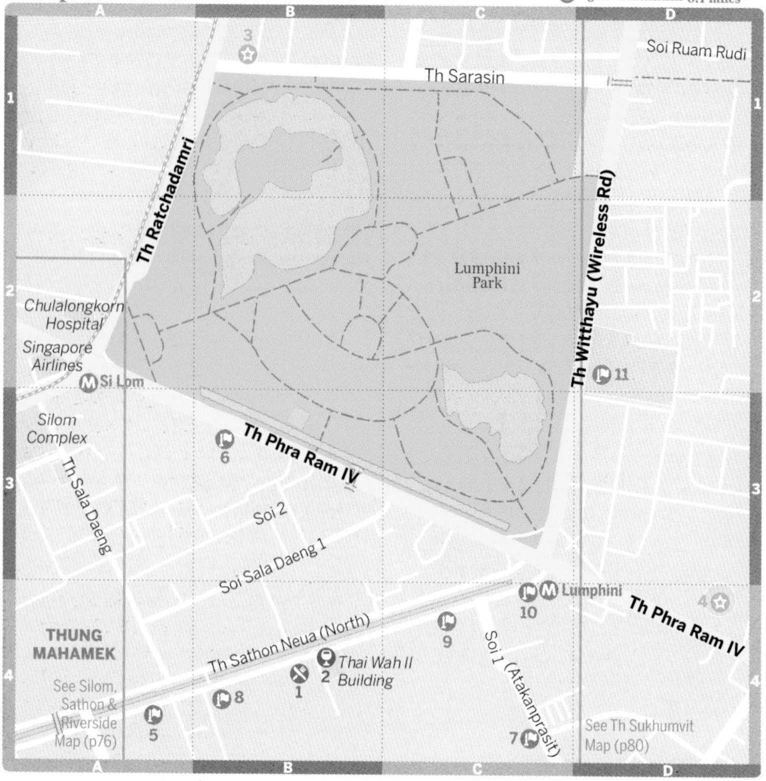

0 — 200 m
0 — 0.1 miles

Lumphini Park & Th Phra Ram IV

Eating
1 nahm......B4

Drinking
2 Moon Bar at Vertigo......B4

Entertainment
3 Brown Sugar......B1
4 Lumphini Stadium......D4

Information
5 Australian Embassy......A4
6 Canadian Embassy......B3
7 Danish Embassy......C4
8 French Consulate......B4
9 German Embassy......C4
10 Irish Embassy......C4
11 Japanese Embassy......D2

MRT Lumphini) Australian chef/author David Thompson is behind what is quite possibly the best Thai restaurant in Bangkok.

Drinking

Once infamous as an anything-goes nightlife destination, in recent years Bangkok has been edging towards teetotalism with strict regulations limiting the sale of alcohol and increasingly conservative closing times.

AMOROSA Bar
Map p66; www.arunresidence.com; rooftop, Arun Residence, 36-38 Soi Pratu Nok Yung; 6-11pm; 123, 508, river ferry Tha Tien) It may be the only bar in the area, but that doesn't mean it's any sort of compro-

mise; Amorosa's rooftop location packs killer views of Wat Arun, making it one of the best spots in Bangkok for a riverside sundowner.

CENTER KHAO SAN Bar

(Map p66; Th Khao San; 24hr; river ferry Tha Phra Athit) One of many front-row views of the human parade on Th Khao San. The upstairs bar hosts late-night bands.

WTF Bar

(Map p80; www.wtfbangkok.com; 7 Soi 51, Th Sukhumvit; 6pm-1am Tue-Sun; BTS Thong Lo;) No, not that WTF; Wonderful Thai Friendship combines a cozy bar and an art gallery in one attractive package. Throw in some of Bangkok's best cocktails and some delicious Spanish-influenced bar snacks, and you won't need another destination for the evening.

IRON FAIRIES Bar

(Map p80; www.theironfairies.com; Soi 55/Thong Lor, Th Sukhumvit; 5pm-midnight Mon-Sat; BTS Thong Lo;) Imagine, if you can, an abandoned fairy factory in Paris c 1912, and you'll get an idea of the design theme at this popular pub/wine bar.

Entertainment

SAXOPHONE PUB & RESTAURANT Live Music

(www.saxophonepub.com; 3/8 Th Phayathai; 6pm-2am; BTS Victory Monument;) This nightlife staple is the big stage of Bangkok's live-music scene. It's a bit too loud for a first date, but the quality and variety of the music makes it a great destination for music-loving buddies on a night out.

BROWN SUGAR Bar

(Map p84; 231/20 Th Sarasin; 6pm-midnight; BTS Ratchadamri;) Plant yourself in a corner of this cosy, maze-like pub, and bump to Zao-za-dung, the nine-piece house band.

FAT GUT'Z Live Music

(Map p80; www.fatgutz.com; 264 Soi 12, Soi 55/Thong Lor, Th Sukhumvit; 6pm-2am; BTS Thong Lo;) This closet-sized 'saloon' combines live music and, er, fish and chips. Live blues every night from 9pm to midnight.

EKAMAI SOI 5 Club

(Map p80; cnr Soi Ekamai 5 & Soi 63/Ekamai, Th Sukhumvit; BTS Ekkamai & access by taxi) This open-air entertainment zone is the destination of choice for Bangkok's young and beautiful – for the moment at least.

TRADITIONAL ARTS PERFORMANCES

CHALERMKRUNG ROYAL THEATRE Traditional Performance

(Sala Chalerm Krung; Map p70; 0 2222 0434; www.salachalermkrung.com; cnr Th Charoen Krung & Th Triphet; tickets 800-1200B; showtime 7.30pm; river ferry Tha Saphan Phut) Today, *kŏhn* performances are held every Thursday and Friday and last about two hours plus intermission. The theatre requests that patrons dress respectfully, which means no shorts, tank tops or sandals.

AKSRA THEATRE Puppet Show

(0 2677 8888, ext 5730; www.aksratheatre.com; 3rd fl, King Power Complex, 8/1 Th Rang Nam; tickets 400-600B; shows 7.30-8.30pm Mon-Wed, dinner shows 6.30-7pm Thu-Sun; BTS Victory Monument) A variety of performances are now held at this modern theatre, but the highlight is performances of the *Ramakian* by using knee-high puppets that require three puppeteers to strike humanlike poses.

NATIONAL THEATRE Traditional Performance

(Map p66; 0 2224 1352; 2 Th Rachini; tickets 60-100B; river ferry Tha Chang) Performances of *kŏhn* (masked dance-drama often depicting scenes from the *Ramayana*) are held on the first and second Sundays of the month, *lá•kon* (Thai dance-dramas) are held on the first Friday of the month, and Thai musical performances are held on the third Friday of the month.

THAI BOXING

Thai boxing's best of the best fight it out at Bangkok's two boxing stadiums: **Lumphini Stadium** (Sanam Muay Lumphini; **Map p84; 0 2251 4303; Th Phra Ram IV; tickets 3rd/2nd class/ringside 1000/1500/2000B; MRT**

War on the Gem Scam

We're begging you, if you aren't a gem trader, then don't buy unset stones in Thailand – period. Countless tourists are sucked into the prolific and well-rehearsed gem scam in which they are taken to a store by a helpful stranger and tricked into buying bulk gems that can supposedly be resold in their home country for 100% profit. Guess what, the gem world doesn't work like that; and what most tourists end up with are worthless pieces of glass.

Lumphini) and **Ratchadamnoen Stadium** (Sanam Muay Ratchadamnoen; Map p66; ☎0 2281 4205; Th Ratchadamnoen Nok; tickets 3rd/2nd class/ringside 1000/1500/2000B; 🚌70, 503, 509, klorng taxi Tha Phan Fah). Fights are held throughout the week, alternating between the two stadiums. Ratchadamnoen hosts the matches at 6.30pm on Monday, Wednesday, Thursday and Sunday. Lumphini hosts matches on Tuesday and Friday at 6.30pm and Saturday at 5pm and 8.30pm.

Shopping

Home to one of the world's largest outdoor markets, numerous giant upscale malls, and sidewalk-clogging bazaars on nearly every street, it's impossible not to be impressed by the amount of commerce in Bangkok.

DEPARTMENT STORES & SHOPPING CENTRES

MBK CENTER Mall

(Mahboonkhrong; Map p72; www.mbk-center.co.th/en; cnr Th Phra Ram I & Th Phayathai; BTS National Stadium & Siam) This colossal mall has become a tourist destination in its own right. This is the cheapest place to buy mobile phones and accessories (4th floor) and name-brand knock-offs (nearly every other floor).

SIAM CENTER & SIAM DISCOVERY CENTER Mall

(Map p72; cnr Th Phra Ram I & Th Phayathai; BTS National Stadium or Siam) These linked sister centres feel almost monastic in their hushed hallways compared to frenetic MBK, just across the street. Siam Discovery Center excels in home decor, with the whole 3rd floor devoted to Asian-minimalist styles and jewel-toned fabrics; we love the earthy, Thai-influenced designs at **Doi Tung**. The attached Siam Center, Thailand's first shopping centre built in 1976, has recently gone under the redesign knife for a younger, hipper look.

SIAM PARAGON Mall

(Map p72; Th Phra Ram I; BTS Siam) The biggest and glitziest of Bangkok's shopping malls, Siam Paragon is more of an urban park than shopping centre. Astronomically luxe brands occupy most floors, while the majority of shoppers hang out in the reflecting pool atrium or basement-level food court. The 3rd floor is home to **Kinokuniya**, Thailand's largest English-language bookstore.

FASHION & TEXTILES

IT'S HAPPENED TO BE A CLOSET Women's Fashion

(Map p72; 1st fl, Siam Paragon, Th Phra Ram I; BTS Siam) Garbled grammar aside, this is a brilliant place to stock up on locally designed and made togs – think Th Khao San meets Siam Paragon.

FLYNOW Women's Fashion

(Map p72; www.flynowbangkok.com; 2nd fl, Gaysorn Plaza, cnr Th Ploenchit & Th Ratchadamri; BTS Chit Lom) A longstanding leader in Bangkok's home-grown fashion scene, Flynow creates feminine couture that has caught the eyes of several international shows.

JIM THOMPSON Silk

(Map p76; www.jimpthompson.com; 9 Th Surawong; ⌚9am-9pm; BTS Sala Daeng, MRT Si Lom) The surviving business of the international promoter of Thai silk, this, the largest Jim Thompson shop, sells

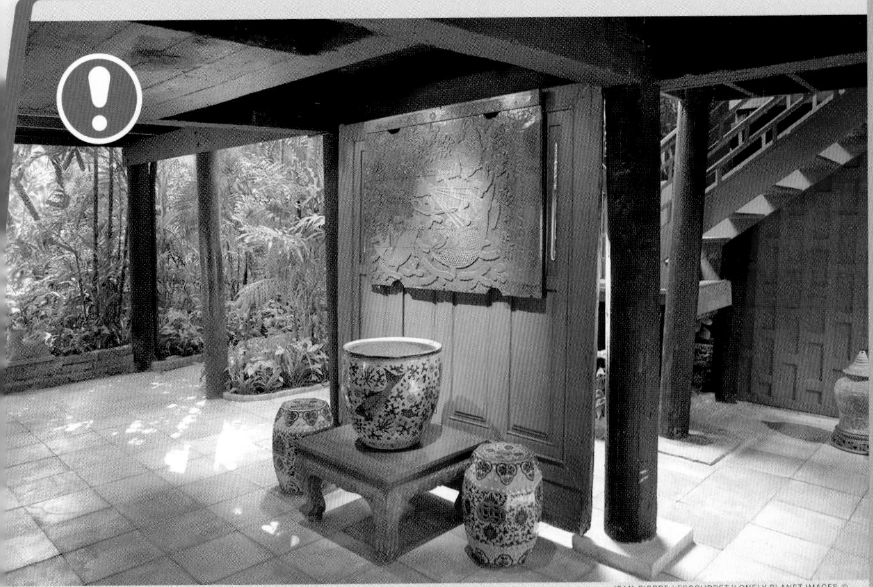

JEAN-PIERRE LESCOURRET/LONELY PLANET IMAGES ©

Don't Miss Jim Thompson House

This leafy **compound** is the former home of the eponymous American silk entrepreneur and art collector. Born in Delaware in 1906, Thompson briefly served in the Office of Strategic Services (forerunner of the CIA) in Thailand during WWII. Settling in Bangkok after the war, his neighbours' handmade silk caught his eye and piqued his business sense; he sent samples to fashion houses in Milan, London and Paris, gradually building a steady worldwide clientele.

In addition to exquisite Asian art, Thompson also collected parts of various derelict Thai homes in central Thailand and had them reassembled in their current location in 1959. His small but splendid Asian art collection and his personal belongings are also on display in the main house.

THINGS YOU NEED TO KNOW

Map p72; www.jimthompsonhouse.com; 6 Soi Kasem San 2; adult/child 100/50B; 9am-5pm, compulsory tours in English & French every 20min; BTS National Stadium, klorng taxi Tha Hua Chang

colourful silk handkerchiefs, placemats, wraps and pillow cushions. Just up the road is a **factory outlet** (Map p76; 149/4-6 Th Surawong; 9am-6pm) that sells discontinued patterns at a significant discount.

MARKETS

CHATUCHAK WEEKEND MARKET Market

(Talat Nat Jatujak; 9am-6pm Sat & Sun; BTS Mo Chit, MRT Chatuchak Park & Kamphaeng Phet)

Among the largest markets in the world, Chatuchak seems to unite everything buyable, from used vintage sneakers to baby squirrels. Plan to spend a full day, as there's plenty to see, do and buy. But come early, ideally around 9am to 10am, to beat the crowds and the heat.

Once you're deep in the bowels of Chatuchack, it will seem like there is no order and no escape, but the market

Thonburi Canals

For an up-close view of the city's famed canals, long-tail boats are available for hire at Tha Chang, Tha Tian, Tha Oriental and Tha Phra Athit.

Trips explore the Thonburi canals **Khlong Bangkok Noi** and, further south, **Khlong Bangkok Yai**, taking in the Royal Barges National Museum, Wat Arun and a riverside temple with fish feeding. Longer trips diverge into **Khlong Mon**, between Bangkok Noi and Bangkok Yai, which offers more typical canal scenery, including orchid farms. On weekends, you have the option of visiting the **Taling Chan floating market**.

is arranged into relatively coherent sections.

TALAT ROT FAI Market

(Th Kamphaeng Phet; 6pm-midnight Sat & Sun; MRT Kamphaeng Phet) Set in a sprawling abandoned rail yard, this market is all about the retro, from antique enamel platters to secondhand Vespas. With mobile snack vendors, VW van-based bars and even a few land-bound pubs, it's also much more than just a shopping destination.

PATPONG NIGHT MARKET Street Market

(Map p76; Patpong Soi 1 & 2, Th Silom; 7pm-1am; BTS Sala Daeng, MRT Si Lom) Drawing more crowds than the ping-pong shows, this market continues the street's illicit leanings with a deluge of pirated goods, particularly watches and clothing. Bargain with intensity as first-quoted prices tend to be astronomically high.

PAK KHLONG MARKET Market

(Map p70; Th Chakkaphet & Th Atsadang; 24hr; river ferry Tha Saphan Phut) A wholesale vegetable market by day but at night transforms into a huge bouquet as the city's largest depot for wholesale flowers.

Getting There & Away

Air

Bangkok has two airports:

Suvarnabhumi International Airport (**0 2132 1888; www.bangkokairportonline.com**) Suvarnabhumi, 30km east of Bangkok, began commercial international and domestic service in September 2006 after several years of delay. The airport's name is pronounced *sù·wan·ná·poom,* and it inherited the airport code (BKK) previously used by the old airport at Don Muang.

Don Muang Airport (**0 2535 1111; www.donmuangairportonline.com**) Bangkok's former international and domestic airport, 25km north of central Bangkok, was retired from commercial service in September 2006, only to be partially reopened five months later to handle overflow from Suvarnabhumi. At the time of writing, rumours of the airport's imminent closure had been circulating, but for now it's still serving some domestic flights.

Boat

Once the city's dominant form of transport, public boats still survive along the mighty Chao Phraya River and on a few interior *klorng*.

CANAL ROUTES

For now, canal taxi boats run along Khlong Saen Saeb (Banglamphu to Ramkhamhaeng) and are an easy way to get from Banglamphu to Jim Thompson House, the Siam Square shopping centres (get off at Tha Hua Chang for both), and other points further east along Sukhumvit – after a mandatory change of boat at Tha Pratunam. These boats are mostly used by daily commuters and pull into the piers for just a few seconds – jump straight on or you'll be left behind. Fares range from 9B to 21B and boats run from approximately 6am to 7pm.

RIVER ROUTES

Chao Phraya Express (**0 2623 6001; www.chaophrayaboat.co.th**) provides one of the city's most scenic (and efficient) transport options, running passenger boats along Mae Nam Chao

Phraya to destinations both south and north of Bangkok.

Tickets range from 13B to 32B and are generally purchased on board the boat, although some larger stations have ticket booths. Either way, hold on to your ticket as proof of purchase.

The company operates express (indicated by an orange, yellow or yellow and green flag), local (without a flag) and tourist boat (larger boat) services. During rush hour, pay close attention to the flag colours to avoid an unwanted journey to a foreign province.

BTS (Skytrain)

The most comfortable option for travelling in 'new' Bangkok (Silom, Sukhumvit and Siam Square) is the *rót fai fáh* (BTS or Skytrain) an elevated rail network that sails over the city's notorious traffic jams.

Trains run frequently from 6am to midnight. Fares vary from 15B to 40B, depending on your destination. Most ticket machines accept 5B and 10B coins only, but change is available from the information booths.

Bus

Allow an hour to reach all bus terminals from most parts of Bangkok.

Eastern bus terminal (**Ekamai; Map p80; ☎0 2391 2504; Soi Ekamai/40, Th Sukhumvit; BTS Ekkamai**) The departure point for buses to Pattaya, Rayong, Chanthaburi and other points east.

Northern & Northeastern bus terminal (**Mo Chit; ☎for northern routes 0 2936 2841, ext 311/442, for northeastern routes 0 2936 2852, ext 611/448; Th Kamphaeng Phet**) Located just north of Chatuchak Park, this hectic bus station is also commonly called *kŏn sòng mŏr chít* (Mo Chit station) – not to be confused with Mo Chit BTS station. Buses depart from here for all northern and northeastern destinations. To reach the bus station, take BTS to Mo Chit or MRT to Chatuchak Park and transfer onto city bus 3, 77 or 509, or hop on a motorcycle taxi.

Southern bus terminal (**Sai Tai Mai; ☎0 2435 1199; Th Bromaratchachonanee, Thonburi**) The city's new terminal lies a long way west of the centre of Bangkok. Commonly called *săi đâi mài*, it's among the more pleasant and orderly in the country. Besides serving as the departure point for all buses south of Bangkok, transport to Kanchanaburi and western Thailand also departs from here. The easiest way to reach the station is by taxi, or you can take bus 79, 159, 201 or 516 from Th Ratchadamnoen Klang or bus 40 from the Victory Monument.

Suvarnabhumi public transport centre (**☎0 2132 1888; Suvarnabhumi Airport**) Located 3km from Suvarnabhumi International Airport, this terminal has relatively frequent departures to points east and northeast including Aranya Prathet (for the Cambodian border), Chanthaburi, Ko Chang, Nong Khai (for the Lao border), Pattaya, Rayong, Trat and Udon Thani. It can be reached from the airport by a free shuttle bus.

Minivan

Privately run minivans, called *rót đôo*, are a fast and relatively comfortable way to get between Bangkok and its neighbouring provinces. The biggest minivan stop is just north of the Victory Monument.

MRT (Metro)

Thais call the metro *rót fai fáh đâi din*. The 20km Blue Line goes from Hualamphong train station to Bang Sue, stopping at 18 stations, including four that link up with the BTS, and one that connects with the airport link. Fares cost 16B to 41B; child and concession fares can be bought at ticket windows. The trains run every seven minutes from 6am to midnight, except during peak hours – 6am to 9am and 4.30pm to 7.30pm – when frequency is less than five minutes.

Train

Hualamphong station (**Map p70; ☎0 2220 4334, general information & advance booking 1690; www.railway.co.th; Th Phra Ram IV; MRT Hualamphong**) Hua Lamphong is the terminus for the main rail services to the south, north, northeast and east.

Bangkok Getaways

You don't have to travel far from the capital to sample the best of Thailand. Within a day's journey from Bangkok are beautiful beaches, ancient temple ruins, historical towns and jungle excursions.

North of Bangkok is the ancient royal capital of Ayuthaya, home to temple ruins. Northwest is Kanchanaburi, which played a minor role in WWII as the site of the Death Railway. Just beyond the town are rugged mountains and outdoor adventures galore.

Due east of Bangkok is a long and pretty coastline dotted by offshore islands, such as pint-sized Ko Samet and jungle-clad Ko Chang.

In the northeast, Isan (*ee·săhn*) offers a glimpse of old-fashioned Thailand: rice fields and water buffaloes. Thailand's first national park, Khao Yai is an easy and rewarding jungle escape for elephant- and monkey-spotting. And scattered throughout the northeast's rice fields are Khmer temple ruins built by Southeast Asia's ancient superpower.

Wat Phra Si Sanphet (p109), Ayuthaya

Wat Yai Chai Mongkhon (p105), Ayuthaya

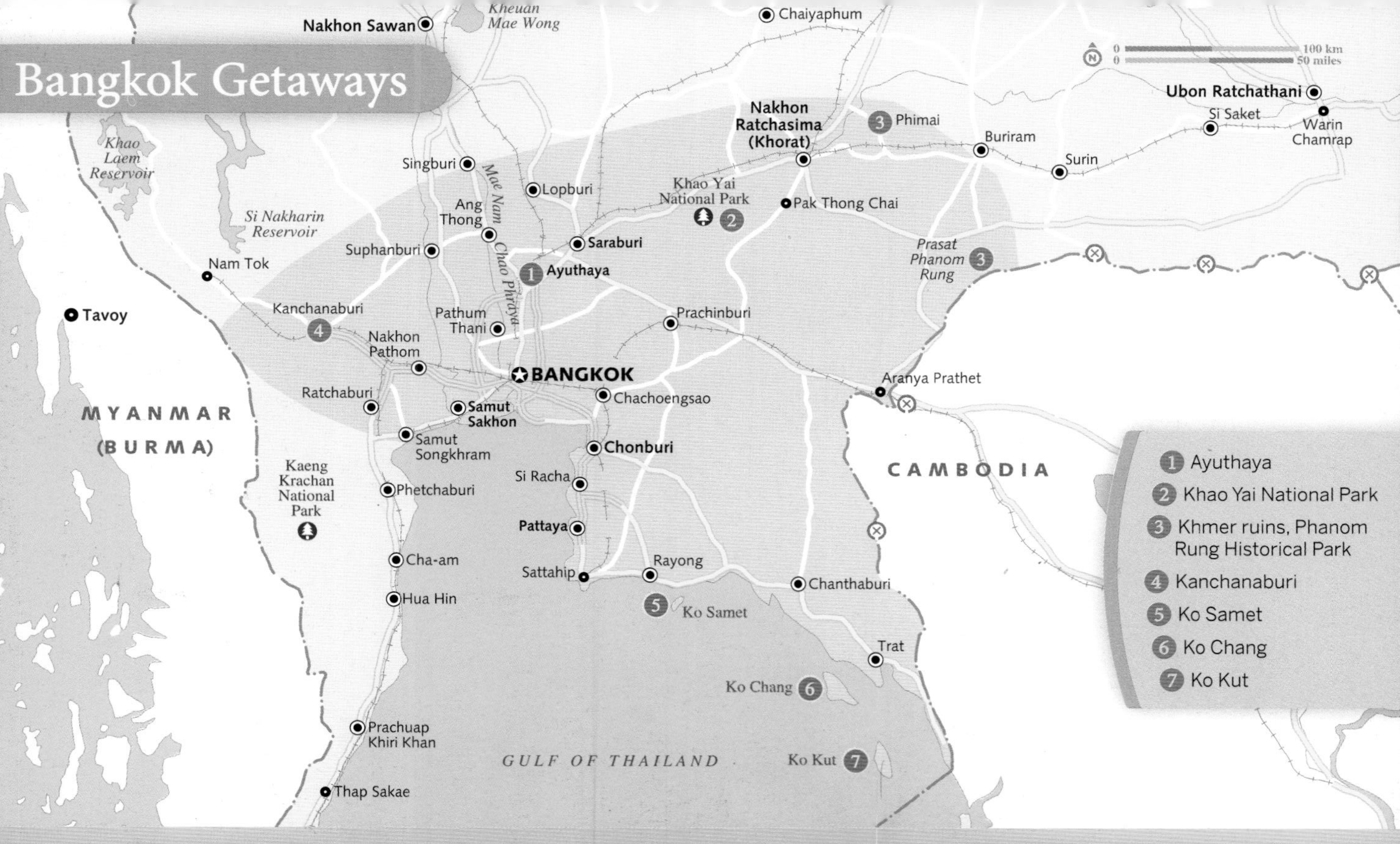
Bangkok Getaways
0 100 km
0 50 miles
Nakhon Sawan
Kheuan Mae Wong
Chaiyaphum
Ubon Ratchathani
Si Saket
Warin Chamrap
Nakhon Ratchasima (Khorat)
Phimai
Buriram
Surin
Khao Laem Reservoir
Si Nakharin Reservoir
Singburi
Lopburi
Ang Thong
Mae Nam Chao Phraya
Khao Yai National Park
Pak Thong Chai
Suphanburi
Saraburi
Prasat Phanom Rung
Nam Tok
Ayuthaya
Tavoy
Kanchanaburi
Pathum Thani
Prachinburi
Nakhon Pathom
BANGKOK
Aranya Prathet
Ratchaburi
Chachoengsao
Samut Sakhon
MYANMAR (BURMA)
Samut Songkhram
Chonburi
Kaeng Krachan National Park
Si Racha
CAMBODIA
Phetchaburi
Pattaya
Cha-am
Sattahip
Rayong
Chanthaburi
Hua Hin
Ko Samet
Trat
Ko Chang
Prachuap Khiri Khan
GULF OF THAILAND
Ko Kut
Thap Sakae
1 Ayuthaya
2 Khao Yai National Park
3 Khmer ruins, Phanom Rung Historical Park
4 Kanchanaburi
5 Ko Samet
6 Ko Chang
7 Ko Kut

Bangkok Getaways Highlights

1

Ayuthaya

An easy day trip north of Bangkok, the former Siamese capital of Ayuthaya (p104) contains a collection of time- and war-worn temples, designated an Unesco World Heritage Site. The city's history offers insight into how Siam avoided colonisation. **Above:** Wat Chai Wattanaram (p107); **Top Right:** Mural, Wat Suwan Dararam (p105); **Bottom Right:** Elephant tour

Need to Know

BEST TIME TO VISIT November to February **TOP TIP** Tour the park aboard an elephant; it gives them meaningful work

For more coverage, see p104

Ayuthaya Don't Miss List

BY LAITHONGRIEN (OM) MEEPAN, FOUNDER/DIRECTOR OF AYUTHAYA ELEPHANT PALACE & ROYAL ELEPHANT KRAAL VILLAGE

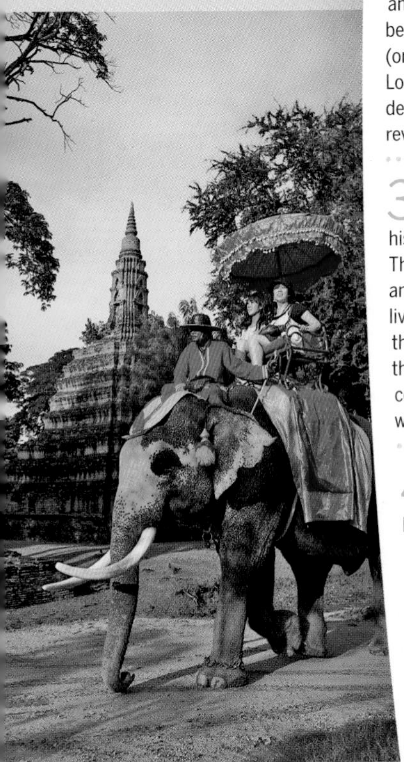

1 AYUTHAYA HISTORICAL STUDY CENTRE

This well-curated museum (p105) depicts the history of Ayuthaya when it was the capital of Siam. There are many interesting displays and models that engage the imagination and inform the intellect about Ayuthaya's role in trade and empire building. Once you piece together Ayuthaya's history, you'll understand how Siam remained independent.

2 WAT SUWAN DARARAM

In the southeast corner of the old city, this beautiful and peaceful temple (p105) is particularly interesting because of the brilliant and historical murals. The *uposatha* (ordination hall) contains murals depicting the life of the Lord Buddha, and the *wí hăhn* (assembly hall) has murals depicting the life of King Naresuan (one of Ayuthaya's most revered warrior kings) and a famous elephant battle.

3 ELEPHANT KRAAL

My elephant conservation organisation runs this historic elephant stockade (p108), the only one left in Thailand. It was here that elephants were rounded up and trained for war. Today, there are over 180 elephants living here. We provide a safe haven for them and support the mahout culture. Without work, the elephants and their mahouts often migrate to Bangkok and other urban centres as beggars, an ignoble and unsafe fate for what was once a royal profession.

4 ELEPHANT RIDE THROUGH THE HISTORIC CITY

Regally clad elephants carry sightseers around Ayuthaya's most famous temples from a stable on Th Pa Thon, in the southern section of the old city. We set up this program to get elephants off the streets as beggars and give them safe, legal and easy work. It is a very beautiful city to see aboard an elephant, and in the past, elephants were a common mode of transport.

Khao Yai National Park

Khao Yai (p126) is Thailand's oldest national park and an Unesco World Heritage Site. The park has good infrastructure, so it is easy to get to different sections to find wildlife, including gibbons and elephants. It is a wonderful wild reserve that is close to Bangkok.

Need to Know

BEST TIME TO VISIT November to March **TOP TIP** A good guide will know where to look for wildlife, depending on seasonality and animal behaviour **For further coverage, see p126**

2

Local Knowledge

Khao Yai National Park Don't Miss List

BY RITTICHAI (NINE) KENGSUNGNOEN, GUIDE AT GREENLEAF GUESTHOUSE

1 **BIRD-WATCHING**

On most days we'll see hornbills, which can be found at fruit-bearing fig trees. There's nothing like hearing the whooshing sound of a great hornbill flying over your head. Khao Yai has one of Thailand's largest populations of hornbills, including the great hornbill (*nók gòk* or *nók gah·hang*), wreathed hornbill (*nók grahm cháhng;* literally, 'elephant-jaw bird'), Indian pied hornbill *(nók kàak)* and brown hornbill *(nók ngêuak sěe nám đahn)*. The park's bird list boasts 315 species.

2 **ANIMAL-WATCHING**

It is also common to see snakes, elephants and gibbons. Animals can often be found at different spots in the park depending on the season. For example, at waterfalls and streams you can find snakes and lots of insects, and at fig trees bearing fruit, you can easily spot gibbons. Elephants are sometimes spotted in the evenings, travelling along the road.

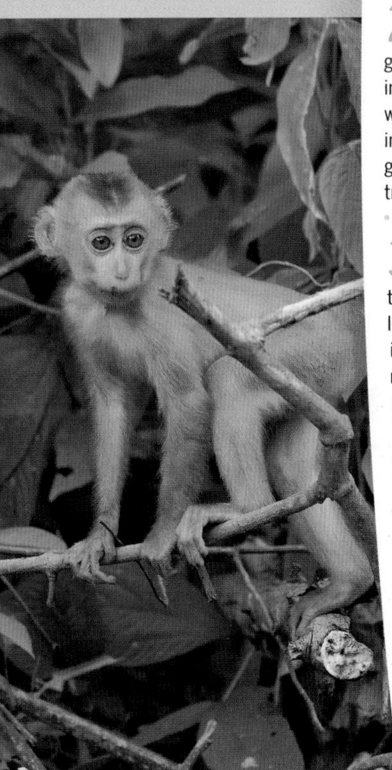

3 **TREKKING**

It is a good idea to hire a guide for trekking because the trails aren't well marked and people do occasionally get lost. A guide will also know where the animals are feeding in the forest. I got involved in guiding after I lost my job as result of the 1997 Asian financial crisis. I started out as a driver, taking foreign tourists into the park on wildlife tours. This made me curious and inspired me to learn about the park's wildlife. It initially began as a hobby, but now I'm working as a guide almost daily and I never feel bored.

4 **NAM TOK HAEW SUWAT**

The park's most famous waterfall (p126) is very beautiful and a good place to freshen up with a dip in the naturally occurring pool.

Khmer Ruins

Smaller versions of Angkor Wat dot the countryside of the rural northeast. Temples, includin Phimai (p125) and Phanom Rung (p128), linked the distant empire's capital to its far-flung frontier outposts. In addition to ornate and ancient architecture, the surrounding countrysid is a fascinating look at rural Thailand: rice paddies, sarong-clad grandmas and long-suffering water buffaloes submerged in muddy ponds. Phanom Rung temple

3

4 Historic Kanchanaburi

The foothills northwest of Bangkok hosted a dramatic WWII subplot. The town of Kan chanaburi (p110) was the site of a brutal Japanese-run prisoner of war (POW) labour camp that constructed a rail rout through the treacherous terrain with rudimentary supplies. Today, two lovingl maintained war cemeteries shelter the Allied dead and several interesting muse ums document the wartime conquest of the jungle. Death Railway Bridge (p111)

FRANK CARTER/LONELY PLANET IMAGES ©

5 Weekend on Ko Samet

Just a few hours west of Bangkok, Ko Samet (p116) is a blissful break from the urban tangle, with nary a túk-túk or skyscraper in sight. Float in the warm amniotic water or follow the footpaths over rocky headlands to the next picturesque cove. Dine under the stars at one of the numerous beachside barbecues and drink a selection of beverages that will keep you blathering into the night.

OLIVER HARGREAVE/GETTY ©

6 Tackle Ko Chang

Sitting in the far western corner of the country, Ko Chang (p119) is the wildest resort island in the country. A thick jungle climbing up vertiginous peaks sits solemnly beside the modern amenities of a fully fledged tourist attraction. Sunbathe with the package tourists on Hat Sai Khao, party with the backpackers on Lonely Beach and trudge through the forest or dive the coral gardens and seamounts.

7 Chill Out on Ko Kut

Ko Chang's semiwild cousin, Ko Kut (p124) excels in the delightful category of rest and relaxation instead of rest and recreation. There is very little to do on the island except for float the day away in the gin-clear waters, bake in the sun and plough through a book. Doing nothing is the island's primary pastime.

Bangkok Getaways Best...

Beaches

- **Hat Sai Khao** (p119) Ko Chang's widest beach is perfect for bar-hopping and sunbathing.
- **Ao Phutsa** (p116) Ko Samet's subdued bay offers tropical scenery without a lot of hubbub.
- **Hat Khlong Chao** (p124) Ko Kut's picture-perfect beach with looking-glass-clear water.
- **Hat Kaibae** (p119) A kid-friendly beach with smooth waves, soft sand to sculpt and family-sized villas.

Museums

- **Thailand-Burma Railway Centre** (p112) Get the facts on Kanchanaburi's small but interesting role in WWII.
- **Ayuthaya Historical Study Centre** (p105) Imagine the city when foreign ships came to call and the temples were capped with gold.
- **Phimai National Museum** (p125) View artwork from the ancient Khmer era.

Temple Ruins

- **Wat Phra Si Sanphet** (p109) Ayuthaya's premier example of its architecturally stylish heyday.
- **Phimai Historical Park** (p125) Khmer-era temple with easy access to Bangkok.
- **Phanom Rung Historical Park** (p128) Sublime Khmer-era temple, further from the tourist trail but closer to perfection.

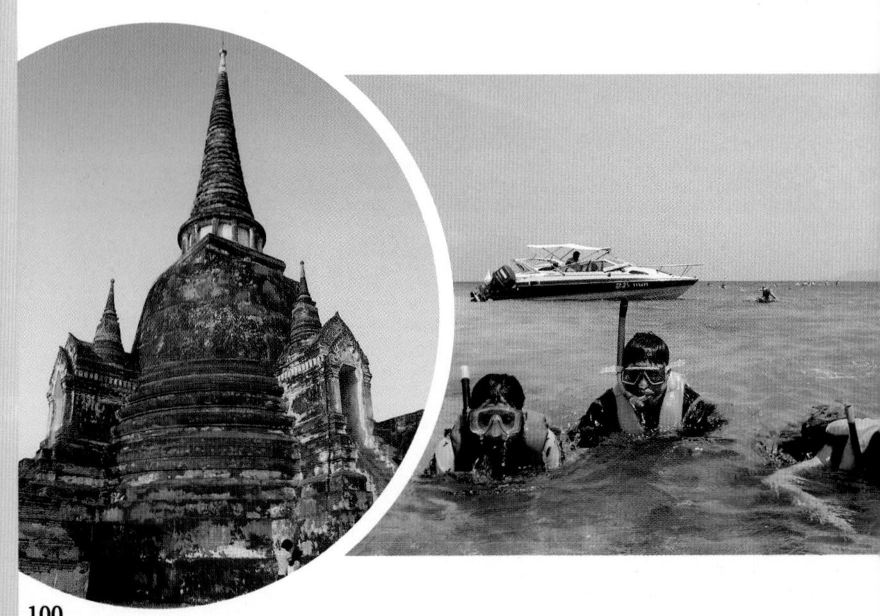

Outdoor Activities

- **Ko Chang** (p121) Dive the deep, paddle the surface or trudge through the forest on this athletic island.
- **Khao Yai National Park** (p126) Spot birds, butterflies and bats on a hike through Thailand's first national park.
- **Kanchanaburi** (p112) Waterfall-spotting, river rafting and elephant riding await in the northwest foothills.

Left: Wat Phra Si Sanphet (p109), Ayuthaya
Above: Snorkellers, Ko Chang (p119)

Need to Know

ADVANCE PLANNING

- **One month before** Watch the movie *Bridge On the River Kwai*.
- **One week before** Book your accommodation if you're visiting the beaches during high season (December to March).
- **One day before** Buy train or bus tickets directly from the station.

RESOURCES

- **Ayuthaya Tourist Authority of Thailand** (TAT; ☎0 3524 6076; 108/22 Th Si Sanphet; ⏲8.30am-4.30pm)
- **Kanchanaburi Tourist Authority of Thailand** (☎0 3451 2500; Th Saengchuto; ⏲8.30am-4.30pm)
- **Nakhon Ratchasima/ Khorat Tourist Authority of Thailand** (☎0 4421 3666; Th Mittaphap; ⏲8.30am-4.30pm)

GETTING AROUND

- **Boats** Travel between the islands and mainland.
- **Bus & minivan** Best way to get to/from Bangkok.
- **Bicycle & motorcycle** Self-touring option in the cities.
- **Sŏrng·tăa·ou** Handy shared taxis in the cities.
- **Train** Bypass Bangkok traffic to Ayuthaya; also links Ayuthaya to Khao Yai.
- **Săhm·lór & túk-túk** Chartered vehicles for in-town trips; negotiate the price beforehand.

BE FOREWARNED

- **Avoid** Sightseeing during the hot season (February to June); Ko Kut closes and Ko Chang slows down during the rainy season (June to October).
- **Dress** Cover to the elbows and the ankles when visiting Ayuthaya's temples and don't pose for pictures in front of Buddha images.
- **Motorcycle safety** Wear a helmet and protective clothing, especially on Ko Chang and Ko Samet.
- **Waterfalls** Thailand's waterfalls are at their peak from June to December.
- **Weekends & holidays** High rates and low vacancy on Ko Chang and Ko Samet.

Bangkok Getaways Itineraries

By sticking close to Bangkok, you can pack a whole lot of history, jungle trekking and ruin-spotting into less than a week's time. You'll also enjoy the slower rhythms of these provincial towns, best navigated on a bicycle.

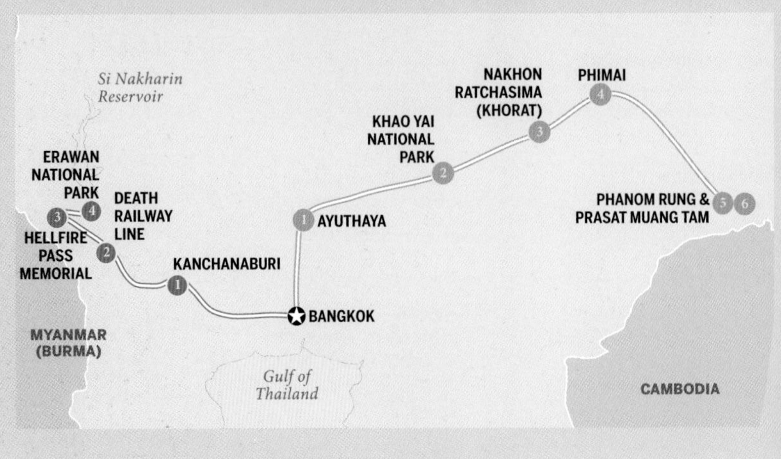

3 DAYS

KANCHANABURI TO ERAWAN NATIONAL PARK

Railroads & Rivers

Just a half-day journey from Bangkok, **(1) Kanchanaburi** offers a quick jungle escape and attractions for WWII history buffs. Kanchanaburi was a base for a WWII Japanese-run POW camp. The town today provides a respectful commemoration of fallen Allied soldiers through several cemeteries and museums.

During WWII, the Japanese military used the labour of POW captives to build a rail line to Burma, a task that resulted in thousands of deaths. Today trains travel over surviving portions of the **(2) Death Railway Line**, mainly over the Mae Nam Khwae.

The **(3) Hellfire Pass Memorial** has transformed one of the Death Railway's most difficult cuttings into a walking trail. The forbidding name refers to the glow from the crew's burning torches, which cast eerie shadows on the inhumane labour, reminiscent of medieval underworld scenes.

(4) Erawan National Park is best known for its seven-tiered waterfall said to resemble Erawan, the three-headed elephant of Hindu mythology. Walking to the first three tiers is simple, but the entire 1.5km hike is tough. Most tourist tours stop here in the morning, but you can make a day of it with your own transport.

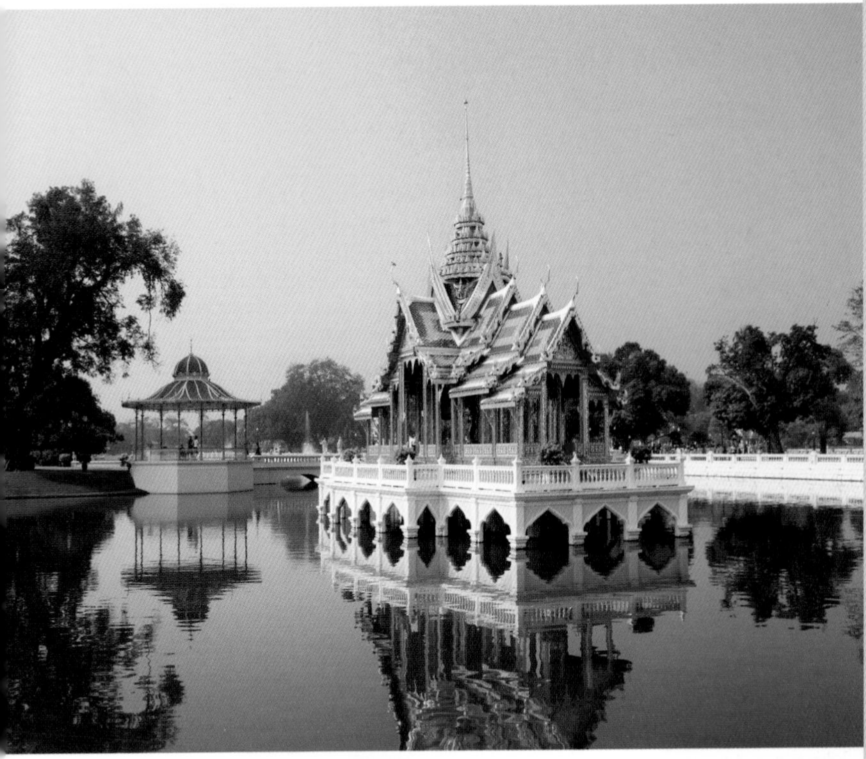

5 DAYS

AYUTHAYA TO PRASAT MUANG TAM

Monuments & Mountains

The fertile central plains have long nurtured monument builders and gave birth to the powerful city-state of Ayuthaya, which ruled much of modern-day Thailand for 400 years. In the northeast, the far-reaching Khmer empire built temple fortresses demarcating its imperial power. Sandwiched in between is Thailand's first national park.

(1) Ayuthaya is a must-see stop on the culture trail and is easily accessible from Bangkok via train or bus. Though many of the great monuments have been destroyed or stolen, Ayuthaya remains historically important. You can visit the most important ruins within a day.

Nature enthusiasts can detour to **(2) Khao Yai National Park**, accessible via train or bus. The park includes a 1351m summit, herds of elephants, troops of monkeys and waterfalls.

(3) Nakhon Ratchasima (Khorat) provides transit access to the Angkor ruins. **(4) Phimai** is easy to reach and has the best tourist infrastructure. But far-flung **(5) Phanom Rung** is considered the apex of Khmer architecture. Nearby, **(6) Prasat Muang Tam** provides a time-worn counterpoint to renovated Phanom Rung.

Bang Pa In Palace (p110), Ayuthaya
JEAN-PIERRE LESCOURRET/LONELY PLANET IMAGES ©

Discover Bangkok Getaways

At a Glance

- **Ayuthaya** (p104) A required stop on the culture trail.
- **Kanchanaburi** (p110) Easy jungle tours and WWII history.
- **Ko Samet** (p116) Bangkok's quick and easy beach playground.
- **Ko Chang** (p119) Modern beach retreat, with diving and jungle treks.
- **Khao Yai National Park** (p126) Spot elephants and monkeys.

Wat Ratburana, Ayuthaya
PETER STUCKINGS/LONELY PLANET IMAGES ©

CENTRAL THAILAND

Ayuthaya พระนครศรีอยุธยา

POP 137,553

Between 1350 and 1767 Ayuthaya was the capital of Siam. As a major trading port during the time of the trade winds, international merchants visited and were left in awe of the hundreds of glittering temples and treasure-laden palaces. At one point the empire ruled over an area larger than England and France combined. Ayuthaya had 33 kings who engaged in more than 70 wars during its 417-year period; however, fine diplomatic skills also ensured no Western power ever ruled Siam.

The last of the empire's battles was in 1767, when an invading Burmese army sacked the city, looting most of its treasures. What was left continued to crumble until major restoration work began. In 1991 Ayuthaya's ruins were designated a Unesco World Heritage Site.

Sights

For simpler navigation, we've divided up the sites into 'on the island' and 'off the island' sections. It is easy to get between the sites by bicycle, and hiring a guide for some historical detail is useful.

Most temples are open from 8am to 4pm; the more famous sites charge an entrance fee. A one-day pass for most sites on the island is available for 220B and can be bought at the museums or ruins.

On the Island

WIHAAN MONGKHON BOPHIT Historical Building

(วิหารมงคลบพิตร; **Map p106**) Next to Wat Phra Si Sanphet is this sanctuary hall, which houses one of the largest bronze Buddha images in Thailand. The 17m-high figure has undergone several facelifts due to lightning strikes and fire.

In 1955 the Burmese Prime Minister visited and donated 200,000B to help restore the building, an act of belated atonement for his country's sacking of the city 200 years earlier.

WAT PHRA MAHATHAT Temple

(วัดพระมหาธาตุ; **Map p106; admission 50B**) The most photographed image in Ayuthaya is here; a sandstone Buddha head that lies mysteriously tangled within a tree's entwined roots. Built in 1374 during the reign of King Borom Rachathirat I, Wat Phra Mahathat also has a central *prang* (Khmer-style stupa) and rows of headless Buddha images. Nobody knows for sure how the Buddha head ended up in the tree. Some say the head was abandoned after the Burmese sacked Ayuthaya, and trees subsequently grew around it. Others believe thieves tried to steal the image, but gave up as it was too heavy.

WAT RATBURANA Temple

(วัดราชบูรณะ; **Map p106; Ratcha-burana; admission 50B**) The *prang* in this temple is one of the best extant versions in the city, with detailed carvings of lotus and mythical creatures. The temple, just north of Wat Phra Mahathat, was built in the 15th century by King Borom Rachathirat II on the cremation site for his two brothers who both died while fighting each other for the throne. Looters raided the site in 1957 and sole many treasures. Some of the culprits were arrested and a subsequent official excavation of the site uncovered many rare Buddha images in the crypt.

WAT SUWAN DARARAM Temple

(วัดสุวรรณดาราราม; **Map p106**) This temple is not one of the most-visited sites but its different architectural styles make it worth seeing. Set in the southeast of the island, King Rama I designed the exterior of the older-style *uposatha* while Rama III was responsible for the interior. The slightly bowed line along the temple's edge and its plain finish are typical of the late Ayuthaya period. Next to it is a *wí·hăhn* (sanctuary) from Rama IV's reign, resplendent with a glittering external mosaic.

AYUTHAYA HISTORICAL STUDY CENTRE Museum

(ศูนย์ศึกษาประวัติศาสตร์อยุธยา; **Map p106; Th Rotchana; adult/student 100/50B; 9am-4.30pm Mon-Fri, to 5pm Sat & Sun**) An impressive diorama of the city's former glories illustrates how spectacular Ayuthaya once was. Other features in this open-plan museum include timelines, examples of traditional village life and videos.

If You Like... Temple Ruins

If you'd like to explore more of Ayuthaya's ruins, hire transport to visit these far-flung sites:

1 **WAT YAI CHAI MONGKHON**
(east of island) A 7m-long reclining Buddha is the defining feature of this temple, built by King U in 1357 to house Sri Lankan monks. The bell-shaped *chedi* (stupa) was later built to honour King Naresuan's victory over Burma.

2 **BAAN TH DUSIT TEMPLES**
(east of island) A rural collection of temples, like Wat Maheyong, Wat Kudi Dao and Wat Ayuthaya.

3 **PHU KHAO THONG**
(northwest of island) At the top of the *chedi*, 79 steps are splendid views of the city. It was originally built by the Burmese during a 15-year occupation of Ayuthaya but was later retrofitted by the Thais to celebrate the occupier's ouster. A statue of King Naresuan, the celebrated liberator, and dozens of fighting cockeral replicas, a symbol of his fearsome fighting style.

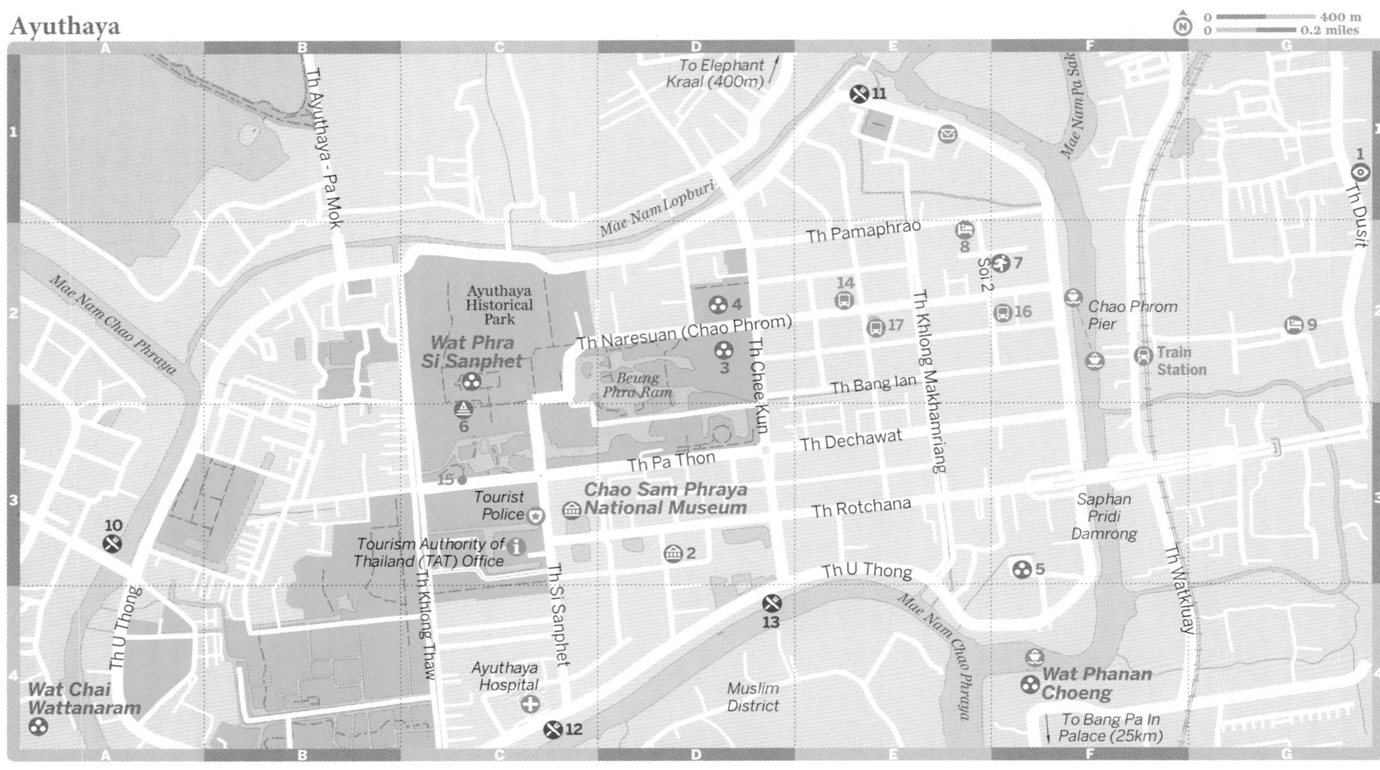
Ayuthaya
0 400 m
0 0.2 miles
To Elephant Kraal (400m)
Th Ayuthaya - Pa Mok
Mae Nam Lopburi
Mae Nam Pa Sak
Th Dusit
Th Pamaphrao
Soi 2
Chao Phrom Pier
Train Station
Ayuthaya Historical Park
Wat Phra Si Sanphet
Th Naresuan (Chao Phrom)
Beung Phra Ram
Th Chee Kun
Th Khlong Makhamriang
Th Bang Ian
Th Dechawat
Th Pa Thon
Mae Nam Chao Phraya
Chao Sam Phraya National Museum
Tourist Police
Th Rotchana
Saphan Pridi Damrong
Tourism Authority of Thailand (TAT) Office
Th U Thong
Th Watkluay
Th Si Sanphet
Th Khlong Thaw
Ayuthaya Hospital
Muslim District
Wat Phanan Choeng
To Bang Pa In Palace (25km)
Wat Chai Wattanaram

Ayuthaya

Top Sights

Chao Sam Phraya National Museum... C3
Wat Chai Wattanaram... A4
Wat Phanan Choeng... F4
Wat Phra Si Sanphet... C2

Sights

1 Ayothaya Floating Market... G1
2 Ayuthaya Historical Study Centre... D3
3 Wat Phra Mahathat... D2
4 Wat Ratburana... D2
5 Wat Suwan Dararam... F3
6 Wihaan Mongkhon Bophit... C3

Activities, Courses & Tours

7 Tour With Thai... F2

Sleeping

8 Baan Lotus Guest House... E2
9 Bann Thai House... G2

Eating

10 Baan Watcharachai... A3
11 Hua Raw Night Market... E1
12 Roti Sai Mai Stalls... C4
13 Sai Thong... D4

Transport

14 Buses to Bangkok... E2
15 Elephant Kraal Taxi... C3
16 Main Bus Terminal... F2
17 Minivans to Bangkok... E2

CHAO SAM PHRAYA NATIONAL MUSEUM Museum

(พิพิธภัณฑสถานแห่งชาติเจ้าสามพระยา; Map p106; adult/child 150B/free; 9am-4pm Wed-Sun) The largest museum in the city has 2400 items on show, ranging from a 2m-high bronze-cast Buddha head to glistening treasures found in the crypts of Wat Phra Mahathat and Wat Ratburana.

Off the Island

You can reach some sites by bicycle, but others require a motorbike. Evening boat tours around the island are another way to see the highlights.

WAT PHANAN CHOENG Temple

(วัดพนัญเชิง; Map p106; admission 20B) Inside this bustling temple is one of Ayuthaya's most revered Buddha images. The 19m-high Phra Phanan Choeng was created in 1325 and sits in the *wí·hăhn* (large hall), surrounded by 84,000 Buddha images that line the walls.

Wat Phanan Choeng, southeast of the old city, can be reached by ferry (5B) from the pier near Phom Phet Fortress. Your bicycle can accompany you across.

AYOTHAYA FLOATING MARKET Market

(ตลาดน้ำอโยธยา; Map p106; 9am-8pm; admission free) Popular with Thais as well as tourists, the floating market sells a range of snacks, artwork and clothes. Set on wooden platforms above the water, the market is covered and so is ideal if the city's fierce heat gets too much. Traditional shows take place throughout the day and long-tail boats (20B) can be hired. The market is to the east of the old city off Th Dusit, near Wat Kudi Dao.

WAT CHAI WATTANARAM Temple

(วัดไชยวัฒนาราม; Map p106; admission 50B) Just 40 years ago this temple was immersed in thick jungle. Today it is one of Ayuthaya's most-photographed sites thanks to its impressive Khmer-style central *prang*, which stands 35m high. Built in 1630 by King Prasat Thong, the temple is a great place to watch sunsets. The site is west of the island and can be reached on bicycle via a nearby bridge.

Audio Guides

Audio guides (150B) can be hired at Wat Phra Si Sanphet, Wat Phra Mahathat and Wat Chai Wattanaram. The English-language guides provide excellent background information and vivid detail that help visitors imagine exactly what once stood on these sites.

ELEPHANT KRAAL Elephant Stockade
(เพนียดคล้องช้าง; off Map p106) Wild elephants were once rounded up and kept in this *kraal* (stockade). Each year the king would watch as the finest beasts were chosen and either put to work or used as war machines. This restored *kraal,* which has 980 teak logs, is northeast of the island.

Activities

TOUR WITH THAI Cycling
(Map p106; ☎0 3523 1084; Th Naresuan; www.tourwiththai.com) Pedalling around the island is the best way to see the ruins. To see more of the surrounding countryside, guides are available and two-day trips are possible.

Sleeping

BAAN LOTUS GUEST HOUSE Guest House $
(Map p106; ☎0 3525 1988; 20 Th Pamaphrao; s 200B, d 400-600B; ❄ 📶) Set in large, leafy grounds, this converted teak schoolhouse has a cool, clean feel and remains our favourite place to crash.

BAAN THAI HOUSE Boutique Hotel $$$
(Map p106; ☎0 35245 555; off Th Dusit; r 2100-2800B; P ❄ 📶 🏊) A gorgeous boutique resort set just off the island. Each of the dozen Thai-style villas is immaculate and set amid lush gardens. A túk-túk (pronounced *đúk đúk;* motorised transport) to the old city costs 80B.

Eating

Ayuthaya's rich heritage has resulted in an equally diverse range of food, from sweet Muslim snacks to seafood. As well as Western-friendly restaurants on Soi 2, Th Naresuan, there are excellent options along the southern part of Th U Thong.

HUA RAW NIGHT MARKET Market $
(Map p106; Th U Thong) This evening market offers simple riverside seating and a range of Thai and Muslim dishes; for the latter look for the green star and crescent.

ROTI SAI MAI STALLS Desserts $
(Map p106; Th U Thong; ⏲10am-8pm) Ayuthaya is famous for the Muslim dessert *roh-đee săi măi.* This is created by rolling together thin strands of melted palm sugar and wrapping them inside the roti. Stalls can be found opposite Ayuthaya Hospital.

SAI THONG Thai $
(Map p106; Th U Thong; dishes 90-150B; ⏲9.30am-10pm) With 180 items on the menu, live music and spectacular food, this old-school restaurant is the best place to eat on the island. As well as

Helping an Old Friend

Elephants helped Thailand win wars, build cities and transport kings. However, today these animals are the ones needing help, as their natural habitat has been slashed back and they are reduced to begging for food in the street. With only 4000 domestic and wild elephants remaining in Thailand, they need all the assistance they can get.

The **Ayuthaya Elephant Palace** (☎0 8066 87727; www.elephantstay.com) does its part by running a hugely successful breeding program and providing brief tourist rides around the ruins. This nonprofit organisation protects elephants by buying sick or abused animals, including bulls that have killed villagers.

PAOLO CORDELLI/LONELY PLANET IMAGES ©

Don't Miss Wat Phra Si Sanphet

The three *chedi* (stupas) at Wat Phra Si Sanphet are perhaps the most iconic image in Ayuthaya. Built in the late 14th century, it was the city's largest temple and was used by several kings. It once contained a 16m-high standing Buddha (Phra Si Sanphet) covered with 250kg of gold, which was melted down by Burmese conquerors.

THINGS YOU NEED TO KNOW

วัดพระศรีสรรเพชญ์; **Map p109; admission 50B**

the regular fare, there are interesting variations, such as chicken marinated in whisky.

BAAN WATCHARACHAI Thai **$$**
(Map p106; off Th Worachate; dishes 100-200B) Located next to Wat Kasatthirat, take a seat on the wooden boat moored outside and feast on *yam blah dùk fòo* (crispy catfish salad).

Information

Ayuthaya Tourist Authority of Thailand **(TAT; ☎0 3524 6076, 108/22 Th Si Sanphet; 8.30am-4.30pm)** Tourist information office.

Getting There & Away

Bus

Ayuthaya's provincial bus stop is on Th Naresuan, a short walk from the guest-house area. Destinations include the following:

Bang Pa In (25B, every 20 minutes; via *sŏrng·tăa·ou*)

Suphanburi (60B, two hours, every 30 minutes) Transfer in town for buses to Kanchanaburi.

Bangkok-bound buses and minivans leave from stops on Th Naresuan to the following areas:

Northern (Mo Chit) station (50B, 1½ hours, every 20 minutes) Also stops at Don Muang airport.

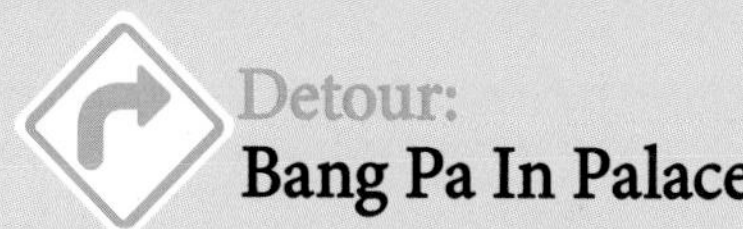

Detour: Bang Pa In Palace

An intriguing assortment of architectural styles makes up Thailand's most eclectic **palace** (บางปะอิน; off Map p106; admission 100B; 8am-4pm). Originally built in the 17th century, the palace was restored during the reign of Rama V (King Chulalongkorn; 1868–1910). Highlights include a replica of the Tiber Bridge in Rome, the stunning Chinese-style **Wehut Chamrun**, the Victorian-influenced observatory **Withun Thatsana**, and a Thai pavilion in the middle of a pond housing a statue of Rama V.

To reach the palace, take a public *sŏrng·tăa·ou* (25B, one hour, frequent) from the provincial bus stop on Th Naresuan. Once the *sŏrng·tăa·ou* drops you at the Bang Pa In bus station, jump on a motorbike taxi (30B) to the palace, which is 4km away. Trains run from Ayuthaya (3rd class 3B, 30 minutes). The train station is closer to the palace than the bus station, but you'll still need a motorbike taxi (20B) to complete the last leg.

Southern (Sai Tai Mai) station (70B, one hour, every 30 minutes from 4.30am to 7pm)

Victory Monument (60B, 1½ hours, hourly from 5.30am to 7pm)

The bus terminal servicing northern Thailand is 5km east of the old city, off Th Rotchana. A túk-túk from the terminal to the old city will cost 100B. Destinations include the following:

Chiang Mai (403B to 806B, nine hours, frequent)

Phitsanulok (224B to 227B, five hours, frequent)

Sukhothai (255B to 328B, six hours, every two hours)

Train

The train station is east of central Ayuthaya. Destinations include:

Bangkok's Bang Sue station (ordinary/rapid/express 15B/20B/315B, 1½ hours, frequent morning and night departures) A convenient station to the Th Khao San area.

Bangkok's Hualamphong station (ordinary/rapid/express 15B/20B/315B, 1½ hours, frequent morning and night departures)

Chiang Mai (ordinary/rapid/express 586B/856B/1198B, six departures a day)

Pak Chong (ordinary/rapid/express 23B/73B/130B, frequent) The nearest station to Khao Yai National Park.

The train station is accessible by a quick cross-river ferry from the centre of town (4B) or *sŏrng·tăa·ou* (50B).

Getting Around

Săhm·lór (three-wheeled pedicabs; also spelt săamláw) or túk-túk are readily available. For trips on the island, the rate is 30B to 40B.

Guest houses rent bicycles (30B) and motorcycles (200B). You can take brief rides around the historical park by elephant (200B to 500B) or by horse and carriage (300B). The elephants stay at a *kraal* on Th Pa Thon.

Kanchanaburi กาญจนบุรี

POP 47,147

The provincial town of Kanchanaburi is an ideal base from which to explore Thailand's wild west.

Today the town is busy and alive but the WWII memorials and museums are a reminder of darker times. Japanese forces used Allied prisoners of war (POWs) and conscripted Southeast Asian labourers to build a rail route to Myanmar (Burma). Roads in the guest house area are named after countries that were involved in the conflict.

Kanchanaburi

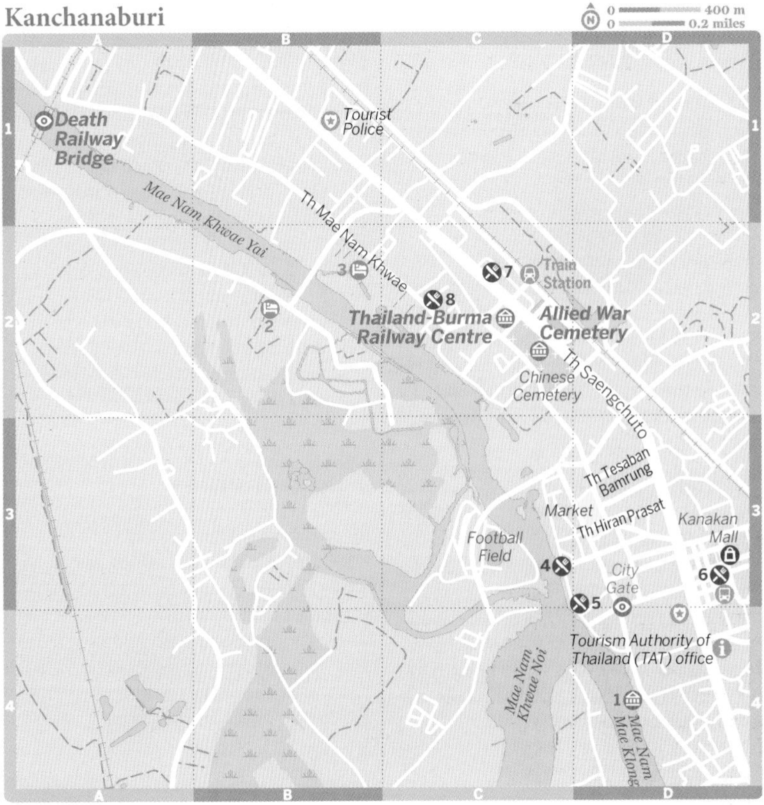

0 — 400 m
0 — 0.2 miles

Kanchanaburi

Top Sights
- Allied War Cemetery C2
- Death Railway Bridge A1
- Thailand-Burma Railway Centre C2

Sights
- 1 Jeath War Museum D4

Sleeping
- 2 Apple's Retreat B2
- 3 Pong Phen B2

Eating
- 4 Floating Restaurants C3
- 5 Jukkru D3
- 6 Market D3
- 7 Night Market C2
- 8 Sri Rung Rueng C2

Sights

DEATH RAILWAY BRIDGE (BRIDGE OVER THE RIVER KWAI) Historical Site

(สะพานข้ามแม่น้ำแคว; Map p111; Th Mae Nam Khwae) The 300m railway bridge is an iconic symbol that represents the efforts of those who toiled to build a crossing here. The centre of the bridge was destroyed by Allied bombs in 1945 so today only the outer curved spans are original. Once you make it to the other side there are cafes and greenery by the waterfront.

The bridge spans Mae Nam Khwae Yai, which is 2.5km from the centre of Kanchanaburi. This means it is walkable from Th Mae Nam Khwae or you can jump on a northbound *sŏrng·tăa·ou* (10B) along

Th Saengchuto. A mini train runs regular trips (20B) over the bridge from the nearby train station.

ALLIED WAR CEMETERY Historical Site

(สุสานทหารพันธมิตรดอนรัก; Map p111; Th Saengchuto; 8am-6pm) Across the street from the Thailand-Burma Railway Centre is the Allied War Cemetery, which is immaculately maintained by the War Graves Commission. Of the 6982 POWs buried here, nearly half were British; the others were mainly from Australia and the Netherlands. It is estimated that at least 100,000 people died while working on the railway, the majority being labourers from nearby Asian countries, though there's not one identifiable grave.

THAILAND-BURMA RAILWAY CENTRE Museum

(ศูนย์รถไฟไทย-พม่า; Map p111; www.tbrconline.com; 73 Th Chaokanen; adult/child 100/50B; 9am-5pm) This informative museum uses video footage, models and detailed display panels to explain Kanchanaburi's role in WWII. A poignant video from POW survivors ensures that the deaths remain a tragedy, not merely a statistic.

JEATH WAR MUSEUM Museum

(พิพิธภัณฑ์สงคราม; Map p111; Th Wisuttharangsi; admission 30B; 8am-5pm) This small museum resembles the bamboo-*ata* in which POWs were kept. The archives focus heavily on surgeon Sir Edward 'Weary' Dunlop, who saved hundreds of lives by operating on injured soldiers and fighting to improve basic medical conditions. The museum is run by the monks of the adjacent **Wat Chaichumphon** (Wat Tai), which in itself is worth a visit. Jeath is an acronym of the countries involved in the construction of the railway: Japan, England, Australia and USA, Thailand and Holland.

Activities

Elephant rides, trips to Thailand's best waterfalls and bamboo rafting are all easily booked via tour agents. More adventurous experiences, including cycling tours, canoeing and overnight jungle trekking, can also be arranged. Some package tours are cancelled if not enough people sign up, so check before booking.

Death Railway Bridge (p111), Kanchanaburi

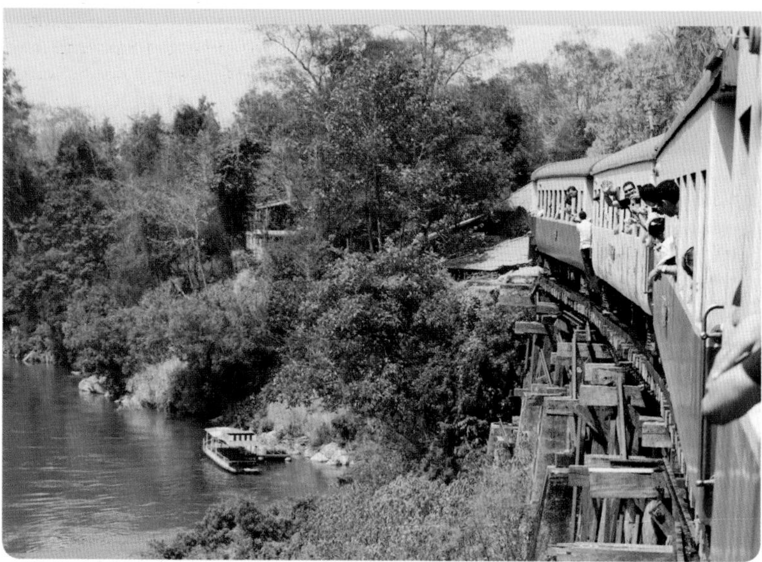

ANDREW BAIN/LONELY PLANET IMAGES ©

Why Bridge the Mae Nam Khwae?

The Thailand-Burma railway was built during the WWII-era Japanese occupation of Thailand (1942–43) and its objective was to link the 415km of rugged terrain between Thailand and Burma (Myanmar) to secure an alternative supply route for the Japanese conquest of other west Asian countries. Some considered the project impossible but the track was completed despite a lack of equipment and appalling conditions.

Construction began on 16 September 1942 at existing stations at Thanbyuzayat in Myanmar and Nong Pladuk (Ban Pong) in Thailand. Japanese engineers estimated it would take five years to link Thailand and Burma by rail. In reality, the Japanese army forced the POWs to complete the 1m-gauge railway in 16 months.

The bridge that spans the Mae Nam Khwae near Kanchanaburi (dubbed the Death Railway Bridge) was used for just 20 months before the Allies bombed it in 1945. Rather than a supply line, the route quickly became an escape path for Japanese troops. After the war, the British took control of the railway on the Burmese side and ripped up 4km of the tracks leading to Three Pagodas Pass for fear of the route being used by Karen separatists.

On the Thai side, the State Railway of Thailand (SRT) assumed control and today continues to operate trains on 130km of the original route between Nong Pladuk, south of Kanchanaburi, to Nam Tok. See the boxed text p115.

AS MIXED TRAVEL Tours
(0 3451 2017; www.applenoi-kanchanaburi.com; Apple's Retreat) A well-organised company with knowledgeable staff.

GOOD TIMES TRAVEL Tours
(0 3462 4441; www.good-times-travel.com; 63/1 Tha Mae Nam Khwae) All the normal day trips are available, plus adventure packages to more remote areas. Cycling tours can be arranged from here.

Sleeping

APPLE'S RETREAT Guest House $
(Map p111; 0 3451 2017; www.applenoi-kanchanaburi.com; 153/4 M.4 Bahn Tamakahm; r 490-690B;) With the most welcoming smiles in town, friendly and knowledgeable staff give the place a homey feel. All the compact, clean rooms look out over a well-maintained garden. In a bid to be eco-friendly, the rooms don't have TVs or fridges.

PONG PHEN Guest House $$
(Map p111; 0 3451 2981; www.pongphen.com; Th Mae Nam Khwae; r 150-1000B;) The best-value option if you want a pool, Pong Phen has rooms that range from backpacker simplicity to more spacious options with balconies. The restaurant offers decent Western and Thai dishes.

U INCHANTREE KANCHANABURI Hotel $$$
(0 3452 1584; www.ukanchanaburi.com; 443 Th Mae Nam Khwae; r from 2850B;) This gorgeous boutique resort 1km north of the bridge has thought of just about everything. Clever touches include a free iPod in every room (you choose the tunes in advance), infinity pool, split-level riverside seating, a gym and a library.

Eating

For more authentic food, check out the **night market** (Th Saengchuto; Thu-Tue)

ANDREAS ROSE/ALAMY ©

Don't Miss Erawan National Park

The majestic seven-tiered waterfall within Erawan National Park is one of the most popular in Thailand. The top level is so-called due its resemblance to Erawan, the three-headed elephant of Hindu mythology. Walking to the first three tiers is easy work, but after that good walking shoes and some endurance are needed to complete the 1.5km hike. Levels two and four are impressive, but be wary of monkeys who may snatch belongings while you're taking a dip.

Buses from Kanchanaburi stop by the entrance of the Erawan waterfall (50B, 1½ hours, hourly from 8am to 5.20pm). The last bus back to Kanchanaburi is at 4pm. Within the park, you can rent bicycles for 20B to 40B per day.

THINGS YOU NEED TO KNOW

อุทยานแห่งชาติเอราวัณ; ☎0 3457 4222; admission 200B; ⏰8am-4pm, levels 1 & 2 5pm

near the train station, which is packed with stalls serving fried treats and blended drinks. Several good-quality **floating restaurants** (Th Song Khwae) are often full of Korean or Thai package-company tourists. The **market** (Th Saeng-chuto) near the bus station is well-known for its excellent *hŏy tôrt* (fried mussels in an egg batter).

JUKKRU Thai $

(Map p111; Th Song Khwae; dishes 60-100B) This well-established restaurant has a regular nightly crowd thanks to its simple but delicious dishes. Look for the blue tables and chairs outside.

SRI RUNG RUENG Thai, Western $

(Map p111; Th Mae Nam Khwae; dishes 60-150B) With pasta, steak, vegetarian and nine pages of drinks to pick from, the menu defines comprehensive. Thai food comes with some Western compromise, but remains tasty and fresh.

Information

Kanchanaburi Tourist Authority of Thailand (☎0 3451 2500; Th Saengchuto; ⏰8.30am-4.30pm) Tourist information office.

Getting There & Away

Bus

Kanchanaburi's bus station is to the south of the town on Th Saengchuto. Destinations include:

Bangkok's Southern (Sai Tai Mai) bus terminal (2nd/1st class 84B/99B, two hours, every 15 minutes between 4am and 8pm)

Bangkok's Northern (Mo Chit) bus terminal (2nd/1st class 95/122B, two hours, every 90 minutes between 6.30am and 6pm) Go here if heading to northern Thailand.

Ratchaburi (2nd/1st class 47B/65B, two hours, frequent) Use this to head south then change to a Phetchaburi- or Hua Hin–bound bus.

Suphanburi (47B, two hours, every 20 minutes until 5.30pm) Connections to Ayuthaya and Lopburi.

Minibuses also run from the bus station. Destinations include:

Bangkok's Victory Monument (110B, two hours, every 10 minutes until 8pm) Stops at the Southern (Sai Tai Mai) bus terminal.

Northern (Mo Chit) terminal (120B, two hours, every 90 minutes until 6pm)

Srimongkol Transport (☎08 4471 8282, 350B) Runs air-conditioned buses to Rayong, stopping at Pattaya.

Train

Kanchanaburi's train station is 2km northwest of the bus station and near the guest house area. Kanchanaburi is on the Bangkok Noi-Nam Tok rail line, which includes a portion of the historic Death Railway built by WWII POWs during the Japanese occupation of Thailand. The State Railway of Thailand (SRT) promotes this as a historic route, and so charges foreigners 100B for any one-way journey along the line, regardless of the distance. Coming from Bangkok Noi station (located in Thonburi), 100B is reasonable, but for short trips in Kanchanaburi it seems steep. The most historic part of the journey begins north of Kanchanaburi as the train crosses the Death Railway Bridge and terminates at Nam Tok station. Destinations include the following:

Nam Tok (two hours, departs 5.30am, 10.30am and 4.19pm) Return journeys from Nam Tok leave at 5.20am, 12.55pm and 3.15pm. Sai Yok Noi waterfall is within walking distance.

Thonburi's Bangkok Noi station (three hours, 7.19am and 2.44pm) Trains leave Bangkok at 7.44am and 1.55pm.

The SRT runs a daily **tourist train** (☎0 3451 1285) from Kanchanaburi to Nam Tok (300B one-way). This train also carries the 100B passengers.

Detour: Hellfire Pass Memorial

To truly understand the suffering that occurred during the construction of the Burma-Thailand Railway in WWII, a visit to this **war memorial** (ช่องเขาขาด; www.dva.gov.au/commem/oawg/thailand.htm; admission by donation; ⏰9am-4pm) is a must. Start at the museum on the top level, look out over the contemplation deck, then walk along the trail that runs alongside the original rail bed.

A walking trail map and excellent audio guide are available. The museum is 80km northwest of Kanchanaburi on Hwy 323 and can be reached by Sangkhlaburi-Kanchanaburi bus (60B, 1½ hours, frequent departures). The last bus back to Kanchanaburi passes here at 4.45pm.

Getting Around

Public Transport

Trips from the bus station to the guest house area will cost 50B on a *săhm·lór* and 30B on a

Beach Admission Fee

Ko Samet is part of a national park and charges all visitors an entrance fee (200/100B adult/child) upon arrival. The fee is collected at the National Parks office in Hat Sai Kaew; *sŏrng·tăa·ou* from the pier will stop at the gates for payment. Hold on to your ticket for later inspections.

motorcycle taxi. Public *sŏrng·tăa·ou* run up and down Th Saengchuto for 10B per passenger (get off at the cemetery if you want the guest house area). The train station is within walking distance of the guest house area.

KO CHANG & EASTERN SEABOARD

Rayong & Ban Phe ระยอง/บ้านเพ

POP 106,737/16,717

You're most likely to be in either of these towns as a transit link en route to Ko Samet. Rayong has frequent bus connections to elsewhere and the little port of Ban Phe has ferry services to Ko Samet. Blue *sŏrng·tăa·ou* link the two towns (25B, 45 minutes, frequent departures).

Getting There & Away

Buses from Rayong go to/from the following destinations:

Bangkok's Eastern (Ekamai) station (127B to 146B, three hours, hourly 6am to 9.30pm)

Bangkok's Northern (Mo Chit) station (146B, four hours, hourly 6am to 7pm)

Bangkok's Southern (Sai Tai Mai) station (150B, five hours, five daily departures)

Bangkok's Suvarnabhumi (Airport) station (165B, 2½ hours, eight daily departures)

Buses from Ban Phe's bus station (near Tha Thetsaban) go to/from Bangkok's Eastern (Ekamai) station (157B, four hours, hourly 6am to 6pm). Ban Phe also has frequent minivan services to the following destinations:

Bangkok's Victory Monument (250B, four hours, hourly 7am to 6pm)

Laem Ngop (350B, four to five hours, two daily departures) For boats to Ko Chang.

Ko Samet เกาะเสม็ด

An island idyll, Ko Samet bobs in the sea with a whole lot of scenery: small sandy coves bathed by clear aquamarine water. You'll have to share all this prettiness with other beach lovers as it's an easy weekend escape from Bangkok as well as a major package-tour destination.

Sights & Activities

Beaches

Starting in the island's northeastern corner, Hat Sai Kaew, or 'Diamond Sand', is the island's widest and whitest stretch of sand and has all the hubbub you'd expect of a top-notch beach resort.

More subdued than its northern neighbour, Ao Hin Khok and Ao Phai are two gorgeous bays separated by rocky headlands. The crowd here tends to be younger and more stylish than the down-to-earth crew in Hat Sai Kaew and the parties are late-nighters.

Further still is wide and sandy **Ao Phutsa** (Ao Tub Tim), a favourite for solitude seekers, families and couples who need access to 'civilisation' but not a lot of other stimulation.

A smaller sister to Hat Sai Kaew, **Ao Wong Deuan** is a long, crescent-shaped bay packed with people, mainly package tourists.

Ao Thian (Candlelight Beach) is punctuated by big boulders that shelter small sandy spots creating a castaway ambience. It is one of Ko Samet's most casual, easygoing beaches and is deliciously lonely on weekdays.

The cove 'caboose' is **Ao Wai**, a lovely beach far removed from everything else (in reality it is only 1km from Ao Thian).

Sleeping

Weekday rates don't rank well on the value scale (fan rooms start at 800B) but look attractive considering weekend and holiday rates increase by as much as 100%.

A word of caution to early risers: Hat Sai Kaew, Ao Hin Khok, Ao Phai and Ao Wong Deuan are the most popular beaches and host well-amplified parties.

SAIKAEW VILLA Hotel **$**
(**☎ 0 3864 4144; Hat Sai Kaew; r 800-2000B; ❄**) The closest option to the pier, Saikaew Villa has big rooms or small rooms, fan or air-con and conjures up a holiday-camp atmosphere. Quality and privacy varies with each room.

TOK'S Hotel **$$**
(**☎ 0 3864 4072; Ao Hin Khok; r 1500B; ❄**) Snazzy villas climb up a landscaped hillside with plenty of shade and flowering plants, making Tok's a respectable midranger.

TUBTIM RESORT Hotel **$$**
(**☎ 0 3864 4025; www.tubtimresort.com; Ao Phutsa; r 800-2500B; ❄ @**) Ranging from fan to fab, Tubtim has a little of everything. More expensive bungalows are pretty and polished, while the cheapies are spare but still within walking distance to the same dreamy beach.

VIKING HOLIDAY RESORT Hotel **$$**
(**☎ 0 3864 4353; www.sametvikingresort.com; Ao Thian (Candlelight Beach); r 1200-2000B; ❄ @**) Ao Thian's most 'upscale' spot with large and comfortable rooms; there's only nine of them so book ahead.

Eating & Drinking

SUMMER RESTAURANT International **$$$**
(**Baan Puu Paan, Ao Noi Na; dishes 250-400B; ⏲ dinner**) In a crisp setting overlooking the harbour, Summer savours a globetrotters' culinary scrapbook, from Indian-style chicken tikka to Cajun chicken breasts.

BAN PLOY SAMED Thai **$$**
(**☎ 0 3864 4188; Ao Noi Na; dishes 300-600B; ⏲ dinner**) Better than having to haul in your meal, you are hauled to this floating restaurant by a boat-and-pulley system.

Ko Samet

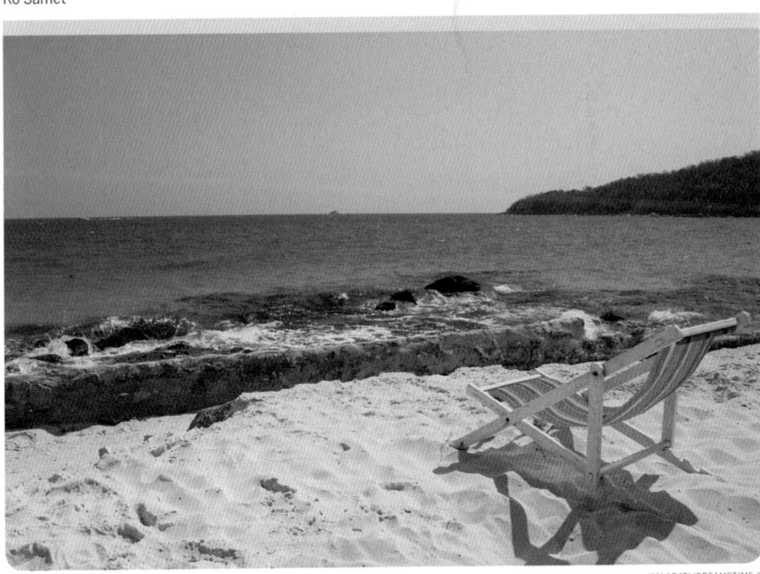

Fresh seafood dishes, especially the whole steamed fish variety, await.

Getting There & Away

Ko Samet is accessible from the mainland piers in Ban Phe. There are dozens of piers in Ban Phe, each used by different ferry companies, but they all charge the same fares (one way/return 50/100B, 40 minutes, hourly 8am to 4pm) and dock at Na Dan, the main pier on Ko Samet. Boats return to the mainland with the same frequency.

Getting Around

Green *sŏrng·tăa·ou* meet arriving boats at the main pier on Ko Samet and provide drop-offs at the various beaches (20B to 80B, depending on the beach).

Trat ตราด

POP 21,590

A major mainland transit point for Ko Chang and coastal Cambodia, Trat is underappreciated for its provincial charms.

Sleeping

Trat has many budget hotels housed in traditional wooden houses on and around Th Thana Charoen. You'll find it hard to spend more even if you want to.

BAN JAIDEE GUEST HOUSE Guest House $

(Map p119; ☎0 3952 0678; 6 Th Chaimongkol; r 200B; wi-fi**)** In a charming neighbourhood, this relaxed traditional wooden house has simple rooms with shared bathrooms (hot-water showers). It's very popular and booking ahead is essential.

RESIDANG GUEST HOUSE Guest House $

(Map p119; ☎0 3953 0103; www.trat-guesthouse.com; 87/1-2 Th Thana Charoen; r 260-600B; air-con, wi-fi**)** Thick mattresses, hot-water showers, wi-fi – what more do you need? Fan rooms come with breezes and balconies.

Getting There & Around

Air

The airport is 40km from town; a taxi to the airport from Trat town costs a ridiculous 5000B. Bangkok Airways (☎Trat Airport 0 3955 1654-5, in Bangkok 0 2265 5555; www.bangkokair.com) flies from Bangkok to Trat (one-way from 2090B, three times daily).

Bus

Trat's bus station is outside of town and serves the following destinations:

- Bangkok's Eastern (Ekamai) station (248B, 4½ hours, hourly 6am to 11.30pm)
- Bangkok's Northern (Mo Chit) station (248B, 5½ hours, two morning departures)
- Bangkok's Suvarnabhumi (Airport) station (248B, four to 4½ hours, five daily departures)

Jetty, Trat

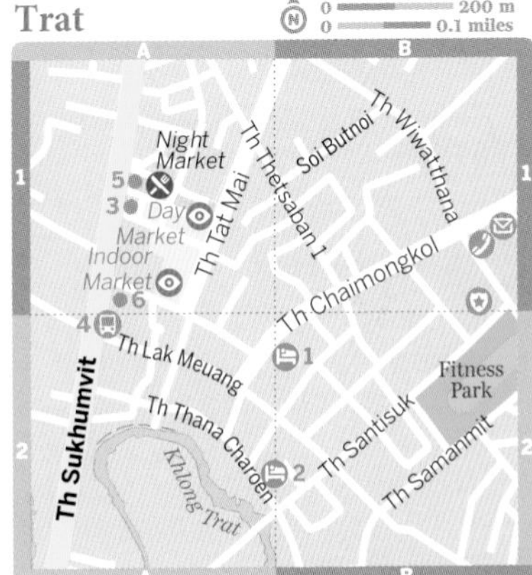

Trat

Sleeping

1 Ban Jaidee Guest House........B2
2 Residang Guest House........A2

Transport

3 Cherdchai Tour ticket office........A1
4 Family Tour (Minivans to Bangkok)........A2
5 Sŏrng·tăa·ou to bus station, Laem Ngop........A1
6 Sŏrng·tăa·ou to Tha Centrepoint (Laem Ngop)........A1

Family Tour (✆08 1996 2216; **Th Sukhumvit cnr Th Lak Meuang**) runs minivans to Bangkok's Victory Monument (300B, five hours, hourly 8am to 5pm) and continues on to Th Khao San (350B).

Local *sŏrng·tăa·ou* leave from Th Sukhumvit near the market for the bus station (20B to 60B, depending on number of passengers).

Boat

The piers that handle boat traffic to/from Ko Chang are located in Laem Ngop, about 30km southwest of Trat.

There are three piers in Laem Ngop each used by different boat companies, but the most convenient services are through Koh Chang Ferry (from Tha Thammachat) and Centrepoint Ferry (from Tha Centrepoint).

From Bangkok, you can catch a bus from Bangkok's Eastern (Ekamai) station all the way to Tha Centrepoint (250B, five hours, three morning departures). This route includes a stop at Suvarnabhumi (Airport) bus station as well as Trat's bus station.

Ko Chang เกาะช้าง

POP 7,033

With steep, jungle-covered peaks erupting from the sea, picturesque Ko Chang (Elephant Island) retains its remote and rugged spirit despite its current status as a package-tour resort akin to Phuket. The island's swathes of sand are girl-next-door pretty but not beauty-queen gorgeous. What it lacks in sand, it makes up for in an unlikely combination: accessible wilderness with a thriving party scene.

Sights

West Coast

HAT SAI KHAO (WHITE SAND BEACH) Beach

(หาดทรายขาว) The longest, most luxurious stole of sand on the island is packed with package-tour hotels and serious sunbathers. Along the main road, the village is busy, loud and brash – but the extremities provide a convenient break.

AO KHLONG PRAO Beach

(อ่าวคลองพร้าว) A relaxed counterpoint to Hat Sai Khao's energy, Khlong Prao's beach is a pretty sweep of sand pinned between hulking mountainous headlands and bisected by two estuaries. At low tide, beachcombers stroll the rippled sand eyeing the critters left naked by the receding water.

HAT KAIBAE Beach

(หาดไก่แบ้) A companion beach to Khlong Prao, Hat Kaibae is a great spot for families and 30-something couples. A slim strip of sand unfurls around an island-dotted bay far enough removed from the package-tour scene that you'll feel self-righteously independent. There's kayaking to the outlying island and low tide provides hours of beachcombing.

LONELY BEACH Beach

The island's backpacker hang-out is the five-o'clock shadow of beaches, a bit scruffy but ready for fun. During the day, most sunbathers are baking off a hangover earned the night before when Lonely Beach becomes the most social place on the island. The music is loud, the drinks are strong and the crowd is youthful and carefree.

BAN BANG BAO Village

(บ้านบางเบ้า) Nearly at the end of the west coast road, Ban Bang Bao is a former fishing community built in the traditional fashion of interconnected piers. Most visitors come for a seafood meal and some decide to stay overnight.

Northern Interior

Ko Chang's mountainous interior is predominately protected as a national park. The forest is lush and alive with wildlife and threaded by silver-hued waterfalls.

BAN KWAN CHANG Elephant Camp

(บ้านควาญช้าง; ☎08 1919 3995; changtone@yahoo.com; ⌚8.30am-5pm) In a beautiful forested setting, this camp offers a quiet and intimate experience with its nine resident elephants. A one-hour visit (900B) involves feeding, bathing and riding an elephant; hotel transfer is included. Be sure to wear mozzie spray.

Activities

KAYAKING

Ko Chang cuts an impressive and heroic profile when viewed from the sea aboard a kayak. Most hotels rent open-top kayaks (from 300B per day) that are convenient for near-shore outings and noncommittal kayakers.

KAYAKCHANG Kayaking

(☎08 7673 1923; www.kayakchang.com; Amari Emerald Cove Resort, Khlong Prao) For more serious paddlers, KayakChang rents high-end, closed-top kayaks (from 1000B per day) that handle better and travel faster.

SALAK KOK KAYAK STATION Kayaking

(☎08 1919 3995; kayak rentals per hr 100B) On the east side of the island, explore the island's mangrove swamps of Ao Salak

Khlong Phu Falls, Ko Chang

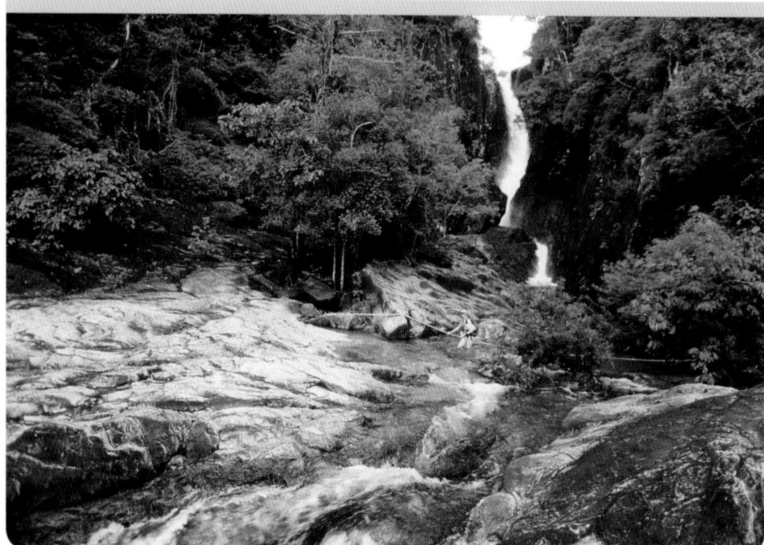

SARA-JANE CLELAND/LONELY PLANET IMAGES ©

Diving & Snorkelling

The dive sites near Ko Chang offer a variety of coral, fish and beginner-friendly shallow waters on par with other Gulf of Thailand dive sites.

The seamounts off the southern tip of the island within the Ko Chang marine park are reached within a 30-minute cruise. Popular spots include **Hin Luk Bat** and **Hin Rap**, rocky, coral-encrusted seamounts with depths of around 18m to 20m. These are havens for schooling fish and some turtles.

Reef-fringed **Ko Wai** features a good variety of colourful hard and soft corals and is great for snorkelling. It is a popular day-tripping island but has simple overnight accommodation for more alone time with the reef.

Diving trips typically cost around 2800B to 3500B. PADI Open Water certification costs 14,500B per person. **BB Divers** (☎0 3955 8040; www.bbdivers.com) is based at Bang Bao with branches at Lonely Beach, Khlong Prao and Hat Sai Khao.

Kok while supporting an award-winning ecotour program. Salak Kok Kayak Station rents self-guided kayaks and is a village-work project designed to promote tourism without deteriorating the traditional way of life.

TREKKING

Mr Tan from **Evolution Tour** (☎0 3955 7078; www.evolutiontour.com) or Lek from **Jungle Way** (☎08 9247 3161; www.jungleway.com) lead one-day treks (800B to 1400B) through Khlong Son Valley.

KOH CHANG TREKKING Trekking, Bird-Watching
(☎08 1588 3324; www.kohchangtrekking.info) Bird-watchers should contact Koh Chang Trekking, which runs one- and two-day trips (1000B to 2000B) to the national park and hikes to the top of Khao Chom Prasat, two nearby rocky tipped peaks.

Sleeping

West Coast

On the west coast, Lonely Beach is still the best budget option, Hat Kai Bae is the best-value option and Hat Sai Khao is the most overpriced.

KEEREEELÉ Hotel **$$**
(☎0 3955 1285; www.keereeele.com; Hat Sai Khao; r 2000B; ❄ 📶 🏊) An excess of 'e's in the name doesn't detract from the merits of this new multi-storey hotel on the interior side of the road. The rooms are modern and comfortable and some have views of the verdant mountains behind. Beach access is 300m via sidewalks so you don't have to play chicken with traffic.

SAI KHAO INN Guest House **$$**
(☎0 3955 1584; www.saikhaoinn.com; Hat Sai Khao; r 800-1800B; ❄) A garden setting on the interior side of the road, Sai Khao Inn has a little bit of everything – bungalows, concrete bunkers, big rooms, even rooms for taxi drivers (according to the brochure).

KB RESORT Hotel **$$**
(☎0 1862 8103; www.kbresort.com; Hat Kaibae; r 2000-3500B; ❄ @ 🏊) Lemon yellow bungalows have cheery bathrooms and pose peacefully beside the sea. Skip the overpriced fan bungalows, though.

PARADISE COTTAGES Hotel **$$**
(☎08 5831 4228; www.paradisecottagekohchang.com; Lonely Beach; r 700-1200B; ❄ 📶) A whole lot of chillin'-out happens at this mellow flashpacker spot. Though it is

National Park Status

Parts of Ko Chang are protected and maintained as a national park. Though their conservation efforts are a bit amorphic, you will be required to pay a 200B park entrance fee when visiting some of the waterfalls (entrance fees are stated in the reviews and payable at the site). **National Park headquarters** (☎0 3955 5080; Ban Than Mayom; ⏰8am-5pm) is on the eastern side of the island near Nam Tok Than Mayom.

Also be aware that nudity and topless sunbathing are forbidden by law in Mu Ko Chang National Marine Park; this includes all beaches on Ko Chang, Ko Kut, Ko Mak, etc.

oceanfront, the beach is too muddy and rocky for swimming.

MANGROVE Hotel $$
(☎08 1949 7888; Lonely Beach; r 1000B) Cascading down a forested hill to a private beach, Mangrove has beautiful yet simple bungalows purposefully designed with accordion-style doors that open to the views and the breezes (a natural air-con). The ambience is a pleasing combo of private rustic-chic.

BANG BAO SEA HUT Hotel $$
(☎08 1285 0570; Ban Bang Bao; r 2500B; ❄) With individual bungalows built on the edge of Bang Bao's pier, this is one of Ko Chang's most unusual places to stay. Each 'hut' (actually much flasher than it sounds) is surrounded by a private deck where breakfast is served, with wooden shutters opening to the sea breeze.

Northern Interior & East Coast

You'll need your own transport and maybe even a posse not to feel lonely out here, but you'll be rewarded with a quieter, calmer experience.

AMBER SANDS Hotel $$
(☎0 3958 6177; www.ambersandsbeachresort.com; Ao Dan Kao; r 2000-2700B; ❄@≋) Sandwiched between mangroves and a quiet red-sand beach, Amber Sands has eight comfortable bungalows with picture windows facing a high-definition sea view. The location feels a world away but it is only 15 minutes from the pier.

SOUK Guest House $
(☎08 1553 3194; Ao Dan Kao; r 700B; @) Next door to Amber Sands, this funky spot has seven pop-art cool (fan only) bungalows at a pleasant price. There are lots of chill-out spaces and an urban vibe in the open-deck restaurant and cocktail bar. Easy access to the ferry pier.

Eating & Drinking

West Coast

OODIE'S PLACE International $$
(☎0 3955 1193; Hat Sai Khao; dishes 150-280B; ⏰lunch & dinner) Local musician Oodie runs a nicely diverse operation with excellent French food, tasty Thai specialities and live music from 10pm. After all these years, it is still beloved by expats.

SAFFRON ON THE SEA Thai $$
(☎0 3955 1253; Hat Kai Mook; dishes 150-350B; ⏰breakfast, lunch & dinner) Owned by an arty escapee from Bangkok, this friendly boutique hotel has a generous portion of oceanfront dining and a relaxed, romantic atmosphere. All the Thai dishes are prepared in the island-style, more sweet than spicy.

IYARA SEAFOOD Seafood $$
(☎0 3955 1353; Khlong Prao; dishes 150-300B; ⏰lunch & dinner) Iyara isn't your standard island seafood warehouse: after dining in the lovely bamboo pavilion, guests are invited to kayak along the nearby estuary.

BARRIO BONITO Mexican $$
(☎08 0092 8208; Lonely Beach; dishes 150-250B; ⏰breakfast, lunch & dinner) This

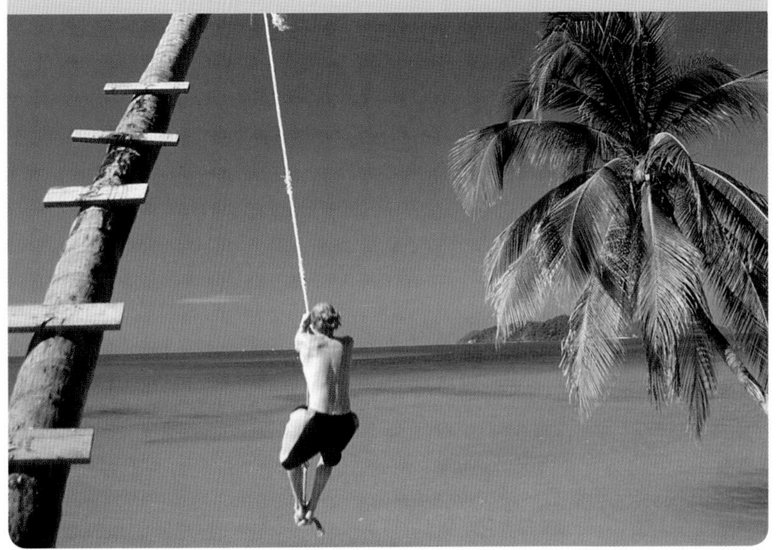

WOODS WHEATCROFT/LONELY PLANET IMAGES ©

breezy, hip place has all the island raving about its seriously good Mexican fare. A French-Mexican couple runs the place with flair and there's a plunge pool should the salsa induce sweating.

RUAN THAI Seafood **$$**
(Ban Bang Bao; dishes 100-300B; lunch & dinner) It's about as fresh as it gets (note your future dinner greeting you in tanks as you enter) and the portions are large. The doting service is beyond excellent – they'll even help you crack your crabs.

Getting There & Away

To/From Mainland

Ko Chang–bound boats depart from the mainland piers collectively referred to as Laem Ngop (see p119 for more information), southwest of Trat. You'll arrive in Ko Chang at either Tha Sapparot or Tha Centrepoint, depending on which pier and boat company you used on the mainland.

Tha Sapparot is the closest to the west coast beaches and receives vehicle ferries from the mainland pier of Tha Thammachat. **Koh Chang Ferry** (**0 3955 5188**) runs this service (one-way 80B, 30 minutes, hourly 6.30am to 7pm).

At the time of writing, the car ferry associated with Tha Centrepoint was competing aggressively for business by offering cheaper prices, more commissions and a Bangkok–Laem Ngop bus service. You cut out some of the land transfers with the new bus service but Tha Centrepoint (on Ko Chang) is further from the west coast beaches, so the time-saving is negligible. **Centrepoint Ferry** (**0 3953 8196**) runs this service (one-way/round-trip 80/100B, 45 minutes, hourly 6am to 7.30pm). Weekend service in high season runs until 9pm.

There is also a new bus route directly from Bangkok's Suvarnabhumi (Airport) station to Ko Chang (308B, six hours) via the car ferry with stops on the mainland at Trat. Another option is a minivan service from Bangkok's Victory Monument that goes all the way to Ko Chang's Tha Sapparot (one-way 300B, four hours, hourly departures).

To/From Neighbouring Islands

Tha Bang Bao in the southern part of the island is the pier used for boat trips to neighbouring islands. There is a daily inter-island ferry (known conflictingly as 'express' or 'slow' boat) operated by **Bang Bao Boats** (**www.bangbaoboat.com**) that does a loop to Ko Wai, Ko Mak, Ko Kut and back. Faster and more frequent speedboat departures do the same circuit.

Getting Around

Shared *sŏrng·tăa·ou* meet arriving boats to shuttle passengers to the various beaches (Hat Sai Khao 50B, Khlong Prao 60B and Lonely Beach 100B). Most hops between neighbouring west coast beaches should cost around 40B to 50B.

Ko Kut

เกาะกูด

All the paradise descriptions apply to Ko Kut: the beaches are graceful arcs of sand, the water is gin clear, coconut palms outnumber buildings and a secluded, unhurried atmosphere embraces you upon arrival. There's nothing in the form of nightlife or even dining, really, but those are the reasons for visiting.

Hat Khlong Chao is one of the island's best and could easily compete with Samui's Hat Chaweng in a beach beauty contest; the clear water is shallow and bathtub smooth. Ao Noi is a pretty boulder strewn beach with a steep drop-off and steady waves for strong swimmers. Ao Phrao is another lovely sweep of sand.

Sleeping

On weekends and holidays during the high season, vacationing Thais fill the resorts.

BANN MAKOK Hotel **$$**

(☎08 1934 5713; Khlong Yai Ki; r 2500-3000B; ❄@) Be the envy of the speedboat patrons when you get dropped off at this boutique hotel tucked into the mangroves. Recycled timbers painted in vintage colours have been constructed into a maze of eight rooms designed to look like a traditional pier fishing village.

TINKERBELL RESORT Hotel **$$$**

(☎08 1813 0058; www.tinkerbellresort.com; Hat Khlong Chao; r incl meals from 7900B; ❄@≈) Natural materials, like towering bamboo privacy fences and thatched roof villas, sew this resort seamlessly into the landscape. The rooms are bright and airy and smack dab on the prettiest beach you've ever seen.

MANGROVE BUNGALOWS Guest House **$**

(☎08 5279 0278; Ban Khlong Chao; r 600-1200B; ❄) Lounging pleasantly along mangrove-forested Khlong Chao, this place has large bungalows sporting polished wood floors and hot-water showers. A restaurant hangs above the lazy canal, and it is a 10-minute walk to the beach.

Information

There are no banks or ATMs, though major resorts can exchange money.

Getting There & Around

To/From Mainland: Ko Kut is accessible from the mainland pier of Laem Sok, 22km southeast of Trat, the nearest bus transfer point.

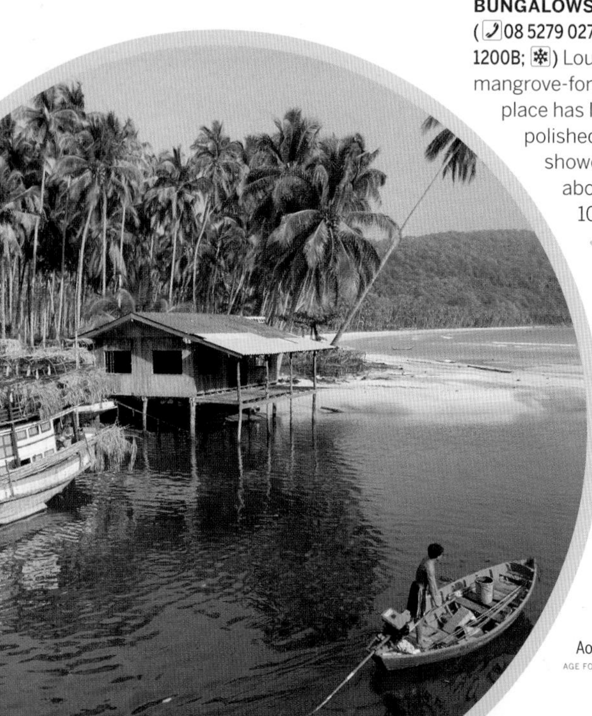

Ao Phrao, Ko Kut

To/From Neighbouring Islands: **Bang Bao Boat** (www.bangbaoboat.com) is the archipelago's inter-island ferry running a daily loop from Ko Chang, departing at 9am, to Ko Kut (one-way 700B, five to six hours). In the opposite direction, you can catch it to Ko Mak (one-way 300B, one to two hours) and Ko Wai (one-way 400B, 2½ hours).

NORTHEASTERN THAILAND

Nakhon Ratchasima (Khorat) นครราชสีมา (โคราช)

POP 215,000

Khorat is a city that grows on you. It has a strong sense of regional identity– people are call themselves *kon koh·râht* instead of *kon ee·săhn* – and is at its best in its quieter nooks, such as inside the east side of the historic moat, where local life goes on in its own uncompromising way.

This urban centre provides transit links to the Angkor ruins of Phimai.

Sleeping

THAI INTER HOTEL Hotel $$
(0 4424 7700; www.thaiinterhotel.com; 344/2 Th Yommarat; r 650-750B;) This little hotel tries to be hip by patching together an odd mix of styles, and it pretty much pulls it off. The lobby is homey and the rooms are comfy. It's got a good (though not so quiet) location near many good restaurants and bars.

Information

Nakhon Ratchasima (Khorat) Tourist Authority of Thailand (0 4421 3666; Th Mittaphap; 8.30am-4.30pm) Tourist information office.

Getting There & Away

Bus

Khorat has two bus terminals. **Terminal 1** (0 4424 2899; Th Burin) in the city centre serves Bangkok and towns within Khorat province. Buses to other destinations, plus more for Bangkok, use **Terminal 2** (0 4425 6006; Hwy 2) north of downtown.

There are now vans to/from Ayuthaya (132B, four hours, every 30 minutes) from Terminal 2 and Pak Chong (60B, one hour, every 20 minutes) from a roadside stop around the corner from Terminal 1.

Getting Around

Túk-túk cost between 30B and 70B to most places around town. Motorcycle taxis and săhm·lór (pedicabs; also spelt *săamláw*), both of which are common, always cost less. **Korat Car Rental** (08 1877 3198; www.koratcarrental.com) is a local firm with a stellar reputation.

Phimai พิมาย

Reminiscent of Cambodia's Angkor Wat, Prasat Phimai once stood on an important trade route linking the Khmer capital of Angkor with the northern reaches of the realm. Phimai is an easy day trip out of Khorat, but if you prefer the quiet life, you could always make Khorat a day trip out of Phimai instead.

Sights

PHIMAI HISTORICAL PARK Khmer Ruin
(อุทยานประวัติศาสตร์พิมาย; 0 4447 1568; Th Anantajinda; admission 100B; 7.30am-6pm) Started by Khmer King Jayavarman V (AD 968–1001) during the late 10th century and finished by his successor King Suriyavarman I (AD 1002–49), this Hindu-Mahayana Buddhist temple projects a majesty that transcends its size. It has been painstakingly reconstructed by the Fine Arts Department and is one of the most complete monuments on the circuit.

PHIMAI NATIONAL MUSEUM Museum
(พิพิธภัณฑสถานแห่งชาติพิมาย; Th Tha Songkhran; admission 100B; 9am-4pm Wed-Sun) Situated on the banks of Sa Kwan, a 12th-century Khmer reservoir, this museum houses a fine collection of Khmer sculptures from Prasat Phimai, including many exquisite lintels and other ruins from around Lower Isan.

Khao Yai Through the Back Door

The drive through the southern stretch of Khao Yai National Park is just as beautiful as the more popular northern region, but wildlife is more abundant, particularly elephants walking along the road at night. **Palm Garden Lodge** (☎08 9989 4470) is in Prachinburi Province, just 12km from the entrance, and for the most part, its day-long **park tours** (1300B per person with four people) are the same as those offered by Pak Chong–based companies but with three key differences: tours visit Haew Narok waterfall (June to November, when it has water), there's the option of a night safari before leaving the park, and Klin is one of Khao Yai's few female guides.

Our favourite is the long-running **Palm Garden Lodge** (☎08 9989 4470; www.palmgalo.com; r 400-650B, bungalows 1200B; ❄@📶), 10km east of the park gate in Ban Khon Kwang. Set in a quiet garden and featuring homey fan and air-con rooms, this is a very relaxing and welcoming place.

Sleeping

OLD PHIMAI GUESTHOUSE Guest House $
(☎08 0159 5363; www.phimaigh.com; Th Chomsudasadet; dm 100B, s 170B, d 200-370B; ❄📶)
This creaking wooden house tucked away down a soi is genuinely homey and attracts many backpackers. The friendly hosts can tell you all about Phimai and also run reasonably priced day trips to Phanom Rung.

Getting There & Away

Buses for Phimai leave from Khorat's Bus Terminal 2 (36B to 50B, 1¼ hours) every half-hour until 10pm.

Khao Yai National Park อุทยานแห่งชาติเขาใหญ่

Up there on the podium with some of the world's greatest parks, **Khao Yai National Park** (☎08 6092 6529; admission 400B) is Thailand's oldest and most visited reserve. Covering 2168 sq km, Khao Yai incorporates one of the largest intact monsoon forests remaining in mainland Asia, which is why it was named a Unesco World Heritage Site (as part of the Dong Phayayen-Khao Yai Forest Complex). The mostly English-speaking staff at the **visitors centre** (⏲8am-8pm) are very helpful.

Some 200 elephants tramp the park's boundaries. Other mammals include tigers, leopards, bears, gaur, barking deer, otters, crocodiles, various gibbons and macaques and some rather large pythons.

Khao Yai has two entrances. By far the busiest is to the north in Nakhon Ratchasima Province, with most travellers passing through the town of Pak Chong. The southern entrance is in Prachinburi Province; see the boxed text, p126, for full details.

Sights & Activities

Khao Yai has plenty of waterfalls. The beauty award, however, goes to 25m **Nam Tok Haew Suwat**, which scooped a starring role in Danny Boyle's film *The Beach*. It has water year-round, and you can swim in the pool at the bottom.

Most of the hotels and resorts around Khao Yai arrange **park tours** and this is really the ideal way to visit because a good guide will show you creatures you never would have seen on your own. The typical day-long program includes some easy walks looking for wildlife and a visit to Haew Suwat waterfall. Bird-watching, camping, trekking and other specialty tours are also available. Greenleaf Guesthouse (p127) has long earned enthusiastic praise for their trips and a new player, **Bobby's Jungle Tours** (☎0 4432 8177; www.bobbysjungletour skhaoyai.com) also appears to have good guides, plus its tours finish at night so there's a better chance of encountering elephants along the park road.

Sleeping

There are at least one hundred places to stay along Th Thanarat (Rte 2090), the road leading to the park, and plenty more in the not-so-pleasant gateway city of Pak Chong.

The best setting for sleeping is, of course, in the park itself. There are **campsites** (per person with own tent 30B, 2–6-person tents 150-400B) and a variety of **rooms & bungalows** (☎0 2562 0760; www.dnp.go.th/parkreserve; 2-8 people 800-3500B) around the park, often quite far from the visitors centre.

GREENLEAF GUESTHOUSE Guest House $
(☎0 4436 5073; www.greenleaftour.com; Th Thanarat, Km7.5; r 200-300B; ) Step past the slightly chaotic common areas and you'll be surprised by the good-value rooms (with cold-water private bathrooms) at the back of this long-running family-owned place.

HOTEL DES ARTISTS Hotel $$$
(☎0 4429 7444; www.hotelartists.com; Th Thanarat, Km17; r incl breakfast 3500B; ❄@☎≋) Breaking from the Khao Yai norm, this tasteful hotel goes for French-colonial chic rather than a nature theme; though with its gorgeous mountain views out the back you won't forget where you are.

Getting There & Away

Sŏrng·tăa·ou travel the 30km from Pak Chong down Th Thanarat to the park's northern gate (40B, 45 minutes), every half-hour from 6am to 5pm. It's another 14km to the visitors centre, and park guards are used to talking drivers into hauling people up there.

All 2nd-class buses between Bangkok (108B to 139B, 2½ hours) and Khorat (60B to 74B, one

Khao Yai National Park

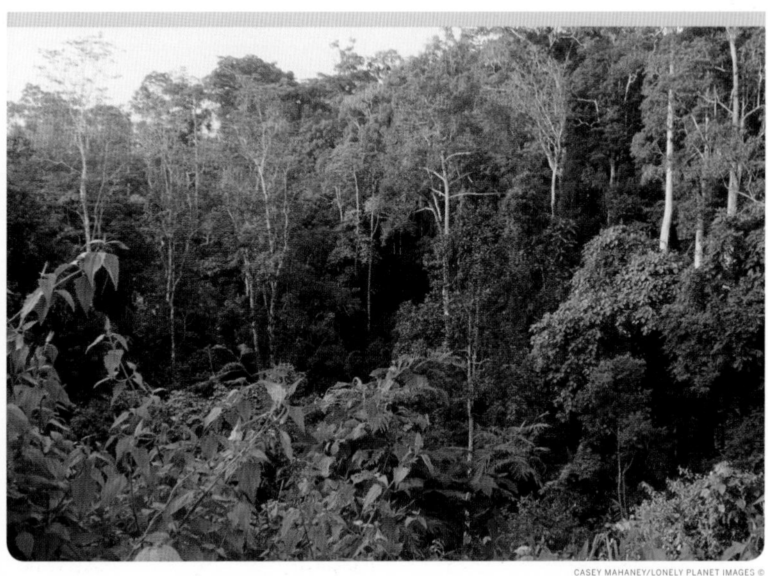

CASEY MAHANEY/LONELY PLANET IMAGES ©

If You Like... Khmer Temples

If you like Phanom Rung, then you'll enjoy these other nearby Khmer ruins:

1 **PRASAT MUANG TAM** **(8km from Phanom Rung; admission 100B; 6am-6pm)** This Khmer temple is an ideal bolt-on to any visit to Phanom Rung, which is only 8km to the northwest. The whole complex was once a shrine to Shiva, dating to the 10th or 11th century. Laterite walls shelter five *prang* and four lotus-filled reservoirs, each guarded by whimsical five-headed *naga*. The principal unrestored *prang* contains a lintel depicting Shiva and his consort Uma riding the sacred bull, Nandi. As at Angkor Wat, the *prang* represent the five peaks of Mt Meru, the abode of the Hindu gods and Barai Muang Tam (a reservoir located across the road) represents the surrounding ocean. A 150B combo ticket allows entry to both Phanom Rung and Muang Tam at a 50B discount.

2 **PRASAT TA MEUAN** **(55km from Phanom Rung; admission free; daylight hr)** A series of three ruins bordering Surin province and the Cambodian border that defined ancient route linking Angkor Wat to Phimai. The ruins include a 12th-century rest stop for pilgrims, a healing station and Shiva shrine that was looted during the Khmer Rouge occupation in the 1980s. Heed the 'danger' signs as landmines still litter the area.

hour) stop in Pak Chong. The bus station for most Bangkok buses is west of the traffic light at Th Thesabarn 8.

There are now also vans to Bangkok's Victory Monument (160B, 2½ hours, hourly) from the traffic light and to Khorat (60B, one hour, every 20 minutes) from *dà·l àht kàak*.

You can also get to Pak Chong by train from Bangkok and Khorat, but it's much faster to go by bus or van. Ayuthaya, on the other hand, has no direct bus service so the train (3rd-class 53B, 2nd-class fan/air-con 83/173B, two to three hours, 13 daily) can be a good option.

Nang Rong นางรอง

POP 20,300

This workaday city is even more forgettable than Buriram, 45km to the north, but it's the most convenient base for visiting Phanom Rung.

Sleeping & Eating

P CALIFORNIA INTER HOSTEL Guest House $
(08 1808 3347; www.pcalifornianangrong.webs.com; Th Sangkakrit; r 250-700B;) This great place on the east side of town offers bright, nicely decorated rooms with good value in all price ranges. English-speaking Khun Wicha, who's a wealth of knowledge about the area, also provides bikes, rents motorcycles (200B per day) and leads tours.

CABBAGES & CONDOMS Hotel $$
(0 4465 7145; Hwy 24; r 240-1500B;) The cheapest (shared bathroom) rooms at this Population & Community Development Association–run resort, set in a garden and ringed by several little lakes, are pretty limp. But move up the price scale (where you get large rooms with stone floors) and this is a pleasant place to stay. It's 6.5km west of town.

Getting There & Away

Nang Rong's **bus terminal** (**0 4463 1517**) is on the west side of town.

Phanom Rung Historical Park อุทยานประวัติศาสตร์เขาพนมรุ้ง

Phanom Rung (Phnom Rung; **0 4478 2715; admission 100B, bike/motorcycle/car fee 10/20/50B; 6am-6pm**), the largest and best restored Khmer monument in Thailand, has a knock-me-dead location. Crowning the summit of an extinct volcano (the name is derived from the Khmer words for 'big mountain'), this sanctuary sits 200m above the paddy fields, and the Dangrek Mountains on the Cambodian border are clearly visible to the southeast.

The temple was erected between the 10th and 13th centuries, the bulk of it during the reign of King Suriyavarman II (r AD 1113–50), which was the apex of Angkor architecture. The complex faces east and four times a year the sun shines through all 15 sanctuary doorways.

One of the most remarkable aspects of Phanom Rung is the **promenade** leading to the main gate. It's the best surviving example in Thailand. It begins on a slope 400m east of the main tower with three earthen **terraces**. The promenade ends at the first and largest of three **naga bridges**. The first is flanked by 16 five-headed *naga* in the classic Angkor style.

The central **ɓrah·sàht** has a gallery on each of its four sides and the entrance to each gallery is itself a smaller version of the main tower.

A 150B combo ticket allows entry to both Phanom Rung and Muang Tam.

Vishnu & the King of Pop

Phanom Rung's most famous sculpture is the **Narai Bandhomsindhu lintel**, a carving depicting a reclining Vishnu ('Phra Narai' in Thai) in the Hindu creation myth. Growing from his navel is a lotus that branches into several blossoms, on one of which sits the creator god, Brahma. Vishnu is asleep on the milky sea of eternity, here represented by a *naga* and alongside him are heads of Kala, the god of time and death. In 1972 it was found on display at the Art Institute of Chicago and Thailand pressed for its return. Superstars Carabao helped the cause with their song 'Thaplang' (Lintel) featuring the line 'Take back Michael Jackson, Give us Phra Narai'. Phra Narai finally came home in 1988.

Getting There & Away

Getting to Phanom Rung without your own vehicle seems complicated, but it's not. *Sŏrng·tăa·ou* (20B, 30 minutes, every half-hour) from in front of the old market *(nâh đà·làht go/uw)* on the east end of town and Chanthaburi-bound buses from the bus station go to Ban Ta Pek where motorcycle taxi drivers charge 200B to Phanom Rung, including waiting time. Chartering a *sŏrng·tăa·ou* at Ban Ta Pek is likely to cost an hefty 800B.

Those coming from or heading to Pak Chong (104B to 140B, 2½ hours, hourly) or Bangkok (Gitjagaan Tours; 275B, five hours, hourly) have the option of getting off at Ban Tako, a well-marked turn-off about 14km east of Nang Rong and waiting for one of the buses or *sŏrng·tăa·ou* from Nang Rong; or just taking a motorcycle taxi (300B return) all the way to Phanom Rung.

Chiang Mai

Snuggled into the foothills of northern Thailand, Chiang Mai is a sanctuary of sorts, with a refreshing combination of city accoutrements and country sensibilities. It is a city of artisans and craftspeople, of university professors and students, of idealists and culture hounds – creating a disposition that is laid-back, creative and reverential.

The city is lauded for its enduring northern Thai (also known as Lanna) characteristics, for the quaint walled quarter filled with temples, and its guardian temple-crowned mountain endowed with mystical attributes.

Outside the urban sphere is accessible, and you'll find scenic countryside and two of Thailand's highest mountain peaks: Doi Inthanon (2565m) and Doi Chiang Dao (2195m). Boasting more natural forest cover than any other province in the north, Chiang Mai offers activities such as cycling, hiking, elephant trekking, bird-watching and river rafting.

Wat Phra That Doi Suthep (p152)

Chiang Mai

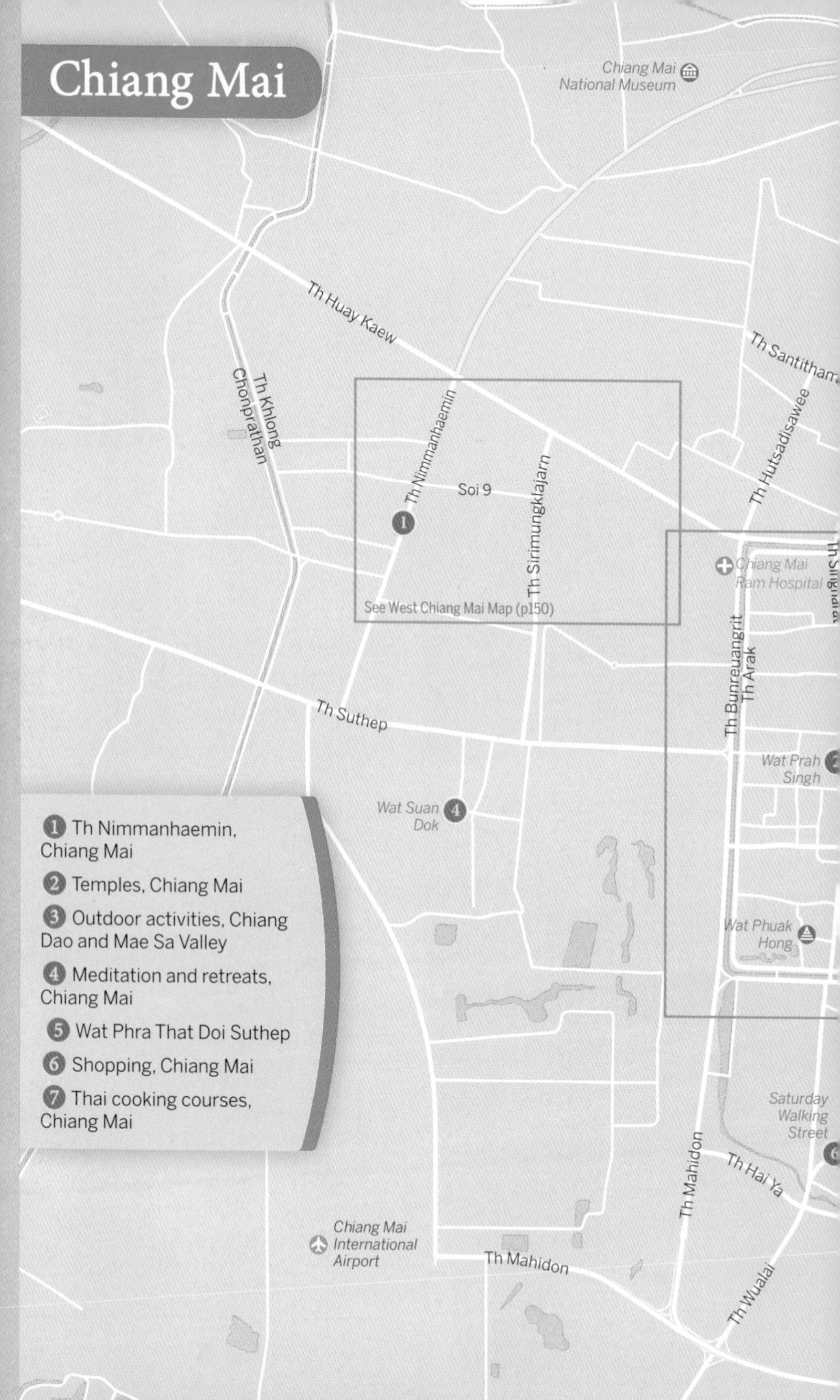

Chiang Mai National Museum
Th Huay Kaew
Th Santitham
Th Khlong Chonprathan
Th Nimmanhaemin
Th Hutsadisawee
Soi 9
Th Sirimungklajarn
Chiang Mai Ram Hospital
See West Chiang Mai Map (p150)
Th Bunreuangrit
Th Arak
Th Suthep
Wat Prah Singh
Wat Suan Dok
Wat Phuak Hong
Saturday Walking Street
Th Hai Ya
Th Mahidon
Chiang Mai International Airport
Th Wualai
1 Th Nimmanhaemin, Chiang Mai
2 Temples, Chiang Mai
3 Outdoor activities, Chiang Dao and Mae Sa Valley
4 Meditation and retreats, Chiang Mai
5 Wat Phra That Doi Suthep
6 Shopping, Chiang Mai
7 Thai cooking courses, Chiang Mai

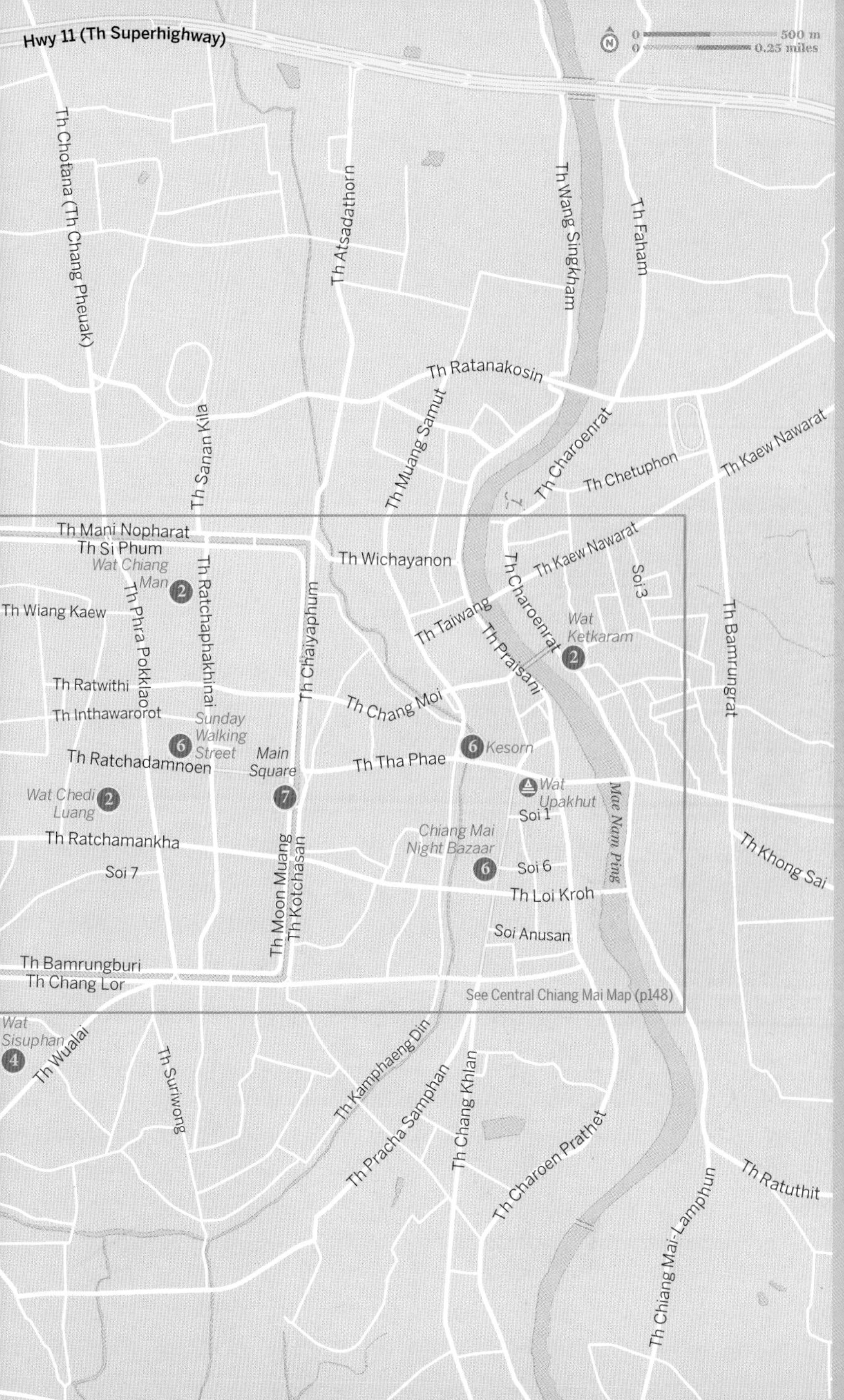

Hwy 11 (Th Superhighway)
0 500 m
0 0.25 miles
Th Chotana (Th Chang Pheuak)
Th Atsadathorn
Th Wang Singkham
Th Faham
Th Ratanakosin
Th Sanan Kila
Th Muang Samut
Th Charoenrat
Th Chetuphon
Th Kaew Nawarat
Th Mani Nopharat
Th Si Phum
Wat Chiang Man
2
Th Wichayanon
Th Ratchaphakhinai
Th Chaiyaphum
Th Wiang Kaew
Th Phra Pokklao
Th Taiwang
Th Praisani
Soi 3
Wat Ketkaram
2
Th Bamrungrat
Th Ratwithi
Th Inthawarorot
Th Chang Moi
Sunday Walking Street
6
6
Kesorn
Th Ratchadamnoen
Main Square
Th Tha Phae
Wat Chedi Luang
2
7
Wat Upakhut
Soi 1
Mae Nam Ping
Th Ratchamankha
Chiang Mai Night Bazaar
Th Khong Sai
Soi 7
6
Soi 6
Th Moon Muang
Th Kotchasan
Th Loi Kroh
Soi Anusan
Th Bamrungburi
Th Chang Lor
See Central Chiang Mai Map (p148)
Wat Sisuphan
4
Th Wualai
Th Suriwong
Th Kamphaeng Din
Th Pracha Samphan
Th Chang Khlan
Th Charoen Prathet
Th Ratuthit
Th Chiang Mai-Lamphun

Chiang Mai's Highlights

1 Th Nimmanhaemin

This road and its offshoots are an incredible hive of energy, bursting with bistros, cafes, trendy bars, boutique shops, art spaces and all manner of creative and fabulous businesses. Shop, eat, mingle, drink, flirt, dance, spa…everything is within a few minutes' walk.

Need to Know

BEST TIME TO VISIT Shops open around 11am and nightlife picks up around 10pm or 11pm **TOP TIP** Pick up *Citylife Chiang Mai* for trends and events **For further coverage, see p144**

Local Knowledge

Th Nimmanhaemin Don't Miss List

BY PIM KEMASINGKI, MANAGING EDITOR, *CITYLIFE CHIANG MAI*

1 SHOPPING

I hardly ever shop outside Th Nimmanhaemin (Nimman) – what's the point? Everything is here. The north end of the road has a smorgasbord of creative boutiques: textiles, ceramics, pewter, fashion and accessories. Ginger (p166) oozes feminine funkiness – girlie accessories, adorable handbags and all things bright and wonderful.

2 NIMMANHAEMIN ART & DESIGN PROMENADE

This four-day event is held around the weekend of 5 December (HM the King's birthday). Soi 1 as well as other shopping areas are closed to traffic and open for serious shopping and nonsensical fun. Stalls selling anything from novelty items to home decor products, roadside bars, eating zones, live music, fashion shows, street art and an overall festive vibe from around 11am to midnight.

3 DINING

Variety is the essence of Chiang Mai's dining scene. **Café de Nimman** (✆0 5321 8405; Rooms Boutique Mall, 61 Th Nimmanhaemin) has delicious Thai dishes at great prices. Su Casa (p162) is a charming little restaurant serving tapas, sangria and delightful champagne cocktails. **Yangze Jiang** (✆0 5326 6550; Soi 5, Th Nimmanhaemin) prepares quintessential Chinese food in a very smart setting.

4 NIGHTLIFE

Th Nimmanhaemin is currently 'it' for nightlife in Chiang Mai, with hordes of students, expats and tourists spilling in and out of bars and clubs every night of the week. Warm-Up (p165) is the land of high-heeled shoes, miniskirts and student exuberance fuelled by the tunes of hip-hop, indie and electro. Glass Onion (p163) is chic and slightly kitsch with fabulous martinis and wines, while adjacent is the new **Cosmos Bar & Wine Shoppe** (✆0 5321 8479; Rooms Boutique Mall, Th Nimmanhaemin), which is just as incandescent.

Chiang Mai's Temples

Chiang Mai's temples showcase traditional Lanna art and preserve folkways and ethnic culture. The old city contains many royal temples built by the Lanna Mengrai dynasty, while outside the old city are village temples that were built by and for Chiang Mai's diverse ethnic groups.

Below: Wat Phra Singh (p145); **Top Right:** Wat Phra That Doi Suthep (p152); **Bottom Right:** Wat Chiang Man (p147)

Need to Know

BEST TIME TO VISIT Early morning **TOP TIP** Learn about the history and symbolic iconography of the temples to appreciate what you're seeing **For further coverage, see p144**

2

Local Knowledge

Chiang Mai's Temples Don't Miss List

BY DR RATANAPORN SETHAKUL, ASSOCIATE PROFESSOR OF HISTORY, PAYAP UNIVERSITY

1 WAT PHRA SINGH

Wat Phra Singh (p145) houses a well-known Buddha image (Phra Singh), which Thai people come to pay respect to regularly. During important festivals the image is moved outside for public merit-making (Buddhist religious rituals). Inside the sanctuary where Phra Singh resides are mural paintings depicting traditional life of ordinary people. My academic research is on Lanna social history and culture so these murals are interesting for me.

2 WAT CHEDI LUANG

Wat Chedi Luang (p145) is well known for the city pillar (*làk meu·ang* or *sao inthakiln*), where an annual merit-making festival takes place prior to the planting season. This pillar shows the historical relationship between the Mon-Khmer people, the indigenous people of Lanna and the Tai people who came to conquer this area in the 13th century. The temple was a centre of Buddhist education from the 15th to the 16th century, educating many domestic and international monastic students. The principal Buddha image is a standing one, which is a different pose from the other temple's images.

3 WAT CHIANG MAN

Wat Chiang Man (p147) was built by King Mengrai and said to be the first temple built in the founding of Chiang Mai as the capital of Lanna. The name is auspicious: *chiang* means 'city' and *man* means 'stability'. The stone inscription at the temple provides important historical evidence.

4 WAT KETKARAM

Wat Ketkaram (Wat Ket; p149) is located on the Ping River in a community of Chinese traders. In the 19th century Chiang Mai became more multiracial with the arrival of Chinese, Hindu and Western merchants and missionaries. After visiting the temple, cross the bridge to enjoy the Talat Warorot (p147), Chiang Mai's biggest market and an example of local life today.

Survey the Scenery

Chiang Mai is Thailand's base for outdoor activities (p151) in the cool, lush northern mountains. There are treks to minority tribal villages, visits to elephant sanctuaries, zipline courses through the forest, rock climbing and mountain biking. Or you can hire your own wheels and head to Chiang Dao (p170) or the Mae Sa Valley (p169) to observe the forest cover graduate t the high-altitude conifer zone.

3

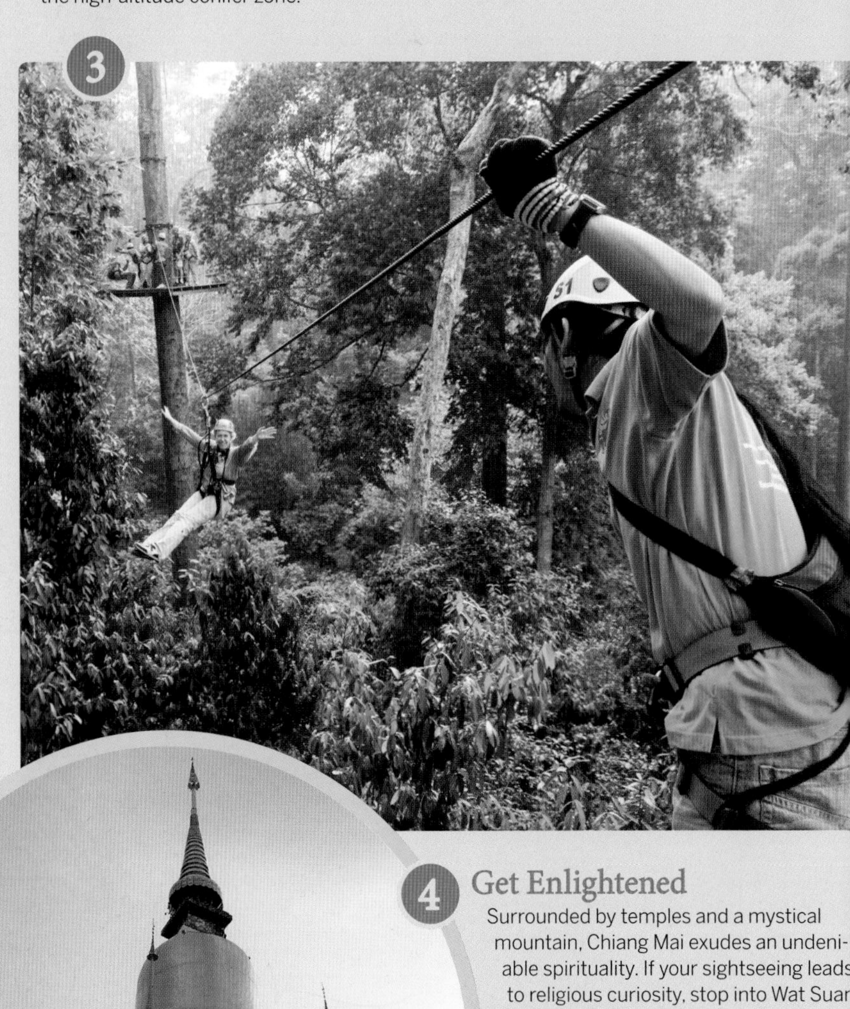

4

Get Enlightened

Surrounded by temples and a mystical mountain, Chiang Mai exudes an undeniable spirituality. If your sightseeing leads to religious curiosity, stop into Wat Suar Dok (p150) or Wat Sisuphan (p149) for one of their monk 'chat' sessions, in which local monks answer questions from foreigners and get to practise thei English. These two temples also offer meditation classes and retreats for a deeper understanding of Buddhism.

Wat Suan Dok

FELIX HUG/LONELY PLANET IMAGES ©

Ascend to Doi Suthep

5

Chiang Mai's guardian mountain ascends from the humid plains into a cool cloud belt where moss and ferns flourish. Nestled on the mountain ridge is Wat Phra That Doi Suthep (pictured; p152), an important religious pilgrimage site for Thai Buddhists. The architecture and views are splendidly photogenic and the temple lore is fittingly mystical. The forested mountain is also a national park criss-crossed by hiking and mountain-biking trails.

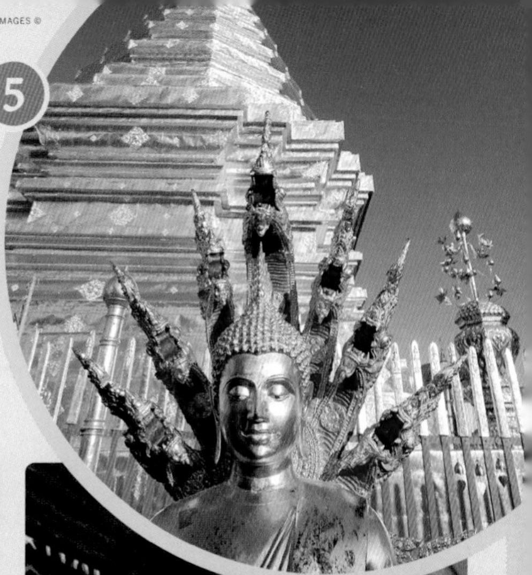

ANDERS RYMAN/ALAMY ©

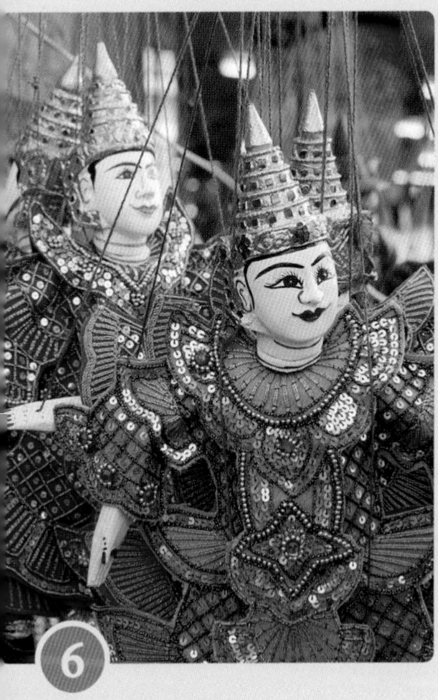

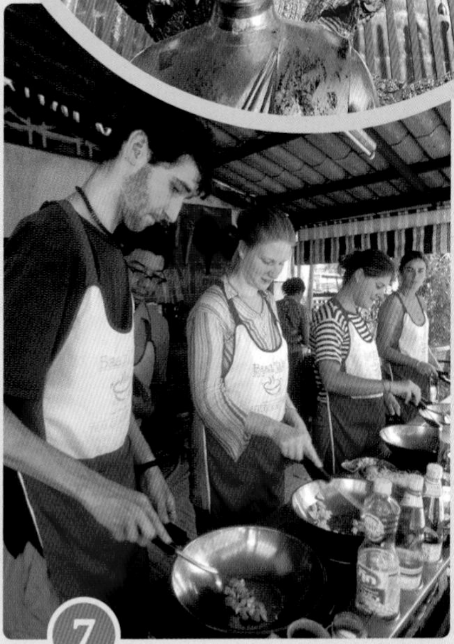

6

Collect Everyday Art

Chiang Mai is Thailand's handicraft centre, producing unique and creative gifts infused with the spirit of old-fashioned traditions. The Saturday Walking Street (p149) and Sunday Walking Street (p144) transform the city's thoroughfares into a crowded but artistic commercial enterprise. The Chiang Mai Night Bazaar (p164) can be mined for factory-made souvenirs, while handicraft stores such as Kesorn (p165) sell everyday art.

7

Master the Mortar & Pestle

You can study Thai cooking in every tourist town, but Chiang Mai adds a little more spice for the aspiring chef: a laid-back approach, regional culinary twists and atmospheric old houses that host cooking classes. Cooking schools such as Chiang Mai Thai Cookery School (p154) introduce Thai culinary ingredients, tour a local market and offer hands-on meal preparation. Your new kitchen skills will come in handy when you're stuck in a dinner rut.

Chiang Mai's Best...

Culture Spots

- **Chiang Mai City Arts & Cultural Centre** (p145) Get educated about the city's history.
- **Chiang Mai National Museum** (p147) Sort out the characteristics of Lanna (northern Thai) art and architecture.
- **Wat Suan Dok** (p150) Do a two-day meditation retreat or chat with a monk about Buddhism.
- **Cooking courses** (p154) Master the mortar and pestle in a Thai cooking class.

Outdoor Activities

- **Trekking** (p151) Chiang Mai is Thailand's base for mountain voyages, elephant rides and visits to high-altitude hill-tribe villages.
- **Elephant sanctuaries** (p151) Become a pachyderm devotee at Chiang Mai's sanctuaries and mahout-training camps.
- **Cycling** (p151) Explore the town or hit the mountain-biking trails in Doi Suthep-Pui National Park (p155).
- **White-Water Rafting** (p151) Brave the rapids of Mae Taeng River from July to March.

Shopping

- **Saturday Walking Street** (p149) Tour the old silver-smithing village during this weekend bazaar.
- **Sunday Walking Street** (p144) Stroll, eat, shop and repeat at this weekend market.
- **Chiang Mai Night Bazaar** (p164) Stock up on souvenirs at this behemoth market.
- **Adorn with Studio Naenna** (p166) Shop for a cause at this village weaving cooperative.

Places to Relax

- **Chiang Mai Women's Prison Massage Centre** (p157) Professional pummelling by ladies in the clink.
- **Dheva Spa** (p157) Luxurious treatment in a fairytale setting.
- **Mae Ping River Cruise** (p153) Soak in the rustic scenery on a river journey.
- **Antique House** (p161) Enjoy the ambiance and the food at this showpiece teak restaurant.

Left: Elephant Nature Park (p152)
Above: Chiang Mai Night Bazaar (164)

Need to Know

ADVANCE PLANNING

- **One month before** Book accommodation and overnight train tickets from Bangkok.
- **One week before** Book air tickets from Bangkok.
- **One day before** Book your cooking course and outdoor activity tour.

RESOURCES

- **1 Stop Chiang Mai** (www.1stopchiangmai.com) For Chiang Mai day trips and outdoor activities.
- **Citylife** (www.chiangmainews.com) Lifestyle magazine with restaurant recommendations.
- **Golden Triangle Rider** (www.gt-rider.com) Maps of the countryside.
- **Nancy Chandler's Map of Chiang Mai** (www.nancychandler.net) Schematic city map.

GETTING AROUND

- **Bicycle** Easy and 'green' get-abouts for central Chiang Mai.
- **Motorcycle** Good self-touring option for outside central Chiang Mai.
- **Sŏrng·tăa·ou** Shared taxis go just about everywhere (30B to 40B).
- **Túk-túk** Chartered vehicles (60B to 80B); remember to bargain.

BE FOREWARNED

- **In temples** Dress and act respectfully. Sit in the 'mermaid' position (legs tucked behind you) in front of Buddha figures.
- **Women travellers** Should not touch monks and should step off the footpath if passing by one.
- **Guides** Hire a guide through the Tourism Authority of Thailand to learn more about northern Thai temples.

Chiang Mai Walking Tour

Chiang Mai's famous temples reside in the historic old city. Start in the cooler morning hours, dress modestly (covering shoulders and knees) and when inside remove your shoes and sit in the 'mermaid' position (legs tucked behind you).

WALK FACTS

- **Start** Wat Phra Singh
- **Finish** Chiang Mai Women's Prison Massage Centre
- **Distance** 2.5km
- **Duration** Two to three hours

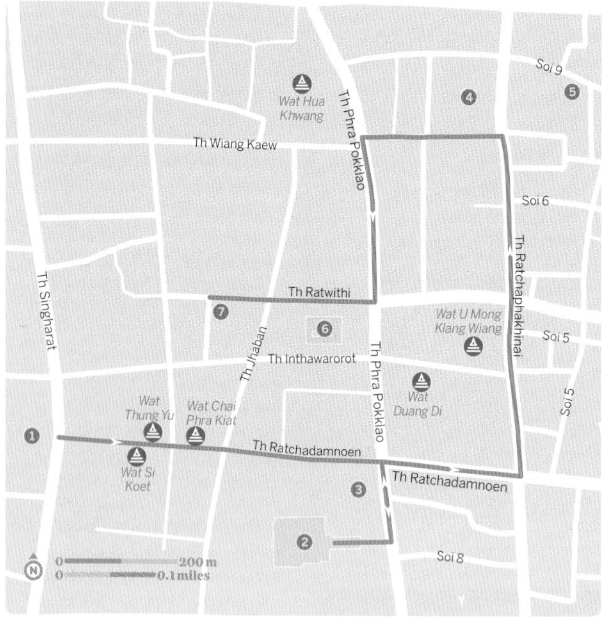

1 Wat Phra Singh

Chiang Mai's most revered Buddha image (Phra Singh) is sheltered in regal style at this beautiful temple, a textbook example of Lanna architecture. During Songkran, Phra Singh is paraded about as part of the city's religious festivities.

2 Wat Chedi Luang

Before condo towers, this now-ruined *chedi* (stupa) was Chiang Mai's tallest structure. The temple once sheltered the famed Emerald Buddha (Phra Kaew), which now resides in Bangkok as a national symbol of Thai Buddhism.

3 Wat Phan Tao

Next door to the Wat Chedi Luang is this tiny teak temple that is more photogenic than venerated. Chiang Mai has a long tradition of woodcarving, inherited from Burmese craftspeople, and the surrounding forests supplied durable teak for the construction of residences and temples. Once you've seen this temple and its delicate ornamentation, you'll instinctively understand what is meant by 'classic Lanna style'.

4 Wat Chiang Man

If it isn't too hot, squeeze in a visit to one more temple. Wat Chiang Man is the city's oldest and features all of Lanna's signature architectural elements. It was renovated in the 1920s by a famous northern monk, who was dedicated to resuscitating dilapidated temples.

5 Blue Diamond

Don't deny your hunger: you've worked up a healthy appetite after a morning of merit-making and sightseeing. At this end of town there aren't a lot of rice joints, so wander over to the backpacker ghetto to indulge your wheat tooth at this cafe. The soi that bisect this neighbourhood give a glimpse into the garden residences of Chiang Mai's old town.

6 Chiang Mai City Arts & Cultural Centre

Synthesise the morning's tour of art, architecture and history into a cohesive narrative at this informative and blissfully air-conditioned museum. The building is recognised as an architectural stand-out as well.

7 Chiang Mai Women's Prison Massage Centre

After a long day, reward yourself with a visit to the Chiang Mai Women's Prison. Wait, not that entrance (unless you have something to confess!). Continue to the building on the south side of the road with the 'Prison Shop' sign, where massages are given by well-behaved inmates. This is a public outreach program to provide job skills for soon-to-be-released prisoners.

Chiang Mai In…

TWO DAYS

Visit the temples highlighted in the Chiang Mai Walking Tour, then explore **Wat Phra That Doi Suthep** (p152). Finish the day at a **riverside restaurant** (p159). The next day do a **Thai cooking course** (p154), or if you're here on the weekend, check out the **Saturday Walking Street** (p149) or **Sunday Walking Street** (p144).

FOUR DAYS

On day three, organise a full-day **outdoor activity** (p151), such as trekking, ziplining, rock-climbing or white-water rafting. The next day, tour the shops and restaurants of **Th Nimmanhaemin** (p166 and p161). Return later for the **nightlife** (p163).

SEVEN DAYS

With an extra few days, you'll have time to retreat into the surrounding countryside for mountain scenery. Hire a motorcycle and follow the mountain ridges through **Mae Sa Valley** (p169), or make an escape to **Chiang Dao** (p170) for bird-watching, hiking and caving.

Ziplining, Flight of the Gibbon (p152), Mae Kampong

Discover Chiang Mai

At a Glance

- **Old City** (p144) Historic quarter.
- **East of the Old City & Riverside** (p147) Craft and souvenir shopping galore.
- **South of the Old City** (p149) Silversmiths on Th Wualai.
- **West of the Old City** (p150) New Chiang Mai and student hang-out.
- **Doi Suthep-Pui National Park** (p155) Forested playground and a holy temple.

Mural, Wat Phra Singh

POP 174,000

History

Chiang Mai (เชียงใหม่) and Thailand's other northern provinces share more of their early development with the Shan state of present-day Myanmar (Burma), neighbouring parts of Laos and even the southern mountains of China than with Bangkok and Thailand's central plains.

Phaya Mengrai (also spelt Mangrai) is credited for founding the Lanna kingdom and expanding it into the Ping River valley. Once he reached the valley, he built a temporary capital at Wiang Kum Kam (p147). Around 1296, King Mengrai relocated the Lanna capital to a more picturesque spot between Doi Suthep and the Ping River and named the auspicious city Nopburi Si Nakhon Ping Chiang Mai (shortened to Chiang Mai, meaning the 'New Walled City'). Traces of the original 1296 earthen ramparts can still be seen today along Th Kamphaeng Din in Chiang Mai.

Sights

Chiang Mai is a very manageable city to navigate. Most visitors base themselves in the old city, which is easily covered on foot or by bike – the famous temples are spread out along Th Ratchadamnoen.

Old City เมืองเก่า

SUNDAY WALKING STREET Market

(ถนนเดินวันอาทิตย์; Map p148; Th Ratchadamnoen; 4pm-midnight Sun) A unique shopping experience, the Sunday Walking Street offers all manner of products and a good dose of provincial culture. It is also a re-

Soi Ban Haw

A remnant from the days when Chiang Mai was a detour on the Silk Road is the Thai-Muslim community along Soi 1 off Th Chang Khlan, near Chiang Mai Night Bazaar. The 100-year-old **Matsayit Chiang Mai (Map p148; Soi 1, Th Charoen Prathet)**, also known as Ban Haw Mosque, was founded by *jeen hor* ('galloping Chinese'), the Thai expression for Yunnanese caravan traders. Within the past two centuries, the city's Muslim community has also grown to include ethnic Yunnanese Muslims escaping unrest in neighbouring Laos and Burma.

There are also a number of simple restaurants and vendors selling Thai-Muslim curries, *kôw soy* (curried chicken and noodles), *kôw mòk gài* (chicken biriani), and *néu·a òp hŏrm* ('fragrant' dried beef), a speciality of Chiang Mai's Yunnanese Muslim community. An evening food vendor does delicious *roh·dee* (Indian flat bread).

minder of an itinerant merchant tradition of the ancient Chinese caravans.

Vendors line Th Ratchadamnoen all the way from the square in front of Pratu Tha Pae to Wat Phra Singh and stretching a few blocks down both sides of Th Phra Pokklao. Many of the products are handmade in and around Chiang Mai, including cotton scarves, leather sandals and wood carvings.

If you're not in town on Sunday, check out the Saturday Walking Street (p149) on Th Wualai.

WAT PHRA SINGH Temple

(วัดพระสิงห์; Th Singharat; donations appreciated) Chiang Mai's most visited temple, Wat Phra Singh owes its fame to the fact that it houses the city's most revered Buddha image, Phra Singh (Lion Buddha), and it has a fine collection of classic Lanna art and architecture.

Phra Singh is housed in Wihan Lai Kham, a small chapel to the rear of the temple grounds next to the *chedi* (stupa). The exterior chapel displays the Lanna characteristics of a three-tiered roofline and carved gables. Inside, the temple features sumptuous *lai·krahm* (gold pattern) stencilling on its interior back wall.

Wat Phra Singh's main *chedi* displays classic Lanna style with its octagonal base. It was built by King Pa Yo in 1345 in honour of his father. Closer to the entrance is the main *wí·hăhn*, which houses a bigger but less important Buddha known as Thong Thip.

CHIANG MAI CITY ARTS & CULTURAL CENTRE Museum

(หอศิลปวัฒนธรรมเชียงใหม่; ☎0 5321 7793; Th Ratwithi; adult/child 90/40B; ⏲8.30am-5pm Tue-Sun) The Chiang Mai City Arts & Cultural Centre offers a fine primer on Chiang Mai history. The 1st floor has engaging displays on religious and cultural elements of northern Thailand. The 2nd floor rooms have been converted into historic settings: there's an early Lanna village, a temple and a train display. From the 2nd floor you can see more of the beauty of this post-colonial building, Chiang Mai's former Provincial Hall, originally built in 1924. It was awarded a Royal Society of Siamese Architects award in 1999 for its faithful architectural restoration.

WAT CHEDI LUANG Temple

(วัดเจดีย์หลวง; Th Phra Pokklao; donations appreciated) Another venerable stop on the temple trail, Wat Chedi Luang is built around a partially ruined Lanna-style *chedi* dating from 1441. It is believed to have been one of the tallest structures in ancient Chiang Mai. The famed Emerald Buddha (Phra Kaew), now held in Bangkok's Wat Phra Kaew (p74), sat in the eastern niche

Chiang Mai & Around

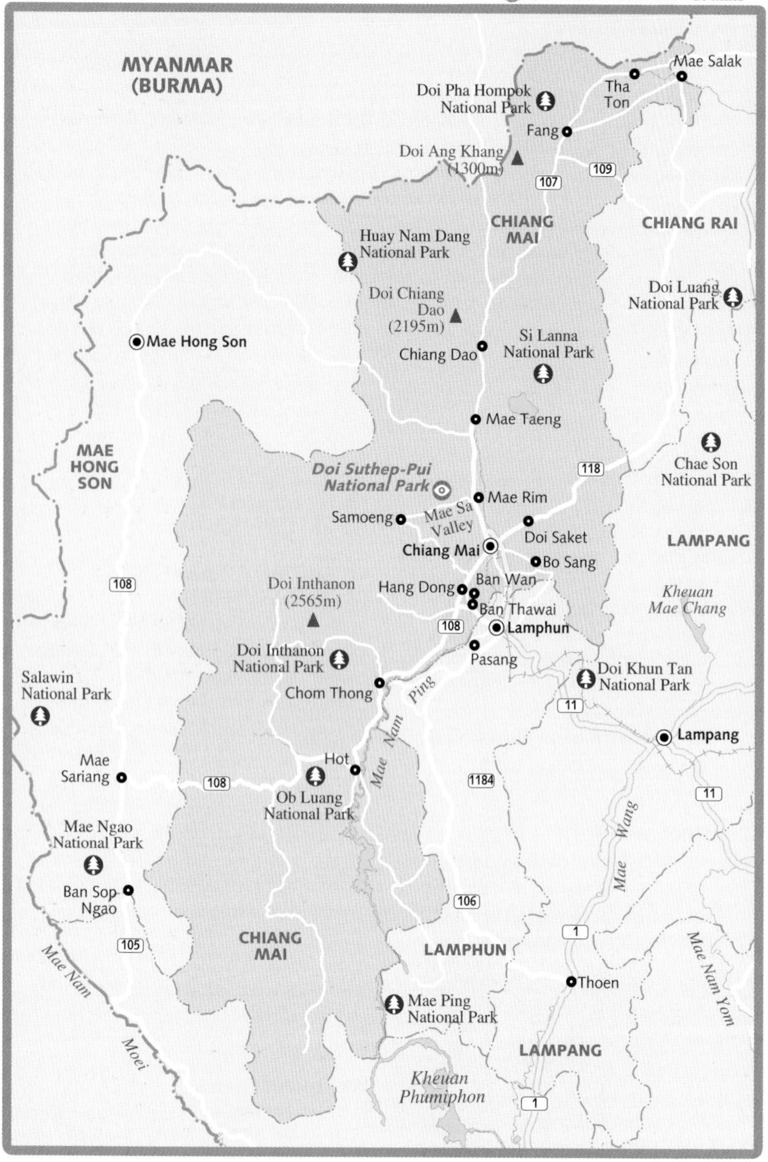

here in 1475. Today there is a jade replica sitting in its place, financed by the Thai king and carved in 1995 to celebrate the 600th anniversary of the *chedi* (according to some reckonings), and the 700th anniversary of the city.

Wat Chedi Luang's other prominent attraction is the *làk meu·ang* (city pillar, believed to house the city's guardian deity) enshrined in a small building to the left of the compound's main entrance.

Have a chat to the monks while you are here (see boxed text, p151).

WAT PHAN TAO Temple

(วัดพันเตา; Map p148; Th Phra Pokklao; donations appreciated) Near Wat Chedi Luang, Wat Phan Tao contains a beautiful old teak *wí·hăhn* that was once a royal residence and is today one of the unsung treasures of Chiang Mai. Constructed entirely of moulded teak panels fitted together and supported by 28 gargantuan teak pillars, the *wí·hăhn* features *naga* bargeboards inset with coloured mirror mosaic. On display inside are old temple bells, some ceramics, a few old northern-style gilded wooden Buddhas, and antique cabinets stacked with old palm-leaf manuscripts.

WAT CHIANG MAN Temple

(วัดเชียงมั่น; Th Ratchaphakhinai; donations appreciated) Considered to be the oldest wát in the city, Wat Chiang Man is believed to have been established by the city's founder, Phaya Mengrai. The wát features typical northern Thai temple architecture.

East of the Old City & Riverside

Passing through Pratu Tha Phae leads to a standard-issue commercial neighbourhood of two-storey concrete shophouses and busy multilaned roads. South of Talat Warorot, on Th Chang Khlan, is the Chiang Mai Night Bazaar (see boxed text, p164). The meandering Mae Ping is another historical attraction.

WIANG KUM KAM Historical Ruins

(เวียงกุมกาม; 8am-5pm) Climb aboard one of the horse-drawn carriages (200B) and relax into the mellow pace of an old-fashioned conveyance. The driver typically passes pleasantries with the locals who live among the old ruins, which are mainly half-buried brick foundations spread out over 3 sq km. The actual ruins are of more historical importance than spectacle but it is the peaceful surrounding village that completes the attraction.

Wiang Kum Kam was the earliest historical settlement in the Chiang Mai area and was established by the Mon as a satellite town for the Hariphunchai kingdom. It was occupied by Phaya Mengrai in 1286 and used as the Lanna capital for 10 years before the construction of Chiang Mai. The city was abandoned in the 16th century due to massive flooding when the Ping River changed its course.

Detour:
Chiang Mai National Museum

Operated by the Fine Arts Department and established in 1973, the Chiang Mai National Museum **(พิพิธภัณฑสถานแห่งชาติเชียงใหม่; 0 5322 1308; www.thailandmuseum.com; off Th Superhighway; admission 100B; 9am-4pm Wed-Sun)** functions as the primary caretaker of Lanna artefacts and as the curator of northern Thailand's history. This museum is a nice complement to the municipally run Chiang Mai City Arts & Cultural Centre (p145) because you'll find more art and artefacts here and the scope of the exhibits reaches beyond the city limits. The best curated section of the museum is the Lanna art section, which displays a selection of Buddha images in all styles, and explains the different periods and influences.

TALAT WAROROT Market

(ตลาดวโรรส; Map p148; cnr Th Chang Moi & Th Praisani; 6am-5pm) Following Th Chang Moi towards the river you'll discover a beehive of activity around Chiang Mai's oldest and most famous marketplace, Talat Warorot. In northern Thai dialect, the market is known as *gàht lŏo·ang* (northern Thai for 'great market'). So much activity surrounds the market buildings that it spreads into the neighbouring area.

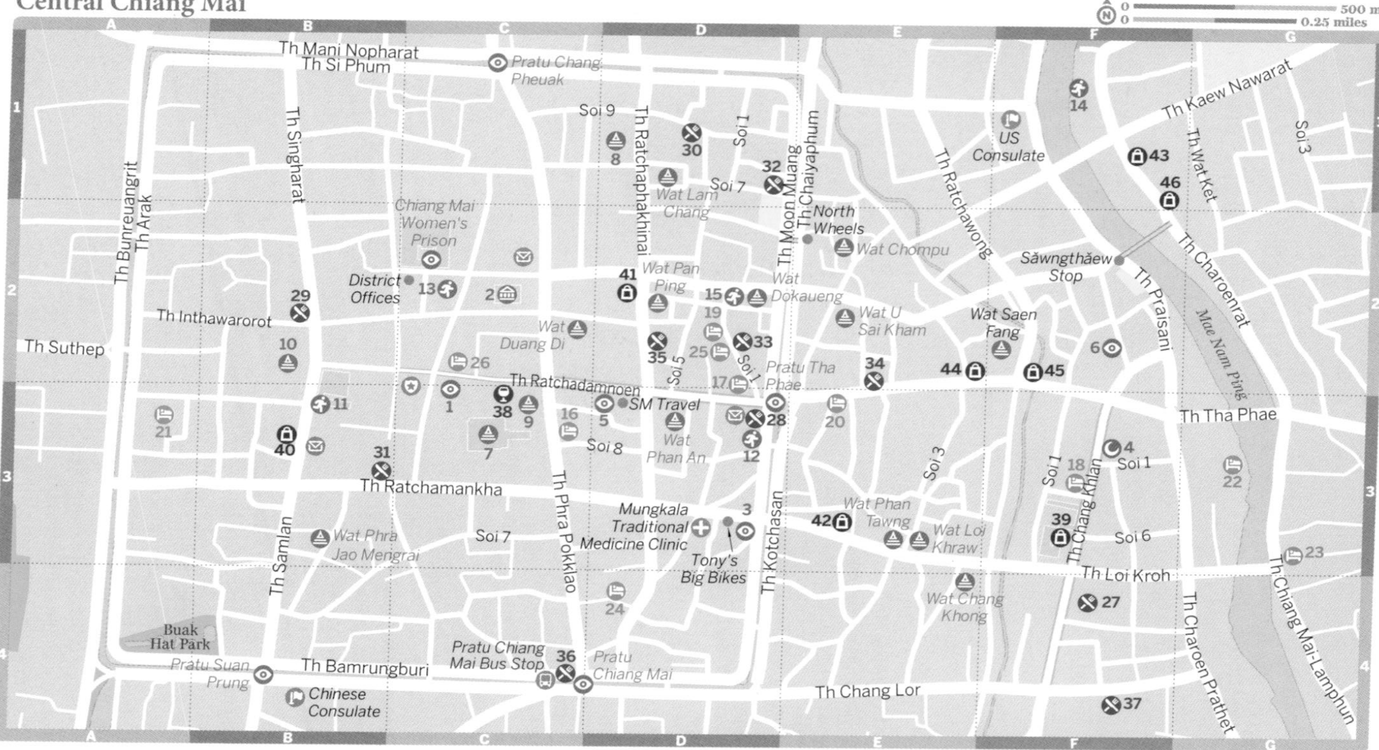
Central Chiang Mai
0 500 m
0 0.25 miles
Th Mani Nopharat
Th Si Phum
Pratu Chang Pheuak
Soi 9
Th Ratchaphakhinai
Soi 1
Th Moon Muang
Th Chaiyaphum
Th Kaew Nawarat
Th Wat Ket
Soi 3
US Consulate
Th Ratchawong
Th Charoenrat
Mae Nam Ping
Sǎwngthǎew Stop
Th Praisani
Soi 7
Wat Lam Chang
North Wheels
Wat Chompu
Th Bunreuangrit
Th Arak
Th Singharat
Chiang Mai Women's Prison
District Offices
Wat Pan Ping
Wat Dokaueng
Wat U Sai Kham
Wat Saen Fang
Th Inthawarorot
Th Suthep
Wat Duang Di
Soi 5
Pratu Tha Phae
Th Ratchadamnoen
SM Travel
Th Tha Phae
Soi 8
Wat Phan An
Soi 3
Soi 1
Th Chang Khlan
Th Ratchamankha
Th Phra Pokklao
Mungkala Traditional Medicine Clinic
Tony's Big Bikes
Th Kotchasan
Wat Phan Tawng
Wat Loi Khraw
Soi 6
Wat Phra Jao Mengrai
Soi 7
Th Samlan
Th Loi Kroh
Wat Chang Khong
Th Charoen Prathet
Th Chiang Mai-Lamphun
Buak Hat Park
Pratu Suan Prung
Th Bamrungburi
Pratu Chiang Mai Bus Stop
Pratu Chiang Mai
Chinese Consulate
Th Chang Lor

Central Chiang Mai

Sights

1 Baan Chang Elephant Park Office C3
2 Chiang Mai City Arts & Cultural Centre C2
3 Elephant Nature Park Booking Office D3
4 Matsayit Chiang Mai F3
5 Sunday Walking Street D3
6 Talat Warorot F2
7 Wat Chedi Luang C3
8 Wat Chiang Man D1
9 Wat Phan Tao C3
10 Wat Phra Singh B2

Activities, Courses & Tours

11 Chiang Mai Mountain Biking B3
12 Chiang Mai Thai Cookery School D3
13 Chiang Mai Women's Prison Massage Centre C2
14 Scorpion Tailed River Cruise F1
15 Siam River Adventures D2

Sleeping

16 3 Sis C3
17 Awanahouse D2
18 dusit D2 Chiang Mai F3
19 Mini Cost D2
20 Mo Rooms E3
21 Rachamankha A3
22 River View Lodge G3
23 Riverside House G3
24 Sa Thu Boutique House D4
25 Vieng Mantra D2
26 Villa Duang Champa C2

Eating

27 Anusan Night Market F4
28 AUM Vegetarian Food D3
29 Baan Nok Noodle B2
30 Blue Diamond D1
31 Heuan Phen B3
32 House D1
33 Lert Ros D2
34 Ratana's Kitchen E2
35 Safe House Court D2
36 Talat Pratu Chiang Mai C4
37 Whole Earth Restaurant F4

Drinking

Tea House .... (see 45)
38 Writer's Club & Wine Bar C3

Shopping

39 Chiang Mai Night Bazaar F3
40 Dor Dek Gallery B3
41 Freedom Wheel Chairs Workshop D2
Kesorn .... (see 45)
42 KukWan Gallery E3
43 La Luna Gallery F1
44 Lost Heavens E2
45 Siam Celadon F2
46 Sop Moei Arts F1

WAT KETKARAM Temple

(**แม่ปิง/วัดเกตการาม; Th Charoenrat**) Chiang Mai's exalted river is Ping River (see boxed text, p153). A community of Chinese traders and Western missionaries populated the eastern riverbank directly across from Talat Warorot. Today the neighbourhood is called Wat Ket, the nickname of the nearby temple, Wat Ketkaram. The temple was built in the 15th century and houses an eclectic museum of attic-like treasures.

South of the Old City

SATURDAY WALKING STREET Market

(**ถนนเดินวันเสาร์; Th Wualai; 4pm-midnight Sat**) The Saturday Walking Street has developed a reputation of having more authentic handicrafts and being less commercial than the Sunday Walking Street. This might be a bit of an exaggeration as most vendors work both markets without exclusion. But the atmospheric old neighbourhood with its silver shops and old ladies wrapped up in Thai silk does give it an authenticity. It's also slightly less hectic, making an evening stroll a bit more pleasant.

WAT SISUPHAN Temple

(**วัดศรีสุพรรณ; Soi 2, Th Wualai; donations appreciated**) This wát was founded in 1502, but little remains of the original structures except for some teak pillars and roof beams in the *wí·hăhn*. The *ubosòht* next door is allegedly the only silver ordination hall in Thailand (although technically they were using a mix of aluminium, compounded silver and pure silver), and the result of the recent renovation is magnificent. The temple hosts a monk chat and meditation instruction (see boxed text, p151). Wat Sisuphan is one of the few wát in Chiang Mai where you can see the Poy Luang (also known as Poy Sang Long) Festival, a Shan-style group ordination of young boys as Buddhist novices, in late March.

West of the Old City

WAT SUAN DOK Temple

(วัดสวนดอก; **Th Suthep; donations appreciated)**
Built on a former flower garden in 1373, this temple is not as architecturally interesting as the temples in the old city but it does have a very powerful photographic attribute: the temple's collection of whitewashed *chedi* sit in the foreground while the blue peaks of Doi Suthep and Doi Pui loom in the background.

Wat Suan Dok is also spiritually united with the temple that sits upon Doi Suthep thanks to an auspicious relic brought to Chiang Mai by Phra Sumana Thera, a visiting monk from Sukhothai. According to legend, the relic miraculously

West Chiang Mai

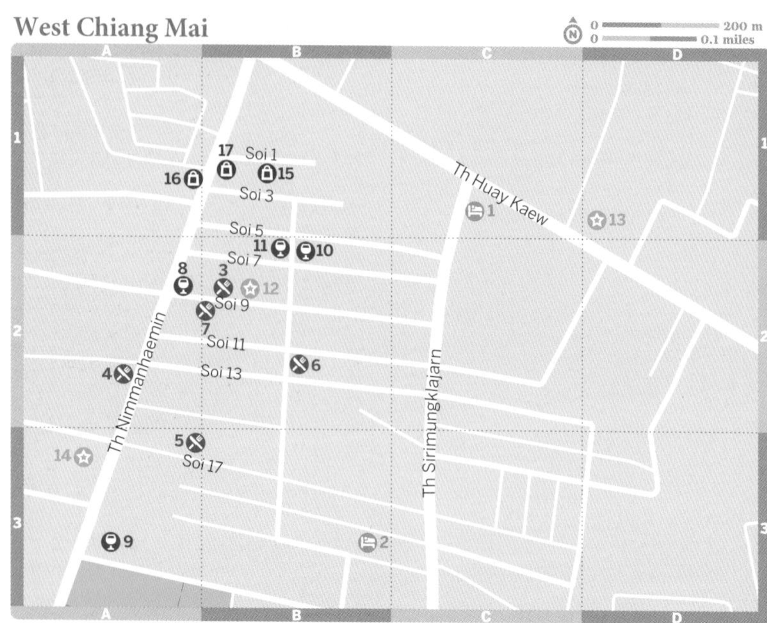

West Chiang Mai

Sleeping
1 H ... C1
2 Pann Malee Home ... B3

Eating
3 94 Coffee ... B2
4 Burmese Restaurant ... A2
5 Khun Churn ... A3
6 Su Casa ... B2
7 Wawee Coffee ... B2

Drinking
8 At 9 Bar ... A2
9 Glass Onion ... A3
10 Outdoors ... B2
11 Pinocchio's ... B2

Entertainment
12 Monkey Club ... B2
13 Sudsanan ... D1
14 Warm-Up ... A3

Shopping
15 Adorn with Studio Naenna ... B1
16 Ginger ... A1
17 Srisanpanmai ... B1

duplicated itself: one piece was enshrined in the temple's large central *chedi* (recently wrapped in gold sheet), while the other was used as a 'guide' for the founding of Wat Doi Suthep.

Today Wat Suan Dok is home to a large population of resident monks and novices, many of them students at the monastery's Mahachulalongkorn Buddhist University. Foreigners often come to Wat Suan Dok for the popular monk chat (see boxed text, p151) and the English-language meditation retreats.

CHIANG MAI ZOO Zoo

(สวนสัตว์/แหล่งเพาะพันธ์ไม้ป่าเขตร้อนเชียงใหม่; ☎0 5322 1179; www.chiangmaizoo.com; 100 Th Huay Kaew; adult/child 100/50B; ⏲8am-5pm) At the foot of Doi Suthep, the Chiang Mai Zoo occupies a lush park setting and boasts a fairly comprehensive assortment of animals plus two special attractions (pandas and an aquarium) that require separate admission fees. The aquarium (adult/child 520/390B) reportedly has Asia's longest viewing tunnel (measuring 113m) and replicates the water environments of Thailand, from the northern rivers to the mangrove swamps and coastal oceans, as well as the Amazon basin.

North of the Old City

Sights north of the old city tend to be too far spread out to visit on foot; it is advisable to hire your own transport.

TRIBAL MUSEUM Museum

(พิพิธภัณฑ์ชาวเขา; ☎0 5321 0872; www.tribalmuseumchiangmai.com; off Th Chang Pheauk) Overlooking a lake in Suan Ratchamangkhala on the northern outskirts of the city, this octagonal museum houses a collection of handicrafts, costumes, jewellery, ornaments, agricultural tools, musical instruments and ceremonial paraphernalia. The museum was closed at the time of research for renovations.

Activities

The surrounding mountains, rivers and byways boast a wave of adrenaline sports that have begun to eclipse the traditional trekking tour.

The countryside is exceptional for two-wheeled outings. Doi Suthep (p155), the city's closest green space, is gaining its own fame for off-road mountain biking. For motorcyclists and long-distance cyclists, the Mae Sa–Samoeng loop is the closest and most stunning escape into the mountains.

Chiang Mai is also one of Thailand's most famous destinations for elephant 'encounters.'

Rock climbers head to Crazy Horse Buttress, an impressive set of limestone cliffs located behind Tham Meuang On, near Sankamphaeng, 45km east of Chiang Mai. The scenery isn't as stunning as Krabi's seaside cliffs, but the ascents reward with pastoral views.

White-water rafting is also possible. The Taeng River is north of Chiang Mai and carves a path through the Doi Chiang Dao National Park and the Huai Nam Dang National Park. The river is a wild and frothy white-water ride for nine months of the year (roughly from July to March), a surprisingly long season in this monsoonal climate. When choosing a white-water outfitter, ask about their safety standards and training.

Monk Chat

Some of the temples in town offer a 'monk chat', where a resident monk or novice fields questions from foreigners. This simple exchange gives them a chance to practise their English while answering questions about daily routines, Buddhist teachings or even how monks stay wrapped up in their robes.

Remember that it is respectful to dress modestly: cover your shoulders and knees. Women should take care not to touch the monks or their belongings or to pass anything directly to them.

JERRY ALEXANDER/LONELY PLANET IMAGES ©

Don't Miss Wat Phra That Doi Suthep

Like a beacon projecting a calming blanket on the urban plains below, Wat Suthep is seen clearly from Chiang Mai, majestically perched atop Doi Suthep's summit. It is one of the north's most sacred temples, and Thai pilgrims flock here to make merit to the Buddhist relic enshrined in the picturesque golden *chedi* (stupa).

The temple was first established in 1383 under King Keu Naone and enjoys a fantastically mystical birth story. A visiting monk from Sukhothai instructed the Lanna king to take the twin of a miraculous relic (enshrined at Wat Suan Dok) to the mountain and establish a temple. The relic was mounted on the back of a white elephant, which was allowed to wander until it 'chose' a site on which a wát could be built to enshrine it. The elephant stopped and died at a spot on Doi Suthep, 13km west of Chiang Mai, where the temple was built in the Year of the Goat.

The temple is reached by a strenuous *naga*-balustrade staircase of 306 steps, a feature that incorporates aspects of meditation with a cardio workout. For the less fit, there's a tram for 20B.

THINGS YOU NEED TO KNOW

วัดพระธาตุดอยสุเทพ; admission 30B

FLIGHT OF THE GIBBON Ziplining

(☎08 9970 5511; www.treetopasia.com; Mae Kampong; 3hr tour 3000B) This adventure outfit in Chiang Mai operates a zipline through the forest canopy some 1300m above sea level. Nearly 2km of wire with 18 staging platforms follow the ridgeline and mimic the branch-to-branch route that a gibbon might take down the mountain.

ELEPHANT NATURE PARK Elephant Park

(Map p148; booking office ☎0 5320 8246; www.elephantnaturepark.org; 1 Th Ratchamankha; 1-/2-

day tours 2500/5800B) Khun Lek (Sangduen Chailert) has won numerous awards for her elephant sanctuary in the Mae Taeng valley, 60km (1½-hour drive) from Chiang Mai. The forested area provides a semi-wild environment for the elephants that have been rescued from abusive situations or retired from a lifetime of work. Visitors can help wash the elephants and watch the herd but there is no show or riding.

BAAN CHANG ELEPHANT PARK Elephant Park

(Map p148; ☎0 5381 4174; www.baanchangelephantpark.com; full-day 1-2 person tour 4200B) Tours involve taking care of an elephant for a day and some training to learn about their behaviour and lifestyle (including feeding and bathing). While you'll ride bareback through the jungle, the centre is firmly against teaching elephants to perform tricks. The training program is in Mae Taeng, 50 minutes north of Chiang Mai.

PEAK Rock Climbing

(☎0 5380 0567; www.thepeakadventure.com; climbing course 1800-2500B) Teaches introductory and advanced rock-climbing courses at Crazy Horse Buttress. The Peak also leads a variety of soft adventure trips, including quad biking, as well as trekking, white-water rafting and a jungle survival cooking course. Note it's best to book directly with the company, and not through a travel agent.

SIAM RIVER ADVENTURES Rafting

(Map p148; ☎089 515 1917; www.siamrivers.com; 17 Th Ratwithi; tour from 1800B) Has the best safety reputation. The guides have swiftwater rescue training and additional staff are located at dangerous parts of the river with throw ropes. Trips can be combined with elephant trekking and village overnights. It also operates kayak trips.

CHIANG MAI MOUNTAIN BIKING Mountain Biking

(Map p148; ☎08 1024 7046; www.mountainbikingchiangmai.com; 1 Th Samlan; tour from 1450-2700B) Offers a variety of guided mountain biking (as well as hike-and-bike) tours through Doi Suthep for all levels.

If You Like... River Cruises

Mae Ping is rural and rustic in most parts with grassy banks and small stilted houses crouching alongside. There are several day and evening boat tours that explore this waterway.

1 **SCORPION TAILED RIVER CRUISE**
(Map p148; ☎08 1960 9398; www.scorpiontailed.com; Th Charoenrat; fare 500B) Focuses on the history of the river using traditional-style craft, known as scorpion-tailed boats. Informative cruises (five daily) last 1½ hours. They depart from Wat Srikhong pier near Rim Ping Condo and stop for a snack at the affiliated Scorpion Tailed Boat Village.

2 **MAE PING RIVER CRUISES**
(☎0 5327 4822; www.maepingrivercruise.com; Wat Chaimongkhon, 133 Th Charoen Prathet) Offers daytime cruises (450B, two hours) in roofed longtail boats. The boats stop at a small farm for fruit snacks after touring the countryside. The 1½-hour Thai dinner cruise (550B) offers a set menu.

CLICK & TRAVEL Cycling

(☎0 5328 1553; www.clickandtravelonline.com; tours 950-1500B) Specialises in half-day and full-day bicycle tours of Chiang Mai. It is a pedal-powered (and family friendly) cultural trip, visiting temples and attractions outside of the city centre.

Courses

BUDDHIST MEDITATION

The following temples offer *vipassana* meditation courses and retreats to English-language speakers. Participants should dress in modest white clothes, which can typically be purchased from the temple. Following Buddhist precepts, there is no set fee but donations are appreciated. Peruse the various websites for course descriptions and daily routines.

WAT SISUPHAN Meditation
(☎0 5320 0332; 100 Th Wualai) Offers a two-hour introduction to meditation using the four postures: standing, walking, sitting and lying down.

WAT SUAN DOK Meditation
(☎0 5380 8411 ext 114; www.monkchat.net; Th Suthep) Offers a two-day meditation retreat every Tuesday to Wednesday. At the end of each month, the temple extends the retreat to a four-day period (Tuesday to Friday).

COOKING

Courses in Thai cuisine are another staple of Chiang Mai's vacation learning scene. Dozens of schools offer cooking classes, typically costing around 1000B a day, either at an in-town location, like an atmospheric old house, or out of town in a garden or farm setting. Students will learn about Thai culinary herbs and spices, tour a local market and prepare a set menu. Of course, you also get to eat the Thai food and travel home with a recipe booklet.

CHIANG MAI THAI COOKERY SCHOOL Cooking
(Map p148; ☎0 5320 6388; www.thaicookeryschool.com; booking office, 47/2 Th Moon Muang) One of Chiang Mai's first cooking schools holds classes in a rural setting outside of Chiang Mai. A portion of the profits funds education of disadvantaged kids.

THAI FARM COOKING SCHOOL Cooking
(Map p148; ☎08 7174 9285; www.thaifarmcooking.com; booking office, 2/2 Soi 5, Th Ratchadamnoen) Teaches cooking classes at its organic farm, located 17km outside of Chiang Mai.

Sleeping

Chiang Mai is kind to the thrifty traveller: there are heaps of competing guest houses, and resulting low rates. A crop of concept/boutique hotels fill in the midrange to top end. The top-end range is dominated mainly by huge corporate-style hotels. The more interesting ones are the intimate boutique hotels that tend to marry antique Lanna elements with modern amenities. At the summit of the

Thai cooking course

ANDERS RYMAN/ALAMY©

MIKEL BILBAO GOROSTIAGA-TRAVELS/ALAMY ©

Don't Miss Doi Suthep-Pui National Park

Looming over the city like guardian spirits and providing a sanctuary of forest and mountain cool air, Chiang Mai's sacred peaks, Doi Suthep (1676m) and Doi Pui (1685m) were used by the city's founders as a divine compass in locating an auspicious position.

Portions of the mountains form a 265-sq-km **national park** that contains a mix of wilderness, hill-tribe villages and tourist attractions, including Wat Phra That Doi Suthep (p152). Most people stick to the main road, visiting the temple, the winter palace and one of the touristy Hmong villages, altogether bypassing the forested interior.

The mountain ascends from the humid lowlands into the cool (and sometimes even cold) cloud belt with moss growing on the curbs and mist wafting across the road. Thriving in the diverse climate are more than 300 bird species and nearly 2000 species of ferns and flowering plants. During the rainy season, butterflies bloom as abundantly as the flowers.

There are hiking and mountain-biking trails as well as camping, bird-watching and waterfall spotting. One of the most scenic waterfalls is **Nam Tok Monthathon** (the park admission fee is collected here), 2.5km off the paved road to Doi Suthep. Pools beneath the falls hold water year-round, although swimming is best during or just after the annual monsoon.

The park fee is collected at some of the park's waterfalls. There is no park fee charged to visit the attractions along the main road, though the attractions have their own admission prices.

The park is about 16km northwest of central Chiang Mai and is accessible via shared *sŏrng·tăa·ou* that leave from the main entrance of Chiang Mai University on Th Huay Kaew. You can also charter a *sŏrng·tăa·ou* for about 500B (round-trip) or rent a motorcycle for much less.

THINGS YOU NEED TO KNOW

อุทยานแห่งชาติดอยสุเทพ - ปุย; ☎0 5321 0244; adult/child under 14yr 100/50B, car 30B; ⏰8am-sunset

scale are the destination resorts that have recreated a village setting complete with rice fields and historic architecture.

Old City

There are heaps of guest houses in the residential sois off Th Moon Muang.

MINI COST Hotel $$
(Map p148; ☎0 5341 8787; www.minicostcm.com; 19/4 Soi 1, Th Ratchadamnoen; r 750-1050B; ❄@) Apartment-style, contemporary rooms with easy chairs, calming colours and a few touches of Thai-style decor are unusual in Chiang Mai in this price range. It's in a terrific spot too, quiet but accessible to everything around Pratu Tha Phae. A real bargain – one of the few genuine midrange accommodations in the city with rooms priced (mostly) under 1000B.

VILLA DUANG CHAMPA Hotel $$
(Map p148; ☎0 5332 7199; www.duangchampa.com; 82 Th Ratchadamnoen; r 2500B, guest house r 700B; ❄@) The hotel occupies a colonial-style building marked by its simplicity, airiness and shuttered windows. Most rooms have an extra sitting area, but No 1 has its own private enclosed balcony with lounge seating – it's a beauty. Stick to the hotel as the dark, cramped guest house rooms are not a good deal.

VIENG MANTRA Hotel $$$
(Map p148; ☎0 5332 6640; www.viengmantra.com; 9 Soi 1, Th Ratchadamnoen; r 2000-4500B; ❄@🛜🏊) This oasis, nestled into its own luxurious gardens, is a class act along bustling Soi 1. Smooth, clean lines and a marriage of concrete and wood dominate the Lanna-style building, while rooms are set around an inner courtyard pool and have balconies with sink-in-and-smile cushioned seating.

3 SIS Hotel $$
(Map p148; ☎0 5327 3243; www.the3sis.com; 1 Soi 8, Th Phra Pokklao; d 1300-1800B; ❄@🛜) Good-sized rooms with double-glazed windows overlooking the street, in the front building, may be the best deal here. However, those in the 'vacation lodge' have lovely wooden floors, clean white walls, fridge and cable TV. Ensuites are OK but check the condition of the shower.

SA THU BOUTIQUE HOUSE Hotel $$
(Map p148; ☎0 5390 3737; www.sathuboutique.com; 31 Soi Prapokklao, Th Ratchaphakhinai; r superior/deluxe 1200/1800B; 🏊) Tucked away off busy Ratchaphakhinai Rd, this small boutique gem is newly opened and beautifully designed, and it has eager staff. The deluxe rooms are much better value with small outdoor courtyards accessed through French doors. Furnishings are in

Trekking

Most companies operating out of Chiang Mai offer the same type of tour: a one-hour mini-bus ride to Mae Taeng or Mae Wang (depending on the duration of the trip), a brief hike to an elephant camp, a one-hour elephant ride to a waterfall, another hour rafting down a river and an overnight in or near a hill-tribe village.

Chiang Mai is not the only base for hill-tribe treks but it is the most accessible. Most guest houses in Chiang Mai act as booking agents in exchange for a commission, which in turn subsidises the cheap room rates. One-day treks usually cost around 1000B, while multiday treks (three days and two nights) cost 1500B. Both prices include transport, guide and lunch; in the case of overnight trips, the price also includes lodging (prices will be a bit more in high season). More expensive treks that offer a better experience may be available; ask around.

sympathy with the minimalist environment and fittings are funky and fun. The only drawback is the poky ensuites.

RACHAMANKHA Hotel $$$
(☎0 5390 4111; www.rachamankha.com; 6 Th Ratchamankha; r from 6000B; ❄@📶🏊) The encore effort by architect Ong-ard Satrabhandu to Tamarind Village, Rachamankha imitates an ancient monastery in Lampang. Considering its reputation, rooms aren't opulent and the superiors are quite small. The deluxe rooms are more generous, however, with four-poster beds and bathrooms that double the living space. The highlight of the hotel is the library, a light-strewn room smelling of polished wood and musty paper.

AWANAHOUSE Guest House $
(Map p148; ☎0 5341 9005; www.awanahouse.com; 7 Soi 1, Th Ratchadamnoen; r 225-850B; ❄@🏊) What started out as a small guest house has grown into a standard multistorey apartment building on a quiet soi. Awana is a bit institutional, but has large and bright rooms, some with balconies, TV and fridge. The bonus here is the rooftop chill-out area with views of the nearby mountains.

East of the Old City

While it isn't as quaint as the old city, Th Tha Phae is just as convenient for sightseeing and nightlife and even closer to the night bazaar. Corporate hotels with business centres and conference capacity occupy the area near the Chiang Mai Night Bazaar.

MO ROOMS Hotel $$
(Map p148; ☎0 5328 0789; www.morooms.com; 263/1-2 Th Tha Pae; r small/medium/large 2800/3200/3500B; ❄@🏊) This outrageous design hotel is completely unique in Chiang Mai and a great choice if you are inspired by art – 'art you can live in'. The 12 rooms are all individually designed according to the animals of the Chinese zodiac. Each is an inspiration from a local artist born under that zodiac sign.

If You Like… Getting Pampered

While there are a few truly exceptional spas in Chiang Mai, the city excels in a more modest category: old-fashioned Thai massage. Many of the temples in the old city have a massage *săh·lah* (often spelt *sala*) on the grounds, continuing an ancient tradition of the monasteries being a repository for traditional knowledge and healing.

1 **CHIANG MAI WOMEN'S PRISON MASSAGE CENTRE**
(Map p148; 100 Th Ratwithi; foot/traditional massage 150-180B; 🕗8am-4.30pm) Offers fantastic full body and foot massages, performed by inmates at the women's prison as a part of their rehabilitation training program. The money earned from these treatments goes directly to the prisoners for use after their release.

2 **DHEVA SPA**
(☎0 5388 8888; www.mandarinoriental.com/chiangmai/spa/; Mandarin Oriental Dhara Dhevi, 51/4 Th Chiang Mai-San Kamphaeng; treatments from 3500B) The grandest spa in all of Chiang Mai is also a cheaper passport into the exclusive and stunning grounds of the luxurious Mandarin Oriental Dhara Dhevi resort than a night's stay there would be.

BAAN KAEW GUEST HOUSE Guest House $$
(☎0 5327 1606; www.baankaew-guesthouse.com; 142 Th Charoen Prathet; r 800B; ❄📶) The two-storey apartment building is set back from the road behind the owner's own residence. Rooms are fairly standard with fridge and cable TV, but upstairs rooms also have small balconies, and are light and airy. It's a good honest deal, very friendly, and in a quiet part of town in its own green patch. It's also conveniently opposite a departure point for river cruises, and elegant Wat Chaimongkhon with its lovely riverside setting.

DUSITD2 CHIANG MAI Hotel $$$
(Map p148; ☎0 5399 9999; www.dusit.com; 100 Th Chang Khlan; r from 3500B; ❄@📶🏊) Designed to impress and overwhelm,

If You Like... Market Meals

Market mavens will love Chiang Mai's covered food and grocery centres, which offer everything from morning noodles to daytime snacking and evening supping.

1 **TALAT PRATU CHIANG MAI**
(Map p148; Th Bamrungburi; 4am-noon & 6pm-midnight) In the early morning, this market is Chiang Mai's communal larder, selling foodstuffs and ready-made dishes. If you want to make merit to the monks, come early and find the woman who sells pre-assembled food donations (20B). Things quiet down by lunchtime, but the burners are re-ignited for a large and popular night market that sets up across the road.

2 **TALAT THANIN**
(off Th Chang Pheuak; 5am-early evening) Market aficionados would be impressed by this efficient and clean covered market. In the prepared food section you'll find Chiang Mai's recent food trends. Continue deeper to the covered food centre for made-to-order noodles and stir-fries.

3 **TALAT TON PHAYOM**
(Th Suthep) Talat Ton Phayom acts as both a local market and a souvenir stop for Thais visiting from other provinces. Take a look at the packaged food area to see the kinds of edible gifts (like bags of *kâap mŏo* and *sâi òo·a*) that make a visit to Chiang Mai complete.

the gleaming white and blinding orange of the lobby in this slick hotel version of an urban hipster is dizzying. The deluxe rooms with couch and cushions alongside windows overlooking Doi Suthep are very good but we'd recommend an upgrade to a suite, which is like a mini-apartment. In this crowded city, you can't help but feel spoilt by walk-in wardrobes.

Riverside

RIVERSIDE HOUSE Guest House $
(off Map p148; 0 5324 1860; www.riversidehousechiangmai.com; 101 Th Chiang Mai-Lamphun; r 500-800B;) Next door to the Tourism Authority of Thailand, this friendly and professional set-up has great cheap rooms arranged around a pretty garden. The best rooms are of course the most expensive, but they are well worth paying extra, being in a new building at the rear of the property. You share a common balcony out front and have your own private balcony at the rear.

RIVER VIEW LODGE Hotel $$
(off Map p148; 0 5327 1109; www.riverviewlodgch.com; 25 Soi 4, Th Charoen Prathet; r 1500-2200B; P) The simple, spacious rooms are a bit overpriced at this breezy riverside lodge with its emphasis on charm and old-fashioned hospitality. But you aren't paying for a spectacular room – go and sit by the pool and drink in the extensive and beautiful gardens, and you'll appreciate the quiet nature of the dead-end soi location.

BAAN ORAPIN B&B $$
(0 5324 3677; www.baanorapin.com; 150 Th Charoenrat; r 2100-3400B;) It's a family affair at Baan Orapin, a pretty garden compound anchored by a stately teak house, which has been in the family since 1914. Luxurious guest residences (a total of 15 rooms) are in separate and modern buildings spread throughout the property.

West of the Old City

Prices tend to be a little higher here than in the backpacker areas but you're closer to Chiang Mai University and in the best area of town for local nightlife.

H Hotel $$
(Map p150; 0 5322 0444; www.h-designhotel.com; 1 Th Sirimungklajarn; r from 1590B;) This new concrete, cubist, monolith style-hotel is quite a find. Staff are tripping over themselves to be helpful, and the architect has gone for space – and a lot of it. The rooms are huge (even the smaller ones) and bathrooms are modern and spacious. To find H, look out for the Mango Chilli Restaurant below.

PANN MALEE HOME Guest House **$$**
(Map p150; ☎0 5328 9147; www.pannmalee.com; off Soi 17, Th Nimmanhaemin; r 1000-1400B; ❄) This converted townhouse really is like staying at somebody's house: the rooms are all individually furnished with the owner's eclectic taste and feel very homely. Apparently each room reflects the personalities of the owner's family members. The extra baht basically buys you more space, fewer stairs and a slightly nicer setting.

Eating

Chiang Mai's restaurant scene is surprisingly down to earth and wholesome. You can also explore the local markets and small shopfronts for the regional speciality of *kôw soy* (sometimes written as *khao soi*), a curried noodle dish claiming Shan-Yunnanese heritage. It's usually accompanied by pickled vegetables and a thick red chilli sauce.

Old City

SAFE HOUSE COURT Thai **$**
(Map p148; 178 Th Ratchaphakhinai; dishes 50-80B; ⏲7am-10pm) Steer away from Western offerings such as sandwiches and go for the cheap and well-prepared Thai dishes here, including regional specialities, spicy salads and good veggie options.

BAAN NOK NOODLE Noodles **$**
(Map p148; Th Singharat; noodles 25-35B; ⏲10am-6pm, closed Wed) For a quick bite on the street, perhaps after a visit to nearby Wat Phra Singh, locals recommend this Thai noodle place. Various types of noodles are served in spicy or clear soup (pork) but the signature dish is *tom yum baan nok* with small noodles.

LERT ROS Northeastern Thai **$**
(Map p148; Soi 1, Th Ratchadamnoen; small/large dish 30/50B; ⏲1-9pm) Whole fish frying on top of cooking drums at the front of this restaurant alerts passers-by to this simple Thai restaurant. Cooking food in the northeastern style, there are various meat and rice dishes strongly spiced, whole tilapia fish, and *sôm·đam* (spicy green papaya salad) to choose from. It's very popular so try early or late for dinner – it's the best cheapie in the area.

HOUSE Asian Fusion **$$$**
(Map p148; ☎0 5341 9011; 199 Th Moon Muang; dishes 200-800B; ⏲6-11pm) This restaurant is definitely the place to treat yourself. It occupies a mid-20th-century house (it once belonged to an exiled Burmese prince) that's now outfitted with colonial accoutrements. The House menu is a pan-Pacific affair, combining imported lamb and salmon with local spices and cooking techniques.

Hawker-style food
OLIVER STREWE/LONELY PLANET IMAGES ©

RACHAMANKHA Thai $$$

(Map p148; ☎0 5390 4111; Rachamankha Hotel, 6 Th Ratchamankha; dishes 300-1000B) Tucked away behind Wat Phra Singh, in the sumptuous grounds of the boutique hotel of the same name, one dines at the Rachamankha to enjoy the crisp white linens and antique atmosphere as much as the food. The menu is Thai-centred, along with hints of Myanmar, Yunnan and Europe at the periphery.

HEUAN PHEN Northern Thai $

(Map p148; ☎0 5327 7103; 112 Th Ratchamankha; dishes 50-150B; ⏰lunch & dinner) At this well-known restaurant everything is on display, from the northern Thai food to the groups of culinary visitors and the antique-cluttered dining room. Try the young jackfruit with a spicy paste. Daytime meals are served in a large canteen out front.

FERN FOREST CAFE Cafe $

(2/2 Soi 4, Th Singharat; desserts 70B; ⏰8.30am-8.30pm) Delectable Western-style desserts (try the carrot cake) or sandwiches are available, but come for the desserts and to loll about in the beautiful garden setting over a fruit drink or coffee. The cool of the garden makes it the perfect place to wait out the heat of the afternoons too.

AUM VEGETARIAN FOOD Vegetarian $

(Map p148; 66 Th Moon Muang; dishes 50-60B; ⏰8am-5pm; 🖉) Aiming square at the health-conscious traveller is AUM's vegetarian delights. There's organic coffee from Laos, seasonal juices and a range of all-veggie Thai-style stir-fries, soups, salads and rice dishes.

BLUE DIAMOND Bakery $

(Map p148; 35/1 Soi 9, Th Moon Muang; mains 50-60B; ⏰7am-9pm Mon-Sat) Always popular but a bit less frenetic than other traveller eating spots around here. Evidence of the quality of the food is in the return clientele. Blue Diamond bakes its own bread and pours fresh local coffee; breakfast is the meal to go for, or possibly a vegetable salad for lunch (Thai vegetarian is big on the menu).

East of the Old City

DA STEFANO Italian $$

(☎0 5387 4187; 2/1-2 Th Changmoi Kao; mains 180-250B; ⏰11.30am-11pm) This unassuming Italian eatery, with its portraits of the Mediterranean hanging on its

Riverside restaurant

walls, is tucked into a soi just outside of the old city. It's one of the best Italian restaurants in Chiang Mai, and you really can't go wrong with the menu, but we'd recommend the rich lasagne, and richer tiramisu.

ANTIQUE HOUSE Northern Thai **$$**
(71 Th Charoen Prathet; dishes 80-200B; ⏲lunch & dinner) Antique House is a quaint two-storey teak house and garden filled with wooden antiques and mellow nightly music. Better to come for dinner rather than lunch – it's a much better time to experience the magic of this beautiful setting.

WHOLE EARTH RESTAURANT Restaurant **$$**
(Map p148; 88 Th Si Donchai; dishes 150-350B; ⏲11am-10pm) This confectionery-coloured teak house wears a garden of hanging vines, kòi ponds and orchids growing in the crooks of tree limbs. It is the sort of place Thais go to treat someone special – where the staff will treat you like royalty and the dishes seem exotic (Thai Indian and vegetarian) without being demanding.

LA-OWN Thai **$**
(Th Charoen Prathet; dishes 40-80B; ⏲lunch & dinner) Tempting aromas waft down the street from this affable restaurant. Dishes are thoughtfully prepared and include lots of seafood and chicken options. We enjoyed the seafood fried-rice with basil.

ANUSAN NIGHT MARKET Food Market **$$**
(Map p148; Anusan Night Bazaar, Th Chang Khlan; dishes 100-350B; ⏲dinner) Anusan is a buzzing food market best known for its Thai-Chinese seafood restaurants. Try **Lena Restaurant** here, where a kilo of succulent grilled prawns will set you back 300B. Or have a stab at the fish in Thai spices and basil leaves.

RATANA'S KITCHEN International Thai **$**
(Map p148; 320-322 Th Tha Phae; dishes 30-150B; ⏲7.30am-11.30pm) For all the talk of Chiang Mai having cool temperatures, it still gets hot by midday. Jump out of the oven and into Ratana's kitchen. It isn't a culinary legend but the dishes and prices are sensible and it's got a prime spot near Pratu Tha Phae for wilting tourists.

Riverside

Past Saphan Nakhon Ping, is Th Faham, known as Chiang Mai's *kôw soy* ghetto. Situated here are **Khao Soi Lam Duan (Th Faham; dishes 40-60B)**, which also serves *kà·nŏm rang pêung* (literally beehive pastry – a coconut-flavoured waffle), **Khao Soi Samoe Jai (Th Faham; dishes 30-65B)** and **Khao Soi Ban Faham (Th Faham; dishes 35-55B)**. *Kôw soy* foodies sometimes spend the day sampling a bowl at each place to decide their favourite.

CHEDI Thai-Indian **$$$**
(☎0 5325 3333; 123 Th Charoen Prathet; mains 500-1000B; ⏲dinner) Fine Indian cuisine is available (the jinga masala is recommended by readers) as well as one of Chiang Mai's few quality wine lists. Shockingly expensive but swamped with first-class service, enjoy gorgeous white-linen dining on the riverbank with floating candles twinkling on the water.

RIVERSIDE BAR & RESTAURANT International Thai **$$**
(Th Charoenrat; dishes 100-200B; ⏲10am-1am) This rambling set of wooden buildings has been the most consistently popular riverside place for over 20 years. The food – Thai, Western and vegetarian – is just a minor attraction compared to the good-times ambience. Some veterans opt to dine on the docked boat before the nightly 8pm river cruise.

West of the Old City

PALAAD TAWANRON Thai **$$**
(☎0 5321 6039; Th Suthep; dishes 120-320B; ⏲lunch & dinner) The Thai menu is extensive and includes plenty of seafood such as serpent-head fish, freshwater prawns and sea bass. There's an extensive outdoor seating area overlooking a small reservoir and the city of Chiang Mai beyond.

KHUN CHURN Vegetarian $
(Map p150; Soi 17, Th Nimmanhaemin; buffet 100B; ⏲lunch; 🌿) Thais love their buffets – it's the all-you-can-eat allure for these food-loving people. There's a plethora of well-prepared vegetarian dishes and salads to choose from and basic fruit drinks are included. The shady outdoor setting will entice you to linger.

SU CASA Tapas $$
(Map p150; ☎0 5381 0088; 28 Soi 11, Th Nimmanhaemin; tapas 70-100B; ⏲lunch & dinner) The chef at this vivacious Mediterranean gem invites Chiang Mai's fresh produce and imported ingredients to tango with him in the kitchen, preparing tapas standards and artful entrees. Try the baby octopus in lemon citrus dressing; the chorizo is also very good here.

PUN PUN Thai, Vegetarian $
(Wat Suan Dok, Th Suthep; mains 30-40B; ⏲breakfast & lunch; 🌿) This shady outdoor eatery quietly churns out top quality Thai vegetarian dishes with little fuss. Food is simple, spicy and delicious. Enter Wat Suan Dok from Suthep road, walk past the temple, and Pun Pun is on your right after the 'monk chat' office.

ROYAL PROJECT RESTAURANT Northern Thai $$
(Th Huay Kaew; mains 70-300B; ⏲9am-6pm) Fine dining Thai-style is dished out at this outlet for the Royal Project, which supports various agricultural initiatives in Thailand.

BURMESE RESTAURANT Burmese $
(Map p150; cnr Th Nimmanhaemin & Soi 14; dishes 30B; ⏲lunch & dinner) This basic eatery behind another eatery with plastic chairs selling fried foods on the pavement, sells delicious Burmese food very cheaply. Try the tamarind leaf salad (our favourite), goat offal curry or catfish balls in gravy.

D-LO Burmese $
(soi off Th Huay Kaew; mains 30-50B; ⏲lunch & dinner) This is a new Burmese restaurant

Left: Eatery, Ping River; Below: Diners at a restaurant
(LEFT) JOHN ELK III/LONELY PLANET IMAGES ©; (BELOW) OLIVER STREWE/LONELY PLANET IMAGES ©

and according to local Burmese food aficionados it serves up very authentic versions of the cuisine. It's located in a soi off Huay Kaew road; look for the sign to the Holiday Garden Hotel – it's about halfway down on the right-hand side.

Drinking

PUB Pub
(189 Th Huay Kaew) In an old Tudor-style cottage set well off the road, this venerable Chiang Mai institution semi-successfully calls up the atmosphere of an English country pub. The Friday-evening happy hour assembles all the old expats who claim to have arrived in the city on the back of elephants.

WRITER'S CLUB & WINE BAR Bar
(Map p148; 141/3 Th Ratchadamnoen) Run by an ex-foreign correspondent, this unassuming traveller hangout is popular with expats and serves a good range of cold beer and cocktails. There's also English pub grub to help anchor a liquid meal.

AT 9 BAR Bar
(Map p150; Th Nimmanhaemin & Soi 9; 6pm-midnight) For a bird's-eye view of all the action on Th Nimmanhaemin pop into this upstairs, open-air bar.

GLASS ONION Bar
(Map p150; Rooms Boutique Mall, Th Nimmanhaemin; 8pm-late) While the barely legals try to blow their eardrums out at Nimmanhaemin's dance clubs, this is the domain of grown-ups desiring cocktails and conversation. The bar also enjoys a gay-friendly reputation.

PINOCCHIO'S Bar
(Map p150; Soi 7, Th Nimmanhaemin) Pinocchio's is a large outdoor bars where the weekend action really hots up. It upmarket, and gets packed with younger Thai students.

VIVIANE PONTI/LONELY PLANET IMAGES ©

Don't Miss Chiang Mai Night Bazaar

Chiang Mai Night Bazaar is one of the city's main night-time attractions, especially for families, and it is the modern legacy of the original Yunnanese trading caravans that stopped here along the ancient trade route between Simao (in China) and Mawlamyaing (on Myanmar's Gulf of Martaban coast). Today the night bazaar sells the usual tourist souvenirs, like what you'll find at Bangkok's street markets.

In true market fashion, vendors form a gauntlet along the footpath of Th Chang Khlan from Th Tha Phae to Th Loi Kroh. In between are dedicated shopping buildings: the Chiang Mai Night Bazaar Building is filled mainly with antique and handicraft stores. Across the street is the Galare Night Bazaar selling upmarket clothes and home decor. The Anusan Market is less claustrophobic and filled with tables of vendors selling knitted caps, carved soaps and other cottage-industry goods. The quality and bargains aren't especially impressive, but the allure is the variety and concentration of stuff and the dexterity and patience it takes to trawl through it all.

THINGS YOU NEED TO KNOW

Map p148; Th Chang Khlan; ⌚7pm-midnight

OUTDOORS Bar

(Map p150; Soi 7, Th Nimmanhaemin) Another large outdoor bar, Outdoors has a mixed crowd of Thais, expats and tourists.

CAFES & TEASHOPS

Almost an attraction in its own right, Soi Kaafae (Coffee Lane on Soi 9, Th Nimmanhaemin) is populated by two bustling coffee shops with lush garden seating and lots of laptop-tapping Thais. On one side of the street is **Wawee Coffee** (Map p150; Soi 9, Th Nimmanhaemin), a local chain that originally started at Mae Sa Elephant Camp and has since expanded to the point of Starbucks saturation. Across the street is **94° Coffee** (Map p150; Soi 9, Th Nimmanhaemin).

TEA HOUSE Teahouse

(Map p148; Th Tha Phae; ⏰9.30-6pm) The mountains of the north also produce Assam tea, served in the Victorian-era Tea House, which shares space with Siam Celadon. It's a beautiful setting for a cup of jasmine tea and a snack.

Entertainment

SUDSANAN Live Music

(Map p150; Th Huay Kaew) Down a driveway opposite a Shell Service Station, this warmly lit wooden house is filled with a lot of local soul. Long-haired Thais and expats, especially from local NGOs, come here to applaud the adept performances that jog from samba to *pleng pêu·a chee·wít* (songs for life).

RIVERSIDE BAR & RESTAURANT Live Music

(9-11 Th Charoenrat) In a twinkly setting on the Ping River, Riverside is a one of the longest-running live-music venues in Chiang Mai. The cover bands made up of ageing Thai hippies stake out centre stage and fill the room with all the singalong tunes from the classic-rock vault.

WARM-UP Nightclub

(Map p150; ☎0 5340 0676, 306 253; 40 Th Nimmanhaemin) The hippest joint in town, and a perennial favourite for the young and beautiful, Warm-Up is one of Chiang Mai's best dance houses.

MONKEY CLUB Nightclub

(Map p150; 7 Soi 9, Th Nimmanhaemin) Merging dinner with dancing and live music in the beautifully-lit tropical garden and featuring local, crooning live bands, Monkey Club attracts a tribe of affluent Thai students and a few expats who might migrate from the garden seats to the glassed-in, all-white bar and club.

GALLERY Live Music

(27 Th Charoenrat) Traditional Thai music from 7pm to 9pm nightly. The beautiful, leafy, riverside setting marries well with the sounds.

Shopping

Chiang Mai is Thailand's handicraft centre, ringed by small cottage factories and workshops. There are several shopping corridors throughout the city, such as the Chiang Mai Night Bazaar (p164), east of the old city, and the Saturday Walking Street (p149) on Th Wualai.

East of the Old City

LOST HEAVENS Tribal Arts

(Map p148; 228-234 Th Tha Phae) This store specialises in museum-quality tribal arts, including textiles, carpets and antiques, as well as ritual artefacts from the Yao (also known as Mien) tribe.

KESORN Tribal Arts

(Map p148; 154-156 Th Tha Phae) A collector's best friend, this cluttered shop has been trading old stuff for years. It specialises mainly in hill-tribe textiles, beads and crafts.

SIAM CELADON Ceramics

(Map p148; www.siamceladon.com; 158 Th Tha Pae; ⏰8am-6pm) This established company sells its fine collection of cracked-glazed celadon ceramics in a lovely teak building. Enjoy the Victorian-era structure and its dainty fretwork longer with a proper English tea at the attached Tea House Siam Celadon (p165).

KUKWAN GALLERY Textiles, Gifts

(Map p148; 37 Th Loi Kroh) Set slightly back from the road, this charming teak building houses natural cotton and silk by the metre. It's a great place to shop for gifts, with scarves, bedspreads and tablecloths available in subtle colours.

DOR DEK GALLERY Crafts, Gifts

(Map p148; ☎08 9859 6683; Th Samlan) Dor Dek Gallery sells the craft projects of street children employed by the Volunteers for Children Development Foundation. The profits from sales are divided among the child artist, the program's educational fund and future supply purchases. It's particularly good for handmade bags, purses and prezzies for the kids.

Riverside

LA LUNA GALLERY Art

(Map p148; ☎0 5330 6678; www.lalunagallery.com; 190 Th Charoenrat) In the old shophouse row on the east bank of the river, this professional gallery picks a fine bouquet of emerging Southeast Asian artists. Many canvases have a social commentary angle and give the viewer a window into the different artistic styles in the region.

VILA CINI Textiles

(☎0 5324 6246; www.vilacini.com; 30-34 Th Charoenrat) Villa Cini sells high-end, handmade silks and cotton textiles that are reminiscent of the Jim Thompson brand. Perhaps the real draw is the store's atmospheric setting: a beautiful teak house with marble floors and a narrow, rickety staircase that leads to a galleried courtyard.

SOP MOEI ARTS Textiles

(Map p148; ☎0 5330 6123; www.sopmoeiarts.com; 150/10 Th Charoenrat) Lots of shops sell hill-tribe crafts, but this one has put a modern makeover on the traditional crafts of the Pwo Karen, a tribal group living in Mae Hong Son Province. The result is some genuinely exquisite textiles including cushion covers, table pieces and wall hangings.

West of the Old City

Close to Chiang Mai University, Th Nimmanhaemin is often referred to as the trendy part of town. It has several malls filled with closet-sized clothing and gift boutiques.

SRISANPANMAI Silk

(Map p150; 6 Soi 1, Th Nimmanhaemin) From the technicolour rainbow patterns of Burma to the wide-hem panel style of Chiang Mai, Srisanpanmai specialises in silks made in the old tradition.

ADORN WITH STUDIO NAENNA Textiles

(Map p150; 22 Soi 1, Th Nimmanhaemin) The pensive colours of the mountains have been woven into these naturally dyed silks and cottons, part of a village weaving project pioneered by Patricia Cheeseman, an expert and author on Thai-Lao textiles.

GINGER Clothing, Accessories

(Map p150; 6/21 Th Nimmanhaemin) For something more night-on-the-townish, check out the shimmery dresses, sparkly mules, fabulous jewellery and colourful accessories.

Information

Tourism Authority of Thailand (TAT; ☎0 5324 8604; Th Chiang Mai-Lamphun; ⏰8.30am-4.30pm)

Tribal clothing, Talat Warorot (p147)

OLIVER STREWE/LONELY PLANET IMAGES ©

Chiang Mai Night Bazaar (p164)

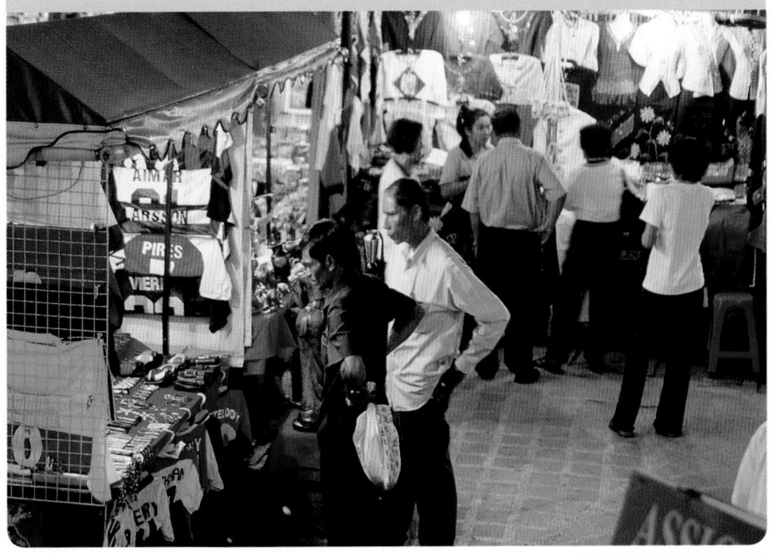

ANTONY GIBLIN/LONELY PLANET IMAGES ©

General tourist information and guide recommendations.

Tourist police (0 5324 7318, 24hr emergency 1155; Th Faham; 6am- midnight) Foreign-language liaisons for the police.

Getting There & Away

Air

Regularly scheduled flights arrive into and depart from Chiang Mai International Airport (Map p146; www.chiangmaiairportonline.com), which is 3km south of the centre of the old city. Unless otherwise noted the following airlines use the Suvarnabhumi Airport for travel from and to Bangkok.

Bangkok Airways (0 5328 9338-9; www.bangkokair.com) Flies daily to Bangkok and continues to Ko Samui.

China Airlines (0 5322 34012250 9898; www.china-airlines.com) Flies to Taipei weekly.

Nok Air (1318; www.nokair.com) Flies to Bangkok Don Muang; note that Nok Air is a subsidiary of Thai Airways.

Orient Thai Airlines (1126; www.flyorientthai.com) Flies to Bangkok's Don Muang four times a day; and three times weekly to Pai (operated by Kan Air).

Silk Air (0 5390 4985; www.silkair.com) Flies to Singapore three times weekly.

Thai Airways International (THAI; 0 5321 1044/7; www.thaiair.com) Flies to Bangkok at least six times daily.

Bus

Arcade Bus Terminal (Th Kaew Nawarat) Chiang Mai's long-distance terminal is about 3km from the old city.

Chang Pheuak Bus Terminal (off Map p148; Th Chang Pheuak) For buses to destinations within Chiang Mai Province, which is north of the old city.

Train

Chiang Mai's train station (Map p146; Th Charoen Muang) is about 2.5km east of the old city.

All Chiang Mai–bound trains originate from Bangkok's Hualamphong station. At the time of writing there were six daily departures from Bangkok to Chiang Mai (and the same number in the opposite direction) and the journey took between 12 and 15 hours.

Sleeping berths are increasingly hard to reserve without booking well in advance; tour groups sometimes book entire cars and available spots are even more scarce during holidays such as Songkran (mid-April), Chulalongkorn Day (October) and Chinese New Year (late February to early March).

Getting Around

To/From Airport

There is only one licensed airport taxi service, charging a flat 150B fare. Many guest houses and hotels also provide airport transfers.

Bicycle

Cycling is a good way to get around Chiang Mai. Rickety cruiser bikes with a fixed gear can be rented for around 60B a day from some guest houses or from various places along the east moat. Chiang Mai Mountain Biking **(Map p146; ☎0 5381 4207; www.mountainbikingchiangmai.com; 1 Th Samlan)** rents well-maintained mountain bikes and city bikes for the day, and it also runs mountain bike tours of the area.

An alternative, handily located option, is SM Travel **(Map p148 ☎0 5320 6844; 87 Th Ratchadamnoen)**, which also hire bikes and is a bit cheaper, reflective of the quality of their bikes (mountain bikes 100B to 200B).

Car & Truck

One of the most well-regarded agencies is North Wheels **(Map p148; ☎0 5387 4478; www.northwheels.com; 70/4-8 Th Chaiyaphum)**, which offers hotel pick-up and delivery, 24-hour emergency road service and comprehensive insurance. Another good bet is Thai Rent a Car **(Petchburee Car Rent; ☎0 5328 1345; www.thairentacar.com; 81/1 Th A-rak)**, located in the southwestern corner of the old city.

Motorcycle

Agencies along Th Moon Muang, and even some guest houses, rent Honda Dream 100cc step-through manual bikes for between 130B and 150B a day, and automatics from 200B); and Honda or Yamaha 125cc to 150cc rent for 250B a day. A few places rent 400cc motorcycles (600B to 900B), while a 650cc can go for 1300B.

Sŏrng·tăa·ou, Túk-Túk & Săhm·lór

The *sŏrng·tăa·ou* are shared taxis: you can flag them down, tell them your destination and if they are going that way they'll nod. Along the way they might pick up other passengers if the stops are en route or close by. Short trips should cost 20B per person (eg between the old city and the river or Th

Stupas, Doi Inthanon National Park

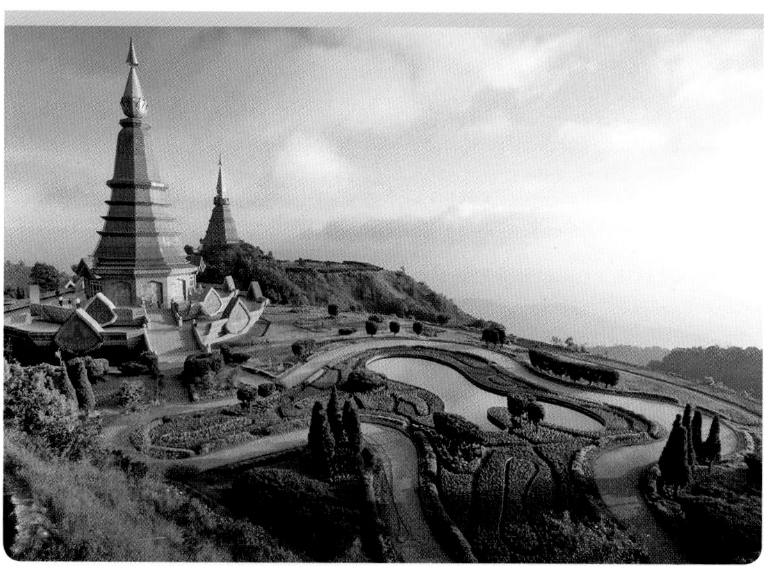

FELIX HUG/LONELY PLANET IMAGES ©

Nimmahemin to the west) and longer trips from 40B per person.

Túk-túks work only on a charter basis and are more expensive than *sŏrng·tăa·ou*. In entertainment areas at night most túk-túk drivers will ask for an optimistic 100B.

If You Like... Shopping Villages

If you like the weekend walking streets and Chiang Mai Night Bazaar (p164), check out these handicraft villages:

1 **BO SANG**
(Map p146) The 'umbrella village' is filled with craft shops selling tourist-grade painted umbrellas, fans, silverware, statuary, celadon pottery and lacquerware.

2 **SAN KAMPHAENG**
Another craft village near Bo Sang, known for its cotton and silk weaving shops and textile showrooms.

3 **HANG DONG**
(Map p146) Rte 108 is a 'furniture highway' specialising in decorative arts, woodcarving, antiques and contemporary furniture.

4 **BAN THAWAI**
(Map p146) A pedestrian-friendly tourist market with 3km of home decor shops.

AROUND CHIANG MAI

Doi Inthanon National Park อุทยานแห่งชาติดอยอินทนนท์

Thailand's highest peak is Doi Inthanon (often abbreviated as Doi In), which measures 2565m above sea level, an impressive altitude for the kingdom, but a tad diminutive compared to its cousins in the Himalayan range. The 1000-sq-km **national park** (☎0 5328 6730; adult/child 200/100B, car/motorbike 30/20B; ⏰8am-sunset) surrounding the peak has hiking trails, waterfalls and two monumental stupas erected in honour of the king and queen. It is a popular day trip from Chiang Mai for tourists and locals, especially during the New Year's holiday when there's the rarely seen phenomenon of frost.

The whole point of the park is to get as high as you can to see life in a colder climate, and the coolness is such a relief from the sweltering plains below. Thais relish bundling up in hats and jackets and posing for pictures among conifers and rhododendrons. Almost at the exact summit there's a *chedi* dedicated to one of the last Lanna kings (Inthawichayanon). From there, a lovely boardwalk through the thick, cool forest leads to a cafe, obligatory souvenir shop and the start of the **Ang Ka nature trail**, a 360m platform walkway through a moss-festooned bog.

The park is one of the top destinations in Southeast Asia for naturalists and birdwatchers.

Mae Sa Valley น้ำตกแม่สา

One of the easiest mountain escapes, the Mae Sa–Samoeng loop travels from the lowland's concrete expanse into the highlands' forested frontier. The 100km route makes a good day trip with private transport. **Golden Triangle Rider** (www.gt-rider.com) publishes a detailed map of the area.

Head north of Chiang Mai on Rte 107 (Th Chang Pheuak) toward Mae Rim, then left onto Rte 1096. The road becomes more rural but there's a steady supply of tour-bus attractions: orchid farms, butterfly parks, snake farms, you name it.

Not far past an elephant camp is the **Queen Sirikit Botanic Gardens** (☎0 5384 1000; www.qsbg.org; Rte 1096; adult/child 30/10B; ⏰8.30am-5pm), featuring a shorn mountainside displaying 227 hectares of various exotic and local flora for conservation and research purposes. The drive to the glasshouse affords some wonderful views and once up here highlights include: the waterlily and lotus collections with some enormous leafy examples, and beautiful two-, even three-tier flowers; and the huge tropical rainforest glasshouse complete with indoor waterfall, where you can walk around on a raised platform giving a bird's-eye view of the forest below. Motorbikes are not allowed in the gardens.

After the botanic gardens the road climbs up into the fertile **Mae Sa Valley**, once a high-altitude basin for growing opium poppies. Now the valley's hill-tribe farmers have re-seeded their terraced fields with sweet peppers, cabbage, flowers and fruits – which are then sold to the royal agriculture projects under the Doi Kham label.

Sitting at the western wedge of the valley, **Proud Phu Fah** (**☎ 0 5387 9389; www.proudphufah.com; Km17, Rte 1096; r 4500-7000B; ❄ @ 🛜 🏊**) is a small boutique hotel with creature-comfort villas designed to give the illusion of sleeping amid the great outdoors. Each villa also has a patio area right on the water's edge. The open-air restaurant serves healthy Thai food (dishes 100B to 150B) with a panoramic view of the valley.

Chiang Dao เชียงดาว

In a lush, jungle setting and slammed up against the limestone cliffs of a mighty *doi* (mountain), Chiang Dao is a very popular escape from the steaming urban plains of Chiang Mai. Local accommodation plays on this theme attracting families and 30-something travellers looking for good eating, plenty of relaxing and northern rural ambience.

Sights

THAM CHIANG DAO Cave

(**ถ้ำเชียงดาว; admission 20B**) In the heat of the day, the coolest place in town is the Chiang Dao Cave, a complex said to extend some 10km to 14km into Doi Chiang Dao.

DOI CHIANG DAO Mountain

(**ดอยเชียงดาว**) Part of the Doi Chiang Dao National Park, Doi Chiang Dao (also called Doi Luang) pokes into the heavens at 2195m above sea level. From the summit, reachable by a two-day hike, the views are spectacular. The southern side of the mountain is believed to be one of the most accessible spots in the world to see the giant nuthatch and Hume's pheasant. Bird-watching and overnight treks can be arranged through local guest houses.

Sleeping

CHIANG DAO NEST Bungalows **$$**

(**☎ 08 6017 1985; http://nest.chiangdao.com; r 550-1600B; @ 🛜 🏊**) Simple, great-value A-frame bungalows get the basics right – comfy beds, privacy and immaculate interiors. Bungalows further away have limited views but plenty of privacy and a lush garden setting.

Painted umbrellas

CHRIS MELLOR/LONELY PLANET IMAGES ©

Elephant sanctuary, Chiang Dao

FELIX HUG/LONELY PLANET IMAGES ©

CHIANG DAO RAINBOW Bungalows **$$**
(☎08 4803 8116; small/large bungalows 650/750B, r 380B) The two recycled teak bungalows are both a great size, have suitably creaky floors, four-poster beds, and shuttered windows overlooking rice fields and mountains. It's a difficult place to find: look for the turn-off, not far from where the bypass road meets Rte 107 (almost opposite Aurora Resort on the bypass road).

Eating

CHIANG DAO NEST International **$$$**
(☎0 6017 1985; dishes 300-500B; ⏲breakfast, lunch & dinner) The Nest's restaurant serves sophisticated fusion-European food in a relaxed garden setting. Wicha, the owner and chef, received her culinary training in the UK and creates a menu that reflects the seasons and the best of the local produce.

CHIANG DAO RAINBOW Thai, Mediterranean **$$**
(☎08 4803 8116; set menu 250B) This highly recommended restaurant offers two menus – northern Thai and Greek-Mediterranean.

Getting There & Around

Chiang Dao is 72km north of Chiang Mai along Rte 107.

Chiang Rai & Northern Thailand

Northern Thailand's 'mountainous' reputation may cause residents of Montana or Nepal to chuckle, but it's the fertile river valleys between these glorified hills that served as the birthplace of much of what is associated with Thai culture.

Not surprisingly, these old hills are the ideal destination for a unique Thai experience. Exploring a Buddhist temple in Lampang, cycling through the ancient ruins of Sukhothai or sipping locally grown coffee in Chiang Rai: northern Thailand's cultural attractions are generally low-key but are eminently rewarding. And for those seeking something more vigorous, the region's rugged geography ensures that there is also ample opportunity for active pursuits such as rafting in Pai or trekking in Mae Hong Son.

Put all this together and it's clear that these old hills are the perfect destination for seeking out a special cultural experience.

Temples, Sukhothai (p205)

Akha woman, Chiang Rai

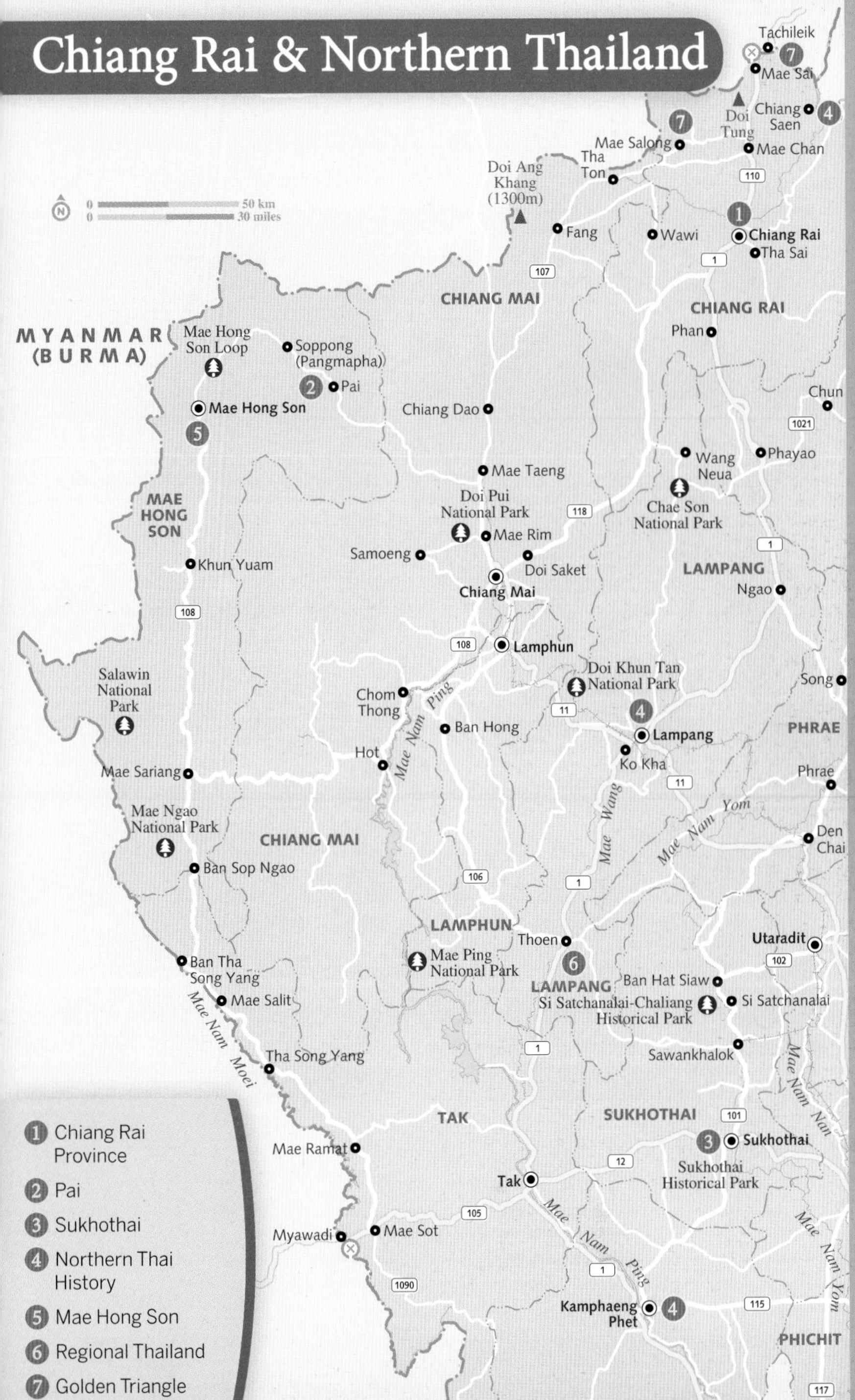
Chiang Rai & Northern Thailand
0 50 km
0 30 miles
MYANMAR (BURMA)
Tachileik
Mae Sai
Doi Tung
Chiang Saen
Mae Chan
Mae Salong
Tha Ton
Doi Ang Khang (1300m)
Fang
Wawi
Chiang Rai
Tha Sai
CHIANG MAI
CHIANG RAI
Phan
Chun
Phayao
Wang Neua
Chae Son National Park
Mae Hong Son Loop
Soppong (Pangmapha)
Pai
Mae Hong Son
Chiang Dao
Mae Taeng
Doi Pui National Park
Mae Rim
Samoeng
Doi Saket
Chiang Mai
MAE HONG SON
Khun Yuam
LAMPANG
Ngao
Lamphun
Doi Khun Tan National Park
Salawin National Park
Chom Thong
Mae Nam Ping
Ban Hong
Lampang
Ko Kha
Song
PHRAE
Phrae
Hot
Mae Sariang
Mae Wang
Mae Nam Yom
Den Chai
Mae Ngao National Park
CHIANG MAI
Ban Sop Ngao
LAMPHUN
Thoen
Utaradit
Ban Tha Song Yang
Mae Ping National Park
LAMPANG
Ban Hat Siaw
Mae Salit
Si Satchanalai-Chaliang Historical Park
Si Satchanalai
Mae Nam Moei
Tha Song Yang
Sawankhalok
Mae Nam Nan
TAK
SUKHOTHAI
Sukhothai
Mae Ramat
Sukhothai Historical Park
Tak
Mae Nam Ping
Myawadi
Mae Sot
Mae Nam Yom
Kamphaeng Phet
PHICHIT
110
107
1
1021
118
108
11
106
102
101
12
105
1090
115
117
1 Chiang Rai Province
2 Pai
3 Sukhothai
4 Northern Thai History
5 Mae Hong Son
6 Regional Thailand
7 Golden Triangle

Chiang Rai & Northern Thailand's Highlights

1

Chiang Rai Province

Chiang Rai Province is connected to Laos and Myanmar (Burma) and has beautiful scenery that makes it special in Thailand. There are fields and forests, mountains and plains and a variety of hill-tribe cultures struggling to maintain their cultural identity and traditional lifestyle.

Above: Akha woman and child; **Top Right:** Phu Chi Fa; **Bottom Right:** Fields near Mae Salong (p196)

Need to Know

BEST TIME TO VISIT November to February when the weather is cool **TOP TIP** Study the culture, customs and traditions before you go **For further coverage, see p186**

Local Knowledge

Chiang Rai Province Don't Miss List

BY PARISUDHA SUDHAMONGKALA (MOO), DIRECTOR OF THE MIRROR FOUNDATION

1 PHU CHI FAH

Phu Chi Fah is an amazing viewpoint on the border with Laos. It is best visited in winter, when the valley below is covered in early morning mist and the sky is clear as the sun rises. It is popular with Thais, but Westerners have yet to discover it in great numbers. It is a two- to three-hour drive from Chiang Rai. Arrive by 4am to hike to the top before sunrise.

2 EATING THE LOCAL DISHES

The local food is delicious and different from standard Thai dishes. Try some of Chiang Rai's local northern Thai restaurants such as Lung Eed Locol Food (p193). Buying locally also helps the sustainability of the rural lifestyle.

3 HILL-TRIBE TREKKING & HOMESTAY

Many tourists come to Chiang Rai Province to visit minority hill-tribe villages. Homestay programs here provide an understanding of the different cultures, hardships and community spirit. Mirror Foundation (p191), among others, organises ecotours to hill-tribe villages and helps educate tourists about the foundation's social justice efforts, including basic education, obtaining Thai citizenship, preventing human trafficking and promotion of handicrafts.

4 COUNTRYSIDE SCENERY

Chiang Rai Province has many beautiful natural and manmade attractions: the hills and mountains, such as Doi Tung (p224), which make up the borders with Burma and Laos; the Mekong River, which flows past Chiang Saen (p200) and defines the northern edge of the province; and steeply sloped fields growing coffee, tea and rice.

5 MAE SALONG

Mae Salong (p196) is a small town nestled in the hills near the border with Burma. It was settled by the Chinese Nationalist army after they were defeated by the communists. Originally relying on opium production to fund the settled army, Mae Salong is now a major tea producer and is also swathed in cherry blossom trees.

Pai

Peaceful Pai resides in a scenic mountain valley northwest of Chiang Mai and specialises in rest and relaxation (and even partying) for lowland city folks. Little planning is needed to appreciate Pai's attractions, which fall somewhere between spiritual and social. **Below:** Pai Canyon; **Top Right:** White-water rafting (p222); **Bottom Right:** Lahu woman and baby

Need to Know

BEST TIME TO VISIT November to February when the weather is cool **TOP TIP** Take time to watch, listen and enjoy the natural environment **For further coverage, see p221**

2

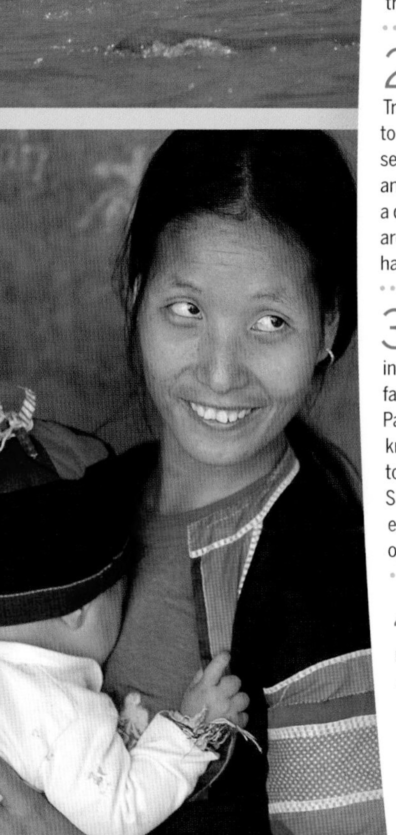

Local Knowledge

Pai Don't Miss List

BY PAYOONG (PIN) ZATHU, OWNER OF PAIRADISE RESORT

1 PAI RIVER

Rafting and kayaking (p222) down the Pai River to Mae Hong Son is a wonderful experience. The river is so peaceful, the landscape is beautiful and camping in the jungle reminds me of my earlier life when I used to travel with my father and our elephant (he worked for a logging company before the ban and then found replacement work taking tourists on elephant treks). I also used to be a trekking guide so I know a little about these woods.

2 PAI VALLEY

The whole of the Pai Valley is an attraction in itself. Travelling around on a motorbike provides an opportunity to explore the countryside and witness the change of seasons. In the rainy season, the forest sprouts mushrooms and bamboo shoots. There are forest treks (p223) that give a different perspective of the valley. And outside of Pai town are hot springs (p222) and waterfalls (p221), but you don't have to have a destination to enjoy it.

3 HILL-TRIBE VILLAGES

There are seven different ethnic groups living together in one small valley – it is a cultural accomplishment. My father is Karen and my mother is Shan so I'm a product of Pai's ethnic harmony. Since my father had elephants we know many of the local hill-tribe villages and I'm happy to visit with old friends there. For tourists, a visit to Ban Santichon (p222), a Yunnanese village, is just one way to experience our ethnic diversity. There are also trekking opportunities to the valley's villages.

4 DO NOTHING

One of the town's slogans is, 'Do nothing in Pai', reminding visitors to slow down, take a deep breath and enjoy the simple things, such as the moment the light changes above the hills.

Sukhothai

You may have had your fill of tumbled-down bricks in Ayuthaya but the ancient capital of Sukhothai (p205) is worth the extra effort. The old city is sheltered in a quiet parklike setting that creates a meditative calm, perfect for enjoying the gravity of the gravity-defying monuments. The surviving Buddha figures exhibit Sukhothai's quintessential artistic tradition: an elegance and fluidity despite their stationary position. And rarely are these lovely ruins overcome by crowds. Worshippers, Wat Mahathat (p207), Sukhothai

3

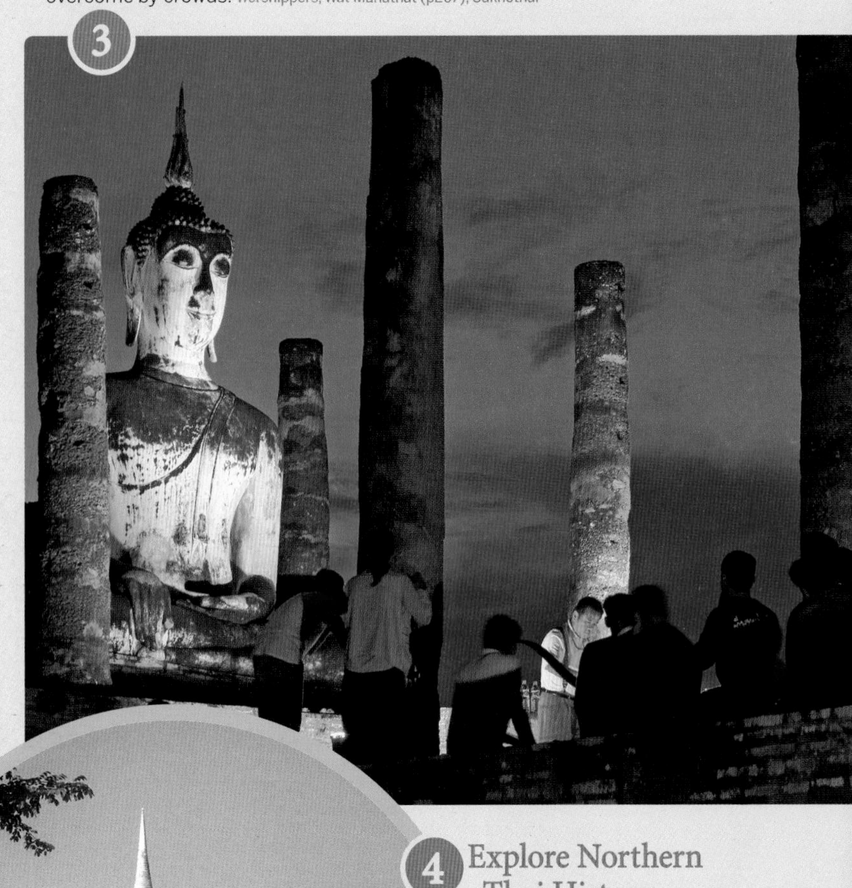

4

Explore Northern Thai History

Sukhothai might have been the first 'Thai' kingdom but the valleys through which the Thais' ancestors migrated from southern China cultivated many minor regional kingdoms that contribute to the emergence of a distinct Thai identity. There are surviving monuments to modest powers now past in Kamphaeng Phet (p214), Chiang Saen (p200) and Lampang (p187). Kamphaeng Phet

AUSTIN BUSH/LONELY PLANET IMAGES ©

Peek into Burma from Mae Hong Son 5

In the mountains overlooking Burma is Mae Hong Son (p216), a provincial capital so far removed from the lowlands that you'll forget that no international borders have been crossed. Peruse the markets for Burmese snacks or wander through temples more akin to Thailand's western neighbour than to Bangkok, or trek into a wilderness of forested peaks and valleys. Buddhist temple near Mae Hong Son

PETER STUCKINGS/LONELY PLANET IMAGES ©

6 Detour to Small Town Thailand

Glimpse ordinary living in northern Thailand's less-than-famous towns. En route to Sukhothai, Phitsanulok (p202) is domestically famous for Wat Phra Si Ratana Mahathat and its beautiful golden Buddha image. En route to Chiang Mai is Lampang (p187), filled with teak temples and horse-drawn sightseeing carts.

Wat Phra Si Ratana Mahathat, Phitsanulok

7 Galloping through the Golden Triangle

The convergence of Thailand, Laos and Myanmar (Burma) was once one of the leading producers of opium poppy. All that is ancient history and the story of the illicit trade is documented at two museums in Sop Ruak (p224), the official 'centre' of the infamous region. Nearby is Mae Sai (p198), a scruffy border town, and Mae Salong (p196), a Yunnanese settlement. Tea, Mae Salong

Chiang Rai & Northern Thailand's Best...

Scenic Journeys

- **Mae Salong** (p196) Slide along the serpentine ridge that bisects this ethnic Chinese village.
- **Mae Hong Son** (p216) Climb mountain switchbacks to this highland outpost.
- **Doi Tung** (p224) Tiptoe past Myanmar (Burma) from Mae Sai to this former opium-growing area.

Eating

- **Laap Khom Huay Pu** (p225) An eatery that worships meat in the tofu town of Pai.
- **Lung Eed Locol Food** (p193) Northern-style grub makes Chiang Rai salivate.
- **Sue Hai** (p198) Slurp homemade Yünnanese-style noodles.
- **Bamee Chakangrao** (p216) Homemade noodles go straight from mixing bowl to soup bowl.

Temples

- **Wat Phra Si Ratana Mahathat** (p213) Phitsanulok's famous bronze Buddha.
- **Wat Rong Khun** (p196) The all-white, ultramodern temple near Chiang Rai.
- **Wat Jong Kham & Wat Jong Klang** (p216) Ornately tiered temples with a scenic lake setting in Mae Hong Son.
- **Wat Mahathat** (p207) Sukhothai's larger-than-life Buddha statue.

Markets

- **Lampang's Walking Street** (p188) Admire an atmospheric shophouse neighbourhood.
- **Chiang Rai's Walking Street** (p195) Traffic is dismissed for a Saturday evening of shopping and noshing.
- **Mae Sai's Gem Market** (p199) Sparkly stones are inspected and traded on the side streets of this border town.
- **Phitsanulok's Night Markets** (p204) Provincial life is in full swing at various night markets and bazaars.

Left: Wat Phra Si Ratana Mahathat (p202), Phitsanulok; **Above:** Farmer, Mae Salong (p196)

Need to Know

ADVANCE PLANNING

- **One month before** Read up on Northern Thai history and culture.
- **One week before** Plan your itinerary.
- **One day before** Buy your train or bus tickets directly from the station.

RESOURCES

- **Lampang Tourism Authority of Thailand** (TAT; ☎0 5423 7229; Th Thakhrao Noi; ⌚10am-4pm Mon-Sat)
- **Chiang Rai TAT** (☎0 5374 4674; Th Singhaclai; ⌚8.30am-4.30pm)
- **Phitsanulok TAT** (☎0 5525 2742; 209/7-8 Th Borom Trailokanat; ⌚8.30am-4.30pm)
- **Sukhothai TAT** (☎0 5561 6228; Th Jarot Withithong; ⌚8.30am-4.30pm)
- **Kamphaeng Phet Tourist Information Centre** (⌚8am-4.30pm)
- **Mae Hong Son TAT** (www.travelmaehongson.org)

GETTING AROUND

- **Air** Fly to Mae Hong Son from Chiang Mai; or from Bangkok to Chiang Mai or Chiang Rai.
- **Bus** Extensive intraregional travel with connections to the hub of Chiang Mai.
- **Bicycle & motorcycle** Self-touring option in the cities.
- **Sŏrng·tăa·ou** Small pick-up trucks that act as shared taxis and public buses.
- **Train** Overnight option for Bangkok to Chiang Mai with detours to Phitsanulok and Lampang.
- **Túk-túk** Chartered vehicles for trips around town; negotiate the price beforehand.

BE FOREWARNED

- **Checkpoints** Travel with an ID as there are military checkpoints around the border.
- **Clothes** In the cool season (November to January) bring a jacket and socks.
- **Motorcycle safety** Wear a helmet and protective clothing.
- **Trekking** Avoid trekking during the hot season (March to May) and the rainy season (June to October); always trek with a licensed TAT guide.
- **Waterfalls** At their peak during and just after the rainy season (June to December).

Chiang Rai & Northern Thailand Itineraries

Tour Thailand's ancient capitals and historical parks. or leapfrog up to the former Golden Triangle border region now a well-behaved agricultural region.

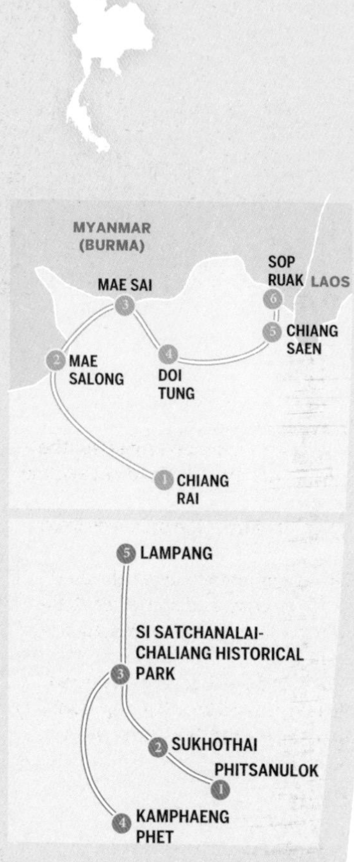

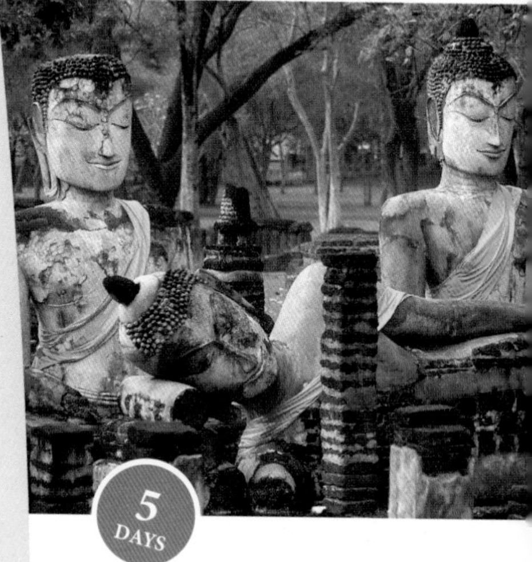

5 DAYS

PHITSANULOK TO LAMPANG

Connect to the Culture Trail

The cradle of the Thai nation sits due north of Bangkok. If you're travelling by train, disembark at **(1) Phitsanulok**, an average provincial town with bus access to Sukhothai. Thai tourists stop here to make merit at Wat Phra Si Ratana Mahathat and eat *gŏoay·đĕe·o hôy kăh* (literally, 'legs-hanging' noodles).

Continue to **(2) Sukhothai** for two to three days of ruin reconnaissance. Sukhothai's dynasty lasted 200 years and included the reign of King Ramkhamhaeng (1275–1317), credited with developing the first Thai script. Deeper into the countryside is **(3) Si Satchanalai-Chaliang Historical Park**, a Sukhothai satellite city where you can view ancient ruins and pottery. The rural setting offers glimpses into the country's agricultural rice basket.

Detour to **(4) Kamphaeng Phet**, a pleasant provincial town with a handful of Sukhothai-era ruins. Then head north to **(5) Lampang**, another historic town filled with teak temples.

Top Left: Buddha statues, Kamphaeng Phet Historical Park (p215); **Top Right:** Fields near Chiang Rai (p190)

CHIANG RAI TO SOP RUAK

Cruise Around the Countryside

Thailand's northernmost province, Chiang Rai has always been a migration route: for the ancestral Tai people of southern China, the pony caravans during the Silk Road era and the pack mules carrying opium from the Golden Triangle.

Start in **(1) Chiang Rai** for a multiday trek led by an NGO that uses the proceeds from their trekking ventures to aid local hill-tribe villages.

Day-trip to **(2) Mae Salong**, an ethnic Chinese village on a mountain ridge cultivated with tea plantations. Or base yourself in **(3) Mae Sai**, a border town and convenient base for exploring the former Golden Triangle area of Chiang Rai Province. Do a driving tour of **(4) Doi Tung** where coffee now grows instead of opium poppies.

Move on to the Mekong border town of **(5) Chiang Saen**, filled with temple ruins and river barges delivering goods from the interior of China. Take a day trip to **(6) Sop Ruak**, the Golden Triangle's official 'centre' and home to museums documenting the region's role in the production of the illicit substance.

Discover Chiang Rai & Northern Thailand

At a Glance

- **Chiang Rai** (p190) Border province known for coffee, trekking and the Golden Triangle.
- **Kamphaeng Phet** (p214) Detour for temple buffs.
- **Mae Hong Son** (p216) Rugged landscape, Burmese influences and Pai.
- **Phitsanulok** (p202) Famous Buddhist temple and rail access to Sukhothai.

Wat Phra Si Ratana Mahathat (p202), Phitsanulok

History

Northern Thailand's history has been characterised by the shifting powers of various independent principalities. One of the most significant early cultural influences in the north was the Mon kingdom of Hariphunchai (modern Lamphun), which held sway from the late 8th century until the 13th century.

In 1238 Sukhothai declared itself an independent kingdom under King Si Intharathit and quickly expanded its sphere of influence. Because of this, and the influence the kingdom had on modern Thai art and culture, Sukhothai is considered by Thais to be the first true Thai kingdom. In 1296 Phaya Mengrai established Chiang Mai after conquering the influential Mon kingdom of Hariphunchai.

Later, Chiang Mai, in an alliance with Sukhothai in the 14th and 15th centuries, became a part of the larger kingdom of Lan Na Thai (Million Thai Rice Fields), popularly referred to as Lanna. The golden age of Lanna was in the 15th century. However, many Thai alliances declined in the 16th century. This weakness led to the Burmese capturing Chiang Mai in 1556 and their control of Lanna for the next two centuries. The Thais regrouped after the Burmese took Ayuthaya in 1767, and under King Kawila, Chiang Mai was recaptured in 1774 and the Burmese were pushed north.

In the late 19th century Rama V of Bangkok made efforts to integrate the northern region with the centre to ward off the colonial threat. The completion of the northern railway to Chiang Mai in 1921 strengthened those links until the northern provinces finally became part of the kingdom of Siam in this early period of the 20th century.

Language

Thailand's regional dialects vary greatly and can even be unintelligible to native speakers of Thai who aren't familiar with the vernacular being spoken. *Găm méuang*, the northern Thai dialect, is no exception and, in addition to an entirely different set of tones to master, possesses a wealth of vocabulary specific to the north. The northern dialect also has a slower rhythm than Thailand's three other main dialects, an attribute reflected in the relaxed, easygoing manner of the people who speak it.

Northern Thai also has its own writing system, based on an old Mon script that was originally used only for Buddhist scripture.

LAMPANG PROVINCE

Lampang ลำปาง

POP 59,000

Boasting lumbering elephants, the elegant mansions of former lumber barons and impressive (and in many cases, lumber-based) Lanna-era temples, Lampang seems to unite every northern Thai cliché – but in a good way.

History

Although Lampang Province was inhabited as far back as the 7th century in the Dvaravati period, legend has it that Lampang city was founded by the son of Hariphunchai's Queen Chama Thewi, and played an important part in the history of the Hariphunchai Kingdom (8th to 13th centuries).

At the end of the 19th and beginning of the 20th century Lampang, along with nearby Phrae, became an important centre for the domestic and international teak trade. A large British-owned timber company brought in Burmese supervisors familiar with the teak industry in Burma to train Burmese and Thai loggers in the area. These well-paid supervisors, along with independent Burmese teak merchants who plied their trade in Lampang, sponsored the construction of more than a dozen temples in the city, a legacy that lives on in several of Lampang's most impressive wát.

Sights

WAT PHRA KAEW DON TAO Temple

(วัดพระแก้วดอนเต้า; admission 20B; ⌚6am-6pm) From 1436 to 1468, this wát was among four in northern Thailand to previously house the Emerald Buddha (now in Bangkok's Wat Phra Kaew, see p74). The main *chedi* (stupa) shows Hariphunchai influence, while the adjacent *mon·dòp* (the small square, spired building in a wát) was built in 1909. The *mon·dòp*, decorated with glass mosaic in typical Burmese style, contains a Mandalay-style Buddha image. A display of Lanna artefacts (mostly religious paraphernalia and woodwork) can be viewed in the wát's **Lanna Museum (admission by donation; ⌚7am-6pm)**.

BAAN SAO NAK Museum

(บ้านเสานัก; 85 Th Radwattana; admission 50B; ⌚10am-5pm) In the old Wiang Neua (North City) section of town, Baan Sao Nak was built in 1895 in the traditional Lanna style. A huge teak house supported by 116 square teak pillars, it was once owned by a local *kun·yĭng* (a title equivalent to 'Lady' in England); it now serves as a local museum. The entire house is furnished with Burmese and Thai antiques, but the real treasure is the structure itself and its manicured garden.

Activities

HORSE CARTS Guided Tour

Lampang is known throughout Thailand as Meuang Rot Mah (Horse Cart City) because it's the only town in Thailand where horse carts are still found, although nowadays they are exclusively used for tourists. A 15-minute horse-cart tour around town costs 150B; for 200B you can get a half-hour tour that goes along the Mae Wang.

SAMAKHOM SAMUNPHRAI PHAK NEUA Massage

(no roman-script sign; ☎08 9758 2396; 149 Th Pratuma; massage per hr 300B, sauna 150B; ⏰8am-7.30pm) Next to Wat Hua Khuang in the Wiang Neua area, accessible via Th Pamaikhet, this rustic place offers traditional northern-Thai massage and herbal saunas. A motorcycle taxi ride here should cost about 20B.

Shopping

WALKING STREET Market

Perhaps wanting to emulate the success of Chiang Mai's street markets, Lampang now has its own along the charming Th Talad Gao (also known as Kat Korng Ta). Dotted with old shophouses showcasing English, Chinese and Burmese architectural styles, the street is closed to traffic on Saturday and Sunday from 4pm to 10pm and fills up with souvenir, handicraft and food stalls. A similar **Cultural Street** is held on Th Wang Nuea from 6am to 9am on Sunday and 6pm to 9pm on Friday.

Sleeping

RIVERSIDE GUEST HOUSE Guest House $$

(☎0 5422 7005; www.theriverside-lampang.com; 286 Th Talad Gao; r 350-900B, ste 1800B; ❄ 📶) Although still within budget range, this leafy compound of refurbished wooden houses is by far the most pleasant place to stay in Lampang.

WIENGLAKOR HOTEL Hotel $$$

(☎0 5431 6430-5; www.wienglakor.com; 138/35 Th Phahonyothin; r 1000-1700B, ste 3000B, incl breakfast; ❄ @ 📶) If you're going to go upscale, this is Lampang's best choice. The lobby is tastefully decorated in a teak and northern Thai temple theme, a design that continues into the rooms.

Walking Street, Lampang

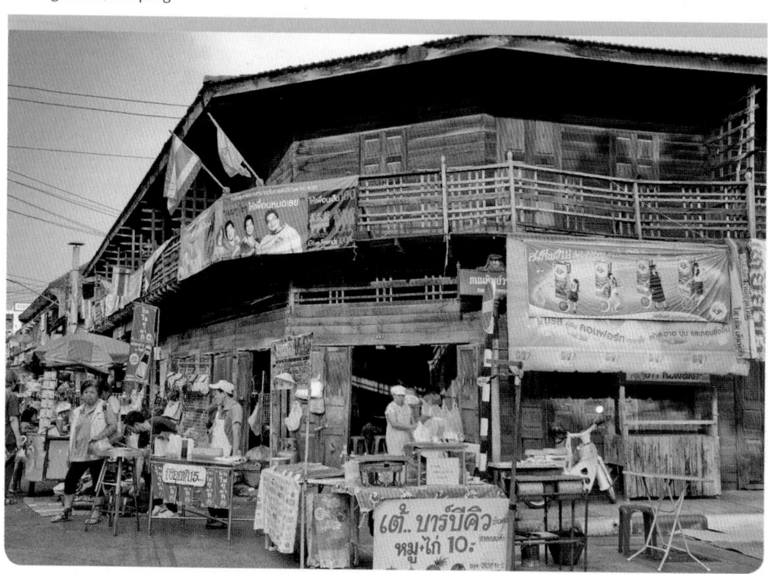

KYLIE MCLAUGHLIN/LONELY PLANET IMAGES ©

Detour: Thai Elephant Conservation Center

Located in Amphoe Hang Chat, 33km from Lampang, this unique facility (**ศูนย์อนุรักษ์ช้างไทย; TECC; 0 5424 7876; www.thailandelephant.org; child/adult incl shuttle bus 40/80B; elephant bathing 9.45am & 1.15pm, public shows 10am, 11am & 1.30pm**) promotes the role of the Asian elephant in ecotourism, and also provides medical treatment and care for sick elephants from all over Thailand.

The elephant show at this 122-hectare centre is less touristy and more educational than most, focusing on how elephants work with logs, as well as the usual painting of pictures and playing oversized xylophones.

For those keen on delving deeper into pachyderm culture, TECC's **Mahout Training School** (**0 5424 7875; www.thailandelephant.org; 1/2/3/30 days 3500/5800/8500/100,000B**) offers an array of scholarships ranging in duration from one day to one month, all with the aim of making you a bona-fide *kwahn cháhng* (elephant caretaker) or mahout.

PIN HOTEL Hotel $$
(**0 5422 1509; 8 Th Suandawg; r 600-900B, ste 1300-1800B, incl breakfast;**) Spotless, spacious and secluded, the rooms here come decked out with cable TV, minibar and large bathrooms. A solid midrange choice.

Eating

For a relatively small town, Lampang boasts a pretty strong repertoire of restaurants, ranging from northern Thai to Western fare, and a few things in between.

Self-caterers or those interested in local eats will want to check out Lampang's **evening market** (**Th Ratsada; 4-8pm**) where steaming baskets of sticky rice and dozens of sides to dip it in are on daily display.

AROY ONE BAHT Thai $
(**cnr Th Suandawg & Th Thipchang; mains 15-40B; 4pm-midnight**) Some nights it can seem like just about everybody in Lampang has gathered at this rambling wooden house, and understandably so: the food is tasty and embarrassingly cheap, the service lightning fast, and the setting in a wooden house-cum-balcony-cum-garden heaps of fun.

PAPONG Northern Thai $
(**125 Th Talad Gao; mains 30-40B; lunch & dinner**) Be sure to stop by this popular local haunt serving *kà·nŏm jeen* (fresh rice noodles topped with various curries). You can't miss it (simply look for a row of bubbling curries in earthenware pots), and ordering is a snap (simply point to whatever looks good)

RIVERSIDE BAR & RESTAURANT International-Thai $$
(**328 Th Thipchang; mains 80-210B; lunch & dinner**) This wooden shack that appears to be on the verge of tumbling into the Mae Wang is extremely popular with visiting and resident foreigners. Live music, a full bar and an expansive menu of local and Western dishes bring in the crowds.

Khun Manee

Lampang is known for its addictive *kôw đaan*, deep-fried rice cakes drizzled with palm sugar, the making of which can be observed at this homey **factory** (**no roman-script sign; 35 Th Ratsada**) off Th Ratsada – look for the yellow arrow.

Information

There are many banks with ATMs along Th Boonyawat, including Siam City Bank and Krung Thai Bank.

M@cnet **(Th Chatchai; per hr 15B; 9am-10pm)** Internet access.

Post office **(Th Prisnee; 8.30am-4.30pm Mon-Fri, 9am-noon Sat)**

Sanuksabai **(8 Th Suandawg; 8am-5pm Mon-Sat)** Next door to Pin Hotel, this agency can arrange air tickets, saving you the trouble of a trip to the airport.

Tourism Authority of Thailand office **(TAT; nationwide call centre 1672, Lampang 0 5423 7229; Th Thakhrao Noi; 10am-4pm Mon-Sat)** The helpful folks here can provide a decent map of the area and details about local sights and activities.

Getting There & Away

Air

Lampang's airport is about 1.5km from the centre of town, at the east end of Asia 1 Hwy. *Sŏrng·tăa·ou* from the airport to downtown cost 50B.

Bangkok Airways **(nationwide call centre 1771, Lampang 0 5482 1522; www.bangkokair.com; Lampang Airport)** conducts flights between Lampang and Bangkok's Suvarnabhumi Airport (2405B, one hour, once daily), and Lampang and Sukhothai (1915B, 30 minutes, once daily).

Bus

The bus terminal in Lampang is nearly 2km from the centre of town, at the corner of Asia 1 Hwy and Th Chantarasurin – 20B by shared *sŏrng·tăa·ou*.

Train

Lampang's historic train station **(0 5421 7024; Th Phahonyothin)** dates back to 1916 and is a fair hike from most accommodation. Major destinations from Lampang include Bangkok (256B to 1272B, 12 hours, six times daily) and Chiang Mai (23B to 50B, three hours, six times daily).

CHIANG RAI PROVINCE

Chiang Rai เชียงราย

POP 62,000

If you take the time to know it, Chiang Rai is a small but delightful city with a relaxed atmosphere, good value accommodation and some tasty eats. It's also the logical base from which to plan excursions to the more remote corners of the province.

Founded by Phaya Mengrai in 1262 as part of the Lao-Thai Lanna kingdom, Chiang Rai didn't become a Siamese territory until 1786, then a province in 1910.

Sights

OUB KHAM MUSEUM Museum

(พิพิธภัณฑ์อูบคำ; www.oubkhammuseum.com; 81/1 Military Front Rd; adult/child 300/200B; 8am-6pm) This privately owned museum houses an impressive collection of

Thai food

JOHN ELK III/LONELY PLANET IMAGES ©

Buses from Lampang

DESTINATION	FARE (B)	DURATION (HR)	FREQUENCY
Bangkok	347-625	9	frequent departures 7.30-11.30am & 6.30-9pm
Chiang Mai	67-134	2	every hr 8am-8.30pm
Chiang Rai	143	3½	3.30pm, 6.30pm & 9.30pm
Phitsanulok	193	4½	every hr 5am-7pm
Sukhothai	162	3½	every hr 5am-7pm

paraphernalia from virtually every corner of the former Lanna kingdom. The items, some of which truly are one of a kind, range from a monkey bone food taster used by Lanna royalty to an impressive carved throne from Chiang Tung, Myanmar (Burma). Guided tours (available in English) are obligatory, and include a walk through a gilded artificial cave holding several Buddha statues, complete with disco lights and fake torches.

The Oub Kham Museum is 2km outside of the centre town and can be a bit tricky to find; túk-túks (pronounced *đúk dúk*) will go here for about 50B.

HILLTRIBE MUSEUM & EDUCATION CENTER Museum

(พิพิธภัณฑ์และศูนย์การศึกษาชาวเขา; Map p192; www.pdacr.org; 3rd fl, 620/25 Th Thanalai; admission 50B; 9am-6pm Mon-Fri, 10am-6pm Sat & Sun) This museum and handicrafts centre is a good place to visit before undertaking any hill-tribe trek. The centre, run by the non-profit Population & Community Development Association (PDA), is underwhelming in its visual presentation, but contains a wealth of information on Thailand's various tribes and the issues that surround them. The curator is passionate about his museum, and will talk about the different hill tribes, their histories, recent trends and the community projects that the museum helps fund. The PDA also runs highly recommended treks.

WAT PHRA KAEW Temple

(วัดพระแก้ว; Map p192; admission free) Originally called Wat Pa Yia (Bamboo Forest Monastery) in the local dialect, this is the city's most revered Buddhist temple. Legend has it that in 1434 lightning struck the temple's octagonal *chedi,* which fell apart to reveal the Phra Kaew Morakot, or Emerald Buddha (actually made of jade). After a long journey that included a long stopover in Vientiane, Laos (see boxed text, p75), this national talisman is now ensconced in the temple of the same name in Bangkok.

Activities

Nearly every guest house and hotel in Chiang Rai offers trekking trips, typically in the Doi Tung, Doi Mae Salong and Chiang Khong areas. Rates at the places below range from 2500B to 4300B per person for two people for a two-night trek.

The following agencies have a reputation for operating responsible treks and cultural tours, and in some cases profits from the treks go directly to community-development projects.

MIRROR FOUNDATION Trekking

(0 5373 7616; www.themirrorfoundation.org; 106 Moo 1, Ban Huay Khom, Tambon Mae Yao) Although its rates are higher than others', trekking with this nonprofit NGO helps support the training of its local guides. Treks range from one to three days, and

Chiang Rai

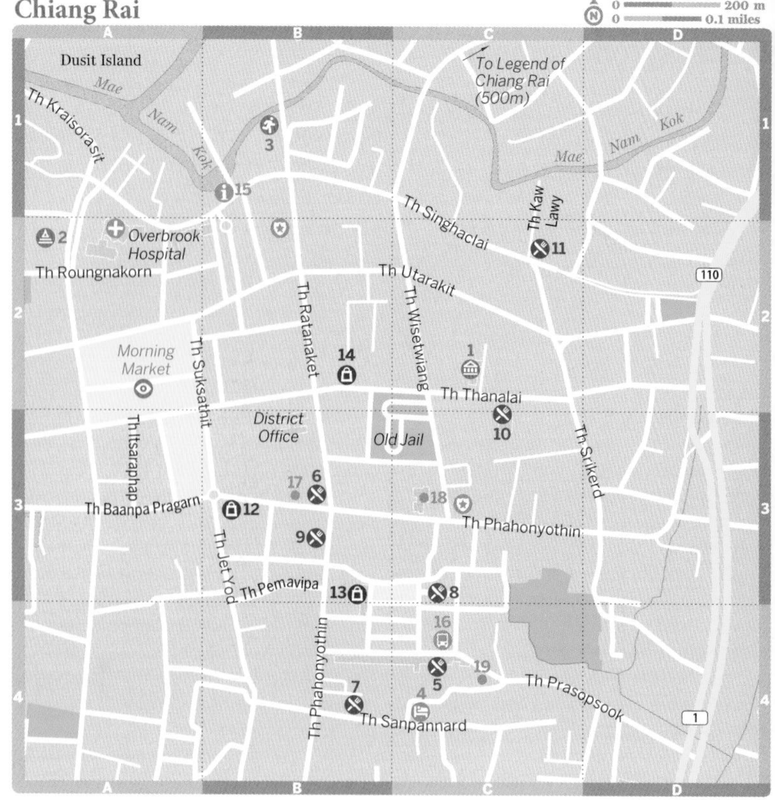

Chiang Rai

Sights

1 Hilltribe Museum & Education Center C2
2 Wat Phra Kaew A2

Activities, Courses & Tours

3 Akha Hill House B1
PDA Tours & Travel .... (see 1)

Sleeping

4 Baan Warabordee C4

Eating

5 BaanChivitMai Bakery C4
6 Doi Chaang B3
7 Nam Ngiaw Paa Nuan B4
8 Night Market C3
9 Old Dutch B3
10 Phu-Lae C3
11 Somkhuan Khao Soi C2

Shopping

12 Fair Trade Shop B3
13 Night Bazaar B3
14 Walking Street B2

Information

15 Tourism Authority of Thailand Office B1

Transport

16 Bus Terminal C4
17 Fat Free B3
18 North Wheels C3
19 Sombat Tour C4

traverse the Akha, Karen and Lahu villages of Mae Yao, north of Chiang Rai.

PDA TOURS & TRAVEL Trekking
(Map p192; 0 5374 0088; www.pda.or.th/chiangrai/package_tour.htm; 3rd fl, 620/25 Th Thanalai, Hilltribe Museum & Education Center; 9am-6pm Mon-Fri, 10am-6pm Sat & Sun) One- to three-day treks are available through this NGO, the profits from which go back into community projects that include HIV/AIDS education, mobile health clinics, education scholarships and the establishment of village-owned banks.

AKHA HILL HOUSET Trekking
(Map p192; 08 9997 5505; www.akhahill.com; Akha River House) This outfit does one- to seven-day treks. They begin with a long-tail boat up the river, before trekking to and around their Akha Hill House about 23km from Chiang Rai, at a height of 1500m. A portion of the profits from the guest houses and their activities go to a local school.

If You Like... Cafe Culture

For such a relatively small town, Chiang Rai has an abundance of high-quality, Western-style cafes. This is largely due to the fact that many of Thailand's best coffee beans are grown in the more remote corners of the province. Some of the more interesting choices include the following:

1 **BAANCHIVITMAI BAKERY**
(Map p192; www.baanchivitmai.com; Th Prasopsook; 7am-9pm Mon-Sat; ❄ @ wi-fi) In addition to a very well-prepared cup of local coffee, you can snack on amazingly authentic Swedish-style sweets at this popular bakery. Profits go to BaanChivitMai, an organisation that runs homes and education projects for vulnerable, orphaned or AIDS-affected children.

2 **DOI CHAANG**
(Map p192; 542/2 Th Ratanaket; 7am-11pm; ❄ @ wi-fi) Doi Chaang is the leading brand among Chiang Rai coffees, and its beans are now sold as far abroad as Canada and Europe.

Sleeping

The two main areas for accommodation are in the centre, clustered around Th Jet Yod and off Th Phahonyothin.

LEGEND OF CHIANG RAI Hotel **$$$**
(off Map p192; 0 5391 0400; www.thelegend-chiangrai.com; 124/15 Moo 21, Th Kohloy; r 3900-5900B, villa 8100B; ❄ @ wi-fi pool) One of the few hotels in town to take advantage of a river location, this upscale resort feels like a traditional Lanna village. Each has a pleasant outdoor sitting area, frosted glass for increased privacy and a cool, outdoor-like bathroom with an oversized shower; villas have small private pools.

BAAN WARABORDEE Hotel **$$**
(Map p192; 0 5375 4488; baanwarabordee@hotmail.com; 59/1 Th Sanpannard; r 600-800B; ❄ @ wi-fi) A delightful small hotel has been made from this modern three-storey Thai villa. Rooms are cool and come decked out in dark woods and light cloths. The owners are friendly and can help with local advice.

Eating

The night market has a decent collection of food stalls offering snacks and meals, from deep-fried wontons to fresh fish. Choose a dish and sit at the nearby tables, or step inside one of several restaurants on and off Th Phahonyothin by the night market.

LUNG EED LOCOL FOOD Northern Thai **$**
(Th Watpranorn; mains 30-60B; 11.45am-9pm Mon-Sat) There's an English-language menu on the wall, but don't miss the sublime *lâhp gài* (minced chicken fried with herbs and topped with crispy deep-fried shallots and garlic). The restaurant is on

Northern Nosh

Traditionally, the residents of Thailand's north ate almost exclusively *kôw něe·o,* sticky rice, known in the local dialect as *kôw nêung*. Coconut milk rarely makes its way into the northern kitchen, and northern Thai cuisine is probably the least spicy of Thailand's regional schools of cooking, often relying on bitter or bitter/hot flavours instead.

There are relatively few restaurants serving northern-style dishes, and the vast majority of authentic local food is sold from stalls in 'to go' bags. However, if you manage to come across a local restaurant, some must-try dishes include:

- *Gaang hang·lair* – Burmese in origin (*hang* is a corruption of the Burmese *hin,* meaning curry), this rich pork curry is often seen at festivals and ceremonies.
- *Kâap mŏo* – deep-fried pork crackling is a common – and delicious – side dish in northern Thailand.
- *Kôw soy* – this popular curry-based noodle dish is most likely Burmese in origin, and was probably introduced to northern Thailand by travelling Chinese merchants.
- *Kà·nŏm jeen nám ngée·o* – fresh rice noodles served with a spaghetti-like pork- and tomato-based broth.
- *Lâhp kôo·a* – literally 'fried *lâhp*', this dish takes the famous Thai minced-meat 'salad' and fries it with a mixture of local bitter/hot dried spices and herbs.
- *Nám prík nùm* – green chillies, shallots and garlic that are grilled then mashed into a paste served with sticky rice, parboiled veggies and deep-fried pork crackling.
- *Nám prík òrng* – a chilli dip of Shan origin made from tomatoes and minced pork – a northern Thai bolognese of sorts.

Th Watpranorn near the intersection with the Superhighway.

NAM NGIAW PAA NUAN Vietnamese-Northern Thai $
(Map p192; Th Sanpannard; mains 10-100B; ⌚9am-5pm) This somewhat concealed place serves a unique mix of Vietnamese and northern Thai dishes. Tasty food, friendly service and a barn-like atmosphere make us wish they served them for dinner as well.

PAA SUK Northern Thai $
(no roman-script sign; Th Sankhongnoi; mains 10-25B; ⌚8am-3pm Mon-Sat) This immensely popular third-generation restaurant specialises in the local dish *kà·nŏm jeen nám ngée·o* (a thin broth of pork or beef and tomatoes served over fresh rice noodles). The restaurant is between Soi 4 and Soi 5 of Th Sankhongnoi (the street is called Th Sathanpayabarn where it intersects with Th Phahonyothin); look for the yellow sign.

PHU-LAE Northern Thai $$
(Map p192; 673/1 Th Thanalai; mains 80-320B; ⌚lunch & dinner; ❄) This air-conditioned restaurant is exceedingly popular with Thai tourists for its tasty, but slightly gentrified northern Thai fare. Recommended local dishes include the *gaang hang·lair,* pork belly in a rich Burmese-style curry, here served with pickled garlic, and *sâi òo·a,* herb-packed sausages.

OLD DUTCH Dutch-International $$
(Map p192; 541 Th Phahonyothin; mains 150-300B; ❄) This cosy, foreigner-friendly restaurant is a good choice if you're tired of rice. There's a variety of well-done

Dutch and other Western-style dishes, as well as a good attached bakery.

SOMKHUAN KHAO SOI Northern Thai $

(Map p192; Th Singhaclai; mains 25B; ⏲8am-3pm Mon-Fri) Friendly Mr Somkhuan serves a tasty bowl of *kôw soy* (a northern Thai curry noodle dish) from a basic street stall under two giant trees.

Shopping

WALKING STREET Market

(Map p192; Th Thanalai; ⏲4-10pm Sat) If you're around on a Saturday evening be sure not to miss the open-air Walking Street, an expansive street market focusing on all things Chiang Rai, from handicrafts to local dishes. The market spans Th Thanalai from the Hilltribe Museum to the morning market.

FAIR TRADE SHOP Handicrafts

(Map p192; www.ttcrafts.co.th; 528/8 Th Baanpa Pragarn; ⏲9am-5pm Mon-Sat) Bright hill-tribe cloths and knick-knacks are available at this shop, the profits of which go to various development projects.

NIGHT BAZAAR Market

(Map p192; ⏲6-11pm) Adjacent to the bus station off Th Phahonyothin is Chiang Rai's night market. On a much smaller scale than Chiang Mai's, it is nevertheless a decent place to find an assortment of handicrafts.

Information

Medical Services

Overbrook Hospital **(Map p192; ☎0 5371 1366; www.overbrookhospital.com; Th Singhaclai)** English is spoken at this modern hospital.

Getting There & Away

Air

Chiang Rai Airport **(☎0 5379 8000)** The airport is 8km north of the city. Taxis run into town from the airport for 200B.

Bangkok's Don Muang Airport (1550B, 1¼ hours, twice daily) via **One-Two-Go** **(Orient Thai; ☎nationwide call centre 1126; www.flyorientthai.com; Chiang Rai Airport)**

Bangkok's Suvarnabhumi Airport (2164B to 3120B, 1¼ hours, six times daily) via **Air Asia** **(☎nationwide call centre 02 515 9999, Chiang Rai 0 5379 3543; www.airasia.com; Chiang Rai airport)** and **THAI** **(☎nationwide call centre 02 356 1111; www.thaiair.com)** City Centre **(☎0 5371 1179; 870 Th Phahonyothin; ⏲8am-5pm Mon-Fri)** Airport Office **(☎0 5379 8202; ⏲8am-8pm)**

Chiang Mai (1399B, 40 minutes, twice daily) via **Kan Air** **(☎nationwide call centre 02 551 6111, Chiang Rai 0 5379 3339; www.kanairlines.com; Chiang Rai Airport)**

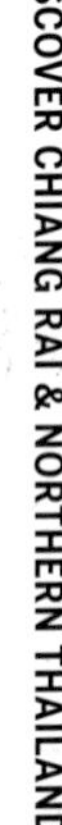

Northen Thai–style food
AUSTIN BUSH/LONELY PLANET IMAGES ©

Detour: Wat Rong Khun

Thirteen kilometres south of Chiang Rai is the unusual and popular **Wat Rong Khun** (วัดร่องขุ่น; 'White Wat'; admission free). Whereas most temples have centuries of history, this one's construction began in 1997 by noted Thai painter-turned-architect Chalermchai Kositpipat.

Seen from a distance, the temple appears to be made of glittering porcelain; a closer look reveals that the look is due to a combination of whitewash and clear-mirrored chips. Walk over a bridge and sculpture of reaching arms (symbolising desire) to enter the sanctity of the wát where instead of the traditional Buddha life scenarios, the artist has painted contemporary scenes representing *samsara* (the realm of rebirth and delusion).

To get to the temple, hop on one of the regular buses that run from Chiang Rai to Chiang Mai or Phayao and ask to get off at Wat Rong Khun (20B).

Getting Around

A túk-túk ride anywhere within central Chiang Rai should cost around 40B. Shared *sŏrng·tăa·ou* cost 20B per person.

Bicycle rental can be arranged at Fat Free (☎0 5375 2532; 542/2 Th Baanpa Pragarn; per day 80-450B; ⏰8.30am-6pm). Motorcycles can be hired at ST Motorcycle (☎0 5371 3652; 1025/34-35 Th Jet Yod; per day 150-1000B; ⏰8am-8pm) – they take good care of their bikes.

The following car rental companies have offices in Chiang Rai.

North Wheels (☎0 5374 0585; www.northwheels.com; 591 Th Phahonyothin; ⏰8am-6pm)

Thai Rent A Car (☎0 5379 3393; www.thairentacar.com; Chiang Rai Airport; ⏰7am-6pm)

Mae Salong (Santikhiri) แม่สลอง (สันติคีรี)

POP 20,000

For a taste of China without crossing any international borders, head to this atmospheric village perched on the back hills of Chiang Rai.

Sights

Markets

A tiny but interesting **morning market** convenes from 6am to 8am at the T-intersection near Shin Sane Guest House. The market attracts town residents and tribespeople from the surrounding districts. An **all-day market** forms at the southern end of town, and unites vendors selling hill-tribe handicrafts, shops selling tea and a few basic restaurants.

Temples

To soak up the great views from **Wat Santakhiri**, go past the market and ascend 718 steps (or drive if you have a car). The wát is of the Mahayana tradition and Chinese in style.

Past the Khumnaiphol Resort and further up the hill is a **viewpoint** with some teashops, and a famous Kuomintang (KMT) general's **tomb**. It is sometimes guarded by a soldier who will describe (in Thai or Yunnanese) the history of the KMT in the area. In the same vein and south of the turn-off to the tomb is the **Chinese Martyr's Memorial Museum**, an elaborate Chinese-style building that is more memorial than museum.

Buses from Chiang Rai

Buses bound for destinations within Chiang Rai Province, as well as slow fan-cooled buses bound for Chiang Mai and Lampang, depart from the bus station in the centre of town.

To Bangkok, **Sombat Tour** (☎0 5371 4971; Th Prasopsook; ⊙6am-7pm) has an office across from the interprovincial bus terminal, but only VIP buses can be boarded here; all other Bangkok-bound buses depart from the new bus station.

DESTINATION	FARE (B)	DURATION (HR)	FREQUENCY
Chiang Khong	65	2½	every hr 5.20am-5.45pm
Chiang Mai	142	7	every 45min 6.30am-noon
Chiang Saen	32	1½	every 20min 6.20am-6.30pm
Lampang	102	5	every 45min 6.30am-noon
Mae Sai	39	1½	every 20min 6am-8pm

If you're heading beyond Chiang Rai (or you're in a hurry), you'll have to go to the **new bus station** (☎0 5377 3989), 5km south of town on Hwy 1. *Sŏrng·tăa·ou* linking it and the old bus station run from 5am to 9pm (10B, 20 minutes).

DESTINATION	FARE (B)	DURATION (HR)	FREQUENCY
Bangkok	448-716	11-12	every hr 7-11.30am & 6.30-9pm
Chiang Mai	142-263	3-7	every hr 6.30am-5.45pm
Kamphaeng Phet	280	7	7am, 8.30am, 1pm
Khon Kaen	316-553	11-12	9am, 10.15am, every 2hr 2pm-9pm
Nakhon Ratchasima (Khorat)	473-710	12-13	6.15am, 11.30am, 1.30pm, 3.30pm, 5pm, 7pm
Lampang	102-286	4-5	every hr 6am-3.45pm
Mae Sai	26-84	1-1½	every 15min 6am-6pm
Mae Sot	354-455	12	7.45am, 8.15am
Phayao	44-141	1½-2	every hr 6am-7.30pm
Phrae	148-244	4	every hr 6am-7.30pm
Phitsanulok	249-374	6-7	every hr 6am-7.30pm
Sukhothai	223-244	8	7.30am, 8.30am, 10.30am, 2.30pm

Activities

Shin Sane Guest House and Little Home Guesthouse have free maps showing approximate trekking routes to Akha, Lisu, Mien, Lahu and Shan villages in the area.

Shin Sane Guest House arranges four-hour **horseback treks** to four nearby villages for 500B for about three or four hours.

Eating

The very Chinese breakfast of *Ƀah·tôrng·gŏh* (deep-fried fingers of dough) and hot soybean milk at the morning market is an inspiring way to start the day. In fact, many Thai tourists come to Mae Salong simply to eat Yunnanese dishes such as *màn·tŏh* (steamed Chinese buns) served with braised pork leg and pickled vegetables,

Home Away From Home

Mae Salong was originally settled by the 93rd Regiment of the Kuomintang (KMT), who had fled to Myanmar (Burma) from China after the 1949 Chinese revolution. The renegades were forced to leave Myanmar in 1961 when the Yangon government decided it wouldn't allow the KMT to remain legally in northern Myanmar. Crossing into northern Thailand with their pony caravans, the ex-soldiers and their families settled into mountain villages and re-created a society like the one they'd left behind in Yunnan.

After the Thai government granted the KMT refugee status in the 1960s, efforts were made to incorporate the Yunnanese KMT and their families into the Thai nation. Until the late 1980s, they didn't have much success. Many ex-KMT persisted in involving themselves in the Golden Triangle opium trade in a three-way partnership with opium warlord Khun Sa and the Shan United Army (SUA). Because of the rough, mountainous terrain and lack of sealed roads, the outside world was rather cut off from the goings-on in Mae Salong, so the Yunnanese were able to ignore attempts by the Thai authorities to suppress opium activity and tame the region.

In an attempt to quash opium activity, and the more recent threat of *yah bâh* (methamphetamine) trafficking, the Thai government has created crop-substitution programs to encourage hill tribes to cultivate tea, coffee, corn and fruit trees.

or black chicken braised with Chinese-style herbs. Homemade wheat and egg noodles are another speciality of Mae Salong, and are served with a local broth that combines pork and a spicy chilli paste. They're available at several places in town.

Countless teahouses sell locally grown teas (mostly oolong and jasmine) and offer complimentary tastings.

SUE HAI Chinese $
(mains 60-150B; ⏲7am-9pm) This very simple family-run teashop-cum-Yunnanese restaurant has an English-language menu of local specialities including local mushroom fried with soy sauce or delicious air-dried pork fried with fresh chilli. They also do filling and tasty bowls of homemade noodles. It's roughly in the middle of town.

NONG IM PHOCHANA Chinese $
(mains 60-150B; ⏲lunch & dinner) Located directly across from Khumnaiphol Resort at the southern end of town, the menu at this open-air restaurant emphasises dishes using local veggies.

Getting There & Away

To get to Mae Salong by bus, take a Mae Sai–bound bus from Chiang Rai to Ban Pasang (20B, 30 minutes, every 20 minutes from 6am to 4pm). From Ban Pasang, blue *sŏrng·tăa·ou* head up the mountain to Mae Salong (60B, one hour, 7am to 5pm). To get back to Ban Pasang, *sŏrng·tăa·ou* park near the 7-Eleven. *Sŏrng·tăa·ou* stop running at around 5pm but you can charter one in either direction for about 500B.

Mae Sai แม่สาย

POP 22,000

At first glance, Thailand's northernmost town, Mae Sai, appears to be little more than a large open-air market. But the city serves as a base for exploring the Golden Triangle, Doi Tung and Mae Salong.

Sleeping

KHANTHONGKHAM HOTEL Hotel **$$**
(0 5373 4222; www.kthotel.com; 7 Th Phahonyothin; r 800-950B, ste 1300-1650B;) This hotel features huge rooms that have been tastefully decorated in light woods and brown textiles. A downside is that many rooms don't have windows.

Eating

An expansive **night market** (5-11pm) unfolds every evening along Th Phahonyothin. During the day, several **snack & drink vendors** (Th Phahonyothin) can be found in front of the police station.

BISMILLAH HALAL FOOD Muslim-Thai **$**
(Soi 4, Th Phahonyothin; mains 25-40B; 6am-6pm) Run by Burmese Muslims, this tiny restaurant does an excellent *biryani*, not to mention virtually everything else Muslim, from roti to samosa.

Shopping

Commerce is ubiquitous in Mae Sai, although most of the offerings are of little interest to Western travellers. One popular commodity is gems, and dealers from as far away as Chanthaburi frequent the small gem market that is opposite the police station. A walk down Soi 4 will reveal several open-air gem dealers diligently counting hundreds of tiny semiprecious stones on the side of the street.

Getting There & Away

On the main Th Phahonyothin road, by Soi 8, is a sign saying 'bus stop'. From here *sŏrng·tăa·ou* stop in Sop Ruak (45B, every 40 minutes 8am to 1pm), terminating in Chiang Saen (50B).

If you're headed to Bangkok, you can avoid going all the way to the bus station by buying your tickets at **Chok-Roong Tawee Tour** (no roman-script sign; 0 5364 0123; near cnr Th Phahonyothin & Soi 9; 8am-5.30pm) – it's next door to the motorcycle dealership.

Destinations from Mae Sai include the following:

Bangkok (483B to 966B, 13 hours, frequent departures from 4pm to 5.45pm)

Food market, Mae Sai

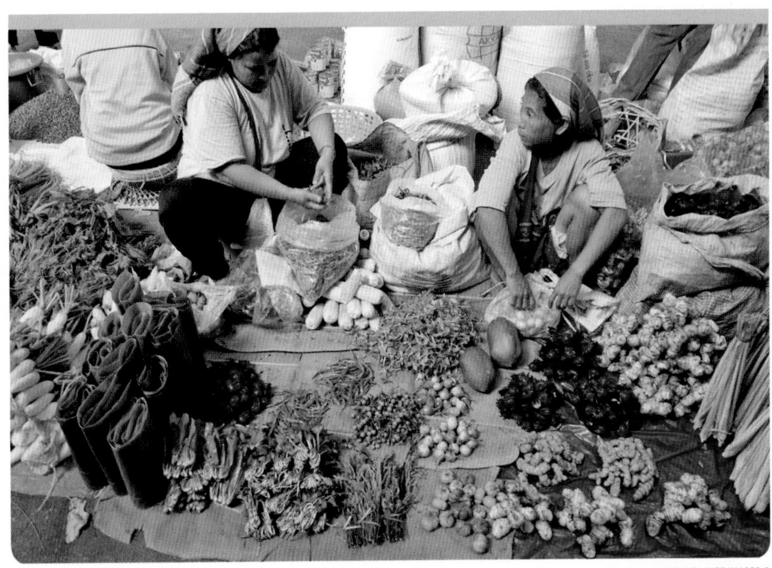

AUSTIN BUSH/LONELY PLANET IMAGES ©

Chiang Mai (165B to 320B, five hours, five departures from 6.45am to 3.30pm)

Chiang Rai (39B, 1½ hours, every 20 minutes from 5.45am to 8pm)

Chiang Saen เชียงแสน

POP 11,000

The dictionary definition of a sleepy river town, Chiang Saen was the site of a Thai kingdom thought to date back to as early as the 7th century. Scattered throughout the modern town are the ruins of the former empire – surviving architecture includes several *chedi*, Buddha images, *wí·hăhn* pillars and earthen city ramparts. Chiang Saen later became loosely affiliated with various northern Thai kingdoms, as well as 18th-century Myanmar (Burma), and never became a Siamese possession until the 1880s.

Today huge river barges from China moor at Chiang Saen, carrying fruit, engine parts and all manner of other imports, keeping the old China–Siam trade route open.

Sights & Activities

WAT CHEDI LUANG Temple

(วัดเจดีย์หลวง; **admission free**) Behind the museum to the east are the ruins of Wat Chedi Luang, which features an 18m octagonal *chedi* in the classic Chiang Saen or Lanna style. Archaeologists argue about its exact construction date but agree it dates to some time between the 12th and 14th centuries.

WAT PA SAK Temple

(วัดป่าสัก; **admission free**) About 200m from the **Pratu Chiang Saen** (the historic main gateway to the town's western flank) are the remains of Wat Pa Sak, where the ruins of seven monuments are visible in a **historical park** (admission 50B). The main mid-14th-century *chedi* combines elements of the Hariphunchai and Sukhothai styles with a possible Bagan influence, and it still holds a great deal of attractive stucco relief work.

WAT PHRA THAT CHOM KITTI & WAT CHOM CHANG Temple

(วัดพระธาตุจอมกิตติ; **admission free**) The remains of Wat Phra That Chom Kitti and Wat Chom Chang can be found about 2.5km north of Wat Pa Sak on a hilltop. The round *chedi* of Wat Phra That Chom Kitti is thought to have been constructed before the founding of the kingdom. The smaller *chedi* below it belonged to Wat Chom Chang. There is nothing much to see at these *chedi*, but there is a good view of Chiang Saen and the river.

WAT PHA KHAO PAN Temple

(วัดผ้าขาวป้าน; **admission free**) Inside the grounds of Wat Pha Khao Pan, a living wát near the river, stands a magnificent Lanna-period *chedi*. The large, square base contains Lanna-style walking Buddhas in niches on all four sides. The Buddha facing east is sculpted in the *mudra* ('calling for rain') pose, with both hands held pointing down at the image's sides – a pose common in Laos but not so common in Thailand.

CHIANG SAEN NATIONAL MUSEUM Museum

(พิพิธภัณฑสถานแห่งชาติเชียงแสน; **702 Th Phahonyothin; admission 100B; 8.30am-4.30pm Wed-Sun**) Near the town entrance, this museum is a great source of local information considering its relatively small size.

MEKONG RIVER TRIPS River Cruise

Five-passenger speedboats leave from the waterfront jet to Sop Ruak (per boat one-way/return 500/600B, one hour).

Sleeping

CHIANG SAEN RIVER HILL HOTEL Hotel $$

(**0 5365 0826; www.chiangsaenriverhill.net; 714 Th Sukapibansai; r incl breakfast 1200B;**) Although the pink exterior and floor tiles don't exactly complement the northern-Thai furnishing touches, this is still probably the best place in town. Rooms are large and equipped with TV, fridge and a small area for relaxing.

Eating & Drinking

Cheap noodle and rice dishes are available at food stalls in and near the market on the river road and along the main road through town from the highway, near the bus stop. Evening food vendors set up at the latter location and stay open till around midnight.

JINDA'S KITCHEN Northern Thai $

(Rte 1290; mains 20-130B; 8am-4pm) This cosy roadside restaurant has been serving up local dishes for more than 50 years. Try the famous northern noodle dishes *kôw soy* or *kà·nŏm jeen nám ngée·o,* or choose a curry or homemade sausage from the English-language menu. Jinda's Kitchen is roughly halfway between Chiang Saen and Sop Ruak.

KIAW SIANG HAI Chinese $$

(no roman-script sign; 44 Th Rimkhong; mains 50-200B; 8am-8pm) Serving the workers of Chinese boats that dock at Chiang Saen, this authentic Chinese restaurant prepares a huge menu of dishes in addition to the namesake noodle and wonton dishes. Try the spicy Szechuan-style fried tofu or one of the Chinese herbal soups. The restaurant can be located by the giant ceramic jars out front.

Information

Visitors centre (0 5377 7084; Th Phahonyothin; 8.30am-4.30pm) Has a good relief display showing the major ruin sites as well as photos of various *chedi* before, during and after restoration.

Getting There & Away

Blue *sŏrng·tăa·ou* that travel to Sop Ruak (20B) and Mae Sai (50B) wait at a stall at the eastern end of Th Phahonyothin from 7.20am to noon. The green *sŏrng·tăa·ou* bound for Chiang Khong (100B) park at a stall on Th Rimkhong, south of the riverside immigration office, from 7.30am to noon. After noon it's only possible to charter the entire vehicle, which costs between 800B and 1000B.

Chiang Saen has no proper bus terminal, rather there is a covered bus shelter at the eastern end of Th Phahonyothin where buses pick up and drop off passengers. From this stop there are frequent buses to Chiang Rai (37B, 1½ hours, 5.30am to 5pm) and two daily departures to Chiang Mai (2nd class air-con/1st class 165/212B, five hours, 7.15am and 9am).

To Bangkok, **Sombat Tour (08 1595 4616; Th Phahonyothin)** offers approximately 12 seats in a daily VIP bus (920B, 12 hours, 5pm), departing from a small office adjacent to Krung Thai Bank.

Seated Buddha, Chiang Saen

Getting Around

Motorbike taxis and săhm·lór will do short trips around town for 20B. They congregate near and across from the bus stop.

A good way to see the Chiang Saen area is on two wheels. Mountain bikes and motorcycles can be rented at motorcycle rental (08 9429 5798; 247/1 Th Phahonyothin; 9am-5pm) and Angpao Chiangsaen Tour (0 5365 0143; www.angpaochiangsaentour.com; Th Phahonyothin; 9am-8pm). The latter can also provide a vehicle with driver, and conducts a variety of local tours.

PHITSANULOK PROVINCE

Phitsanulok พิษณุโลก

POP 84,000

Phitsanulok sees relatively few independent travellers, but a fair amount of package tourists, perhaps because the city is a convenient base from which to explore the attractions of historical Sukhothai, Si Satchanalai and Kamphaeng Phet.

Sights

WAT PHRA SI RATANA MAHATHAT Temple

(**วัดพระศรีรัตนมหาธาตุ; admission free; 6am-9pm**) The full name of this temple is Wat Phra Si Ratana Mahathat, but the locals call it Wat Phra Si or Wat Yai. The main *wí·hăhn* appears small from the outside, but houses the Phra Phuttha Chinnarat, one of Thailand's most revered and copied Buddha images. This famous bronze statue is probably second in importance only to the Emerald Buddha in Bangkok's Wat Phra Kaew.

The story goes that construction of this wát was commissioned under the reign of King Li Thai in 1357. When it was completed, King Li Thai wanted it to contain three high-quality bronze images, so he sent for well-known sculptors from Si Satchanalai, Chiang Saen and Hariphunchai (Lamphun), as well as five Brahman priests. The first two castings worked well, but the third required three attempts before it was decreed the best of all. Legend has it that a white-robed sage appeared from nowhere to assist

Incense, Wat Phra Si Ratana Mahathat, Phitsanulok

GLENN BEANLAND/LONELY PLANET IMAGES ©

in the final casting, then disappeared. This last image was named the Chinnarat (Victorious King) Buddha and it became the centrepiece in the *wí·hăhn*.

The image was cast in the late Sukhothai style, but what makes it strikingly unique is the flame-like halo around the head and torso that turns up at the bottom to become dragon-serpent heads on either side of the image. The head of this Buddha is a little wider than standard Sukhothai, giving the statue a very solid feel.

Come early (ideally before 7am) if you're looking for quiet contemplation or simply wish to take photos, and regardless of the time, be sure to dress appropriately – no shorts or sleeveless tops.

WAT RATBURANA Temple

(วัดราชบูรณะ; admission free; 6am-8.30pm) Across the street from Wat Phra Si Ratana Mahathat, Wat Ratburana draws fewer visitors but in some ways is more interesting than its famous neighbour. There is a large wooden boat decked with garlands that originally served to transport King Rama V on an official visit to Phitsanulok. Today the boat is thought to grant wishes to those who make an offering and crawl under its entire length three or nine times. Next to the *wí·hăhn* is a sacred tree with ladders on either side that visitors climb up, leave an offering, then ring a bell and descend, repeating the action a total of three or nine times. Directly adjacent to the tree is an immense gong that when rubbed the right way creates a unique ringing sound.

Near each of these attractions you'll find somebody stationed who, in addition to selling the coins, incense and flowers used as offerings, will also instruct visitors in exactly how to conduct each particular ritual, including how many times to pass, what to offer and what prayer to say.

If You Like... Museums

The following museums are south of Phitsanulok on Th Wisut Kasat; a túk-túk here should cost about 60B.

1 **SERGEANT MAJOR THAWEE FOLK MUSEUM**

(26/43 Th Wisut Kasat; adult/child 50/20B; 8.30am-4.30pm) The Sergeant Major Thawee Folk Museum displays a remarkable collection of tools, textiles and photographs from Phitsanulok Province. This fascinating museum is spread throughout five traditional-style Thai buildings with well-groomed gardens, and the displays are all accompanied by informative English descriptions.

2 **BUDDHA CASTING FOUNDRY**

(admission free; 8am-5pm) Across the street and also belonging to Dr Thawee is a small Buddha Casting Foundry where bronze Buddha images of all sizes are cast. Visitors are welcome to watch and there are even detailed photo exhibits demonstrating the lost-wax method of metal casting.

3 **GARDEN BIRDS OF THAILAND**

(adult/child 50/20B; 8.30am-5pm) Attached to the foundry is Dr Thawee's latest project, Garden Birds of Thailand. This collection of aviaries contains indigenous Thai birds including some endangered species, like the very pretty pink-chested jamu fruit-dove, and the prehistoric-looking helmeted hornbill. Unfortunately, the cages are generally rather small and don't reflect the birds' natural environments.

Sleeping

GOLDEN GRAND HOTEL Hotel $$

(0 5521 0234; www.goldengrandhotel.com; 66 Th Thammabucha; r incl breakfast 690-850B;) The rooms are so tidy we're wondering if they've ever even been slept in, and friendly staff and great views of the city from the upper floors provide even more incentive to stay here.

Night market, Phitsanulok

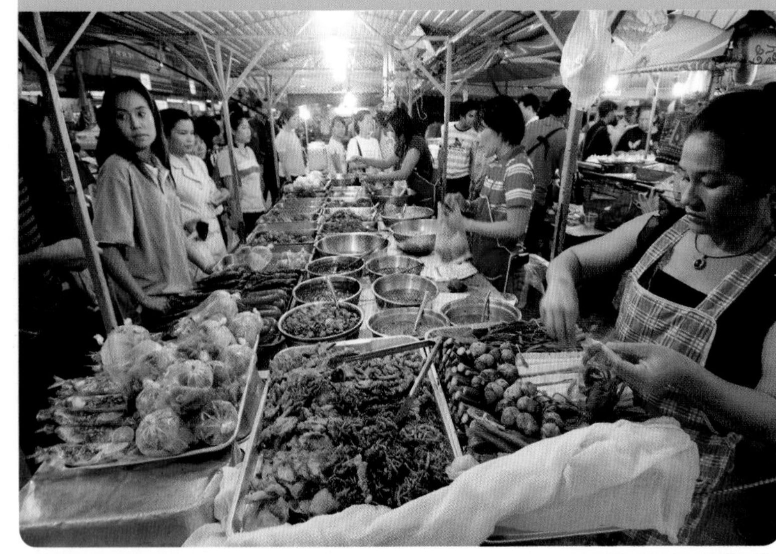

AUSTIN BUSH/LONELY PLANET IMAGES ©

YODIA HERITAGE HOTEL Hotel **$$$**
(08 1613 8496; www.yodiaheritage.com; 89/1 Th Phuttha Bucha; r 2950B, ste 4200-8900B, incl breakfast;) This new boutique hotel takes the crown as Phitsanulok's most upscale accommodation. Located along a quiet stretch of the Mae Nam Nam, suites are huge and feature similarly large tubs and a semiprivate swimming pool.

Eating

Phitsanulok takes its cuisine seriously. The city is particularly obsessive about night markets, and there are no fewer than three dotted in various locations around town. The most well known, Phitsanulok's **Night Bazaar** (mains 40-80B; 5pm-3am), focuses mainly on clothing, but a few riverfront restaurants specialise in *pàk bûng loy fáh* (literally 'floating-in-the-sky morning glory vine'), where the cook fires up a batch of *pàk bûng* in the wok and then flings it through the air to a waiting server who catches it on a plate. If you're lucky, you'll be here when a tour group is trying to catch the flying vegetables, but is actually dropping *pàk bûng* all over the place. Another **night market** (mains 20-40B; 5pm-midnight) lines either side of Th Phra Ong Dam north of Th Authong, and there's a very busy **night market** (mains 20-60B; 4-8pm) just south of the train station that features mostly takeaway items including *kôw nĕe·o hòr,* (tiny banana-leaf parcels of sticky rice with various toppings); there are two vendors opposite each other near the Th Ekathotsarot entrance to the market.

Another dish associated with Phitsanulok is *gŏoay·đĕe·o hôy kăh* (literally, 'legs-hanging' noodles). The name comes from the way customers sit on the floor facing the river, with their legs dangling below. **Rim Nan** (no roman-script sign; 5/4 Th Phaya Sua; mains 20-35B; 9am-4pm), north of Wat Phra Si Ratana Mahathat, is one of a few similar restaurants along Th Phutta Bucha that offer noodles and 'alternative' seating.

BAN MAI Thai **$$**
(93/30 Th Authong; mains 60-150B; 11am-2pm & 5-10pm;) Dinner at this local favourite is like a meal at your grand-parents': opinionated conversation resounds, frumpy furniture abounds, and an overfed Siamese cat appears to

rule the dining room. Don't expect home cooking though; Ban Mai specialises in unusual but perfectly executed dishes that aren't easily found elsewhere, like the *gaang pèt Ъèt yâhng* (a curry of smoked duck) or *yam đà·krái* (lemongrass 'salad').

Information

Golden House Tour (☎0 5525 9973; 55/37-38 Th Borom Trailokanat; ⏰7am-7pm Mon-Sat) This experienced travel agency can book airline tickets and arrange ground transport in and around Phitsanulok.

Tourism Authority of Thailand (TAT; ☎nationwide call centre 1672, Phitsanulok 0 5525 2742; tatphlok@tat.or.th; 209/7-8 Th Borom Trailokanat; ⏰8.30am-4.30pm) Off Th Borom Trailokanat, with helpful staff who hand out free maps of the town and a walking-tour sheet.

Getting There & Away

Air

Phitsanulok's **airport** (☎0 5530 1002) is 5km south of town. Golden House Tour has a board at the airport indicating its minivan service from the airport to hotels (200B per person). Túk-túk go to the airport from town for 150B.

Nok Air (☎nationwide call centre 1318; www.nokair.co.th; Phitsanulok Airport) operates flights between Phitsanulok and Bangkok's Don Muang airport (1290B, 50 minutes, twice daily).

Bus & Minivan

Phitsanulok's **bus station** (☎0 5521 2090) is 2km east of town on Hwy 12.

Train

Phitsanulok's train station is within walking distance of accommodation and offers a left-luggage service. The station is a significant train terminal and virtually every northbound and southbound train stops here; major destinations from Phitsanulok include Bangkok (80B to 1164B, five to seven hours, 11 times daily) and Chiang Mai (143B to 1145B, seven to nine hours, six times daily).

Getting Around

Rides on the town's Darth Vader–like săhm·lór start at about 60B. Outside the train station there's a sign indicating túk-túk prices for different destinations around town.

Budget (☎0 5530 1020; www.budget.co.th) has a car-rental office at the airport that charges from 1500B per day.

SUKHOTHAI PROVINCE

Sukhothai สุโขทัย

POP 37,000

The Sukhothai (Rising of Happiness) Kingdom flourished from the mid-13th century to the late 14th century. This period is often viewed as the 'golden age' of Thai civilisation – the religious art and architecture of the era are considered to

Buses from Phitsanulok

DESTINATION	FARE (B)	DURATION (HR)	FREQUENCY
Bangkok	224-380	5	every hr 7.20am-midnight
Chiang Rai	249-320	5	every hr 8am-midnight
Chiang Mai	211-317	6	every hr 8am-midnight
Kamphaeng Phet	53-74	3	every hr 5am-6pm
Lampang	155-265	4	every hr 8am-midnight
Sukhothai	28-50	1	every hr 5.40am-6pm

be the most classic of Thai styles. The remains of the kingdom, today known as the *meuang gòw* (old city), feature around 45 sq km of partially rebuilt ruins, which are one of the most visited ancient sites in Thailand.

Located 12km east of the historical park on the Mae Nam Yom, the market town of New Sukhothai is not particularly interesting; yet its friendly and relaxed atmosphere, good transport links and attractive accommodation make it a good base from which to explore the old city ruins.

History

The area was the site of a Khmer empire until 1238, when two Thai rulers, Pho Khun Pha Muang and Pho Khun Bang Klang Hao, decided to unite and form a new Thai kingdom.

Sukhothai's dynasty lasted 200 years and spanned nine kings. The most famous was King Ramkhamhaeng, who reigned from 1275 to 1317 and is credited with developing the first Thai script – his inscriptions are also considered the first Thai literature. Ramkhamhaeng eventually expanded his kingdom to include an area even larger than that of present-day Thailand. But a few kings later in 1438, Sukhothai was absorbed by Ayuthaya.

Sights

The Sukhothai ruins are one of Thailand's most impressive Unesco World Heritage Sites. The **Sukhothai Historical Park** (อุทยานประวัติศาสตร์สุโขทัย) includes the remains of 21 historical sites and four large ponds within the old walls, with an additional 70 sites within a 5km radius.

The architecture of Sukhothai temples is most typified by the classic lotus-bud *chedi*, featuring a conical spire topping a square-sided structure on a three-tiered base. Some sites exhibit other rich architectural forms introduced and modified during the period, such as bell-shaped Sinhalese and double-tiered Srivijaya *chedi*.

Despite the popularity of the park, it's quite expansive, and solitary exploration is usually possible. Some of the most impressive ruins are outside the city walls, so a bicycle or motorcycle is essential to fully appreciate everything.

The ruins are divided into five zones, the central, northern and eastern of which each has a separate 100B admission fee.

CENTRAL ZONE

This is the historical park's main **zone** (**Map p207; admission 100B, plus per bicycle/motorcycle/car 10/30/50B; ⏲6.30am-8pm**) and is home to what are arguably some of the

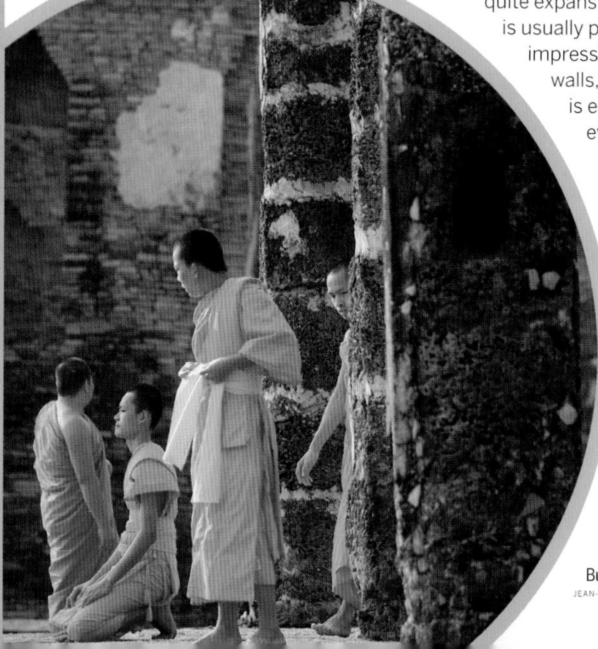

Buddhist monks, Sukhothai (p205)

Sukhothai Historical Park

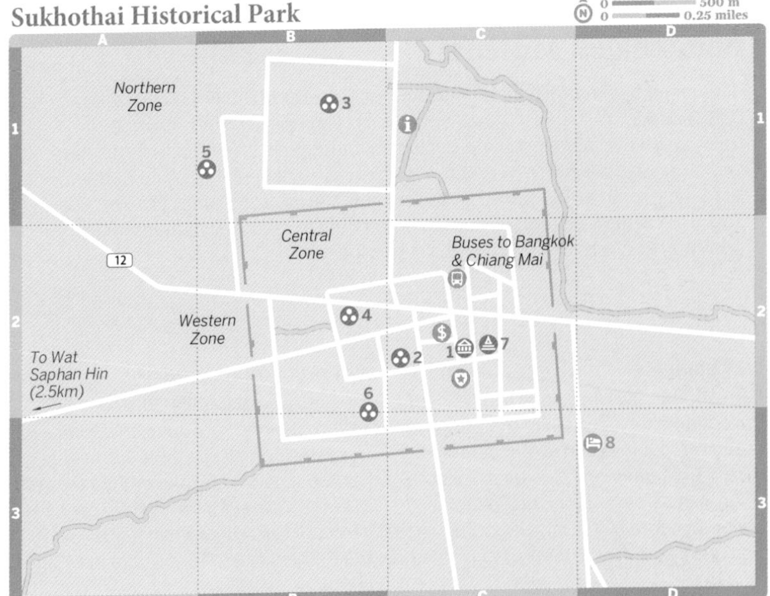

park's most well-preserved and impressive ruins.

WAT MAHATHAT Temple

(วัดมหาธาตุ; **Map p207**) Completed in the 13th century, the largest wát in Sukhothai is surrounded by brick walls (206m long and 200m wide) and a moat that is believed to represent the outer wall of the universe and the cosmic ocean. The *chedi* spires feature the famous lotus-bud motif, and some of the original stately Buddha figures still sit among the ruined columns of the old *wí·hăhn*. There are 198 *chedi* within the monastery walls – a lot to explore in what many consider was once the spiritual and administrative centre of the old capital.

RAMKHAMHAENG NATIONAL MUSEUM Museum

(พิพิธภัณฑสถานแห่งชาติรามคำแหง; **Map p207; 0 5561 2167; admission 150B; 9am-4pm)** A good starting point for exploring the historical park ruins is Ramkhamhaeng National Museum. A replica of the famous Ramkhamhaeng inscription, said to be the earliest example of Thai writing, is kept here among an impressive collection of Sukhothai artefacts.

WAT SI SAWAI Temple

(วัดศรีสวาย; **Map p207**) Just south of Wat Mahathat, this Buddhist shrine (dating from the 12th and 13th centuries) features three Khmer-style towers and a picturesque moat. It was originally built by the Khmers as a Hindu temple.

Sukhothai Historical Park

Sights

1 Ramkhamhaeng National Museum C2
2 Wat Mahathat C2
3 Wat Phra Phai Luang B1
4 Wat Sa Si B2
5 Wat Si Chum B1
6 Wat Si Sawai B2
7 Wat Trapang Thong C2

Sleeping

8 Orchid Hibiscus Guest House D3
Thai Thai .... (see 8)

Sangkhalok Museum

This small but comprehensive **museum** (off Map p210; ☎0 5561 4333; 203/2 Mu 3, Th Muangkao; adult/child 100/50B; ⏰8am-5pm) is an excellent introduction to ancient Sukhothai's most famous product and export, its ceramics. It displays an impressive collection of original 700-year-old Thai pottery found in the area, plus some pieces traded from Vietnam, Burma and China. The 2nd floor features examples of non-utilitarian pottery made as art, including some beautiful and rare ceramic Buddha statues.

WAT SA SI Temple

(วัดสระศรี; Map p207) Also known as 'Sacred Pond Monastery', Wat Sa Si sits on an island west of the bronze monument of King Ramkhamhaeng (the third Sukhothai king). It's a simple, classic Sukhothai-style wát containing a large Buddha, one *chedi* and the columns of the ruined *wí·hăhn*.

WAT TRAPANG THONG Temple

(วัดตระพังทอง; Map p207) Next to the Ramkhamhaeng National Museum, this small, still-inhabited wát with its fine stucco reliefs is reached by a footbridge across the large lotus-filled pond that surrounds it. This reservoir, the original site of Thailand's Loi Krathong festival, supplies the Sukhothai community with most of its water.

NORTHERN ZONE

This **zone** (Map p207; admission 100B, plus per bicycle/motorcycle/car 10/30/50B; ⏰7.30am-5.30pm), 500m north of the old city walls, is easily reached by bicycle.

WAT SI CHUM Temple

(วัดศรีชุม; Map p207) This wát is northwest of the old city and contains an impressive *mon·dòp* with a 15m, brick-and-stucco seated Buddha. This Buddha's elegant, tapered fingers are much photographed. Archaeologists theorise that this image is the 'Phra Atchana' mentioned in the famous Ramkhamhaeng inscription.

WAT PHRA PHAI LUANG Temple

(วัดพระพายหลวง; Map p207) Outside the city walls in the northern zone, this somewhat isolated wát features three 12th-century Khmer-style towers, bigger than those at Wat Si Sawai. This may have been the centre of Sukhothai when it was ruled by the Khmers of Angkor prior to the 13th century.

WESTERN ZONE

This **zone** (Map p207; admission 100B, plus per bicycle/motorcycle/car 10/30/50B; ⏰7.30am-5.30pm), at its furthest extent 2km west of the old city walls, is the most expansive, and in addition to Wat Saphan Hin, several mostly featureless ruins can be found. A bicycle or motorcycle is necessary to explore this zone.

WAT SAPHAN HIN Temple

(วัดสะพานหิน; off Map p207) Located on the crest of a hill that rises about 200m above the plain, the name of the wát, which means 'stone bridge', is a reference to the slate path and staircase that leads up to the temple, which are still in place. The site is 3km west of the former city wall and gives a good view of the Sukhothai ruins to the southeast and the mountains to the north and south.

All that remains of the original temple are a few *chedi* and the ruined *wí·hăhn*, consisting of two rows of laterite columns flanking a 12.5m-high standing Buddha image on a brick terrace.

Activities

CYCLING SUKHOTHAI Cycling

(off Map p210; 0 5561 2519; www.cycling-sukhothai.com; half-/full day 600/750B, sunset tour 300B) Belgian cycling enthusiast Ronny offers a variety of fun and educational bicycle tours of the area. A resident of Sukhothai for nearly 20 years, his rides follow themed itineraries such as the Dharma & Karma Tour, which includes a visit to bizarre **Wat Tawet**, a temple with statues depicting Buddhist hell, or the Historical Park Tour, which includes stops at lesser-seen wát and villages.

Sleeping

Clean, cheerful hotels and guest houses abound, with many places offering attractive bungalows, free pick-up from the bus station, free wi-fi and free use of bicycles.

There are an increasing number of options near the park, many of them in the upscale bracket. Prices tend to go up during the Loi Krathong festival.

New Sukhothai

RUEAN THAI HOTEL Hotel $$$

(Map p210; 0 5561 2444; www.rueanthaihotel.com; 181/20 Soi Pracha Ruammit; r 1200-3600B;) At first glance, you may mistake this eye-catching complex for a temple or museum. The rooms on the upper level are very Thai and feature worn teak furnishings and heaps of character. Poolside rooms are slightly more modern, and there's a concrete building with simple air-con rooms out the back. Call for free pick-up from the bus station.

AT HOME SUKHOTHAI Hotel $

(Map p210; 0 5561 0172; www.athomesukhothai.com; 184/1 Th Vichien Chamnong; r incl breakfast 400-800B;) Located in the 50-year-old childhood home of the proprietor, the attractive structure could easily pass as a newborn after recent renovations. Combining original wooden furnishings with new, the results blend seamlessly, and the simple but comfortable rooms really do feel like home.

LOTUS VILLAGE Hotel $$

(Map p210; 0 5562 1484; www.lotus-village.com; 170 Th Ratchathani; r & bungalows incl breakfast 720-2850B;) Village is an apt label for this peaceful compound of elevated wooden bungalows. Smaller rooms in an attractive wooden building are also available, and a Burmese/Indian design theme runs through the entire place.

Wat Mahathat (p207), Sukhothai Historical Park

New Sukhothai

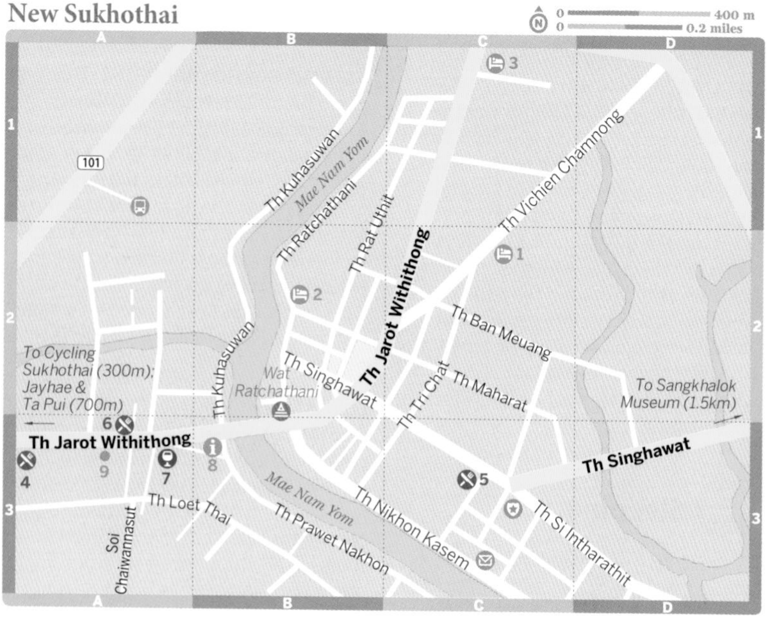

New Sukhothai

Sleeping

1 At Home Sukhothai C2
2 Lotus Village B2
3 Ruean Thai Hotel C1

Eating

Chopper Bar .... (see 7)
4 Chula A3
5 Dream Café C3
6 Night Market A3

Drinking

7 Chopper Bar A3

Information

8 Tourism Authority of Thailand Office B3

Transport

9 Sŏrng·tăa·ou to Sukhothai Historical Park A3

Sukhothai Historical Park

ORCHID HIBISCUS GUEST HOUSE Hotel $$

(Map p207; ☎0 5563 3284; orchid_hibiscus_guest_house@hotmail.com; 407/2 Rte 1272; r/bungalows 900/1300B; ❄@📶🏊) This collection of rooms and bungalows is set in relaxing, manicured grounds with a swimming pool as a centrepiece and the self-professed 'amazing breakfast' as a highlight. Rooms are spotless and fun, featuring various design details and accents.

The guest house is on Rte 1272 about 500m off Rte 12 – the turn-off is between Km 48 and Km 49 markers.

THAI THAI Hotel $$

(Map p207; ☎08 4932 1006; thai_thai_guesthouse@hotmail.com; Rte 1272; bungalows incl breakfast 1000-1200B; ❄@📶) Next door to Orchid Hibiscus Guest House, Thai Thai takes the form of 10 wooden bungalows in an attractive garden and fully outfitted with TV, fridge, hot water and air-con.

Eating & Drinking

Sukhothai's signature dish is *gŏo·ay đĕe·o sù·kŏh·tai* (Sukhothai-style noodles), which feature a slightly sweet broth with different types of pork, ground peanuts and thinly sliced green beans.

The dish is available at **Jayhae** (off Map p210; Th Jarot Withithong; dishes 25-40B; 7am-4pm) and **Ta Pui** (off Map Map p210; Th Jarot Withithong; dishes 25-35B; 7am-3pm), located across from each other on Th Jarot Withithong, about 1.3km west of the Mae Nam Yom.

Don't miss New Sukhothai's tiny **night market** (Map p210; Th Jarot Withithong).

DREAM CAFÉ Thai $$

(Map p210; 86/1 Th Singhawat, New Sukhothai; dishes 80-150B; lunch & dinner;) A meal at Dream Café is like dining in a museum or an antique shop. Eclectic but tasteful furnishings and knick-knackery abound, staff are equal parts competent and friendly, and most importantly of all, the food is good. The helpful menu lays down the basics of Thai food, explaining what to order and how to eat it. Try one of the well-executed *yam* (Thai-style 'salads') or one of the dishes that feature freshwater fish, a local speciality.

CHULA Thai $

(Map p210; Th Jarot Withithong, New Sukhothai; dishes 30-90B; lunch & dinner) It has all the charm of an airport hangar, but the food at this local favourite is solid. Pick-and-choose from prepared dishes, or do the same with the raw ingredients displayed out front, which will be fried before your eyes.

CHOPPER BAR Bar

(Map p210; Th Prawet Nakhon, New Sukhothai; 5pm-12.30am) Travellers and locals congregate from dusk till hangover for food, drinks, live music and flirtation at this place, within spitting distance of Sukhothai's tiny guest house strip.

Information

Tourism Authority of Thailand office (TAT; nationwide call centre 1672, Sukhothai 0 5561 6228; Th Jarot Withithong; 8.30am-4.30pm) Near the bridge in New Sukhothai, this new office has a pretty good selection of maps and brochures.

Getting There & Away

Air

Sukhothai's airport is 27km from town off Rte 1195, about 11km from Sawankhalok. There is a minivan service (180B) between the airport and new Sukhothai. **Bangkok Airways** (nationwide call centre 1771, Sukhothai 0 5564 7224; www.bangkokair.com; Sukhothai Airport) operates flights to Bangkok's Suvarnabhumi International Airport (3480B, 80 minutes, twice daily) and Lampang (2115B, 30 minutes, once daily).

Buses from Sukhothai

DESTINATION	FARE (B)	DURATION (HR)	FREQUENCY
Bangkok	255-380	6-7	every 30min 7.50am-11pm
Chiang Mai	218	6	every 30min 7.15am-4.30pm
Chiang Rai	249	9	6.40am, 9am, 11.30am
Kamphaeng Phet	55-70	1½	7.50am-11pm
Lampang	162	3	every 30min 7.15am-4.30pm
Phitsanulok	28-39	1	every 30min 6am-6pm
Sawankhalok	19-27	1	every hr 6am-6pm
Si Satchanalai	46	1½	11am

Admission Fees

An all-inclusive admission fee of 220B allows entry to Si Satchanalai, Wat Chao Chan (at Chaliang) and the Si Satchanalai Centre for Study & Preservation of Sangkalok Kilns.

Bus

Sukhothai's **bus station** (☎0 5561 4529; Rte 101) is almost 1km northwest of the centre of town.

Getting Around

A ride by săhm·lór within New Sukhothai should cost no more than 40B. *Sŏrng·tăa·ou* run frequently between New Sukhothai and Sukhothai Historical Park (20B, 30 minutes, 6am to 5.30pm), leaving from Th Jarot Withithong near Poo Restaurant, and making a stop at Sukhothai's bus station.

Transport from the bus terminal into the centre of New Sukhothai costs 60B in a chartered vehicle. Motorbike taxis charge 40B. If going directly to Old Sukhothai, *sŏrng·tăa·ou* charge 180B and motorcycle taxis 150B.

The best way to get around the historical park is by bicycle, which can be rented at shops outside the park entrance for 30B per day.

Motorbikes can be rented starting at about 250B for 24 hours and are available at at Poo Restaurant and nearly every guest house in New Sukhothai.

Si Satchanalai-Chaliang Historical Park อุทยานประวัติศาสตร์ศรีสัชนาลัย

Set among the hills, the 13th- to 15th-century ruins of the old cities of Si Satchanalai and Chaliang, about 50km north of Sukhothai, are in the same basic style as those in the Sukhothai Historical Park, but the setting is more peaceful and almost seems untouched. The park covers roughly 720 hectares and is surrounded by a 12m-wide moat. Chaliang, 1km southeast, is an older city site (dating to the 11th century), though its two temples date to the 14th century, and the remains of an ancient pottery industry can be found north of the park.

Wat Phra Si Ratana Mahathat (p202), Phitsanulok

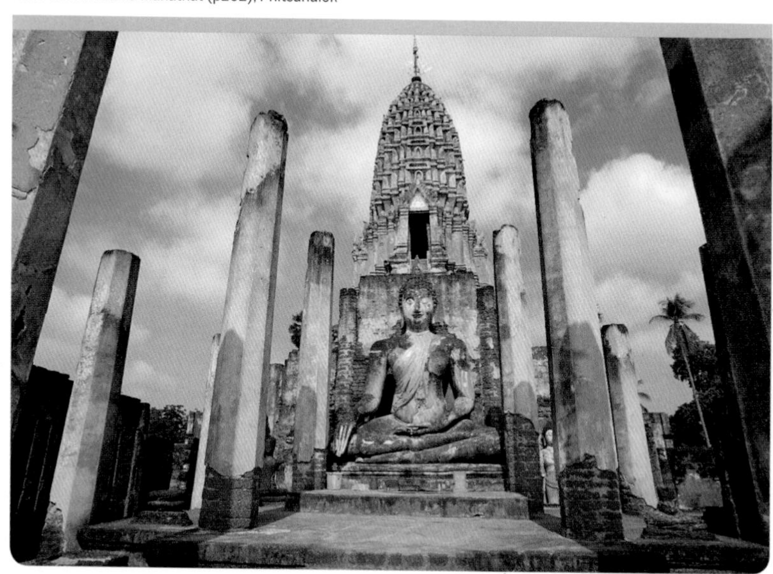

Sights

Si Satchanalai

This **zone** (admission 100B, plus per car 50B; 8am-4.30pm) contains the vast majority of ruins. An **information centre** (8.30am-5pm) at the park distributes free park maps and has a small exhibit outlining the history and major attractions. Bicycles can be rented near the entrance gate to the park (20B).

WAT CHANG LOM Temple

(วัดช้างล้อม) This fine temple, marking the centre of the old city of Si Satchanalai, has elephants surrounding a bell-shaped *chedi* that is somewhat better preserved than its counterpart in Sukhothai. An inscription says the temple was built by King Ramkhamhaeng between 1285 and 1291.

WAT KHAO PHANOM PHLOENG Temple

(วัดเขาพนมเพลิง) On the hill overlooking Wat Chang Lom to the right are the remains of Wat Khao Phanom Phloeng, including a *chedi*, a large seated Buddha and stone columns that once supported the roof of the *wí·hăhn*. From this hill you can make out the general design of the once-great city. The slightly higher hill west of Phanom Phloeng is capped by a large Sukhothai-style *chedi* – all that remains of Wat Khao Suwan Khiri.

WAT CHEDI JET THAEW Temple

(วัดเจดีย์เจ็ดแถว) Next to Wat Chang Lom, these ruins contain seven rows of *chedi*, the largest of which is a copy of one at Wat Mahathat in Sukhothai. An interesting brick-and-plaster *wí·hăhn* features barred windows designed to look like lathed wood (an ancient Indian technique used all over southeast Asia). A *prasat* (small ornate building with a cruciform ground plan and needlelike spire) and *chedi* are stacked on the roof.

WAT NANG PHAYA Temple

(วัดนางพญา) South of Wat Chedi Jet Thaew, this *chedi* is Sinhalese in style and was built in the 15th or 16th century, a bit later than the other monuments at Si Satchanalai. Stucco reliefs on the large laterite *wí·hăhn* in front of the *chedi* – now sheltered by a tin roof – date from the Ayuthaya period when Si Satchanalai was known as Sawankhalok. Goldsmiths in the district still craft a design known as *nahng pá·yah*, modelled after these reliefs.

Detour: Sawanworanayok National Museum

In Sawankhalok town, near Wat Sawankhalam on the western river bank, this state-sponsored **museum** (0 5564 1571; 69 Th Phracharat, Sawankhalok; admission 50B; 9am-4pm) houses an impressive collection of 12th- to 15th-century artefacts. The ground floor focuses on the area's ceramic legacy, while the 2nd floor features several beautiful bronze and stone Sukhothai-era Buddha statues.

Chaliang

This older site, a short bike ride from Si Satchanalai, has two temples of note. Admission isn't always collected at Wat Chao Chan.

WAT PHRA SI RATANA MAHATHAT Temple

(วัดพระศรีรัตนมหาธาตุ; admission 20B; 8am-5pm) These ruins consist of a large laterite *chedi* (dating back to 1448–88) between two *wí·hăhn*. One of the *wí·hăhn* holds a large seated Sukhothai Buddha image, a smaller standing image and a bas-relief of the famous walking Buddha, exemplary of the flowing, boneless Sukhothai style. The other *wí·hăhn* contains some less distinguished images.

WAT CHAO CHAN Temple

(วัดเจ้าจันทร์; admission 100B; ⏲8am-5pm) These wát ruins are about 500m west of Wat Phra Si Ratana Mahathat. The central attraction is a large Khmer-style tower similar to later towers built in Lopburi and probably constructed during the reign of Khmer King Jayavarman VII (1181–1217). The tower has been restored and is in fairly good shape. The roofless *wí·hăhn* on the right contains the laterite outlines of a large standing Buddha that has all but melted away from exposure and weathering.

Sawankhalok Kilns

At one time, more than 200 huge pottery **kilns** (admission free) lined the banks of Mae Nam Yom in the area around Si Satchanalai. In China – the biggest importer of Thai pottery during the Sukhothai and Ayuthaya periods – the pieces produced here came to be called 'Sangkalok', a mispronunciation of Sawankhalok. Ceramics are still made in the area and a local ceramic artist even continues to fire his pieces in an underground wood-burning oven.

In addition to the centre below, several barely recognisable kiln sites can be found along the road that runs north of Si Satchanalai.

SI SATCHANALAI CENTRE FOR STUDY & PRESERVATION OF SANGKALOK KILNS Museum

(ศูนย์ศึกษาและอนุรักษ์เตาสังคโลก; admission 100B; ⏲9am-4pm) Located 5km northwest of the Si Satchanalai ruins, this centre has large excavated kilns and many intact pottery samples. The exhibits are interesting despite the lack of English labels.

KAMPHAENG PHET PROVINCE

Kamphaeng Phet กำแพงเพชร

POP 30,000

Located halfway between Bangkok and Chiang Mai, Kamphaeng Phet literally means 'Diamond Wall', a reference to the apparent strength of this formerly walled city's protective barrier. This level

Left: Ruins, Kamphaeng Phet Historical Park;
Below: Merit-makers, Kamphaeng Phet
(LEFT) AUSTIN BUSH/LONELY PLANET IMAGES ©; (BELOW) AUSTIN BUSH/LONELY PLANET IMAGES ©

of security was necessary, as the city previously helped to protect the Sukhothai and later Ayuthaya kingdoms against attacks from Burma or Lanna. Parts of the wall can still be seen today, and the impressive ruins of several religious structures also remain.

Sights

KAMPHAENG PHET HISTORICAL PARK Historical Park

(อุทยานประวัติศาสตร์กำแพงเพชร; ☎0 5571 1921; admission 100-150B, motorbike/car 20/50B; 🕗8am-5pm) A Unesco World Heritage Site, this park features the ruins of structures dating back to the 14th century, roughly the same time as the better-known kingdom of Sukhothai. Kamphaeng Phet's Buddhist monuments continued to be built until the Ayuthaya period, nearly 200 years later, and thus possess elements of both Sukhothai and Ayuthaya styles, resulting in a school of Buddhist art quite unlike anywhere else in Thailand.

Sleeping

THREE J GUEST HOUSE Guest House **$**

(☎0 5571 3129; www.threejguesthouse.com; 79 Th Rachavitee; r 250-700B; ❄@📶) This pleasant collection of bungalows in a pretty garden has a very hospitable and friendly host. The cheapest ones share a clean bathroom and the more expensive have air-con. There's heaps of local information; bicycles and motorcycles are available for rent, and the owner can also arrange visits to his country resort near Klong Wang Chao.

CHAKUNGRAO RIVERVIEW Hotel **$$**

(☎0 5571 4900-8; www.chankungraoriverview.com; 149 Th Thesa; r 1000-1300B, ste 5000B, incl breakfast; ❄@📶) Kamphaeng Phet's poshest digs has some nice rooms despite its unremarkable facade.

Eating & Drinking

A busy night market sets up every evening near the river just north of the Navarat Hotel.

BAMEE CHAKANGRAO Thai $

(no roman-script sign; Th Ratchadamnoen; dishes 25-30B; 8.30am-3pm) Thin wheat and egg noodles *(bà·mèe)* are a speciality of Kamphaeng Phet, and this famous restaurant is one of the best places to try them. The noodles are made fresh every day behind the restaurant; pork satay is also available.

KAMPHAENG PHET PHOCHANA Thai $

(no roman-script sign; dishes 25-50B; 6am-1am) This popular place puts out just about every Thai fave from *pàt tai* to *kôw man gài* (Hainanese-style chicken rice). It's also a good place to try *chŏw góoay*, grass jelly, a product made in Kamphaeng Phet. Look for the rainbow-coloured facade near the roundabout.

MAE PING RIVERSIDE Restaurant, Bar

(no roman-script sign; 50/1 Moo 2, Nakhon Chum; dishes 40-120B; lunch & dinner) Offers draught beer, live music and cool breezes. It's one of the first places along the road that parallels the river.

Information

Tourist Information Centre (8am-4.30pm) Across from the national museum, this centre has some maps and pamphlets. There is another more history-focused centre at the group of ruins north of the city wall.

Getting There & Away

The **bus station** (0 5579 9844) is about 1km west of the Mae Nam Ping. From the same station, *sŏrng·tăa·ou* depart for Sukhothai (39B, two hours, every hour from 1pm to 8pm).

Getting Around

The least expensive way to get from the bus station into town is to hop on a red *sŏrng·tăa·ou* (15B per person) to the roundabout across the river. From there take a săhm·lór anywhere in town for 20B to 30B. Motorcycle taxis from the bus station to most hotels downtown cost 40B.

MAE HONG SON PROVINCE

Mae Hong Son แม่ฮ่องสอน

POP 6,000

Mae Hong Son, with its remote setting and surrounding mountains, fits many travellers' preconceived notion of how a northern Thai city should be. A palpable Burmese influence and a border town feel don't dispel this image, and best of all, there's hardly a túk-túk or tout to be seen. This doesn't mean Mae Hong Son is uncharted territory; the tour groups have been coming here for years, but the city's potential as a base for activities, from spa treatment to trekking, ensures that your visit can be quite unlike anyone else's.

History

Mae Hong Son has been isolated from Thailand geographically, culturally and politically for most of its short existence. The city was founded as an elephant training centre in the early 19th century, and remained little more than this until 1856, when fighting in Burma caused thousands of Shan to pour into the area. In the years following, Mae Hong Son prospered as a centre for logging and remained an independent kingdom until 1900, when King Rama V incorporated the area into the Thai kingdom.

Sights

With their bright colours, whitewashed stupas and glittering zinc fretwork, Mae Hong Son's Burmese- and Shan-style temples will have you scratching your head wondering just which country you're in.

WAT JONG KHAM & WAT JONG KLANG Temple

(วัดจองคำ/วัดจองกลาง; admission free) Wat Jong Kham was built nearly 200 years ago by Thai Yai (Shan) people, who make up

JOHN BORTHWICK/LONELY PLANET IMAGES ©

Don't Miss Wat Phra That Doi Kong Mu

Climb the hill west of town, Doi Kong Mu (1500m), to visit this Shan-built **wát** (วัดพระธาตุดอยกองมู; admission free), also known as Wat Plai Doi. The view of the sea of fog that collects in the valley each morning is impressive; at other times of the day you get wonderful views of the town and surrounding valleys. Two Shan *chedi,* erected in 1860 and 1874, enshrine the ashes of monks from Myanmar's Shan State. Around the back of the wát you can see a tall, slender, standing Buddha and catch views west of the ridge.

about half of the population of Mae Hong Son Province. Wat Jong Klang houses 100-year-old glass *jataka* paintings and a **museum** (admission by donation; 8am-6pm) with 150-year-old wooden dolls from Mandalay that depict some of the more gruesome aspects of the wheel of life. Wat Jong Klang has several areas that women are forbidden to enter – not unusual for Burmese-Shan Buddhist temples.

The temples are lit at night and reflected in Nong Jong Kham – a popular photo op for visitors.

Activities

Mae Hong Son's location at the edge of mountainous jungle makes it an excellent base for treks into the countryside. Trekking here is not quite the large-scale industry it is elsewhere, and visitors willing to get their boots muddy can expect to find relatively untouched nature and isolated villages.

Long-tail boat trips on the nearby Mae Pai are gaining popularity, and the same guest houses and trekking agencies that organise treks from Mae Hong Son can arrange river excursions.

NATURE WALKS Trekking
(☎0 5361 1040, 08 9552 6899; www.trekkingthailand.com) Although the treks here cost more than elsewhere, John, a native of Mae Hong Son, is the best guide in town. Treks here range from day-long nature walks to multiday journeys across the province. John can also arrange custom nature-based tours such as the orchid-viewing tours he conducts from March to May.

FRIEND TOUR Trekking
(☎0 5361 1647; PA Motorbike, 21 Th Pradit Jong Kham; ⏲7.30am-7.30pm) With nearly 20 years' experience, this recommended outfit offers trekking, elephant riding and rafting, as well as day tours.

NAM RIM TOUR Trekking
(☎0 5361 4454; 21 Th Pradit Jong Kham) Mr Dam advertises 'Bad sleep, bad jokes', but his treks get good reports.

POOKLON COUNTRY CLUB Spa
(☎08 6198 0722; Ban Mae Sanga; ⏲8am-6.30pm) This self-professed 'country club' is touted as Thailand's only mud treatment spa. Discovered by a team of geologists in 1995, the mud here is pasteurised and blended with herbs before being employed in various treatments (facial 60B). There's thermal mineral water for soaking (60B), and on weekends, massage (per hour 200B).

Pooklon is 16km north of the Mae Hong Son in the Mok Champae district.

Sleeping

Because it's a tourist town, accommodation prices fluctuate with the seasons, and outside of the high season (November to January) it's worth pursuing a discount.

RESIDENCE@MAEHONGSON Hotel $$
(☎0 5361 4100; www.theresidence-mhs.com; 41/4 Th Ni-wet Pi-sarn; r 900-1400B; ❄@📶) One of the more recent places to go up, this cheery yellow building houses 11 inviting rooms. Teak furnishings abound, and lots of windows ensure ample natural light. There's also a sunny communal rooftop area, a friendly English-speaking owner, and bicycles provided free of charge.

ROMTAI Hotel $$
(☎0 5361 2437; www.maehongson-romtai.com; Th Chamnansathit; r 600-1200B, bungalows 1500-1700B; ❄📶) Hidden behind both the lakeside temples and a bland-looking reception area, this place has a huge variety of accommodation, ranging from spacious, clean rooms to bungalows overlooking a lush garden with fishponds.

FERN RESORT Hotel $$$
(☎0 5368 6110; www.fernresort.info; 64 Moo 10, Tambon Pha Bong; bungalows incl breakfast 2500-3500B; ❄@📶🏊) This long-standing eco-friendly resort is one of the more pleasant places to stay in northern Thailand. The 40 Shan-style wooden bungalows are set among tiered rice paddies and streams and feature stylishly decorated interiors. Nearby nature trails lead to the adjacent Mae Surin National Park, and to encourage community-based tourism, most of the employees come from local villages. The downside is that the resort is 7km south of town, but free pick-up is available from the airport and bus terminal, and regular shuttles run to/from town stopping at the Fern Restaurant.

SANG TONG HUTS Hotel $$
(☎0 5362 1680; www.sangtonghuts.com; Th Makhasanti; bungalows 800-3000B; @📶🏊) This popular set of bungalows in a wooded area just outside of town is one of the more character-filled places to stay. There's a huge variety of bungalows, all of them spacious and well designed. It's popular among repeat visitors to Mae Hong Son, so it pays to book ahead. Sang Tong Huts is about 1km northeast of Th Khunlum Praphat, just off Th Makhasanti – if going towards Pai, turn left at the town's northernmost stoplight and follow the signs.

Evening market, Mae Hong Son

AUSTIN BUSH/LONELY PLANET IMAGES ©

Eating & Drinking

Mae Hong Son's morning market is a fascinating place to have breakfast. Several vendors at the north end of the market sell unusual dishes such as *tòo·a òon* (a Burmese noodle dish supplemented with thick chickpea porridge and deep-fried bits of vegetables, chickpea flour cakes and tofu). Other vendors along the same strip sell a local version of *kà·nŏm jeen nám ngée·o,* often topped with *kahng pòrng* (a Shan snack of battered and deep-fried vegetables).

The city also has two good night markets; the night market near the airport offers mostly takeaway northern Thai–style food while the night market at the southern end of Th Khunlum Praphat has more generic Thai food.

BAN PHLENG Northern Thai $

(no roman-script sign; 108 Th Khunlum Praphat; mains 45-100B; ⏲lunch & dinner Mon-Sat) This popular open-air restaurant does a handful of very tasty local dishes – you're safe going with anything that says 'Maehongson style' on the English-language menu. Ban Phleng is just south of town – look for the white banners at the side of the road.

MAE SI BUA Northern Thai $

(51 Th Singhanat Bamrung; mains 20-30B; ⏲lunch) Like the Shan grandma you never had, Auntie Bua prepares a huge variety of different Shan curries, soups and dips on a daily basis. Try her delicious *gaang hang·lair,* an incredibly rich curry of pork belly with a flavour not unlike American-style barbecue sauce.

FERN RESTAURANT International Thai $$

(Th Khunlum Praphat; mains 70-180B; ⏲10.30am-10pm) The Fern is almost certainly Mae Hong Son's most upscale restaurant, but remember, this is Mae Hong Son. Nonetheless, service is professional and the food is decent. The expansive menu covers Thai, local and even European dishes. There is live lounge music some nights.

SUNFLOWER CAFÉ Bar

(Th Pradit Jong Kham; ⏲7am-midnight) This open-air place combines draught beer, live lounge music and views of the lake.

Rice fields near Pai

KYLIE MCLAUGHLIN/LONELY PLANET IMAGES ©

Sunflower also does meals (35B to 180B) and runs tours.

Information

Srisangwal Hospital (**☎0 5361 1378; Th Singhanat Bamrung**) A full-service facility that includes an emergency room.

Tourism Authority of Thailand office (**TAT; ☎nationwide call centre 1672, Mae Hong Son 0 5361 2982; www.travelmaehongson.org; Th Ni-wet Pi-sarn; ⏰8.30am-4.30pm**) Basic tourist brochures and maps can be picked up here.

Getting There & Away

Air

For many people the time saved flying from Chiang Mai to Mae Hong Son versus bus travel is worth the extra baht. There are four flights daily (1590B to 1890B, 35 minutes), operated by **Kan Air** (**☎nationwide call centre 02 551 6111, Mae Hong Son 0 5361 3188; www.kanairlines.com; Mae Hong Son Airport**) and **Nok Air** (**☎nationwide call centre 1318, Mae Hong Son 0 5361 2057; www.nokair.co.th; Mae Hong Son Airport**).

A túk-túk into town costs about 80B.

Bus

Mae Hong Son's bus station is 1km south of the city. **Prempracha Tour** (**☎0 5368 4100**) conducts bus services within the province and **Sombat Tour** (**☎0 5361 3211**) conducts services between Mae Hong Son and Bangkok.

Other bus destinations from Mae Hong Son include the following:

Bangkok (718B to 838B, 15 hours, three departures from 2pm to 4pm)

Chiang Mai (northern route, 127B, eight hours, 8.30am and 12.30pm)

Chiang Mai (southern route, 178B, nine hours, frequent departures from 6am to 9pm)

Pai (70B, 4½ hours, 8.30am and 12.30pm)

Minivan

Air-conditioned minivans, a popular way to get around the province, also depart from the bus station.

Chiang Mai (250B, six hours, every hour from 7am to 3pm)

Pai (150B, 2½ hours, every hour from 7am to 4pm)

Soppong (150B, 1½ hours, every hour from 7am to 4pm)

Getting Around

The centre of Mae Hong Son can easily be covered on foot, and it is one of the few towns in Thailand that doesn't seem to have a motorcycle taxi at every corner. Because most of Mae Hong Son's attractions are outside of town, renting a motorcycle or bicycle is a wise move.

PA Motorbike (☎0 5361 1647; 21 Th Pradit Jong Kham; ⏰7.30am-7.30pm) Opposite Friend House, rents motorbikes (250B per day) and trucks (1500B to 2500B per day).

PJ (☎08 4372 6967; Th Khunlum Praphat; ⏰8am-7.30pm) Rents motorbikes (150B per day).

Titan (Th Khunlum Praphat; ⏰10am-10pm) Rents good-quality mountain bikes (80B per day).

Pai ปาย

POP 2000

Pai's popularity has yet to impact its setting in a nearly picture-perfect mountain valley. There's heaps of quiet accommodation outside the main drag, a host of natural, lazy activities to keep visitors entertained, a vibrant art and music scene, and the town's Shan roots can still be seen in its temples, quiet back streets and fun afternoon market.

Sights

There are a few waterfalls around Pai that are worth visiting, particularly after the rainy season (October to early December). The closest and the most popular, **Nam**

Trouble in Pairadise?

Despite its immense popularity, Pai has largely been able to remain a positive example of tourism development in Thailand. Natural and cultural conservation have long been fundamental aspects of Pai's tourism sector. And the town has been able to remain loyal to its rural roots, which form the basis of a lively art and music scene that leave most visitors with an overwhelmingly positive impression.

Tourism has also brought prosperity to the formerly isolated farming community. Land in desirable parts of the town is said to sell for as much as US$65,000 an acre, and many locals are now employed in various tourist service-related jobs or supplement their income by selling handicrafts. Roads and other infrastructure have improved, and in 2007 Pai's commercial airport commenced flights.

On the other hand, the huge influx of visitors to Pai has also resulted in a host of new problems. The town is beginning to experience difficulties in dealing with increasing amounts of rubbish and sewage. Locals complain of being kept awake by the sound of live music and partying. Drug use is widespread. And the city's police force has garnered considerable negative press where it concerns tourists and tourism, ranging from a brief crackdown on so-called 'illegal dancing' in the city's bars to the controversial shooting death of a Canadian tourist in early 2008.

Closing times at the town's bars are now strictly enforced, wastewater treatment is in the process of being made mandatory, and a new dump is being considered. But if Pai continues to maintain its current level of popularity, it remains to be seen whether or not the town can maintain the same level of responsible development that made it such an attractive destination to begin with.

Tok Mo Paeng, has a couple of pools that are suitable for swimming. The waterfall is a total of 8km from Pai along the road that also leads to Wat Nam Hoo – a long walk indeed, but suitable for a bike ride or short motorcycle trip. Roughly the same distance in the opposite direction is **Nam Pembok**, just off the road to Chiang Mai.

WAT PHRA THAT MAE YEN Temple

(วัดพระธาตุแม่เย็น) This temple sits atop a hill and has good views overlooking the valley. Walk 1km east from the main intersection in town, across a stream and through a village, to get to the stairs (353 steps) that lead to the top. Or take the 400m sealed road that follows a different route to the top.

BAN SANTICHON Village

(บ้านสันติชน) Approximately 4km outside of Pai, a small market, delicious Yunnanese food, tea tasting, pony rides and Yunnanese **adobe-style accommodation** (☎08 1024 3982; bungalows 1000-1500B) make the KMT village of Ban Santichon not unlike a Chinese-themed amusement park.

THA PAI HOT SPRINGS Hot Springs

(บ่อน้ำร้อนท่าปาย; adult/child 200/100B; 6am-7pm) Across the Mae Nam Pai and 7km southeast of town via a paved road are the Tha Rai Hot Springs, a well-kept local park 1km from the road. A scenic stream flows through the park; the stream mixes with the hot springs in places to make pleasant bathing areas. The water is also diverted to a couple of nearby spas; see p222.

Activities

Massage

There are plenty of traditional Thai massage places around town charging around 150B an hour.

PAI TRADITIONAL THAI MASSAGE Massage

(PTTM; ☎0 5369 9121; www.pttm1989.com; 68/3 Soi 1, Th Wiang Tai; massage per 1/2hr 180/350B, sauna per visit 80B, 3-day massage course 2500B; 9am-9pm) This long-standing and locally owned outfit offers very good northern-Thai massage, as well as a sauna (cool season only) where you can steam yourself in *sà·mŭn·prai* (medicinal herbs). Three-day massage courses begin every Monday and Friday and last three hours per day.

Rafting & Kayaking

Rafting, and to a lesser extent kayaking, along the Mae Nam Pai during the wet season (approximately June to February) is a popular activity. The most popular trip runs from Pai to Mae Hong Son, which depending on the amount of water, can traverse rapids in scale from grade one to grade five. Rates are all-inclusive

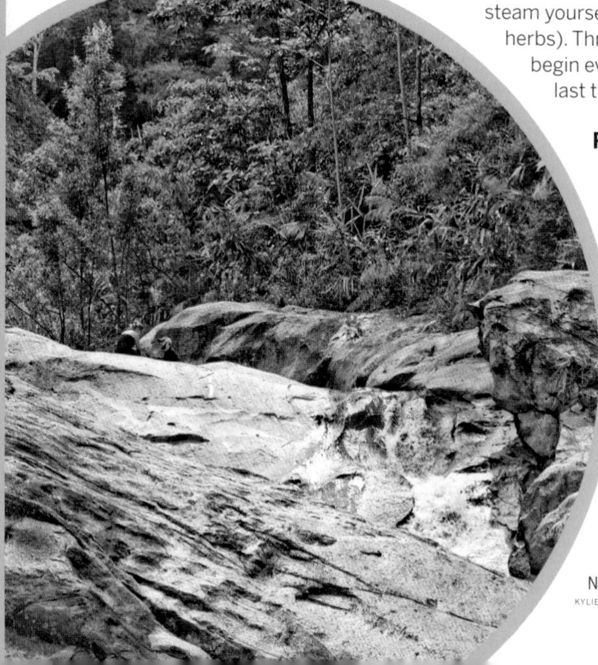

Nam Tok Mo Paeng, Pai

(rafting equipment, camping gear, dry bags and insurance) and run from about 1200B to 1500B per person for a one-day trip and from 1800B to 2500B per person for two days.

PAI ADVENTURE Rafting
(☎0 5369 9385; www.thailandpai.net; Th Chaisongkhram) The one- to three-day white-water rafting trips offered by this recommended outfit can be combined with trekking and other activities.

THAI ADVENTURE RAFTING Rafting
(☎0 5369 9111; www.thairafting.com; Th Chaisongkhram) This French-run outfit leads one- and two-day trips. On the way, rafters visit a waterfall, a fossil reef and hot springs. One night is spent at the company's permanent riverside camp.

Trekking

Guided treks range in cost from about 700B to 1000B per person per day, in groups of two or more, and are all-inclusive. Most treks focus on the Lisu, Lahu and Karen villages in and around neighbouring Soppong.

Courses

PAI COOKERY SCHOOL Cooking
(☎08 1706 3799; Soi Wanchaloem; lessons 600-1000B; ⏰11am-1pm & 2-6.30pm) With a decade of experience, this outfit offers a variety of courses spanning three to six dishes. The course typically involves a trip to the market for ingredients. Contact a day in advance.

MAM YOGA HOUSE Yoga
(☎08 9954 4981; www.mamyoga.paiexplorer.com; Th Rangsiyanon; 1-day course from 200B; ⏰10am-noon & 3-5pm) Just north of the police station, Mam offers Hatha yoga classes and courses in small groups.

S WIRASUT Thai Boxing
(☎08 0678 5269; lessons 400B; ⏰8am-noon & 2-5pm) Chalee and Kot lead instruction in Thai boxing at this rustic gym about 1km outside of town, on the turn-off just before Fluid.

Sleeping

Keep in mind that prices fluctuate significantly in Pai, and nearly all the midrange and top-end accommodation cut their prices, sometimes by as much as 60%, during the off season.

RIM PAI COTTAGE Hotel $$$
(☎0 5369 9133; www.rimpaicottage.com; Th Chaisongkhram; bungalows incl breakfast 1300-5000B; ❄📶) The homelike bungalows here are spread out along a secluded and beautifully wooded section of the Nam Pai. There are countless cosy riverside corners to relax at, and a palpable village-like feel about the whole place. Rim Pai is an excellent deal in the low season when the prices drop dramatically.

PAI RIVER VILLA Hotel $$
(☎0 5369 9796; www.wangchangpuek.com; r 1000B, bungalows 1200-2500B, incl breakfast; ❄📶) This place boasts some of the more attractive midrange riverside bungalows in town. The air-con bungalows are spacious and attractive and have wide balconies that encourage lazy riverside relaxing and mountain viewing. The fan bungalows are a significantly tighter fit, and there's an adjacent house with 11 rooms.

PAI COUNTRY HUT Hotel $
(☎08 4046 4458; Ban Mae Hi; bungalows incl breakfast 500B; 📶) The bamboo bungalows here are utterly simple, but are tidy and have bathrooms and inviting hammocks. Although it's not exactly riverside, it's the most appealing of several similar places in the area.

BULUNBURI Hotel $$$
(☎0 5369 8302; www.bulunburi.com; 28 Moo 5 Ban Pong; bungalows incl breakfast 1350-3300B; ❄@) Set in a tiny secluded valley of rice fields and streams, the seductively bucolic location is as much a reason to stay here as the attractive accommodation. The hotel is about 2.5km from the centre of town along the road to Mae Hong Son –

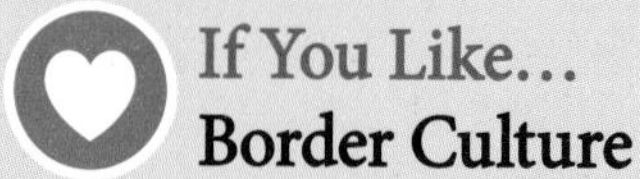

If You Like... Border Culture

If you like the border atmosphere of Mae Sai (p198), then delve deeper into the so-called Golden Triangle:

1 DOI TUNG ROYAL VILLA
(0 5376 7011; www.doitung.org; admission 70B; 6.30am-5pm) A royal summer palace sitting atop Doi Tung is now open as a public museum. The affiliated royal initiative provided education to the local farmers on sustainable agricultural methods to stop slash-and-burn practices and replace opium as a cash crop.

2 SOP RUAK
The borders of Myanmar (Burma), Thailand and Laos meet at this official 'centre' of the Golden Triangle. To commemorate those lawless days there's both a **House of Opium** (www.houseofopium.com; admission 50B; 7am-7pm) and a Hall of Opium (admission 200B; 8.30am-4pm Tue-Sun) plus Mekong River Cruises (1hr cruise; 400B/boat). Stay overnight at **Anantara Golden Triangle Resort & Spa** (0 5378 4084; www.anantara.com; r 16,500, ste 18,000B, incl breakfast;), an award-winning resort.

look for the well-posted turn-off, about 1km from Pai.

PAIRADISE Hotel $$
(0 5369 8065; www.pairadise.com; 98 Moo 1 Ban Mae Hi; bungalows 800-1500B;) Popular with the Western yoga-and-meditation set, this tidy resort looks over the Pai Valley from atop a ridge just outside town. The bungalows are stylish, spacious and include gold leaf lotus murals, beautiful rustic bathrooms and terraces with hammocks. All surround a waterfall-fed pond that is suitable for swimming. The hotel is nearly 1km east of Pai.

SUN HUT Hotel $$
(0 5369 9730; www.thesunhut.com; 28/1 Ban Mae Yen; bungalows incl breakfast 900-1900B;) Located in a jungle-like setting with a stream running through it, this long-standing and rustic resort is one of the more unique places in the area. Bungalows are nicely spaced apart and more expensive ones have porches and lots of charm. Service is friendly and gentle; there's an organic garden, a vegetarian restaurant, and an attractive communal area with hammocks and napping guests. The hotel is 300m east of the Mae Nam Pai along the road that leads to Tha Pai Hot Springs.

AMY'S EARTH HOUSE Guest House $$
(08 6190 2394; www.amyshouse.net; Ban Mae Khong; bungalows 600B;) Amy's claims to have been the first adobe accommodation in Pai. Mud bungalows are simple, but spacious, have open-air showers, and are on a landscaped hillside looking over the valley. The hotel is about 3.5km from the centre of town off the road to Mae Hong Song – look for the well-posted turn-off just after the airport runway, about 1.3km from Pai.

PAI TREEHOUSE Hotel $$$
(08 1911 3640; www.paitreehouse.com; 90 Moo 2 Mae Hi; bungalows incl breakfast 1200-12,000B;) It's every child's fantasy hotel: wooden bungalows suspended from a giant old tree. Even if you can't score one of the three elusive tree-house rooms (they're popular), there are several other attractive bungalows, many near the river. On the vast grounds you'll also find elephants and floating decks on the Mae Nam Pai, all culminating in a family-friendly atmosphere. The resort is 6km from Pai, just before Tha Pai Hot Springs.

Eating

At first glance, Pai has a seemingly impressive range of restaurants for such a small town, but a few meals will reveal that the quality of food is generally pretty mediocre. Even the Thai food is fairly dull, and your best dining options are, quite paradoxically, probably Chinese and Israeli. And to make things worse, if

Yunnanese Muslim–style dishes

JERRY ALEXANDER/LONELY PLANET IMAGES ©

you're here outside of the tourist season (approximately November to February), many of the town's better restaurants can be closed, although the options listed below should be open year-round.

During the day, there's takeaway food at **Saengthongaram market** (Th Khetkelang). For tasty take-home local eats, try the **evening market** (gàht láang; Th Raddamrong) that unfolds every afternoon from about 3pm to sunset. And every evening during the tourist season several vendors set up along Th Chaisongkhram and Th Rangsiyanon, selling all manner of food and drink from stalls and refurbished VW vans.

LAAP KHOM HUAY PU Northern Thai $

(no roman-script sign; Ban Huay Pu; mains 35-60B; 9am-10pm) Escape the dreadlocks and tofu crowd and get your meat on at this unabashedly carnivorous local eatery. The house special, and the dish you must order, is *lâhp kôo·a* (minced beef or pork meat fried with local herbs and spices). Accompanied by a basket of sticky rice, a plate of bitter herbs and a cold Singha, it's the best meal in Pai. The restaurant is on the road to Mae Hong Son, about 1km north of town, just past the turn-off to Belle Villa and Baan Krating.

MAMA FALAFEL Israeli $

(Soi Wanchaloem; set meals 80-90B; 11am-8pm) This friendly native of Pai has been cooking up tasty felafel, hummus, schnitzel and other Jewish/Israeli faves since 2002. Set meals win in both quality and quantity.

KHANOM JEEN NANG YONG Thai $

(no roman-script sign; Th Chaisongkhram; mains 20B; lunch & dinner) This place specialises in *kà·nŏm jeen* (thin rice noodles served with a currylike broth). They do a particularly rich and spicy *kà·nŏm jeen ṇám ngée·o*, great with deep-fried pork rinds, but don't worry about getting the names right – simply point to whichever clay pot looks the tastiest. It's in the same building as Pai Adventure.

JE-IN PAI Vegetarian $

(Pure Vegetarian Food; Th Raddamrong; mains 40-80B; 10am-8pm) Opposite the District Office, this simple open-air place serves tasty and cheap vegan and vegetarian Thai food. During lunch, choose from the metal trays out front.

NONG BEER Thai $

(cnr Th Khetkalang & Th Chaisongkhram; mains 30-60B; 10am-8pm) The atmosphere at this extremely popular place is akin to a food court (you have to exchange cash for tickets, and everything is self-serve), but it's a good place for cheap and authentic Thai eats ranging from *kôw soy* to curries ladled over rice.

WITCHING WELL International $

(Th Wiang Tai; dishes 40-80B) This foreigner-run place is where to come if you're looking for authentic sandwiches, pasta, cakes and pastries. They also do the kind of breakfasts you're not going to find elsewhere in Pai.

Drinking & Entertainment

As a general guide to 'downtown' Pai's entertainment scene, most of the open-air and VW van–based cocktail bars are along Th Chaisongkhram; Th Wiang Tai is where you'll find the mostly indoor and chilled reggae-type places; the 'guest house' style restaurant/bars with a diverse soundtrack are mostly found on Th Rangsiyanon; and a few live music bars can be found along the eastern end of Th Ratchadamnoen.

BEBOP Live Music

(Th Rangsiyanon; 6pm-1am) This legendary box is popular with travellers and has live music nightly (from about 9pm), playing blues, R&B and rock.

TING TONG Bar

(Th Rangsiyanon; 7pm-1am) A sprawling compound of bamboo decks, concrete platforms, hidden tables and towering trees, this is one of the larger bars in town. Reggae/dub defines but doesn't rule the play list, and there's occasional live music.

Information

Pai Explorer (www.paiexplorer.com) is the free local English-language map. The *Pai Events Planner* (PEP) is a free monthly map that covers cultural events, travel destinations and some restaurant and bar openings, and can be picked up around town.

Getting There & Away

Air

Pai's airport is around 1.5km north of town along Rte 1095 and offers a daily connection to Chiang Mai (1890B, 25 minutes) on **Kan Air (nationwide call centre 02 551 6111, Pai 0 5369 9955; www.kanairlines.com; Pai Airport).**

Bus

Pai's tiny bus station runs ordinary (fan-cooled) and minibus (propane-fuelled) departures to Chiang Mai and destinations in Mae Hong Son.

White-water rafting (p222), Pai River, Pai
JOHN BORTHWICK/LONELY PLANET IMAGES ©

Chiang Mai (72B to 150B, three to four hours, frequent departures from 8am to 4pm)

Mae Hong Son (70B, 4½ hours, 11am and 1pm)

Minivan

Minivans also depart from Pai's bus terminal. You can also book tickets at aYa Service (☎0 5369 9940; www.ayaservice.com; 22/1 Moo 3 Th Chaisongkhram), which runs hourly air-con minivan buses to Chiang Mai (150B, three hours, frequent departures from 8am to 4pm), as well as a single departure to Chiang Rai (550B, five hours) and Mae Sai (850B, six hours) at 5.30am, and Chiang Khong (650B, seven hours) at 8pm.

Chiang Mai (150B, three hours, every hour from 7am to 4.30pm)

Mae Hong Son (150B, 2½ hours, every hour from 8.30am to 5.30pm)

Getting Around

Most of Pai is accessible on foot. For local excursions you can rent bicycles or motorcycles at several locations around town.

aYa Service (☎0 5369 9940; www.ayaservice.com; Th Chaisongkhram; bikes per 24hr 80-700B) This busy outfit has more than 100 bikes. There are a couple of similar places in the immediate vicinity.

North Wheels (www.northwheels.com; Th Khetkelang; motorcycle/car per 24hr 150/1500B; 7am-8pm)

Ko Samui & the Gulf Coast

The Gulf Coast easily mixes convenience with coastal getaways, ranging from international beach resorts to rustic, coral-fringed islands.

Known as the 'royal' coast, the Upper Gulf has long been the favoured retreat of the Bangkok monarchy and elite. Every Thai king, dating from Rama IV, has found an agreeable spot to build a royal getaway. Today domestic tourists flock to Hua Hin in the same pursuit of leisure, as well as to pay homage to the revered kings. Indeed this is the country's surf-and-turf destination, offering historic sites, pleasant provincial life and long sandy beaches, all within an easy commute from Bangkok.

The Lower Gulf features Thailand's ultimate island trifecta: Ko Samui, Ko Pha-Ngan and Ko Tao. This family of spectacular islands lures millions of tourists every year with powder-soft sands, emerald waters, pumping parties and world-class diving and snorkelling.

Ko Tao (p264)

Ang Thong Marine National Park (p267)

Ko Samui & the Gulf Coast

Ko Samui & the Gulf Coast's Highlights

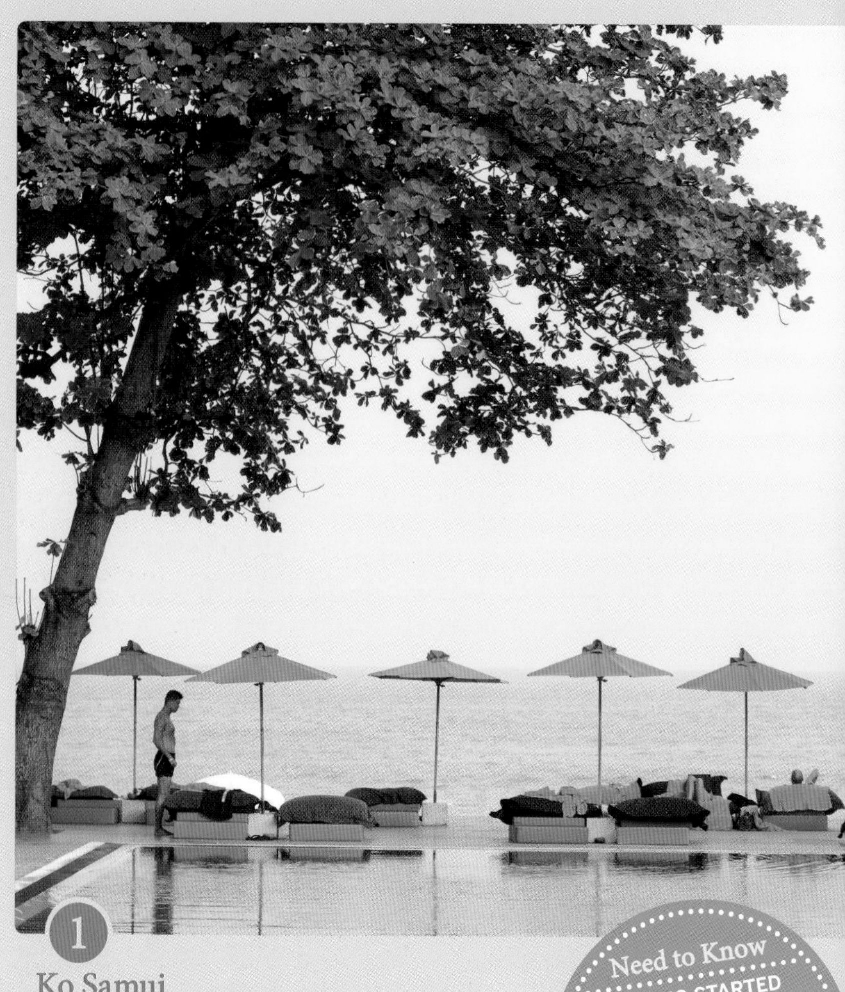

1

Ko Samui

Ko Samui is a tropical paradise that offers beautiful beaches, amazing jungle and an interesting traditional way of life. There's also fine dining and lots of people-watching at the popular beaches, as well as quiet corners for coastal castaways. **Above:** Library (p252), Chaweng; **Top Right:** Zazen (p257), Bo Phut; **Bottom Right:** Swimmers, Ko Samui's interior jungle

Need to Know

GETTING STARTED Check out Saithip's TV projects: Samui Channel and *My Green Journey* **TOP TIP** Motorcycle drivers should take care on Samui **For more coverage, see p250**

Ko Samui Don't Miss List

BY SAITHIP NOOCHSAMNIENG, TV DIRECTOR, SAMUI DIGITAL & *MY GREEN JOURNEY*

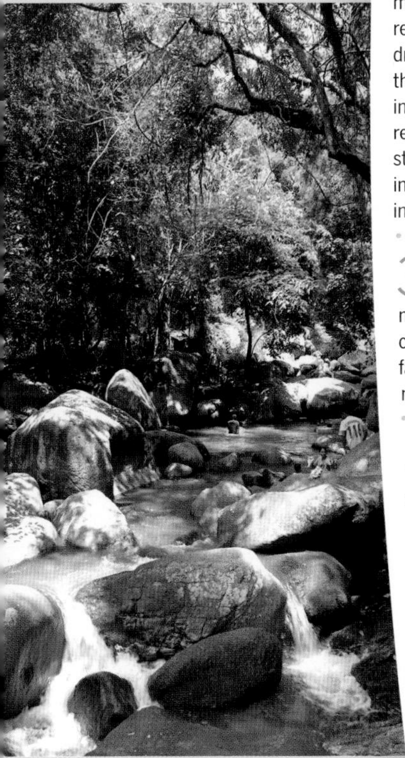

1 NAM TOK HIN LAT

Samui isn't all white-sand beaches and clear seas. There are still patches of interior jungle where waterfalls cascade and pool through rugged terrain. Nam Tok Hin Lat (p250) is accessible by a pleasant walking trail. It takes about an hour from the road to reach the waterfall and there's a refreshing swimming hole to cool you down.

2 BO PHUT

The northern beach of Bo Phut (p253) and its atmospheric Fisherman's Village (so named because of the village's traditional profession) has to be one of the most romantic places on Samui. There are plenty of cosy restaurants (p255) for candlelit dinners and evening sunset drinks. Despite tourism, there are still many locals living in the village and many are extended families that have lived in the village for generations. Many of the elderly residents refuse to have loud noises from pubs and bars so it also stays quiet and peaceful around here. The village is very interesting and charming in the way that the residents have integrated modern tourism with a traditional lifestyle.

3 HUA THANON

Hua Thanon (p256) still retains much of its local multicultural appeal: Chinese, Muslim and Buddhist communities live together in this fishing village. The old-fashioned fishing boats dock in the shallow harbour and a market sells local specialities.

4 CHOENG MON

Choeng Mon (p253) has been my secret beach for all these years. I especially like the beach just behind Imperial Boat House hotel. There is small restaurant owned by a local who goes out fishing to catch the fresh fish for his guests. Sometimes when the tide is low you can also walk to a small island nearby called Ko Fan.

Hua Hin

A favourite weekend getaway for Bangkok's elite (including the royal family), Hua Hin is a friend indeed if beach time is short and the need for comfort is high. It is the closest to the capital with long, sandy beaches, fantastic seafood and classy city accoutrements.

Need to Know

GETTING STARTED Hotels south of town are more secluded **TOP TIP** Get out and explore the coast south of Hua Hin **For more coverage, see p244**

2

Local Knowledge

Hua Hin Don't Miss List

BY SIRANEE MEESITH, EXECUTIVE ASSISTANT, TOUR DE ASIA BICYCLING TOURING & HUA HIN BIKE TOURS

1 HUA HIN BEACH

The city's long stretch of coastline starts south of the harbour at a rocky headland that inspired the town's name (Hua Hin means 'Stone Head'). From here Hua Hin Beach (p244) goes on for kilometres all the way to Khao Takiab, which is adorned by a giant Buddha.

2 JEK PIA COFFEESHOP

Whenever people in Hua Hin don't feel like cooking, they can easily be encouraged to go to Jek Pia Coffeeshop (p247). It is a simple open-air restaurant serving breakfast and dinner. In the morning it is a culinary immersion; Thais like to eat noodles and rice for breakfast (and lunch – and dinner). Jek Pia has the usual morning noodle and rice dishes, including rice soups and stir-fried chicken or pork over rice. No breakfast is complete without Thai-style coffee, which is very sweet and strong. A Jek Pia breakfast is easily wrapped up with a walk on Hua Hin Beach.

3 BAAN SILAPIN

Baan Silapin (p245) is an art village that is always fun to visit on Saturdays when they have a (mini) jazz band and art classes for kids. They also have amazing paintings for sale, but you don't have to buy anything. It is nice just to look around and then consider taking an art class after you've been inspired to make your own masterpiece. Khun Nang leads art classes for adults on Tuesday and Thursday, and children on Saturday.

4 BIKING HUA HIN

Everything within Hua Hin town is accessible by bicycle and just outside of town the roads and trails offer even better cycling. I love to ride my bike and, though Thailand is hot, cycling usually creates a cool breeze. You can take a bike tour, or rent a bike (p249).

Beach Bumming on Ko Pha-Ngan

Ko Pha-Ngan (p259) has mythic status among globetrotters looking for the perfect place to adore the sea, sand and sky. It is an easygoing island known for picturesque surroundings and amnesiac days of doing nothing, or recovering from doing too much the night before. The sandy peninsula of Hat Rin hosts the rowdy Full Moon parties, reminiscent of a university booze-fest, while the north and the east coast are sleepy hangover cures well suited to unstructured days.

3

4

Dive into the Blue on Ko Tao

Get schooled in scuba on Ko Tao (p264). Loads of dive shops deliver low price, high-quality dives at great nearby sites. Ko Tao's location is ideal for beginners: waters are clear and relatively calm, the neon reefs are filled with marine life and the ocean temperatures are as warm as bathwater. Snorkellers can strap on a mask right after breakfast and hit the near-shore reefs with little planning.

NOBORU KOMINE/LONELY PLANET IMAGES ©

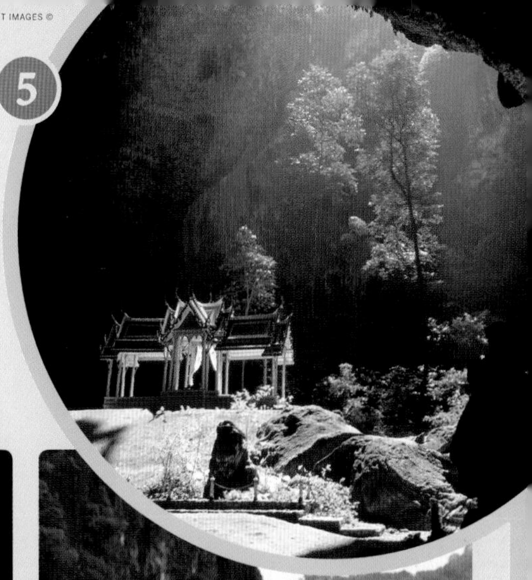

Khao Sam Roi Yot

Allegedly 300 mountains occupy this national park (p248), south of Hua Hin. You can climb to the top for a landscape view of these hump-backed outcroppings or crawl inside for an internal survey of the mountain's guts. Pretty beaches buffer these limestone towers, combining the best of surf and turf. The park's interior mangroves are beloved by migratory bird species.
Tham Phraya Nakhon (p248)

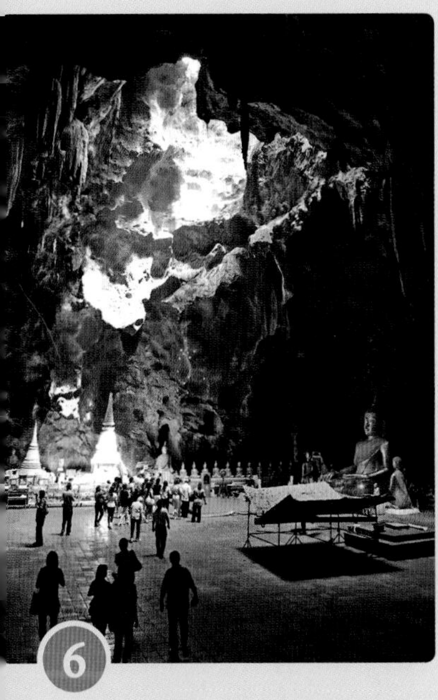

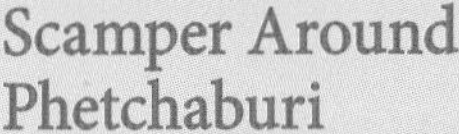

AUSTIN BUSH/LONELY PLANET IMAGES ©

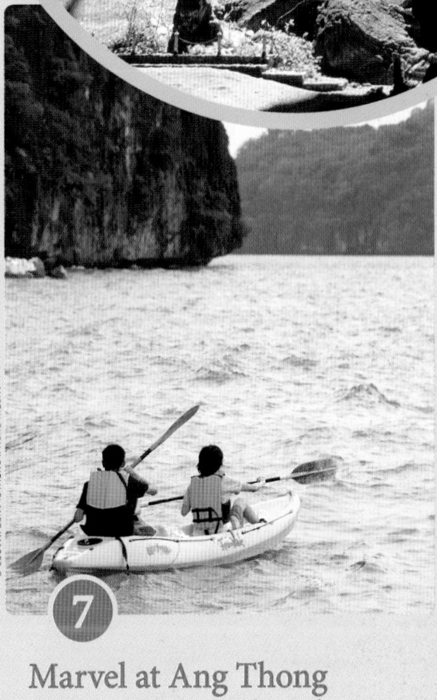

Scamper Around Phetchaburi

An easy daytrip from Hua Hin or Bangkok, Phetchaburi (p242) served as the royal getaway for Rama IV (King Mongkut). The town's central hill was crowned with the king's palace, perfectly poised for viewing the night sky, the monarch's preferred hobby. Nearby, cave-riddled mountains host several shrines that have been further adorned by the artistic handiwork of subterranean irrigation. Tham Khao Luang (p242)

Marvel at Ang Thong Marine National Park

Float between the mysterious limestone islands of Ang Thong Marine National Park (p267) rising out of the sea. Blonde skirts of beach fringe the towering peaks, dimpled and carved by millennia of crashing waves. Paddle up close to view the cliff-clinging creatures and plants that survive the sea's diurnal tides.

Ko Samui & the Gulf Coast's Best...

Diving & Snorkelling Spots

- **Ko Tao** (p264) First stop for beginners to get dive certified; snorkel spots are steps from shore.
- **Ko Pha-Ngan** (p260) Fun dives, fewer divers.
- **Ang Thong Marine National Park** (p267) Underwater sightseeing tours to a surreal landscape of craggy limestone islands and cerulean seas.

Seafood

- **Hua Hin** (p246) Mingle with holidaying Thais at this seafood capital.
- **Ko Samui** (p255) Destination dining for superb gastronomy and seaside settings.
- **Ko Tao** (p266) The island that plays hard eats well, with adept regional specialties.

Party Places

- **Ko Pha-Ngan** (p263) The poster-child of beach revelry, Ko Pha-Ngan's monthly raves are a smear of day-glo body paint, fire-twirlers, chest-thumping beats and drunken abandon.
- **Woo Bar** (p258) Sling back cocktails as the sun sinks into the sea.
- **Chaweng** (p258) Ko Samui's most popular beach reigns day and the night with beachside bars, raucous discos and an assortment of party people.

Spas & Health Resorts

- **Spa Resort** (p253) Ko Samui's first health retreat delivers health and wellness in a seaside setting.
- **Tamarind Retreat** (p253) Spa among the trees and the boulders at this top-notch retreat.
- **Sanctuary** (p262) Release your inner hippie at Ko Pha-Ngan's homage to all things New Age.

Left: Seafood market; **Above:** Snorkellers, Ang Thong Marine National Park (p267)

Need to Know

ADVANCE PLANNING

- **One month before** Book accommodation and train/air tickets.
- **One week before** Book a dive trip.
- **One day before** Buy bus/boat combination tickets; available through travel agents.

RESOURCES

- **Tourism Hua Hin** (www.tourismhuahin.com)
- **Hua Hin Observer** (www.observergroup.net)
- **Backpackers Information Centre** (www.backpackersthailand.com)
- **Koh Tao Community** (www.kohtao-community.com)

GETTING AROUND

- **Boat** From the mainland (Chumphon and Surat Thani) to the Samui islands; interisland services too.
- **Bus** Mainland journeys connect Bangkok to port towns on both coasts.
- **Motorcycle** Self-touring option available on the islands.
- **Sŏrng·tăa·ou** Small pick-up trucks that act as shared taxis and public buses.
- **Train** Overnight journeys from Bangkok to Chumphon and Bangkok to Surat Thani.
- **Túk-túk** Chartered vehicles for trips within towns; remember to bargain.

BE FOREWARNED

- **Motorcycle travel** Wear a helmet and protective clothing and drive carefully in wet conditions; don't put valuables in front baskets.
- **Drugs** Don't buy drugs, especially on Ko Pha-Ngan.
- **Women** Don't travel alone from bars on Ko Samui and Ko Pha-Ngan. Don't sunbathe topless.
- **Bus/boat tickets** Be sure you have tickets for both modes of travel before paying.

Ko Samui & the Gulf Coast Itineraries

Take a long weekend or a five-day escape to the Gulf Coast's prime attractions. Next time you can come back and be a beach hermit.

3 DAYS

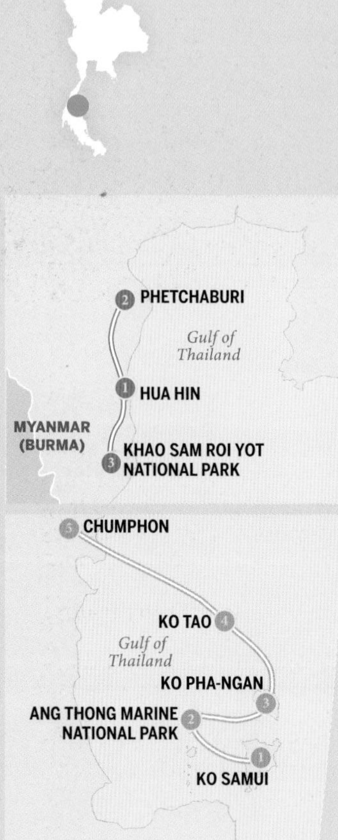

HUA HIN TO PHETCHABURI

Quick Beach Break

If you're short on time, **(1) Hua Hin** is an ideal commute by road from the capital, without the hassle of a ferry transfer. The beachfront hotels meet international standards and the nightly food market specialises in unbeatable seafood specialties, enjoyed by domestic and international tourists alike. For many Thais, the night market is the sole reason for a visit. But the mainland beach is another powerful contender, with its powder-soft sand and a rocky headland adorned by a golden Buddha and hilltop temple. It is an unbeatable convergence of city conveniences and attractions with coastal distractions.

Take a break from the beach and head to **(2) Phetchaburi** for a bit of culture, a nearby provincial town boasting a hilltop palace and a Gaudi-esque cave temple.

Alternatively, day trip to **(3) Khao Sam Roi Yot National Park**, a nature preserve filled with limestone caves, the country's largest freshwater marsh and migrating bird species.

Left: Tham Phraya Nakhon (p248), Khao Sam Roi Yot National Park
Right: Ang Thong Marine National Park (p267)

KO SAMUI TO CHUMPHON

Toast the Samui Sisters

The Gulf coast's premier island, **(1) Ko Samui** appeals to every kind of traveller and is easily accessible from Bangkok by air. Base yourself in lovely Chaweng to be close to the action, or retreat to the northern beaches of Mae Nam and Bo Phut, both with laid-back appeal. Consider dabbling in the island's various health treatments, from beachside yoga to three-day fasts. Rent a motorcycle and tour the sleepy backwater villages in the southern part of the island.

Swim among the craggy and curiously shaped limestone islands of **(2) Ang Thong Marine National Park**, a popular day trip from Samui.

If your timing is right, you can ferry over to **(3) Ko Pha-Ngan** for the monthly beachside raves. Welcome the rising sun and hop on a ferry back to Samui for some well-earned sleep.

Devote a few days to a snorkelling or diving tour of **(4) Ko Tao**, a small island sheltering colourful coral gardens. The west coast is monopolised by the diving scene, while the rocky coves of the east coast are for solitude seekers. Ferry to the mainland port of **(5) Chumphon** to catch an overnight train back to Bangkok.

Discover Ko Samui & the Gulf Coast

At a Glance

- **Hua Hin** (p244) Seaside town for seafood and aristocrats.
- **Chumphon** (p249) Mainland transfer to Samui islands.
- **Ko Tao** (p264) Dive-centric island.
- **Ko Pha-Ngan** (p259) Mellow hang-out island.
- **Ko Samui** (p250) Well-rounded resort island.
- **Surat Thani** (p269) Mainland transfer to Samui islands and Andaman coast.

Ko Samui (p250)

-SID-/DREAMSTIME ©

Phetchaburi (Phetburi) เพชรบุรี

An easy escape from Bangkok, Phetchaburi should be on every cultural traveller's itinerary. It has temples and palaces like Ayuthaya, outlying jungles and cave shrines like Kanchanaburi, and access to the coast. The town offers a delightful slice of provincial life with busy markets, old teak shophouses and visiting groups of Thai students.

Sights & Activities

THAM KHAO LUANG Cave

(ถ้ำเขาหลวง; **8am-6pm**) About 4km north of town is Tham Khao Luang, a dramatic stalactite-filled chamber that is one of Thailand's most impressive cave shrines and a favourite of Rama IV. The cave is accessed through a steep set of stairs. It's central Buddha figure is often illuminated with a heavenly glow when sunlight filters in through the heart-shaped skylight. On the opposite end of the chamber is a row of sitting Buddhas casting shadows on the cavern wall.

PHRA RAM RATCHANIWET Historic Site

(พระรามราชนิเวศน์; **Ban Peun Palace; 0 3242 8083; admission 50B; 8am-4pm Mon-Fri**). This incredible art deco creation is 1km south of town. Construction of the royal summer palace began in 1910 at the behest of Rama V (who died just after the project was started). It was designed by German architects, who used the opportunity to showcase contemporary innovations in construction and interior design.

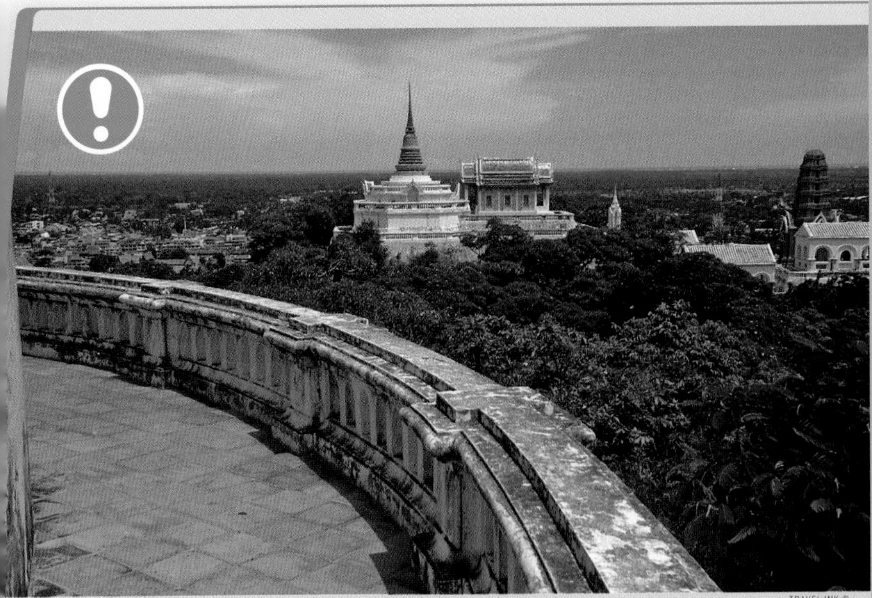
TRAVEL INK ©

Don't Miss Phra Nakhon Khiri Historical Park

This national historical park sits regally atop Khao Wang (Palace Hill), surveying the city with subdued opulence. Rama IV (King Mongkut) built the palace and surrounding temples in 1859 to be used as a retreat from Bangkok. The hilltop location allowed the king to pursue his interest in astronomy and stargazing.

The palace was built in a mix of European and Chinese styles and each breezy hall is furnished with royal belongings. Cobblestone paths lead from the palace through the forested hill to three summits, each topped by a chedi. The white spire of **Phra That Chom Phet** skewers the sky and can be spotted from the city below.

There are two entrances to the site. The front entrance is across from Th Ratwithi and involves a strenuous walk along a footpath that passes a troop of unpredictable monkeys. The back entrance is on the opposite side of the hill and has a **tram** (one way adult/child 40B/free; 8.30am-5.30pm) that goes to the summit. The park is a popular school-group outing and you'll be as much of a photo-op as the historic buildings.

A **Monday night market** lines the street in front of Khao Wang with the usual food and clothing stalls.

THINGS YOU NEED TO KNOW

อุทยานประวัติศาสตร์พระนครคีรี; 0 3240 1006; admission 150B; 8.30am-5pm

Getting There & Away

Most air-conditioned buses and minivans stop out of town on Th Phetkasem in front of the Big C department store. Destinations include Cha-am (50B, 40 minutes, frequent departures) and Hua Hin (50B, two hours). Motorcycle taxis await and can take you into town for around 50B.

Frequent rail services run to/from Bangkok's Hualamphong station. Fares vary depending on the train and class (3rd class 84B to 144B, 2nd class 188B to 358B, three hours).

Getting Around

Motorcycle taxis go anywhere in the town centre for 40B to 50B. *Sŏrng·tăa·ou* cost about the same.

Hua Hin หัวหิน

POP 98,896

Thailand's original beach resort is no palm-fringed castaway island and it is all the better for it. Instead it is a delightful mix of city and sea, with a cosmopolitan ambiance, lively markets, tasty street eats, long, wide beaches and fully functional city services (meaning no septic streams bisect the beach like those *other* places).

Today all the international hotel chains have properties in Hua Hin, and a growing number of wealthy expats retire to the nearby housing estates and condominiums. Middle-class and high-society Thais from Bangkok swoop into town on weekends, making parts of the city look a lot like upper Sukhumvit.

Hua Hin is a bustling Thai town, seafood is plentiful and affordable, there's cheap public transport for beach hopping and it takes a lot less time and effort (and money) to get here from Bangkok than to the southern islands.

Sights

The city's beaches are numerous, wide and long; swimming is safe, and Hua Hin continues to enjoy some of the peninsula's driest weather. During stormy weather, watch out for jellyfish.

Hua Hin Town เมืองหัวหิน

A former fishing village, Hua Hin town retains its roots with an old teak shophouse district bisected by narrow soi, pier houses that have been converted into restaurants or guest houses, and a busy fishing pier still in use today.

HAT HUA HIN Beach

(หาดหัวหิน; public access via eastern end of Th Damnoen Kasem) When viewed from the main public entrance, Hua Hin's beach might seem like a lot of hype. Don't be dismayed; this is the people-watching spot.

If you're after swimming and sunbathing, continue south to where the 5km-long beach stretches into a Buddha-adorned headland (Khao Takiab). The sand is a fine white powder that is wide

Hua Hin

and long, and the sea is a calm gray-green.

HUA HIN HILLS VINEYARD Vineyard

(ไร่องุ่นหัวหินฮิลล์ วินยาร์ด; ☎08 1701 8874; www.huahinhillsvineyard.com; Th Hua Hin-Pa Lu-U; ⏲10am-6pm) Part of the New Latitudes wine movement, this vineyard is nestled in a scenic mountain valley 45km west of Hua Hin. The loamy sand and slate soil feeds several Rhone grape varieties that are used in its Monsoon Valley wine label.

A vineyard shuttle leaves the affiliated **Hua Hin Hills Wine Cellar store** (☎0 3252 6351, Market Village, Th Phetkasem, South Hua Hin) at 10.30am and 3pm and returns at 1.30pm and 6pm; return ticket is 200B.

South Hua Hin

South of Hua Hin are a series of beaches framed by dramatic headlands that make great daytrips when Hua Hin beach feels too urban.

KHAO TAKIAB Viewpoint

(เขาตะเกียบ) About 7km south of Hua Hin, Monumental Chopstick Mountain guards the southern end of Hua Hin beach and is home to a giant standing Buddha. Atop the 2722m mountain is a Thai-Chinese temple (**Wat Khao Lat**). The many resident monkeys are not to be trusted, but the views are great.

HAT KHAO TAO Beach

(13km south of Hua Hin) A barely inhabited beach stretches several kilometres south from Khao Takiab to Khao Tao (Turtle Mountain). It is blissfully free of civilization: there are no high rises, no beach chairs, no sarong sellers and no horseback riders.

Detour: Baan Silapin

Local painter Tawee Kase-ngam established this **artist collective** (บ้านศิลปิน; ☎0 3253 4830; www.huahinartistvillage.com; Th Hua Hin-Pa Lu-U; ⏲10am-5pm Tue-Sun) in a shady grove 4km west of Th Phetkasem. The galleries and studio spaces highlight the works of 21 artists, many of whom opted out of Bangkok's fast-paced art world in favour of Hua Hin's more relaxed atmosphere and scenic landscape of mountains and sea. Outlying clay huts shelter the playful sculptures of Nai Dee and Mae A-Ngoon. Khun Nang, a skilful and charismatic teacher, leads **art classes** (9.30am-11.30am; 300/200B adult/child) for adults on Tuesday and Thursday, and for children on Saturday.

Activities

Hua Hin is an ideal kiteboarding spot: it has a long, consistent windy season. It's also home to the country's first golf course, and continues to be an international and domestic golfing destination.

KITEBOARDING ASIA Kiteboarding

(☎08 8230 0016; www.kiteboardingasia.com; South Hua Hin; beginner courses 11,000B) This 10-year-old company operates four beachside shops that rent equipment and offer lessons.

HUA HIN GOLF CENTRE Golf

(☎0 3253 0476; www.huahingolf.com; Th Selakam; ⏲noon-10pm) The friendly staff at this pro shop can steer you to the most affordable, well-maintained courses where the monkeys won't try to run off with your balls. The company also organises golf tours and rents equipment.

BLACK MOUNTAIN GOLF COURSE Golf

(☎0 3261 8666; www.bmghuahin.com; green fees 2500B) The city's newest course is everyone's favourite.

HUA HIN BIKE TOURS Cycling
(☎08 1173 4469; www.huahinbiketours.com; 4/34 Soi Hua Hin 96/1, Th Phetkasem, South Hua Hin; tours 1500-2500B) A husband-and-wife team operates this cycling company that leads half-, full- and multiday tours to a variety of attractions in and around Hua Hin.

Sleeping

BAAN BAYAN Hotel $$$
(☎0 3253 3540; www.baanbayan.com; 119 Th Phetkasem, South Hua Hin; r 4000-11,000B; ❄🏊) A colonial beach house built in the early 20th century, Baan Bayan is perfect for travellers seeking a luxury experience without the overkill of a big resort. The airy, high-ceilinged rooms are painted a relaxing buttery yellow, the staff are attentive and the location is absolute beachfront.

BAAN LAKSASUBHA Hotel $$$
(☎0 3251 4525; www.baanlaksasubha.com; Th 53/7 Naresdamri; r 4200-7900B; ❄📶🏊) Next door to the Sofitel, this petite resort, owned by a Bangkok aristocrat, specialises in family-friendly cottages. The decor is so crisp and subdued that it is almost plain, meandering garden paths lead past the pool to the beach and there's a dedicated kid's room with toys and books.

VERANDA LODGE Hotel $$$
(☎0 3253 3678; www.verandalodge.com; 113 Soi Hua Hin 67, Th Phetkasem, South Hua Hin; r 3000-5000B; ❄📶🏊) Beachfront without the whopping price tag, this top-end hotel has a variety of options, from modern hotel rooms to luxurious garden bungalows.

Eating

NIGHT MARKET Seafood $$
(Th Dechanuchit btw Th Phetkasem & Th Sasong; dishes from 60B; ⏰5pm-midnight) An attraction that rivals the beach, Hua Hin's night market tops locals' lists of favourite spots to eat. Ice-packed displays of spiny lobsters and king prawns appeal to the big-spenders, but the simple stir-fry stalls offer food that is just as tasty.

Seafood market

ANTONIOSEN/DREAMSTIME ©

SANG THAI RESTAURANT Thai $

(Th Naresdamri; dishes 120-350B; ⏲lunch & dinner) One of many beloved pier-side restaurants, Sang Thai soaks in the view and specialises in whole steamed fish that arrives still sizzling to your table.

JEK PIA COFFEESHOP Seafood $$

(51/6 Th Dechanuchit; dishes 80-160B; ⏲breakfast, lunch & dinner) More than just a coffeeshop, this 50-year-old restaurant is another culinary destination specialising in an extensive array of stir-fried seafood dishes.

HUA HIN KOTI Seafood $$

(☎0 3251 1252; 16/1 Th Dechanuchit; dishes 80-250B; ⏲lunch & dinner) Across from the night market, this Thai-Chinese restaurant is a national culinary luminary. Thais adore the fried crab balls, while foreigners swoon over *dôm yam gûng* (shrimp soup with lemongrass).

Information

Medical Services

Hospital San Paolo (**☎0 3253 2576; 222 Th Phetkasem**) Just south of town; has emergency facilities.

Bangkok Hospital Hua Hin (**☎0 3261 6800; www.bangkokhospital.com/huahin; Th Phetkasem btw Soi Hua Hin 94 & 106;**) The latest outpost of the luxury hospital chain.

Tourist Information

Hua Hin Tourist Information Office (**☎0 3251 1047; cnr Th Phetkasem & Th Damnoen Kasem, Hua Hin; ⏲8.30am-4.30pm Mon-Fri**) Conveniently located tourism office. There's another branch (**☎0 3252 2797; Th Naebkehardt, Hua Hin; ⏲9am-7.30pm Mon-Fri, 9.30am-5pm Sat & Sun**).

Getting There & Away

Air

The airport (**www.huahinairport.com**) is 6km north of town but only has charter services through Nok Mini (**☎0 2641 4190; www.nokmini.com**).

Bus

Hua Hin's long-distance bus station (**Th Phetkasem btw Soi Hua Hin 94 & 98**) is south of town and serves the following destinations:

Chiang Mai (785B, 12 hours, three daily departures)

Phuket (856B, nine hours, one nightly departure)

Surat Thani (480B, seven hours, two daily departures)

Bangkok buses (160B, three hours, every two hours from 8am to 9pm) also leave from a bus company's in-town office (Th Sasong), near the night market.

Ordinary buses depart from a station (**cnr Th Phetkasem & Th Chomsin**), north of the market, and go to the following destinations:

Cha-am (50B, 30 minutes) Minivans to Bangkok's Sai Tai Mai (Southern) bus station and Victory Monument (180B, three hours, every 30 minutes from 4am to 8pm) leave from an office on Th Naebkehardt.

Lomprayah (**☎0 3253 3739; Th Narasdamri**) Offers a bus-boat combination from Hua Hin to Ko Tao (1000B, 8½ hours; one morning and one night departure).

Phetchaburi (50B, 1½ hours)

Train

There are frequent trains running to/from Bangkok's Hualamphong station (2nd class 212-302B, 3rd class 94-154B, four hours) and other stations on the southern railway line.

Getting Around

Green *sŏrng·tăa·ou* depart from the corner of Th Sasong and Th Dechanuchit, near the night market and travel south on Th Phetkasem to Khao Takiab (20B). Pranburi-bound buses depart from the same stop.

Motorcycles (250B to 500B per day) can be hired from shops on Th Damnoen Kasem. Thai Rent A Car (**☎0 2737 8888; www.thairentacar.com**) is a professional car-rental agency with competitive prices, a well-maintained fleet and hotel drop-offs.

If You Like... Beach Getaways

If you like Hua Hin's long sandy coastline, then explore its 'country cousin' of Pranburi, 35km south of Hua Hin and best accessed by private transport.

1 **AWAY HUA HIN**
(☎08 9144 6833; www.away-huahin.com; south of Khao Kalok; r from 5000B;) A boutique resort without pretence, Away has reconstructed seven antique teak houses on this coastal patch of paradise.

2 **LA A NATU BED & BAKERY**
(☎0 3268 9941; www.laanatu.com; south of Khao Kalok; r from 5000B;) Turning the humble Thai rice village into a luxury experience is all the rage but La a natu does it with a little more panache than most. And then there's the semi-private beach right at your doorstep.

3 **DOLPHIN BAY RESORT**
(☎0 3255 9333; www.dolphinbayresort.com; Dolphin Bay; r from 1500B; @) The resort that defined Dolphin Bay as a family-friendly retreat offers a low-key, holiday-camp ambiance. The gang will love it.

4 **BRASSIERE BEACH**
(☎0 3263 0555; www.brassierebeach.com; Dolphin Bay; r from 5000B;) A delicious combination of privacy and personality, these nine stucco villas are sandwiched between Khao Sam Roi Yot National Park and a secluded beach.

Khao Sam Roi Yot National Park อุทยานแห่งชาติเขาสามร้อยยอด

Towering limestone outcrops form a rocky jigsaw-puzzled landscape at this 98-sq-km **park** (☎0 3282 1568; adult/child 200/100B), which means Three Hundred Mountain Peaks. There are also caves, beaches and coastal marshlands to explore for outdoor enthusiasts and bird-watchers. With its proximity to Hua Hin, the park is well visited by daytrippers and contains a mix of public conservation land and private shrimp farms, so don't come expecting remote, virgin territory.

Sights & Activities

HAT LAEM SALA Beach

Laem Sala is a sandy beach flanked on three sides by limestone hills and casuarinas. It's not accessible via vehicle road. Instead follow the turn-off from Tham Kaew to the ocean where there are beachfront restaurants; this is Bang Pu where you can hire boats to Laem Sala (300B round-trip). Alternatively you can follow the steep footpath for a 20-minute hike to the beach where you'll find a small visitors centre, restaurant, bungalows and camp sites.

THAM PHRAYA NAKHON Cave

The park's most popular attraction and the primary reason for visiting Laem Sala is to pay homage to this revered cave. A royal săh·lah built for Rama V in 1890 sits bathing in streams of light. The 450m trail, which starts from Hat Laem Sala, is steep, rocky and at times slick so don't wear your ballet flats. Once there you'll find two large caverns with sinkholes – the meeting hall is the second of the two.

THUNG SAM ROI YOT Bird-Watching

The country's largest freshwater marsh is recognized as a natural treasure and provides an important habitat for songbirds and water birds, amphibians and other wetland species. It sits in the western corner of the park accessible from Hwy 4 (Th Phetkasem) at the Km275.6 marker; hold on to your entrance fee ticket to avoid having to pay again.

Getting There & Away

The park is about 40km south of Hua Hin, and best visited by car. There are two main entrances into the park. The turn-off for the northern entrance is at Km256 marker on Hwy 4 (Th

Phetkasem). The southern entrance is off the Km286.5 marker.

Travel agencies in Hua Hin run daytrips to the park. **Hua Hin Bike Tours** (08 1173 4469; www.huahinbiketours.com; tours 1500-2500B) offer cycling and hiking tours.

Chumphon ชุมพร

POP 55,835

Chumphon is a transit town funnelling travellers to and from Ko Tao or westward to Ranong or Phuket.

Sleeping

MORAKOT HOTEL Hotel $$
(0 7750 2999; 102-112 Th Tawee Sinka; r 800-950B;) The multistorey lime-green building has recently received a fresh upgrade, making it a solid midrange choice for provincial VIPs.

CHUMPHON GARDENS HOTEL Hotel $$
(0 7750 6888; 66/1 Th Tha Taphao; r 500B;) Spacious rooms with cable TVs are a great distraction while you hang around and wait.

Information

New Infinity Travel (0 7757 0176; 68/2 Th Tha Taphao; 8am-10pm; @) A great travel agency with knowledgeable and friendly staff; it also sells paperbacks and rents four rooms.

Getting There & Away

Air

Solar Air (0 7755 8212; www.solarair.co.th) flies to Bangkok (2900B, one hour, once daily).

Boat

You have many boat options for getting to Ko Tao (p264), though departure times are limited to mainly morning and night. Most ticket prices include pier transfer.

Slow boat (250B, six hours, midnight) The cheapest, slowest and most scenic option, as everyone stretches out on the open deck of the fishing boat with the stars twinkling overhead.

Car ferry (350B, six hours, 11pm Mon-Sun) A more comfortable ride with bunk or mattress options available on board.

Songserm express boat (450B, three hours, 7am) Faster, morning option leaving from Tha Talaysub, about 10km from town.

Lomprayah catamaran (600B, 1¾ hours, 7am & 1pm) A popular bus-boat combination that leaves from Tha Tummakam, 25km from town; the ticket office is beside Chumphon train station.

Bus

There are several in-town bus stops to save you a trip out to the main bus station. **Choke Anan**

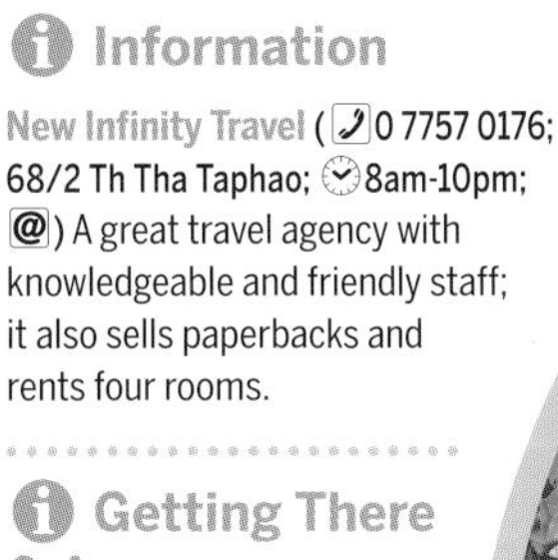

Monkey, Khao Sam Roi Yot National Park

Tour (☎0 7751 1757; soi off of Th Pracha Uthit), in the centre of town, has daily departures to the following destinations:

Bangkok's Southern (Sai Tai Mai) station (375-550B, eight hours, five departures)

Ranong (320B; two hours; four departures)

Phuket (320B; 3½ hours; four departures)

Suwannatee Tour (☎0 7750 4901), 700m southeast of train station road, serves the following destinations:

Bangkok's Southern (Sai Tai Mai) station (270-405B 2nd class-VIP buses, three departures)

Prachuap Khiri Khan (120B)

Hua Hin (170B)

Phetchaburi (205B)

Minivan companies are numerous and depart from individual offices throughout town:

Surat Thani (170B, three hours, every hour) Departs from an unnamed soi on Th Krom Luang Chumphon; the soi is east of an optical shop.

Ranong (120B, 2½ hours, every hour 7am to 3pm) Departs from Th Tha Taphao; arrives at Ranong bus station (not in the town).

Train

There are frequent services to/from Bangkok (2nd class 292B to 382B, 3rd class 235B, 7½ hours). Overnight sleepers range from 440B to 770B.

Southbound rapid and express trains – the only trains with 1st and 2nd class – are less frequent and can be difficult to book out of Chumphon between November and February.

Ko Samui เกาะสมุย

POP 40,230

Ko Samui is a choose-your-own-adventure kinda place that strives, like a genie, to grant every tourist their ultimate holiday wish. You want ocean views, daily massages and personal butlers? Poof – here are the keys to your private poolside villa. Is it a holistic aura-cleansing vacation you're after? Shazam – take a seat on your yoga mat before your afternoon colonic. Wanna party like a rockstar? Pow – trance your way down the beach with the throngs of whisky-bucket-toting tourists.

Sights

Ko Samui is quite large – the island's ring road is almost 100km.

CHAWENG Beach

(Map p251) This is the most popular spot. It's the longest and most beautiful beach on the island. The sand is powder soft, and the water is surprisingly clear, considering the number of boats and bathers.

HIN-TA & HIN-YAI Landmark

(Map p251) At the south end of Lamai, the second-largest beach, you'll find these infamous stone formations (also known as Grandfather and Grandmother Rocks). These genitalia-shaped rocks provide endless mirth to giggling Thai tourists.

HUA THANON Neighbourhood

Hua Thanon is home to a vibrant Muslim community, and its anchorage of high-bowed fishing vessels is a veritable gallery of intricate designs.

BO PHUT Neighbourhood

Although the northern beaches have coarser sand and aren't as striking as the beaches in the east, they have a laid-back vibe and stellar views of Ko Pha-Ngan. Bo Phut stands out with its charming Fisherman's Village; a collection of narrow Chinese shophouses that have been transformed into trendy resorts and boutique hotels.

NAM TOK NA MUANG Waterfall

(Map p251) At 30m, this is the tallest waterfall on Samui and lies in the centre of the island about 12km from Na Thon. The water cascades over ethereal purple rocks, and there's a great pool for swimming at the base. This is the most scenic – and somewhat less frequented – of Samui's falls.

NAM TOK HIN LAT Waterfall

(Map p251) Near Na Thon, this is worth visiting if you have an afternoon to

Ko Samui

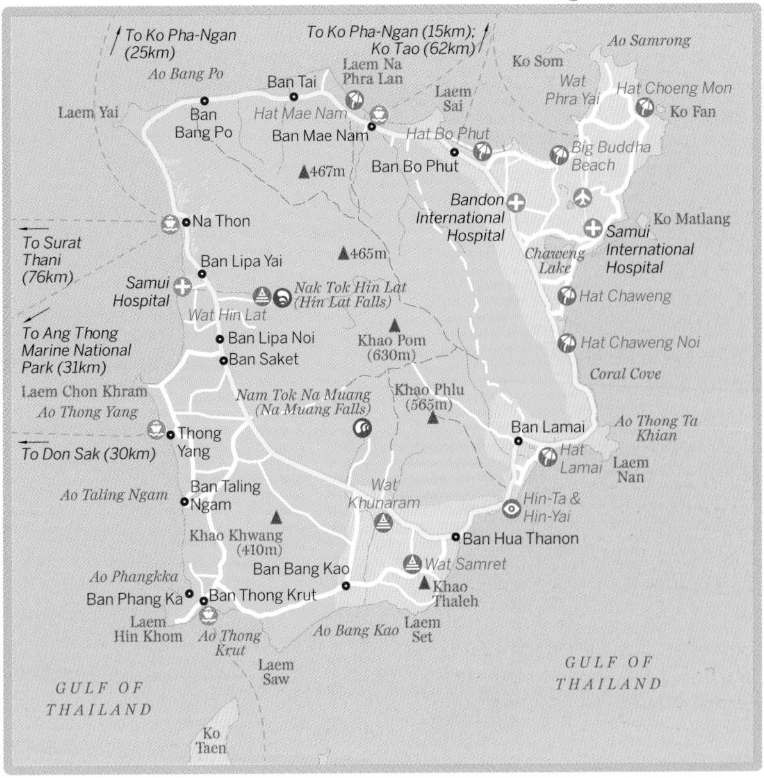

kill before taking a boat back to the mainland. After a mildly strenuous hike over streams and boulders, reward yourself with a dip in the pool at the bottom of the falls. Keep an eye out for the Buddhist temple that posts signs with spiritual words of moral guidance and enlightenment. Sturdy shoes are recommended.

Activities

If you're serious about diving, head to Ko Tao and base yourself there for the duration of your diving adventure. If you're short on time and don't want to leave Samui, there are plenty of operators who will take you to the same dive sites (at a greater fee, of course).

Competition for Samui's five-star accommodation is fierce, which means that the spas are of the highest calibre. The Spa Resort in Lamai is the island's original health destination, and is still known for its effective 'clean me out' fasting regime.

100 DEGREES EAST Diving

(0 7742 5936; www.100degreeseast.com; Bang Rak) Highly recommended.

BLUE STARS Kayaking, Snorkelling

(0 7741 3231; www.bluestars.info; trips 2600B) For those interested in snorkelling and kayaking, book a day trip to the stunning Ang Thong Marine National Park. Blue Stars, based in Hat Chaweng on Ko Samui, offers guided sea-kayak trips in the park.

Sleeping

Chaweng

JUNGLE CLUB Bungalows **$$**
(☎08 1894 2327; www.jungleclubsamui.com; bungalows 800-4500B; ❄@📶🏊) This isolated mountain getaway is a huge hit with locals and tourists alike. There's a relaxed back-to-nature vibe – guests chill around the stunning horizon pool or tuck themselves away for a catnap under the canopied roofs of an open-air *săh·lah* (often spelt *sala*). Taxis from the main road cost 50B; it's 100B from central Chaweng.

LIBRARY Resort **$$$**
(☎0 7742 2767; www.thelibrary.name; r from 13,300B; ❄@📶🏊) The entire resort is a sparkling white mirage accented with black trimming and slatted curtains. The large rectangular pool is not to be missed – it is tiled in piercing shades of red, making the term 'bloodbath' suddenly seem appealing.

BAAN CHAWENG BEACH RESORT Resort **$$$**
(☎0 7742 2403; www.baanchawengbeachresort.com; bungalows 3500-7000B; ❄@📶🏊) A pleasant option for those who want top-end luxury without the hefty bill, Baan Chaweng is one of the new kids on the block and is keeping its prices relatively low.

TANGO BEACH RESORT Resort **$$**
(☎0 7742 2470; www.tangobeachsamui.com; r 1600-4600B; ❄@📶🏊) A midrange all-star, Tango features a string of bungalows arranged along a teak boardwalk that meanders away from the beach.

PANDORA BOUTIQUE HOTEL Resort **$$$**
(☎0 7741 3801; www.pandora-samui.com; r 2700-4900B; ❄📶🏊) As adorable as it is memorable, Pandora looks like it just fell out of a comic book – maybe *Tintin and the Mystery of Surprisingly Cheap Accommodation in Chaweng*? Rooms are outfitted with cheerful pastels, wooden moulding, and the occasional stone feature.

Chaweng (p250), Ko Samui

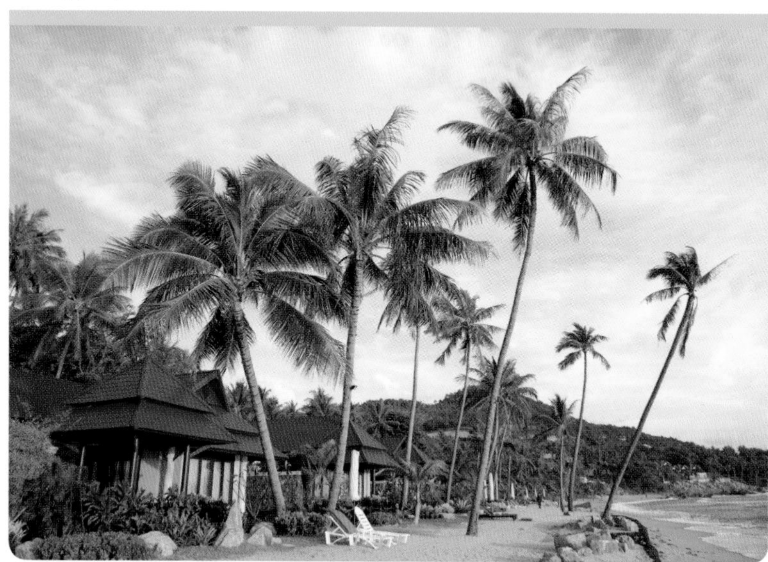

CHAWENG GARDEN BEACH Resort **$$**
(☎0 7796 0394; www.chawenggarden.com; r 1850-8500B; ❄@📶🏊) A popular 'flashpacker' choice, this campus of accommodation has a large variety of room types serviced by an extra-smiley staff.

Lamai

ROCKY RESORT Resort **$$$**
(☎0 7741 8367; www.rockyresort.com; Hua Thanon; r 4890-17,000B; ❄📶🏊) Our favourite spot just south of Lamai, Rocky finds the right balance between an upmarket ambience and an unpretentious, sociable atmosphere. The pool has been carved in between a collection of boulders, mimicking the rocky beach nearby (hence the name).

SAMUI JASMINE RESORT Resort **$$$**
(☎0 7723 2446; r & bungalows 3800-5000B; ❄📶🏊) Pleasant Samui Jasmine offers great deals. Go for the lower-priced rooms – most have excellent views of the ocean and the crystal-coloured lap pool.

SPA RESORT Bungalows **$$**
(☎0 7723 0855; www.spasamui.com; Lamai North; bungalows 800-2800B; ❄📶) This health spa has a bevy of therapeutic programs on offer, and no one seems to mind that the lodging is cheap by Lamai's standards. Programs include colonics, massage, aqua detox, hypnotherapy and yoga, just to name a few. Accommodation tends to book up quickly, so it's best to reserve in advance (via email). Nonguests are welcome to partake in the programs.

If You Like... Health & Wellbeing

Look after yourself in Ko Samui, where you can practise yoga, have a massage or take part in a detox and wellness program.

1 **TAMARIND RETREAT**
(☎0 7723 0571; www.tamarindretreat.com) Tucked far away from the beach within a silent coconut-palm plantation, Tamarind's small collection of villas and massage studios is seamlessly incorporated into nature: some have granite boulders built into walls and floors, others offer private ponds or creative outdoor baths.

2 **YOGA THAILAND**
(☎0 7792 0090; www.yoga-thailand.com; Phang Ka; retreats from €680; ❄@📶) Secreted away along the southern shores, Yoga Thailand is ushering in a new era of therapeutic holidaying with its state-of-the-art facilities and dedicated team of trainers.

3 **ABSOLUTE SANCTUARY**
(☎0 7760 1190; www.absoluteyogasamui.com) What was once a friendly yoga studio has blossomed into a gargantuan wellness complex, featuring plenty of accommodation and an exhaustive menu of detox and wellness programs.

Northern Beaches

CHOENG MON

IMPERIAL BOAT HOUSE HOTEL Resort **$$$**
(☎0 7742 5041-52; www.imperialhotels.com; Hat Choeng Mon; r 4000-5500B, boat ste 6000-6700B; ❄📶🏊) This sophisticated retreat has a three-storey hotel and several free-standing bungalows made from imported-teak rice barges, whose bows have been transformed into stunning patios. Oxidised copper cannons blast streams of water into the boat-shaped swimming pool.

BO PHUT

The beach isn't breathtaking, but Bo Phut has the most dynamic lodging in all of Samui. A string of vibrant boutique cottages starts deep within the clutter of Fisherman's Village and radiates outward along the sand.

L'HACIENDA Guest House **$$**
(☎0 7724 5943; www.samui-hacienda.com; r 1400-3500B; ❄📶🏊) Polished terracotta and rounded archways give the entrance a Spanish mission motif. Similar decor permeates the eight adorable rooms, which

sport loads of personal touches such as pebbled bathroom walls and translucent bamboo lamps. There's a charming surprise waiting for you on the roof, and we're pretty sure you'll love it as much as we did.

ZAZEN Resort **$$$**
(☎ 0 7742 5085; www.samuizazen.com; r 6010-17,200B; ❄ @ 📶 🏊) What was once a simple place has now transformed into the boutique-iest boutique resort on Samui. Every inch of this charming getaway has been thoughtfully and creatively designed. It's 'Asian minimalism meets modern Rococo' with a scarlet accent wall, terracotta goddesses, a dash of feng shui, and a generous smattering of good taste. Guests relax poolside on comfy beach chairs gently shaded by canvas parasols. The walk-in prices are scary, so it's best to book in advance.

LODGE Hotel **$$**
(☎ 0 7742 5337; www.apartmentsamui.com; r 1400-2500B; ❄ 📶 🏊) The Lodge feels like a colonial hunting chalet with pale walls and dark wooden beams jutting across the ceiling. Every room has scores of wall hangings and a private balcony overlooking the beach. The 'pent huts' on the top floor are very spacious. Reservations are a must – this place always seems to be full.

MAE NAM & BANG PO

MAENAM RESORT Bungalows **$$**
(☎ 0 7742 5116; www.maenamresort.com; bungalows 1400-3000B; ❄ @ 📶) Palm-bark cottages are set in several rows amid a private, jungle-like garden. The cottages are decked out in a mix of wicker and wooden furnishings, and vary in price according to their distance from the beach. Suites are a steal for families.

SHANGRILAH Bungalows **$**
(☎ 0 7742 5189; bungalows 300-2000B; ❄) A backpacker's Shangri La indeed – these are some of the cheapest huts around and they're in decent condition.

Left: Chaweng (p250), Ko Samui; **Below:** Jetty, Bo Phut (p250), Ko Samui
(LEFT) PARASOLA.NET / ALAMY ©; (BELOW) AUSTIN BUSH/LONELY PLANET IMAGES ©

Eating

Influenced by the mainland, Samui is peppered with *kôw gaang* (rice and curry) shops, usually just a wooden shack displaying large metal pots of southern Thai–style curries. Folks pull up on their motorcycles, lift up the lids to survey the vibrantly coloured contents, and pick one for lunch. *Kôw gaang* shops are easily found along the Ring Rd (Rte 4169) and sell out of the good stuff by 1pm.

Lured by high salaries and spectacular weather, world-class chefs regularly make an appearance on the island.

Chaweng

For the best ambience, get off the road and head to the beach, where many bungalow operators set up tables on the sand and turn on glittery fairy lights at night.

LAEM DIN MARKET Market $

(dishes from 30B; ⏲4am-6pm, night market 6pm-2am) A busy day market, Laem Din is packed with stalls selling fresh fruits, vegetables and meats that stock local Thai kitchens. Pick up a kilo of sweet green oranges or wander the stalls trying to spot the ingredients in last night's curry. For dinner, come to the adjacent night market and sample the tasty southern-style fried chicken and curries.

PAGE Asian Fusion $$$

(dishes 180-850B; ⏲breakfast, lunch & dinner) If you can't afford to stay at the ultra-swanky Library, have a meal at its beachside restaurant. Lunch is a bit more casual and affordable, but you'll miss the designer lighting effects that light up the evening.

PREGO Italian $$$

(www.prego-samui.com; mains 200-700B; ⏲dinner) This smart ministry of culinary style serves up fine Italian cuisine in a barely-there dining room of cool marble and modern geometry. Reservations are accepted for seatings at 7pm and 9pm.

DR FROGS Steakhouse **$$$**
(mains 380-790B; lunch & dinner) Perched atop a rocky overlook, Dr Frogs combines incredible ocean vistas with delicious international flavours (namely Italian and Thai). Delectable steaks and crab cakes, plus friendly owners, put this spot near the top of our dining list.

BETELNUT@BURI RASA Asian Fusion **$$$**
(mains 600-800B; dinner) Fusion can be confusing, and often disappointing, but Betelnut will set you straight. Chef Jeffrey Lords claims an American upbringing and European culinary training, but most importantly he spent time in San Francisco. The menu is a pan-Pacific mix of curries and chowder, papaya and pancetta.

WAVE SAMUI International **$**
(dishes from 60B; breakfast, lunch & dinner) Everyone says that Samui is going upmarket, but the most crowded restaurants at dinnertime are still the old-fashioned budget spots, like this one. This jack-of-all trades (guest house-bar-restaurant) serves honest food at honest prices and fosters a travellers ambience with an in-house library and a popular happy hour (3pm to 7pm).

Lamai

As Samui's second-most populated beach, Lamai has a surprisingly limited assortment of decent eateries when compared to Chaweng next door. Most visitors dine wherever they're staying.

ROCKY'S International **$$$**
(dishes 300-800B; lunch & dinner) Easily the top dining spot on Lamai, Rocky's gourmet dishes are actually a bargain when you convert the baht into your native currency. Try the signature beef tenderloin with blue cheese – it's like sending your tastebuds on a Parisian vacation. On Tuesday evenings, diners enjoy a special Thai-themed evening with a prepared menu of local delicacies. Rocky's is located at the Rocky Resort just south of Lamai.

LAMAI DAY MARKET Market **$**
(dishes from 30B; 6am-8pm) The Thai equivalent of a grocery store, Lamai's market is a hive of activity, selling food necessities and takeaway food. Visit the covered area to pick up fresh fruit or to see vendors shredding coconuts to make coconut milk. It's next door to a petrol station.

HUA THANON MARKET Market **$**
(dishes from 30B; 6am-6pm) Slip into the rhythm of this village market slightly south of Lamai; it's a window into the food ways of southern Thailand. Follow the market road to

Thai food

the row of food shops delivering edible Muslim culture: chicken biryani, fiery curries or toasted rice with coconut, bean sprouts, lemongrass and dried shrimp.

Northern Beaches

Some of Samui's finest establishments are located on the northern coast. Boho Bo Phut has several trendy eateries to match the string of yuppie boutique hotels.

CHOENG MON

DINING ON THE ROCKS Asian Fusion **$$$**

(☎0 7724 5678; reservations-samui@sixsenses.com; Choeng Mon; menus from 2200B; ⏰dinner) Samui's ultimate dining experience takes place on nine cantilevered verandahs of weathered teak and bamboo that yawn over the gulf. After sunset (and a glass of wine), guests feel like they're dining on a wooden barge set adrift on a starlit sea. Each dish on the six-course prix-fixe menu is the brainchild of the cooks who regularly experiment with taste, texture and temperature. Dining On The Rocks is located at the isolated Six Senses Samui.

BO PHUT

SHACK BAR & GRILL Steakhouse **$$$**

(www.theshackgrillsamui.com; mains 480-780B; ⏰dinner) Head here for hands down the best steaks on the island. The Shack imports the finest cuts of meat from Australia and slathers them in a rainbow of tasty sauces from red wine to blue cheese. Booth seating and jazz over the speakers give the joint a distinctly Western vibe, though you'll find all types of diners come here to splurge.

ZAZEN Asian Fusion **$$$**

(dishes 550-850B, set menu from 1300B; ⏰lunch & dinner) The chef describes the food as 'organic and orgasmic', and the ambient 'yums' from elated diners definitely confirm the latter. This romantic dining experience comes complete with ocean views, dim candle lighting and soft music. Reservations recommended.

VILLA BIANCA Italian **$$**

(dishes from 200B; ⏰lunch & dinner) A fantastic Italian spot on Samui, Villa Bianca is a sea of crisp white tablecloths and woven lounge chairs.

MAE NAM & BANG PO

ANGELA'S BAKERY International **$$**

(Mae Nam; dishes 80-200B; ⏰breakfast & lunch) Duck through the screen of hanging plants into this beloved bakery that smells of fresh bread and hospitality. Angela's sandwiches and cakes have kept many Western expats from wasting away in the land of rice.

BANG PO SEAFOOD Seafood **$$**

(Bang Po; dishes from 100B; ⏰dinner) A meal at Bang Po Seafood is a test for the tastebuds. It's one of the only restaurants that serves traditional Ko Samui fare (think of it as island roadkill, well, actually it's more like local sea-kill). Recipes call for ingredients such as raw sea urchin roe, baby octopus, sea water, coconut, and local turmeric.

West Coast

The quiet west coast features some of the best seafood on Samui. Na Thon has a giant day market on Th Thawi Ratchaphakdi. It's worth stopping by to grab some snacks before your ferry ride.

FIVE ISLANDS Seafood **$$$**

(www.thefiveislands.com; Taling Ngam; dishes 150-500B, tours 3000-6500B; ⏰lunch & dinner) Five Islands defines the term 'destination dining' and offers the most unique eating experience on the island. Before your meal, a traditional long-tail boat will take you out onto the turquoise sea to visit the haunting Five Sister Islands, where you'll learn about the ancient and little-known art of harvesting bird nests to make bird's-nest soup, a Chinese delicacy. The lunch tour departs around 10am, and the dinner program leaves around 3pm. Customers are also welcome to dine without going on the tour and vice versa.

Drinking & Entertainment

Chaweng & Lamai

Making merry in Chaweng is a piece of cake. Most places are open until 2am and there are a few places that go strong all night long.

BEACH REPUBLIC Lounge

(**Hat Lamai**) Recognised by its thatch-patched awnings, Beach Republic would be the perfect spot to shoot one of those MTV Spring Break episodes. There's an inviting wading pool, comfy lounge chairs and an endless cocktail list.

Q-BAR Lounge

(**www.qbarsamui.com; Hat Chaweng**) Overlooking Chaweng Lake, Q-Bar is a little piece of Bangkok nightlife planted among the coconut trees. The upstairs lounge opens just before sunset, treating cocktail connoisseurs to various highbrow tipples and a drinkable view of southern Chaweng – mountains, sea and sky. After 10pm, the night-crawlers descend upon the downstairs club where DJs spin the crowd into a techno amoeba. A taxi there will cost between 200B and 300B.

ARK BAR Bar

(**www.ark-bar.com; Hat Chaweng**) The 'it' destination for a Wednesday-night romp on Samui. Drinks are dispensed from the multicoloured bar draped in paper lanterns, and guests lounge on pyramidal pillows strewn down the beach. The party usually starts around 4pm.

GOOD KARMA Bar

(**Hat Chaweng**) Open all day, this snazzy lounge lures the hip 'hi-so' (Thai high society) crowd with canopied daybeds and a hidden pond.

GREEN MANGO Bar

(**Hat Chaweng**) This place is so popular it has an entire soi named after it. Samui's favourite power drinking house is very big, very loud and very faràng (Western). Green Mango has blazing lights, expensive drinks and masses of sweaty bodies swaying to dance music.

Northern & West Coast Beaches

WOO BAR Lounge

(**Mae Nam**) The W Retreat's signature lobby bar gives the word 'swish' a whole new meaning, with cushion-clad pods of seating plonked in the middle of an expansive infinity pool that stretches out over the infinite horizon. This is, without a doubt, the best place on Samui for a sunset cocktail.

NIKKI BEACH Lounge

(**www.nikkibeach.com/kohsamui; Lipa Noi**) The acclaimed luxury brand has brought its international *savoir faire* to the secluded west coast of Ko Samui. Expect everything you would from a chic address in St Barts or St Tropez: haute cuisine, chic decor and gaggles of jetsetters.

Information

Dangers & Annoyances

The rate of road accident fatalities on Samui is quite high. This is mainly due to the large number of tourists who rent motorcycles, only to find out that the winding roads, sudden tropical rains and frenzied traffic can be lethal.

Medical Services

Ko Samui has four private hospitals, all near Chaweng's Tesco-Lotus supermarket on the east coast (where most tourists tend to gather).

Bandon International Hospital (**Map p251; 0 7742 5840, emergency 0 7742 5748**)

Bangkok Samui Hospital (**Map p251; 0 7742 9500, emergency 0 7742 9555**) Your best bet for just about any medical problem.

Samui International Hospital (**Map p251; 0 7742 2272; www.sih.co.th; Hat Chaweng**) Emergency ambulance service is available 24 hours and credit cards are accepted. Near the Amari Resort in Chaweng.

Tourist Information

Ko Samui Tourist Authority of Thailand (**TAT; 0 7742 0504; Na Thon; 8.30am-4.30pm**)

Hat Rin, Ko Pha-Ngan

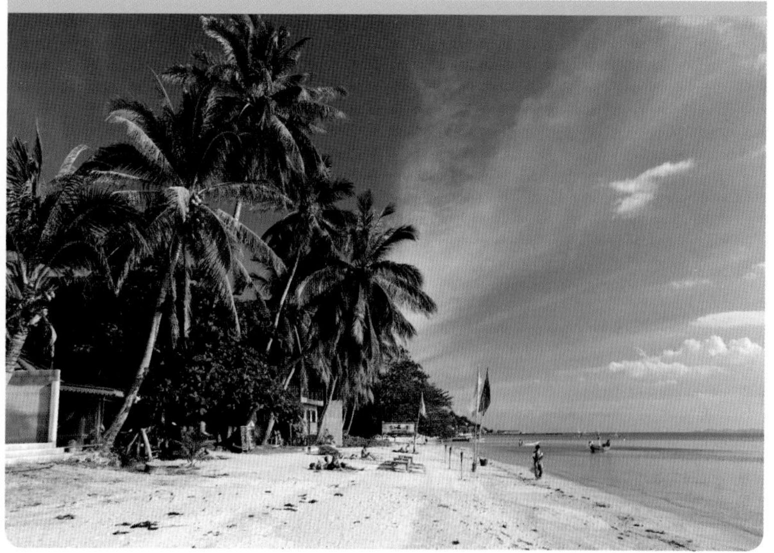

ADS/ALAMY ©

Getting There & Away

Air

Bangkok Airways (www.bangkokair.com) operates flights roughly every 30 minutes between Samui and Bangkok's Suvarnabhumi Airport (50 minutes). Bangkok Air also flies direct from Samui to Phuket, Pattaya, Chiang Mai, Singapore and Hong Kong.

Firefly (www.fireflyz.com.my) operates direct flights from Samui to Kuala Lumpur's Subang airport.

During the high season, make your flight reservations far in advance as seats do sell out. If Samui flights are full, try flying into Surat Thani from Bangkok and taking a short ferry ride to Samui.

Boat

There are frequent boat departures between Samui and Surat Thani. The hourly Seatran ferry is a common option. Ferries take one to five hours, depending on the boat.

There are almost a dozen daily departures between Samui and Ko Pha-Ngan. These leave from the Na Thon, Mae Nam or Big Buddha pier and take from 20 minutes to one hour. The boats departing from Big Buddha service Hat Rin, and the other boats alight at Thong Sala. From the same piers, there are also around six daily departures between Samui and Ko Tao. These take 1¼ to 2½ hours.

Getting Around

Motorbikes You can rent motorcycles (and bicycles) from almost every resort on the island. The going rate is 200B per day, but for longer periods try to negotiate a better rate.

Sŏrng·tăa·ou Drivers of *sŏrng·tăa·ou* love to try to overcharge you, so it's always best to ask a third party for current rates, as they can change with the season. It's about 50B to travel between beaches, and no more than 100B to travel halfway across the island. Figure about 20B for a five-minute ride on a motorcycle taxi.

Taxis Taxi service on Samui is quite chaotic due to the plethora of cabs. Taxis typically charge around 500B for an airport transfer. Some Chaweng travel agencies can arrange minibus taxis for less.

Ko Pha-Ngan เกาะพงัน

POP 11,000

In the family of southern Gulf islands, Ko Pha-Ngan sits in the crystal sea between Ko Samui, its business-savvy older brother, and little Ko Tao, the spunky younger brother full of dive-centric energy. Ko

Pha-Ngan is the slacker middle child: a chilled out beach bum with tattered dreadlocks, a tattoo of a Chinese serenity symbol, and a penchant for white nights and bikini-clad pool parties.

The scenic cape of Hat Rin has long been the darling destination of this laid-back paradise. Sunrise Beach started hosting the world-famous Full Moon parties long before Alex Garland's *The Beach* inspired many to strap on a rucksack. Today, thousands still flock to the kerosene-soaked sands for an epic trance-a-thon fuelled by adrenaline and a couple of other substances...

Activities

Diving group sizes tend to be smaller on Ko Pha-Ngan since the island has less divers in general. The clear favourite snorkelling spot is **Ko Ma**, a small island in the northwest connected to Ko Pha-Ngan by a charming sandbar. A major perk of diving from Ko Pha-Ngan is the proximity to **Sail Rock** (Hin Bai), the best dive site in the Gulf of Thailand and a veritable beacon for whale sharks.

LOTUS DIVING Diving

(☎0 7737 4142; www.lotusdiving.net) This dive centre has top-notch instructors and owns not one, but two beautiful boats (that's two more vessels than most of the other operations on Ko Pha-Ngan).

ECO NATURE TOUR Tour

(☎08 4850 6273; 1500B) This exceedingly popular oufit offers a 'best of' island trip, which includes elephant trekking and snorkelling and a visit to the Chinese temple, a stunning viewpoint and Phang waterfall. The day trip departs at 9am and returns around 3pm.

Sleeping

For now, Ko Pha-Ngan can revel in its three distinct classes of lodging: pinch-a-penny shacks, trendy midrange hang-outs, and blow-the-bank luxury.

Pha-Ngan also caters to a subculture of seclusion-seekers who crave a deserted slice of sand. The northern and eastern coasts offer just that – a place to escape.

Beachside accommodation, Hat Rin, Ko Pha-Ngan

Hat Rin

Needless to say, the prices listed here are meaningless during periods of maximum lunar orbicularity. Also, during Full Moon events bungalow operations expect you to stay for a minimum number of days (around four or five). If you plan to arrive on the day of the party (or even the day before), we strongly suggest booking a room in advance, or else you'll probably have to sleep on the beach (which you might end up doing anyway). Full Mooners can also stay on Samui and take one of the hourly speedboat shuttles (from 550B) to access the festivities.

SARIKANTANG Resort **$$$**
(**0 7737 5055; www.sarikantang.com; Hat Seekantang; bungalows 1400-6200B;**) Don't get too strung out over trying to pronounce the resort's name – you can simply call this place 'heaven'. Cream-coloured cabins framed with teak posts and lintels are sprinkled among swaying palms and crumbling winged statuettes. Inside, the rooms look like the set of a photo shoot for an interior design magazine.

PHA-NGAN BAYSHORE RESORT Resort **$$**
(**0 7737 5227; www.phanganbayshore.com; Hat Rin Nok; r 1700-3200B;** @) After a much-needed overhaul in 2009, this hotel-style operation has primed itself for the ever-increasing influx of flashpackers in Hat Rin. Sweeping beach views and a giant swimming pool make Pha-Ngan Bayshore one of the top addresses on Sunrise Beach.

SEA BREEZE BUNGALOW Bungalows **$$**
(**0 7737 5162; Ban Hat Rin; bungalows 500-8000B;**) Sea Breeze gets a good report card from our readers, and we agree; the labyrinth of secluded hillside cottages is an ideal hammocked retreat for any type of traveller. Several bungalows, poised high on stilts, deliver stunning views of Hat Rin and the sea.

West Coast Beaches

The atmosphere is a pleasant mix between the east coast's quiet seclusion and Hat Rin's sociable vibe, although some of the beaches along the western shores (particularly towards the south) aren't as picturesque as some of the other parts of the island.

HAT SALAD

Hat Salad is our favourite beach on the west coast, and it isn't short on quality digs set along the inviting sand.

COOKIES SALAD Resort **$$**
(**0 7734 9125, 08 3181 7125; www.cookies-phangan.com; bungalows 1500-3000B;**) The resort with a tasty name has delicious Balinese-styled bungalows orbiting a two-tiered lap pool tiled in various shades of blue. Shaggy thatching and dense tropical foliage gives the realm a certain rustic quality, although you won't want for creature comforts.

Northern Beaches

Stretching from Chalok Lam to Thong Nai Pan, the dramatic northern coast is a wild jungle with several stunning and secluded beaches. It's the most scenic coast on the island.

BOTTLE BEACH (HAT KHUAT)

This isolated dune has garnered a reputation as a low-key getaway, and has thus become quite popular. During high season, places can fill up fast so it's best to try to arrive early. Grab a long-tail taxi boat from Chalok Lam for 50B to 120B (depending on the boat's occupancy).

SMILE Bungalows **$**
(**08 1956 3133; smilebeach@hotmail.com; bungalows 400-700B**) At the far west corner of the beach, Smile features an assortment of wooden huts that climb up a forested hill. The two-storey bungalows (700B) are our favourite.

THONG NAI PAN

These beaches have been increasing in popularity over the last few years, as bamboo bungalows are being razed to make room for elaborate resorts.

ANANTARA RASANANDA Resort **$$$**
(☎0 7723 9555; www.rasananda.com; villas from 5000B; ❄@) Rasananda represents the future of Ko Pha-Ngan. This attempt at five-star luxury is a sweeping sand-side property with a smattering of semi-detached villas, many bedecked with private plunge pools.

LONGTAIL BEACH RESORT Bungalows **$**
(☎0 7744 5018; www.longtailbeachresort.com; bungalows 390-1150B; ❄) Effortlessly adorable, and one of the last remaining batches of beach bungalows in the area, Longtail offers backpackers a taste of Pha-Ngan's past with its charming thatch-and-bamboo abodes.

East Coast Beaches

Robinson Crusoe, eat your heart out. The east coast is the ultimate hermit hang-out. For the most part you'll have to hire a boat to get to these beaches, but water taxis are available in Thong Sala and Hat Rin.

HAT THIAN

SANCTUARY Bungalows **$$**
(☎08 1271 3614; www.thesanctuarythailand.com; dm 200B, bungalows 450-5450B) A friendly enclave promoting relaxation, the Sanctuary is an inviting haven offering splendid lodgings while also functioning as a holistic retreat (think yoga classes and detox sessions). Accommodation, in various manifestations of twigs, is scattered around the resort, married to the natural surroundings.

Eating

Ko Pha-Ngan is no culinary capital, especially since most visitors quickly absorb the lazy lifestyle and end up eating at their accommodation. Those with an adventurous appetite should check out the island's centre of local commerce, Thong Sala.

Left: Hat Rin (p261), Ko Pha-Ngan; **Below:** Full Moon party-goers, Hat Rin, Ko Pha-Ngan

Drinking

Hat Rin is the beating heart of the legendary Full Moon fun, and the area can get pretty wound up even without the influence of lunar phases. The following party venues, except Pirates Bar, flank Hat Rin's infamous Sunrise Beach from south to north.

ROCK Bar

(Hat Rin) Great views of the party from the elevated terrace on the far south side of the beach.

CACTUS BAR Bar

(Hat Rin) Smack in the centre of Hat Rin Nok, Cactus pumps out a healthy mix of old-school tunes, hip-hop and R&B.

MELLOW MOUNTAIN Bar

(Hat Rin) Also called 'Mushy Mountain' (you'll know why when you get there), this trippy hang-out sits at the northern edge of Hat Rin Nok delivering stellar views of the shenanigans below.

PIRATES BAR Bar

(Hat Chaophao) This wacky drinkery is a replica of a pirate ship built into the cliffs. When you're sitting on the deck and the tide is high (and you've had a couple drinks), you can almost believe you're out at sea. These guys host the well-attended Moon Set parties, three days before Hat Rin gets pumpin' for the Full Moon fun.

Information

Dangers & Annoyances

Nowadays there's a system of paved roads on which you can ride motorcycles, but much of it is a labyrinth of rutty dirt-and-mud paths. The island is also very hilly, and even if the road is paved, it can be too difficult for most riders to take on. The *very* steep road to Hat Rin is a perfect case in point.

Signs promoting sights and activities, Ko Tao

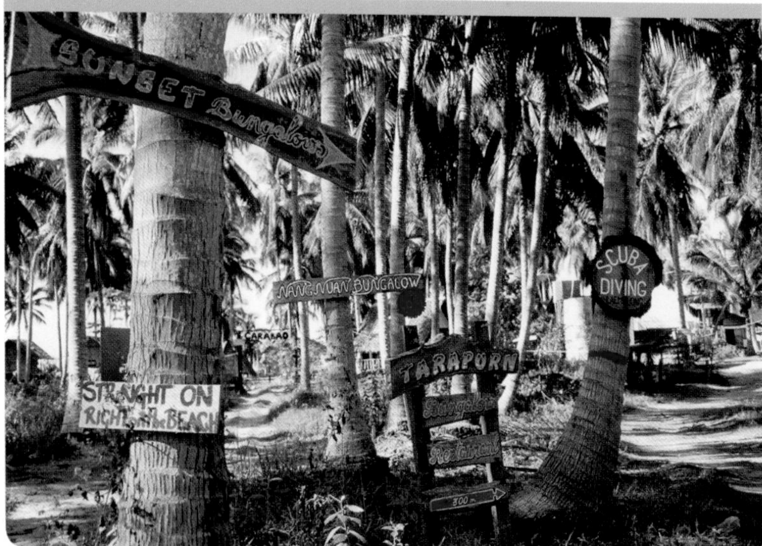

RICHARD NEBESKY/LONELY PLANET IMAGES ©

Getting There & Away

Rough waves are known to cancel ferries between October and December.

Ko Samui

There are around a dozen daily departures between Ko Pha-Ngan and Ko Samui. These boats leave throughout the day from 7am to 6pm and take from 20 minutes to an hour. All leave from either Thong Sala or Hat Rin on Ko Pha-Ngan.

Ko Tao

Ko Tao-bound Lomprayah ferries depart from Thong Sala on Ko Pha-Ngan at 8.30am and 1pm and arrive at 9.45am and 2.15pm. The Seatran service departs from Thong Sala at 8.30am and 2pm daily.

Getting Around

Motorbikes You can rent motorcycles all over the island for 150B to 250B per day. If you plan on riding over dirt tracks it is imperative that you rent a bike comparable to a Honda MTX125 as gearless scooters cannot make the journey.

Sŏrng·tăa·ou The trip from Thong Sala to Hat Rin is 100B; further beaches will set you back around 150B.

Water taxi Long-tail boats depart from Thong Sala, Chalok Lam and Hat Rin, heading to a variety of far-flung destinations such as Hat Khuat (Bottle Beach) and Ao Thong Nai Pan. Expect to pay anywhere from 50B for a short trip, and up to 300B for a lengthier journey.

Ko Tao เกาะเต่า

POP 1382

Today, thousands of visitors come to worship the turquoise waters offshore, and quite often they stay. Diving enthusiasts cavort with sharks and rays in a playground of tangled neon coral. Hikers and hermits can re-enact an episode from *Lost* in the dripping coastal jungles. And when you're Robinson Crusoe-ed out, hit the pumpin' bar scene that rages on until dawn.

Activities

Diving

Ko Tao is *the* place to lose your scuba virginity. The shallow bays scalloping the island are the perfect spot for newbie divers to take their first stab at scuba.

Expect large crowds and booked-out beds in December and January, and between June and August, and a monthly glut of wannabe divers after every Full Moon party on Ko Pha-Ngan next door.

BAN'S DIVING SCHOOL Diving
(☎0 7745 6466; www.amazingkohtao.com; Sairee Beach) A well-oiled diving machine and relentlessly expanding conglomerate, Ban's certifies more divers per year than any other scuba school in the world. Refurbishments in 2009 have given it a five-star feel.

BIG BLUE DIVING Diving
(☎0 7745 6415, 0 7745 6772; www.bigbluediving.com; Sairee Beach) If Goldilocks were picking a dive school, she'd probably pick Big Blue – this midsize operation (not too big, not too small) gets props for fostering a sociable vibe while maintaining a high standard of service.

CRYSTAL DIVE Diving
(☎0 7745 6107; www.crystaldive.com; Mae Hat) Crystal is the Meryl Streep of diving operators, winning all the awards for best performance year after year. It's one of the largest schools on the island (and around the world), although high-quality instructors and intimate classes keep the school feeling quite personal.

Snorkelling

Snorkelling is a popular alternative to diving, although scuba snobs will tell you that strapping on a snorkel instead of an air tank is like eating spray cheese when there's Camembert on the table.

Most snorkel enthusiasts opt for the do-it-yourself approach on Ko Tao, which involves swimming out into the offshore bays or hiring a long-tail boat to putter around further out. Guided tours are also available and can be booked at any local travel agency. Tours range from 500B to 700B (usually including gear, lunch and a guide/captain) and stop at various snorkelling hotspots around the island.

If You Like... Diving

Each dive school chooses a smattering of dive sites for the day, dependant on weather and ocean conditions.

1 **CHUMPHON PINNACLE**
(36m maximum depth) 13km west of Ko Tao; has a colourful assortment of sea anemones along the four interconnected pinnacles. The site plays host to schools of giant trevally, tuna and large grey reef sharks.

2 **JAPANESE GARDENS**
(12m maximum depth) Between Ko Tao and Ko Nang Yuan. A low-stress dive site perfect for beginners.

3 **SAIL ROCK**
(34m maximum depth) Best accessed from Ko Pha-Ngan; features a massive rock chimney with a vertical swim-through, and large pelagics like barracuda and kingfish. This is one of the top spots in southeast Asia to see whale sharks.

4 **SOUTHWEST PINNACLE**
(33m maximum depth) Offers divers a small collection of pinnacles that are home to giant groupers and barracudas.

5 **WHITE ROCK**
(29m maximum depth) Home to colourful corals, angelfish, clown fish and territorial triggerfish.

Freediving

Over the last couple of years, freediving (exploring the sea using breath-holding techniques rather than scuba gear) has grown rapidly in popularity. Several small schools have opened up across the island. We recommend the capable staff at **Apnea Total** (☎08 7183 2321; www.apnea-total.com; Sairee Beach) who have earned several awards in the freediving world and possess a special knack for easing newbies into this heart-pounding sport.

Detour: Ko Nang Yuan

Photogenic Ko Nang Yuan, just off the coast of Ko Tao, is easily accessible by the Lomprayah catamaran, and by water taxis that depart from Mae Hat and Sairee. **Ko Nangyuan Dive Resort** (0 7745 6088; www.nangyuan.com; bungalows 1200-9000B;) has a rugged collection of wood and aluminium bungalows, which wind across three coolie-hat-like conical islands connected by an idyllic beige sandbar. The resort also boasts the best restaurant on the island, but then again, it's the only place to eat…

Sleeping

Sairee Beach

Giant Sairee is the longest and most developed strip on the island, with a string of dive operations, bungalows, travel agencies, minimarkets and internet cafes.

SUNSET BURI RESORT Bungalows $$
(0 7745 6266; bungalows 700-2500B;) A long beach-bound path is studded with beautiful white bungalows featuring enormous windows and flamboyant, temple-like roofing.

KOH TAO CORAL GRAND RESORT Bungalows $$$
(0 7745 6431; www.kohtaocoral.com; bungalows 3350-6950B;) The plethora of pink facades at this family-friendly option feels a bit like Barbie's dream Thai beach house. Cottage interiors are coated in cheery primary colours framed by white truncated beams, while pricier digs have a more distinctive Thai flavour, boasting dark lacquered mouldings and gold-foiled art.

East Coast Beaches

The serene eastern coast is, without a doubt, one of the best places in the region to live out your island paradise fantasies.

HIN WONG

A sandy beach has been swapped for a boulder-strewn coast, but the water is crystal clear. The road to Hin Wong is paved in parts, but sudden sand pits and steep hills can toss you off your motorbike.

HIN WONG BUNGALOWS Bungalows $
(0 7745 6006; bungalows from 300B) Pleasant wooden huts are scattered across vast expanses of untamed tropical terrain It all feels a bit like *Gilligan's Island* (minus the millionaire castaways).

TANOTE BAY (AO TANOT)

This is the only bay on the east coast that is accessible by a decent road.

FAMILY TANOTE Bungalows $$
(0 7745 6757; bungalows 700-3500B) As the name suggests, this scatter of hillside bungalows is run by a local family who take pride in providing comfy digs to solitude seekers. Strap on a snorkel mask and swim around with the fish at your doorstep, or climb up to the restaurant for a tasty meal and pleasant views of the bay.

Eating

With super-sized Samui lurking on the horizon, it's hard to believe that quaint little Ko Tao holds its own in the gastronomy category.

Sairee Beach

DARAWAN International $$
(mains 160-400B; lunch & dinner) Like a top-end dining venue plucked from the posh shores of Samui nearby, regal Darawan is the island's newest place to take a date. Designer lighting, efficient waiters and a tasty Wagyu burger seal the deal.

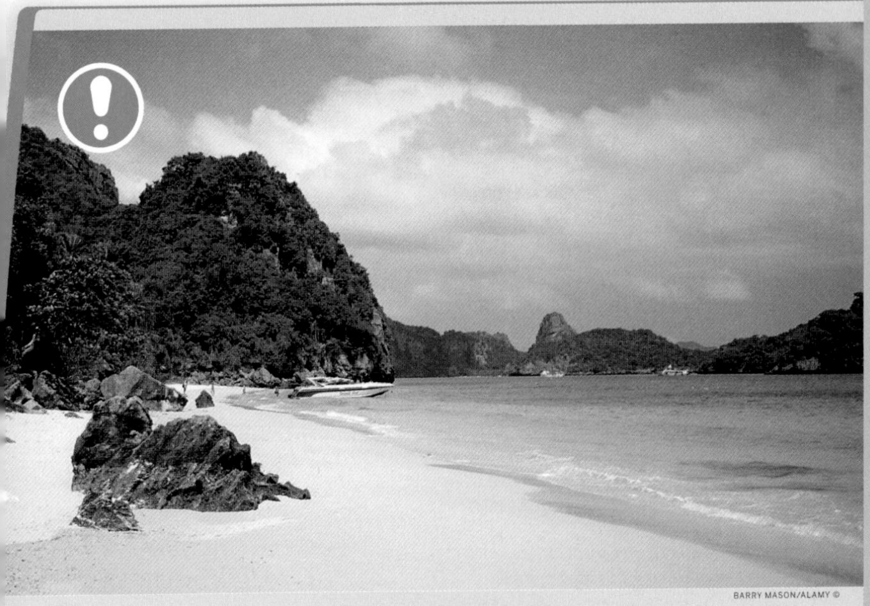

BARRY MASON/ALAMY ©

Don't Miss Ang Thong Marine National Park

The 40 jagged jungle islands of Ang Thong Marine National Park stretch across the cerulean sea like a shattered emerald necklace – each piece a virgin realm featuring sheer limestone cliffs, hidden lagoons and perfect peach-coloured sands. February, March and April are the best months to visit this ethereal preserve of greens and blues; crashing monsoon waves means that the park is almost always closed during November and December.

Every tour stops at the park's head office on **Ko Wua Talap**, the largest island in the archipelago. The island's **viewpoint** might just be the most stunning vista in all of Thailand. From the top, visitors have sweeping views of the jagged islands nearby as they burst through the placid turquoise water in easily anthropomorphised formations. The trek to the lookout is an arduous 450m trail that takes roughly an hour to complete. Hikers should wear sturdy shoes and walk slowly on the sharp outcrops of limestone.

The **Emerald Sea** (also called the Inner Sea) on Ko Mae Ko is another popular destination. This large lake in the middle of the island spans an impressive 250m by 350m and has an ethereal minty tint. You can look but you can't touch; the lagoon is strictly off-limits to the unclean human body. A second dramatic viewpoint can be found at the top of a series of staircases nearby.

The best way to experience Ang Thong is through one of many guided tours departing from Ko Samui and Ko Pha-Ngan. The tours usually include lunch, snorkelling equipment, hotel transfers and (fingers crossed) a knowledgeable guide. Dive centres on Ko Samui and Ko Pha-Ngan offer scuba trips to the park, although Ang Thong doesn't offer the world-class diving that can be found around Ko Tao and Ko Pha-Ngan.

THINGS YOU NEED TO KNOW

อุทยานแห่งชาติหมู่เกาะอ่างทอง

ZANZIBAR Sandwiches **$$**

(sandwiches 90-140B; breakfast, lunch & dinner) The island's outpost of sandwich yuppie-dom slathers a mix of unpronounceable condiments betwixt two slices of wholegrain bread.

KANYA Thai **$**

(mains 60-130B; breakfast, lunch & dinner) Tucked at the back of Sairee Village on the road to Hin Wong, four-table Kanya serves an assortment of international dishes, but you'll be missing out if you stray from the delectable array of home-cooked Thai classics. The *đôm yam ɓlah* is divine.

Mae Hat

WHITENING International **$$**

(dishes 160-300B; dinner) Although it looks like a pile of forgotten driftwood during the day, this beachy spot falls somewhere between being a restaurant and being a chic seaside bar. Foodies will appreciate the tasty twists on indigenous and international dishes while beertotalers will love the beachy, bleached-white atmosphere that hums with gentle lounge music.

PRANEE'S KITCHEN Thai **$**

(dishes 50-120B; breakfast, lunch & dinner;) An old Mae Hat fave, Pranee's serves scrumptious curries and other Thai treats in an open-air pavilion sprinkled with lounging pillows, wooden tables and TVs. English movies (with hilariously incorrect subtitles) are shown nightly at 6pm.

Information

Dangers & Annoyances

The roads on Ko Tao are horrendous, save the main drag connecting Sairee Beach to Chalok Ban Kao.

Getting There & Away

Rough waves are known to cancel ferries between October and December. Note that we advise purchasing your boat tickets *several* days in advance if you are accessing Ko Tao from Ko Pha-Ngan after the Full Moon party.

Bangkok, Hua Hin & Chumphon

From Ko Tao, the high-speed catamaran departs for Chumphon at 10.15am and 2.45pm (1½ hours); the Seatran leaves the island at 4pm (two hours); and a Songserm fast boat makes the same journey at 2.30pm (three hours). There's also a midnight boat from Chumphon arriving early in the morning. It returns from Ko Tao at 11pm.

Ko Pha-Ngan

The Lomprayah catamaran offers a twice-daily service, leaving Ko Tao at 9.30am and 3pm and arriving on Ko Pha-Ngan around 10.50am and 4.10pm. The Seatran Discovery Ferry offers an identical service. The Songserm Express Boat departs daily at 10am and arrives on Ko Pan-Ngan at 11.30am.

Long-tail boats, Mae Hat

Ko Samui

The Lomprayah catamaran offers a twice-daily service, leaving Ko Tao at 9.30am and 3pm and arriving on Samui around 11.30am and 4.40pm. The Seatran Discovery Ferry offers an identical service. The Songserm Express Boat departs daily at 10am and arrives on Samui at 12.45pm.

Getting Around

Sŏrng·tăa·ou Rides from Sairee to Chalok Ban Kao cost 80B per person, or 150B for solo tourists.
Motorbikes Daily rental rates begin at 150B for a scooter. Larger bikes start at 350B.
Water taxis Boat taxis depart from Mae Hat, Chalok Ban Kao and the northern part of Sairee Beach (near Vibe Bar). Boat rides to Ko Nang Yuan will set you back at least 100B.

Surat Thani อำเภอเมืองสุราษฎร์ธานี

POP 128,990

Known in Thai as 'City of Good People', Surat Thani was once the seat of the ancient Srivijaya empire. Today, this busy junction has become a transport hub that indiscriminately moves cargo and people around the country. Travellers rarely linger here as they make their way to the deservedly popular islands of Ko Samui, Ko Pha-Ngan and Ko Tao.

Sleeping

WANGTAI HOTEL Hotel $$
(☎0 7728 3020; www.wangtaisurat.com; 1 Th Talad Mai; r 790-2000B; ❄@🛜🏊) Across the river from the TAT office, Wangtai tries its best to provide a corporate hotel atmosphere.

Getting There & Away

In general, if you are departing Bangkok or Hua Hin for Ko Pha-Ngan or Ko Tao, consider taking the train or a bus-boat package that goes through Chumphon rather than Surat. You'll save time, and the journey will be more comfortable. Travellers heading to/from Ko Samui will most likely pass through. If you require any travel services, try **Holiday Travel** (Th Na Meuang) or **Pranthip Co** (Th Talat Mai) – both are reliable and English is spoken.

Air

Although flights from Bangkok to Surat Thani are cheaper than the flights to Samui, it takes quite a bit of time to reach the gulf islands from the airport, which isn't ideal. If you want to fly through Surat, there are daily shuttles to Bangkok on **Thai Airways International** (THAI; ☎0 7727 2610; 3/27-28 Th Karunarat).

Boat

In the high season travellers can usually find bus-boat services to Ko Samui and Ko Pha-Ngan directly from the Phun Phin train station. Be warned that the Raja service can be a very frustrating experience, especially for travellers who are tight on time.

Bus & Minivan

Andaman-bound buses (usually destined for Phuket) depart every hour from 7am to 3.30pm, stopping at Takua Pa for those who want to access Khao Sok National Park. The 'new' bus terminal (which is actually a few years old now, but still referred to as new by the locals) is located 7km south of town on the way to Phun Phin. This hub services traffic to and from Bangkok.

Train

When arriving by train you'll actually pull into Phun Phin, a cruddy town 14km west of Surat. If you plan on travelling during the day, go for the express railcars. Night travellers should opt for the air-con couchettes.

N50
N50

Phuket & the Andaman Coast

The Andaman Coast is the ultimate land of superlatives: the tall*est* karst formations, the soft*est* sands, the blu*est* water – the list goes on.

Along the coast, boats from Khao Lak idle between the Similan and Surin Islands, dropping scuba buffs deep down into the greatest dive sites around. Further south, Phuket, the biggest island, is the region's hedonistic launching pad, offering a glimpse of what's to come.

The Andaman's signature pinnacles of jagged jungle-clad karst come to a stunning climax in Krabi. Ko Phi-Phi Don's unimaginable beauty exceeds even the highest expectations. And at Railay, rock-climbers take in the scenery as they dangle like ornaments on a giant Christmas tree.

The catch is that the destination is no secret and the beaches are crowded with backpackers, package tourists and everyone else in between.

Long-tail boats, Krabi Province (p307)

Thai massage

Phuket & the Andaman Coast

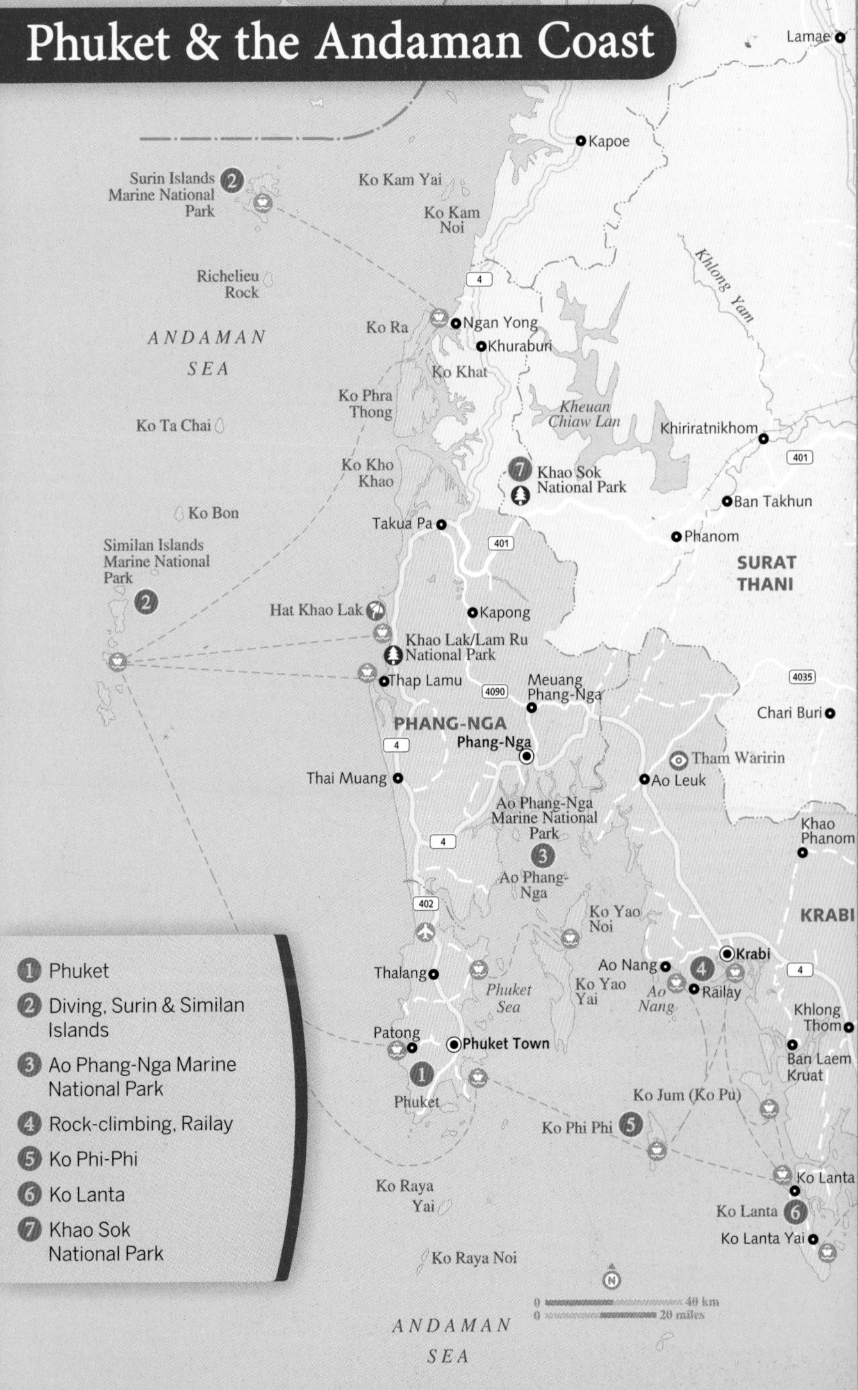

Phuket & the Andaman Coast's Highlights

1

Phuket

Phuket is both a beach getaway and a culinary destination. The island is endowed with an abundance of fresh fish and seafood, and local farmers grow an array of produce. As a trading crossroads, Phuket has inherited Chinese, Indian, Malay and Western culinary traditions. Plus there are dining and cooking opportunities beside the sea. **Bottom Right:** Vegetarian Festival (p295)

Need to Know

BEST TIME TO VISIT November to March **TOP TIP** Eating Thai food is a social event: order lots of dishes and share them with friends and family **For further coverage, see p290**

Local Knowledge

Phuket Don't Miss List

BY RATTANA PHOLTAISONG, SOUS CHEF & COOKING COURSE INSTRUCTOR, MOM TRI'S BOATHOUSE

1 PHUKET'S BEACHES

The white sands, the view of sea and sky: Hat Kata (p297) is my favourite and it is lucky that I work there so I can pop out every now and then for a break. Hat Mai Khao (p306) is a quiet alternative. It is a natural environment without a lot of hotels or other tourist development. Sometimes you can even see the turtles coming ashore to lay their eggs.

2 DINE & RELAX LIKE A CHEF

The simple waterfront restaurant **Pak Nam Seafood** (☎0 7624 0240; Th Ratsadanuson, Phuket Town) is located in a small village where the seafood is 'walked' from the sea to the restaurant's kitchen. The prices are aimed at Phuket's locals. A popular Phuket dish is *gaang sôm Ƀlah* (southern-style sour fish curry). For relaxing, **At Surakul** (☎0 7630 4409; 14/19 Th Vichit, Thalang) has live Thai country music and is fun for groups of friends.

3 PHUKET TOWN

For shopping, browse the old shops in Phuket Town (p294). A lot of the old buildings were built in the Sino-Portuguese style and walking around this historic area is a great way to discover new restaurants and shops.

4 COOKING COURSES

Mom Tri's Boathouse (p292) cooking classes are hands-on workshops right by the sea so students can learn with a view. Classes explain the building blocks of Thai food and the flavour progression as the sugar, lemon and fish sauce are added. I grew up in the northeast surrounded by home cooks so I've merged the best of both worlds: Isan with Phuket.

5 PHUKET'S VEGETARIAN FESTIVAL

According to legend, Chinese Thais started the Vegetarian Festival (p295) in order to purify themselves of bad luck. Not to be missed is the dragon fighting event. Two costumed dragon dancers climb up on long poles and try to knock each other down with long poles. Eventually one loses and falls to the ground to be caught by their dragon team members.

Diving the Surin & Similan Islands

These two Andaman marine parks offer the best diving in Thailand. The water can be so blue and clear. The topography and marine life varies at each dive site so that it rivals other southeast Asian spots, known for a greater abundance of aquatic life.

Need to Know

BEST TIME TO VISIT December to May **TOP TIP** Dive in a small group with a company that focuses environmental stewardship **For further coverage, see p290 & p288**

2

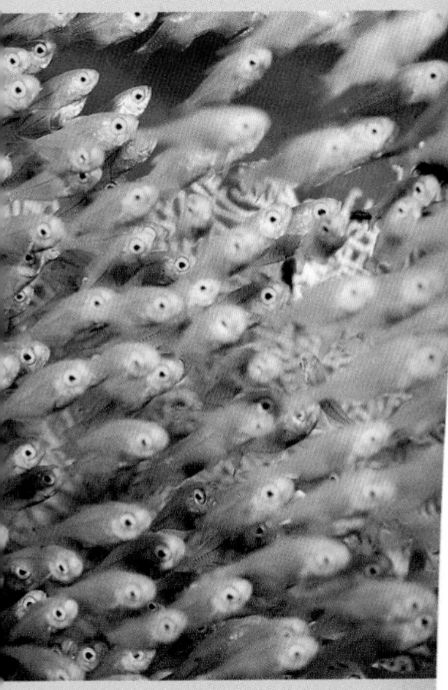

Local Knowledge

Surin & Similan Islands Don't Miss List

BY ORAYA (GAE) SENIWONG NA AYUTTHAYA, DIVE INSTRUCTOR, AT WICKED DIVING, KHAO LAK

1 NORTH POINT

The huge boulder formations at this dive site are majestic. The water is often very blue and clear. The dive starts in a deep water area and finishes in a shallow reef where you commonly see turtles.

2 WEST OF EDEN

Another boulder site, West of Eden is a fun dive because you can drift along in the current (saving your strength for other dives). The colours of the soft corals and sea fans are an amazing collection of pinks and purples in the deeper part. It is also less crowded than other spots in the park.

3 TACHAI PINNACLE

The northern part of this pinnacle dive is beloved because of its schools of fish and soft corals. But the real deal is the challenge of the current. Diving here taught me a lot about currents: how to read and predict them, and even though it can be a bit of a struggle, it is always a truly fun dive.

4 RICHELIEU ROCK

Probably the most famous dive site in the Andaman Sea, Richelieu Rock has lots of things to see, from soft corals to schools of fish. For soft-coral fans, Richelieu Rock is their pick. The downside is its popularity; it can be very busy when big live-aboard boats arrive.

5 KO BON RIDGE

Ko Bon is known for possible encounters with Manta rays and so it can get pretty busy with divers. But on a calm day hovering over the ridge you can have an amazing time observing plenty of fish zooming around. And, yes, if you get lucky, you can see a manta: wow!

Paddle into Prehistory

Crowning Phuket Island is stunning Ao Phang-Nga Marine National Park (p288), a turquoise bay filled with gigantic karst formations. Once a part of a regional mountain chain, these submerged peaks are a vertical testament to the earth's ever-changing topography. Despite their rocky permanence, the sea and rain chips away the easily dissolved material until it is pock-marked and full of Swiss-cheese–like caves.

3

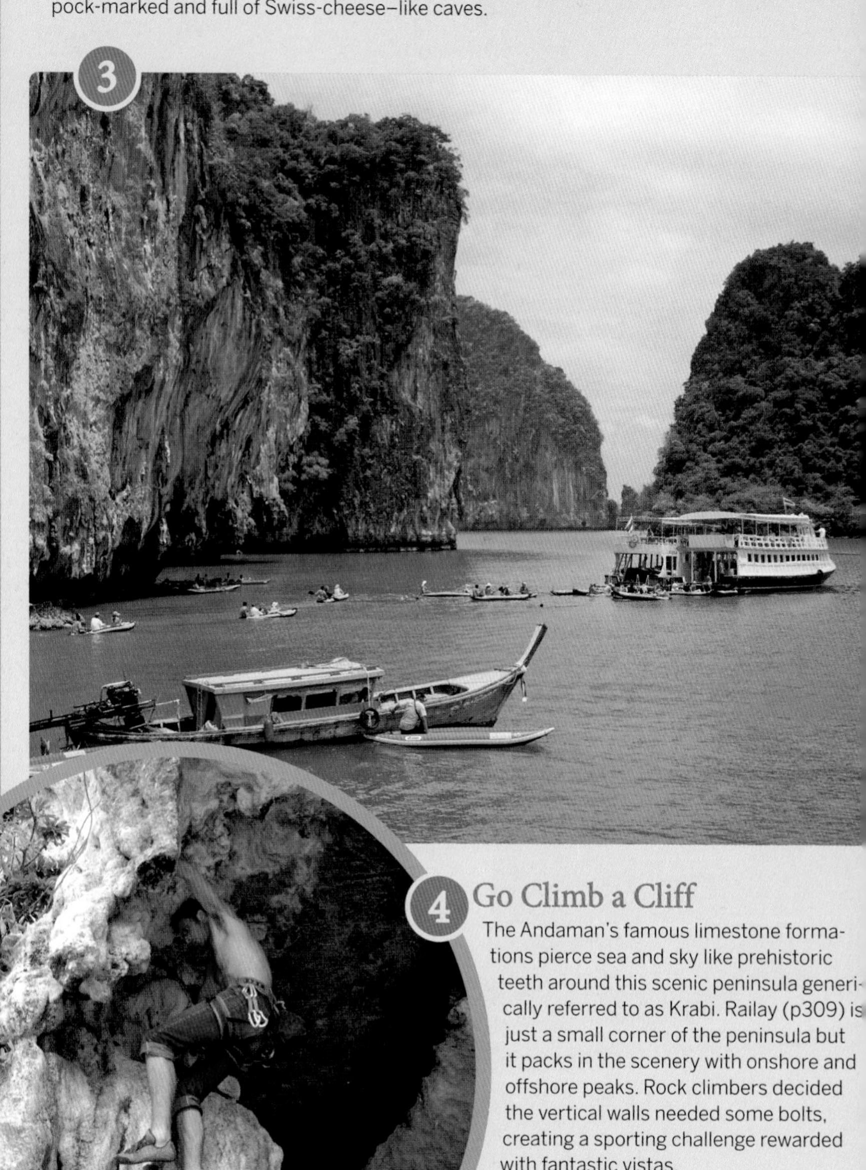

4 Go Climb a Cliff

The Andaman's famous limestone formations pierce sea and sky like prehistoric teeth around this scenic peninsula generically referred to as Krabi. Railay (p309) is just a small corner of the peninsula but it packs in the scenery with onshore and offshore peaks. Rock climbers decided the vertical walls needed some bolts, creating a sporting challenge rewarded with fantastic vistas.

Ogle Ko Phi-Phi

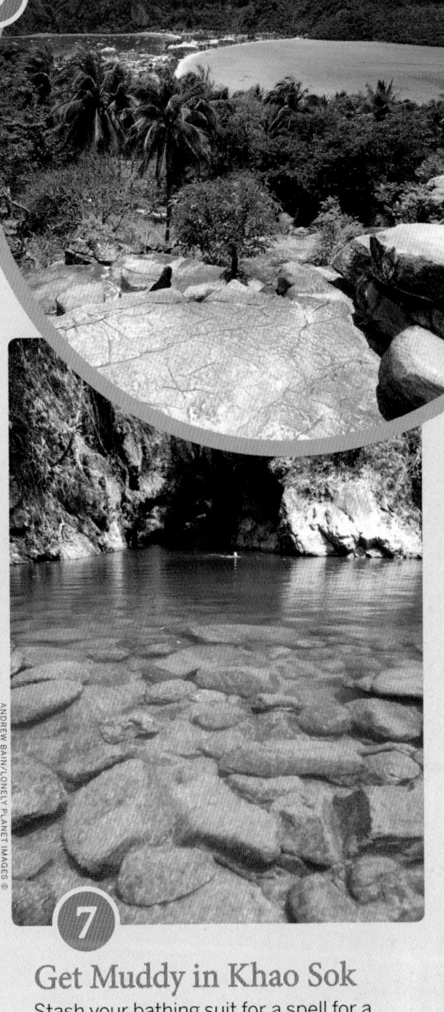

5

Come worship upon the white-sand altar of Ko Phi-Phi (p311), one of the most beautiful beaches on planet earth. The bearded limestone cliffs, ribbons of emerald and turquoise water and voluptuous contours of sand are a sensory feast. Soak it all in with an afternoon swim or an all-night booze fest. True to its coquettish looks, Phi-Phi is courted by crowds of beach-lovers and long abandoned a hermit lifestyle.

6

Kick Back on Ko Lanta

If Ko Phi-Phi is just too pretty and popular for you, then placid Ko Lanta (p314) is just your type. The island excels in the personality department with a laid-back island vibe and cultural insights into the Thai-Muslim fishing community. It is a marathon book-reading place popular with families and quieter types who no longer howl at the moon.

7

Get Muddy in Khao Sok

Stash your bathing suit for a spell for a sweaty and muddy good time. The interior rainforest of Khao Sok National Park (p284) is an example of nature at its most primordial. Among the muddy trails and forested karst mountains are monkeys, bugs galore, birds and the rare *Rafflesia kerrii*, a Malay peninsular flower with a fragrance of rotten meat.

Phuket & the Andaman Coast's Best...

Diving & Snorkelling

- **Surin Islands Marine National Park** (p287) Famous seamount of Richelieu Rock and soft coral earn top marks from divers.
- **Similan Islands Marine National Park** (p288) Protected park with great visibility and marine life for all diving levels.
- **Ko Lanta** (p314) Undersea pinnacles of Hin Muang and Hin Daeng attract large pelagic fish.

Karst Scenery

- **Ao Phang-Nga Marine National Park** (p288) Dramatic missile-shaped islands guard an aquamarine bay.
- **Ko Phi-Phi Leh** (p315) Ko Phi-Phi's uninhabited sister is decorated with soaring cliffs and gem-coloured lagoons.
- **Railay** (p309) Rock-climb, kayak, snorkel or simply admire these limestone outcroppings.

Fine Dining

- **Rum Jungle** (p297) Tropical open-air restaurant delivers top-notch seafood and Mediterranean fare.
- **Ka Jok See** (p296) Eclectic, trinket-filled restaurant that turns Thai dining into an event.
- **Tatonka** (p305) Alfresco dining with a globetrotter's menu.

Spas

- **Bua Luang Spa** (p306) Combines the best of Thai and Ayurvedic healing in a luxurious setting.
- **Sala Resort & Spa** (p307) Get wrapped up like human sushi at this celebrity-worthy spa.
- **Hideaway Day Spa** (p305) The first and one of the best spas with a tranquil lagoon setting.
- **Raintree Spa** (p294) Retro-colonial cool meets the spa scene.

Left: Divers, Surin Islands Marine National Park (p287); **Above:** Railay (p309), Krabi Province

(LEFT) JOHN ELK III/LONELY PLANET IMAGES ©; (ABOVE) SAIKO3P/DREAMSTIME ©

Need to Know

ADVANCE PLANNING

- **One month before** Book accommodation.
- **One week before** Book your dive trip and domestic plane trip.
- **One day before** Book a table at one of Phuket's high-end restaurants.

RESOURCES

- **Jamie's Phuket** (www.jamie-monk.blogspot.com)
- **One Stop Phuket** (www.1stopphuket.com)
- **Railay.com** (www.railay.com)

GETTING AROUND

- **Boat** Everything that floats will take you where roads can't; less so during the rainy season (June to October).
- **Bus** Good way to get between mainland towns or to/from Bangkok.
- **Minivan** Faster and more flexible option than the bus.
- **Motorcycle** Self-touring option on Phuket and Ko Lanta.
- **Sŏrng·tăa·ou** Small pick-up trucks that act as public buses on the mainland and Phuket.
- **Taxi & túk-túk** Chartered vehicles that charge a lot on the islands; remember to bargain.

BE FOREWARNED

- **Dive trips** Book your trip directly with the dive shop, not with an agent.
- **Motorcycle travel** Always wear a helmet when riding a motorcycle and don't put valuables in the front basket.
- **Rainy season** Except for Phuket, much of the Andaman Coast closes between June and October as seas can be too rough for transport and diving.
- **Drownings** Common on Phuket's west coast beaches, especially during the rainy season.
- **Sunbathing** Ladies, don't go topless.

Phuket & the Andaman Coast Itineraries

You can pop to Phuket in a hurry, but give yourself more time to savour the coast and peep underneath the surface.

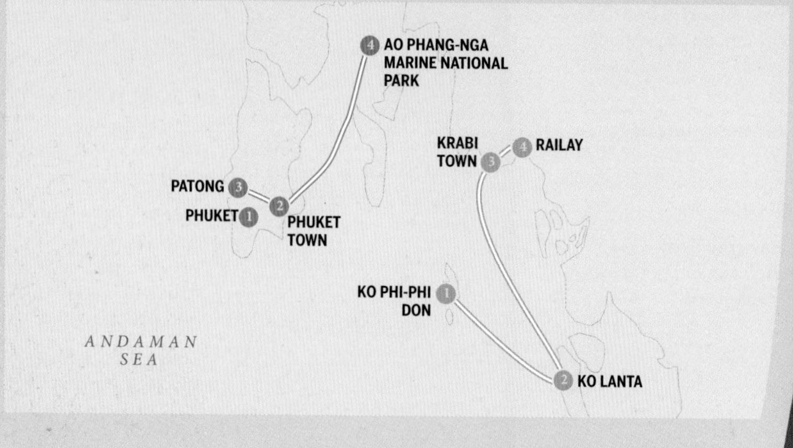

3 DAYS

PHUKET TO AO PHANG-NGA MARINE NATIONAL PARK

Phuket in a Nutshell

You can fly to Phuket from Bangkok for a long weekend without wasting much time in transit. The largest of Thailand's islands, **(1) Phuket** has lovely west-coast beaches that are lined with professional resorts and intimate boutiques, umbrella lounge-chairs and warm, clear water. The international standards of leisure apply in Phuket and there are plenty of extra amenities besides swimming and sunbathing. Treat yourself to a spa session, a cooking class and a fine meal.

Explore the old Sino-Portuguese architecture and Chinese shrines of **(2) Phuket Town** and cool down at a local eatery or cafe to savour old Phuket, one of Thailand's few resort islands with a lengthy historical record.

Once the sun has set, the night creatures descend on **(3) Patong**, a rowdy strip of neon lights, ladyboy cabarets, screaming discos and a touch of port-town seediness.

Devote one day to **(4) Ao Phang-Nga Marine National Park**, a protected bay cluttered with more than 40 peaked karst islands. Vast mangrove forests border the bay, providing fertile fishing grounds for local villagers.

KO PHI-PHI DON TO RAILAY

Go 'Ko' Hopping

South of Phuket, small islands and beaches are cradled together in a scenic coastal neighbourhood. Travellers visit them in succession as if they were all cherished family members.

From Phuket, boat down to **(1) Ko Phi-Phi Don**, the beauty queen of the Thai islands with just the right proportions of mod-cons and party power.

Then boat to **(2) Ko Lanta**, which has exceptional dive sites and lots of 'island' personality. Hire a motorcycle and cruise the local fishing villages and roadside food shacks to get in touch with Lanta's local population of Muslim and Buddhist Thais as well as *chow lair* (also spelt *chao leh,* sea gypsies). This kicked-back island doesn't have the flawless good looks of Ko Phi-Phi, but it has a whole lot of soul.

Another boat journey will take you to **(3) Krabi Town**, where you can transfer to a long-tail boat headed for **(4) Railay**. This coastal peninsula is hemmed in by limestone stacks, both on- and offshore. Rock climbers creep up the pitted vertical walls, while kayakers prefer a surface view. You're just a step away from Krabi Town for a quick air return to Bangkok.

Hat Nai Thon (p306), Sirinat National Park, Phuket Province

Discover Phuket & the Andaman Coast

At a Glance

- **Khao Lak** (p285) Mainland departure point for live-aboard dive trips.
- **Surin & Similan Islands Marine National Parks** (p287 & p288) Top dive sites in the Andaman Sea.
- **Ao Phang-Nga Marine National Park** (p288) Stunning karst island–filled bay; day-trip from Phuket.
- **Phuket** (p290) Thailand's number-one beach resort island.

Khao Lak

JOHN ELK III/LONELY PLANET IMAGES ©

PHANG-NGA PROVINCE

Khao Sok National Park

อุทยานแห่งชาติเขาสก

Many believe this lowland jungle – the wettest spot in Thailand – to be over 160 million years old, making it one of the oldest rainforests on the planet. It features dramatic limestone formations and waterfalls that cascade through juicy thickets drenched with rain.

The best time of year to visit is the dry season between December and April.

Sights & Activities

Khao Sok's vast terrain makes it one of the last viable habitats for **large mammals**. There are more than 300 bird species, 38 bat varieties and one of the world's largest flowers, the rare *Rafflesia kerrii*, which is found only here in Khao Sok.

Chiaw Lan, created in 1982 by an enormous shale-clay dam called Ratchaprapha (Kheuan Ratchaprapha or Chiaw Lan), sits about an hour's drive (65km) east of the visitors centre.

Tham Nam Thalu cave contains striking limestone formations and subterranean streams, while **Tham Si Ru** features four converging passageways used as a hideout by communist insurgents between 1975 and 1982.

Elephant trekking, kayaking and rafting are popular park activities. The hiking is also excellent, and you can arrange park tours from any guest house.

Tsunami Early Warning System

On the morning of 26 December 2004, an earthquake off the coast of the Indonesian island of Sumatra sent enormous waves crashing against much of Thailand's Andaman Coast, claiming around 8000 lives and causing millions of dollars of damage to homes and businesses. In 2005 Thailand officially inaugurated a national disaster warning system, which was created in response to the country's lack of preparedness in 2004.

For non-Thai speakers, the centre has installed warning towers along the high-risk beachfront areas that will broadcast announcements in various languages accompanied by flashing lights. The **call centre** (☎1860) also handles questions and tips from the public regarding potential or unfolding disasters.

Sleeping

ART'S RIVERVIEW JUNGLE LODGE Guest House $$
(☎08 6470 3234; www.krabidir.com/artsriverviewlodge; bungalows 650B) In a monkey-filled jungle bordering a river with a natural limestone cliff-framed swimming hole, this is the prettiest location in Khao Sok. Wood bungalows are simple but big, and all have river views.

JUNGLE HUTS Guest House $
(☎0 7739 5160; www.khao-sok-junglehuts.com; huts 300-1200B) Basic but good-value huts sit in a forest of fruit trees near a river or high up on stilts connected by a vertiginous walkway.

Information

The park headquarters (☎0 7739 5025; www.khaosok.com; park admission 200B) and visitors centre are 1.8km off Rte 401, close to the Km 109 marker.

Getting There & Around

Minivans to Surat Thani (250B, one hour), Krabi Town (300B, two hours) and a handful of other destinations leave daily.

Khao Lak เขาหลัก

Hat Khao Lak is a beach for folks who shun the glitz of Phuket's bigger resort towns, but still crave comfort, shopping and plenty of facilities. With warm waves to frolic in, long stretches of golden sand backed by forested hills, and easy day trips to the Similan and Surin Islands, Khao Sok and Khao Lak/Lam Ru National Parks or even Phuket, the area is a central base for exploring the North Andaman Coast – above and below the water.

Activities

Diving or snorkelling day excursions to the Similan and Surin islands are immensely popular, but if you can, opt for a live-aboard trip. Since the islands are around 60km from the mainland (about three hours by boat), if you visit on a live-aboard you'll have a more relaxing trip and experience the islands sans day-trippers. All dive shops offer live-aboard trips from around 10,000/19,000B for two-/three-day packages and day trips for 4900B to 6500B.

On these miltiday trips, you'll wake up with the dawn and slink below the ocean's surface up to four times each day in what's commonly considered to be one of the top 10 diving realms in the world.

Although geared towards divers, all dive shops welcome snorkellers who can hop on selected dive excursions or live-aboards for a discount of around 40%; otherwise, tour agencies all around town offer even cheaper snorkelling trips to the Similan Islands for around 2700B.

WICKED DIVING Diving

(☎0 7648 5868; www.wickeddiving.com) An exceptionally well-run and environmentally conscious outfit that runs diving and snorkelling overnight trips offering a range of live-aboard options including Whale Sharks & Mantas, Turtle & Reefs and Sharks & Rays conservation trips, run in conjunction with **Ecocean** (www.whaleshark.org).

SIMILAN DIVING SAFARIS Diving

(☎0 7648 5470; www.similan-diving-safaris.com) As far as live-aboards are concerned, this is probably the best bang for your baht. Day trips are also available.

Sleeping

LA FLORA RESORT Hotel $$$

(☎0 7642 8000; www.lafloraresort.com; r 5700-7700B, villas 9000-10,500B;) On gorgeous Hat Bang Niang, this resort exudes barefoot class; it's both elegant and supremely relaxing. Cabana-style villas are large and modern with sexy beachfront infinity pools and there's a kid-friendly pool in the centre of things.

NANGTHONG BEACH RESORT Hotel $$

(☎0 7648 5911; www.nangthong2.com; r 2000-2200B, bungalows 2500-3000B;) The best choice in Khao Lak proper has large, well-appointed rooms, and even larger bungalows, with ceramic-tile floors, dark-wood furnishings, a bourgeoning garden, impeccable service and the best stretch of sand in town.

GREENBEACH Hotel $$

(☎0 7648 5845; greenbeach_th@yahoo.com; bungalows 1300-2300B;) On an excellent stretch of Khao Lak beach and extending back into a garden, this place has a warm family-style soul. The wood bungalows have glass doors, air-con and fan, shady terraces and views of a towering, ancient banyan tree. Even the cheapest rooms have sea views.

Surin Islands Marine National Park

FELIX HUG/LONELY PLANET IMAGES ©

Eating

MAMA'S RESTAURANT Restaurant **$$**
(Th Petchkasem; dishes 60-300B) Nobody, and we do mean nobody, does seafood better than Mama, who's set up across from Boat 813. Her fish cakes are insane, so is the barracuda sautéed in yellow curry.

Information

For diving-related emergencies, call the **SSS Ambulance** (☎08 1081 9444), which rushes injured persons down to Phuket for treatment. The ambulance can also be used for car or motorcycle accidents. There is also one nurse in Bang Niang who caters to diving related injuries.

Getting There & Away

Any bus running along Hwy 4 between Takua Pa (50B, 45 minutes) and Phuket (100B, two hours) will stop at Hat Khao Lak if you ask the driver. **Khao Lak Discoveries** runs hourly minibuses to/from Phuket International Airport (600B, one hour 15 minutes).

Surin Islands Marine National Park อุทยานแห่งชาติหมู่เกาะสุรินทร์

The five gorgeous islands that make up this **national park (www.dnp.go.th; admission 400B; ⏲mid-Nov–mid-May)** sit about 60km offshore, a measly 5km from the Thai–Burma marine border. Healthy rainforest, pockets of white-sand beach in sheltered bays and rocky headlands that jut into the ocean characterise these granite-outcrop islands. The clearest of water makes for great marine life, with underwater visibility often up to 35m. The islands' sheltered waters also attract *chow lair* (also spelt *chao leh;* sea gypsies), who live in a village onshore during the monsoon season from May to November. Around here they are known as Moken, derived from the local word *oken* meaning 'salt water'.

Khuraburi is the jumping-off point for the park. The pier is about 9km north of town, as is the mainland **national park office (☎0 7649 1378; ⏲8am-5pm)**, which has good information, maps and helpful staff.

Sights & Activities

DIVING & SNORKELLING

Dive sites in the park include **Ko Surin Tai** and **HQ Channel** between the two main islands. **Richelieu Rock** (a seamount 14km southeast) is also technically in the park and happens to be one of the best – if not the best – dive sites on the Andaman Coast. Whale sharks are sometimes spotted here during March and April. There's no dive facility in the park itself, so dive trips (four-day live-aboards around 20,000B) must be booked from the mainland; see Khao Lak (p287) for more information.

Snorkelling isn't as good as it used to be due to recent bleaching of the hard corals, but you'll still see fish and soft corals. If you'd like a serene snorkelling experience, charter your own long-tail boat from the national park (half day 1000B), or better yet, directly from the Moken themselves in **Ban Moken**. The most beautiful, vibrant soft corals we saw were at **Ao Mae Yai**, an enormous North Island bay around the corner from Chong Khod. The best section of reef is between the white buoys along the northern peninsula. **Ao Suthep**, off the South Island, has vast schools of iridescent fish and shallow blue holes with milky bottoms.

VILLAGE TOUR

The national park offers a **Moken Village Tour (per person 300B)**. You'll stroll through the village where you should ask locals for permission to hike the 800m **Chok Madah trail** over the jungled hills to an empty beach. Tours depart at 9.15am and must be reserved the day before.

Getting There & Away

Several tour operators run day tours (2900B including food and park lodging) to the park. The best in safety, service and value is **Greenview** (☎0 7640 1400; Khuraburi pier).

Wildlife in Ao Pang-Nga Marine National Park

The marine limestone environment at Ao Pang-Nga favours a long list of reptiles, including Bengal monitor lizards, flying lizards, banded sea snakes, dogface water snakes, shore pit vipers and Malay pit vipers. Keep an eye out for a two-banded monitor *(Varanus salvator)*, which looks like a crocodile when seen swimming in the mangrove swamp and can measure up to 2.2m in length.

Amphibians in the Ao Phang-Nga region include marsh frogs, common bush frogs and crab-eating frogs. Avian residents of note are helmeted hornbills (the largest of Thailand's 12 hornbill species, with a body length of up to 127cm), the edible-nest swiftlets *(Aerodramus fuciphagus)*, white-bellied sea eagles, ospreys and Pacific reef egrets.

In the mangrove forests and on some of the larger islands reside over 200 species of mammals, including white-handed gibbons, serows, dusky langurs and crab-eating macaques.

Similan Islands Marine National Park

อุทยานแห่งชาติหมู่เกาะสิมิลัน

Known to divers the world over, beautiful **Similan Islands Marine National Park** (www.dnp.go.th; admission 400B; Nov-May) is 60km offshore. Its smooth granite islands are as impressive above water as below, topped with rainforest, edged with white-sand beaches and fringed with coral reefs. Unfortunately recent coral bleaching has killed many of the hard corals but soft corals are still intact, the fauna is there and it remains a lovely place to dive.

Hat Khao Lak is the jumping-off point for the park. The pier is at Thap Lamu, about 10km south of town.

Sights & Activities

The Similan Islands offer diving for all levels of experience, at depths from 2m to 30m. There are rock reefs at **Ko Payu** (Island 7) and dive-throughs at **Hin Pousar** (Elephant Head), with marine life ranging from tiny plume worms and soft corals to schooling fish and whale sharks. No facilities for divers exist in the national park itself, so you'll need to take a dive tour.

Getting There & Away

Agencies in Khao Lak (p285) and Phuket (p290) book day/overnight tours (from around 3000/5000B) and dive trips (three-day live-aboards from around 15,000B) – this is about how much you would pay if you tried to get to the islands on your own steam.

Ao Phang-Nga Marine National Park

อุทยานแห่งชาติอ่าวพังงา

Established in 1981 and covering an area of 400 sq km, **Ao Phang-Nga Marine National Park** (0 7641 1136; www.dnp.go.th; admission 200B; 8am-4pm) is noted for its classic karst scenery. There are over 40 islands with huge vertical cliffs, some with caves that are accessible at low tide and lead into hidden *hôrngs* (lagoons surrounded by solid rock walls). The bay itself is composed of large and small tidal channels including Khlong Ko Phanyi, Khlong Phang-Nga, Khlong Bang Toi and Khlong Bo Saen. These channels run through vast mangroves in a north–south direction and today are used by fisherfolk and island inhabitants as aquatic highways. These mangroves are the largest remaining primary mangrove forests in Thailand.

In the peak season the bay can become a package-tour superhighway. But if you explore in the early morning or stay out a bit late, you'll find a slice of beach, sea and a limestone karst to call your own. The best way to experience the park is by kayak.

 Sights & Activities

JOHN GRAY'S SEACANOE Kayaking
(☎0 7622 6077; www.johngray-seacanoe.com) John Gray was the first kayak outfitter in the bay and remains the most ecologically minded. He's constantly clamouring for more protection for his beloved *hôrngs* among local national park rangers and their supervisors in Bangkok. His **Hong By Starlight day trip** (per person 3950B) dodges the crowds, involves plenty of sunset paddling and will introduce you to Ao Phang-Nga's famed bioluminescence once night falls. See also p290.

KO NOK & KO KLUI Island
Set halfway between Phuket and Krabi, these two islands are far enough from tour epicentres that you'll usually have them to yourself. Ko Klui, the big island north of Ko Yao Noi, has tidal access to a huge *hôrng,* which some call the **Blue Room**, and a pristine white-sand beach with plenty of hornbills and monkeys.

KO PHING KAN (JAMES BOND ISLAND) Island
The biggest tourist drawcard in the park is the so-called 'James Bond Island', known to Thais as **Ko Phing Kan** (literally 'Leaning on Itself Island'). Used as a location setting for *The Man with the Golden Gun,* the island is now full of vendors hawking coral and shells that should have stayed in the sea.

Getting There & Around

From the centre of Ao Phang-Nga drive about 6km south on Hwy 4, turn left onto Rte 4144 (the road to Tha Dan) and travel 2.6km to the park headquarters. Without your own transport you'll need to take a *sŏrng·tăa·ou* to Tha Dan (30B).

From the park office, you can hire a boat (1500B, maximum four passengers) for a three-hour tour of the surrounding islands.

Ko Yao เกาะยาว

With mountainous backbones, unspoilt shorelines, a large variety of bird-life and a population of friendly Muslim fisherfolk, **Ko Yao Yai** and **Ko Yao Noi** are laid-back vantage points for soaking up Ao Phang-Nga's beautiful scenery. The islands are part of the Ao Phang-Nga Marine National Park but are most easily accessed from Phuket.

Please remember to respect the beliefs of the local Muslim population and wear modest clothing when away from the beaches.

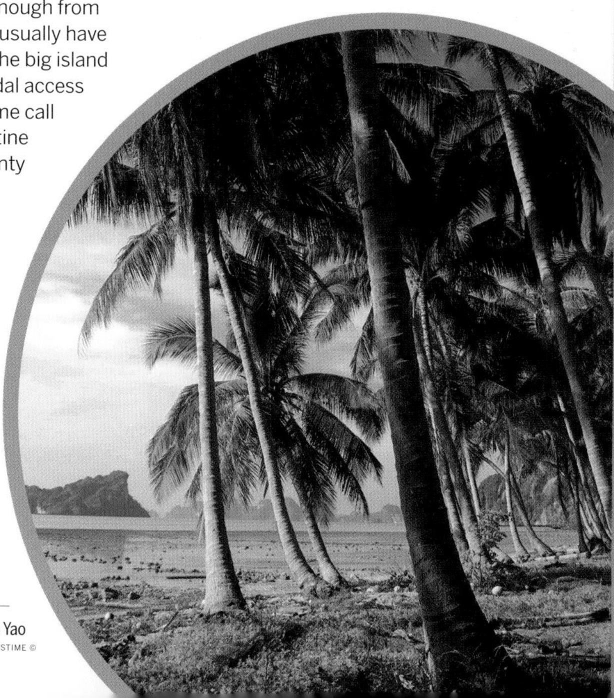

Ko Yao

Activities

Bring along or rent a mountain bike (200B per day from most guest houses) if you want to explore each of the islands' numerous dirt trails, or join up with Phuket's **Amazing Bike Tours** (☎08 7263 2031; www.amazingbiketoursthailand.com; day trip 2900B).

KOH YAO DIVER Diving
(☎08789 575 517; www.kohyaodiver.com) Leads dive trips from both islands. Half-day three-island snorkelling tours (1700B, maximum six passengers) through Ao Phang-Nga are easily organised from any guest house or with long-tail captains on the beaches.

MOUNTAIN SHOP ADVENTURES Rock Climbing
(☎08 9971 0380, 08 4841 1540; www.themountainshop.org; Tha Khao) Offers full-day rock climbing trips around Ko Yao Noi from 2500B, as well as fishing, snorkelling and kayaking trips.

Getting There & Away

From Phuket

For Ko Yao Noi, hourly long-tails (150B, 20 minutes) or three daily speedboats (200B, 20 minutes) leave Tha Bano Rong north of Phuket Town between 7.30am and 5.40pm.

To Ko Yao Yai, catch a speedboat or ferry from Tha Rasada near Phuket Town. Ferries depart at 8.30am, 10.30am and 2pm (one hour, 100B). Speedboats (30 minutes, 150B) make the run at 4pm and 5pm. On Fridays the schedule shifts to accommodate prayer times.

PHUKET PROVINCE ภูเก็ต

POP 83,800

Dubbed the 'pearl of the Andaman' by marketing execs, this is Thailand's original flavour of tailor-made fun in the sun. Jet-setters come in droves, getting pummelled during swanky spa sessions and swigging sundowners at one of the many fashion-forward nightspots. And you don't have to be an heiress to tap into Phuket's trendy to-do list. There's deep-sea diving, high-end dining and white beaches that beckon you and your book – whatever your heart desires.

Activities

Diving & Snorkelling

Phuket enjoys an enviable central location for diving. The much-talked-about Similans sit to the north, while dozens of dive sites orbit Ko Phi-Phi Don (p311) and Ko Lanta (p314) to the south.

Typical one-day dive trips to nearby sites cost around 3500B, including two dives and equipment. Nondivers (and snorkellers) are often permitted to join these dive trips for a significant discount.

Snorkelling is best along Phuket's west coast, particularly at the rocky headlands between beaches.

SEA FUN DIVERS Diving
(☎0 7634 0480; www.seafundivers.com; 29 Soi Karon Nui, Patong) An outstanding and very professional diving operation. Standards are extremely high and service is impeccable.

OFFSPRAY LEISURE Diving, Snorkelling
(☎08 1894 1274; www.offsprayleisure.com; 43/87 Chalong Plaza; trips from 2950B) A dive and snorkelling excursion company specialising in small-load, intimate trips to the reefs around Ko Phi-Phi.

Sea Kayaking

Several companies based on Phuket offer canoe tours of scenic Ao Phang-Nga Marine National Park.

JOHN GRAY'S SEACANOE Kayaking
(☎0 7625 4505-7; www.johngray-seacanoe.com; 124 Soi 1, Th Yaowarat) The original, still the most reputable and by far the most ecologically sensitive company on the island.

Ko Phuket

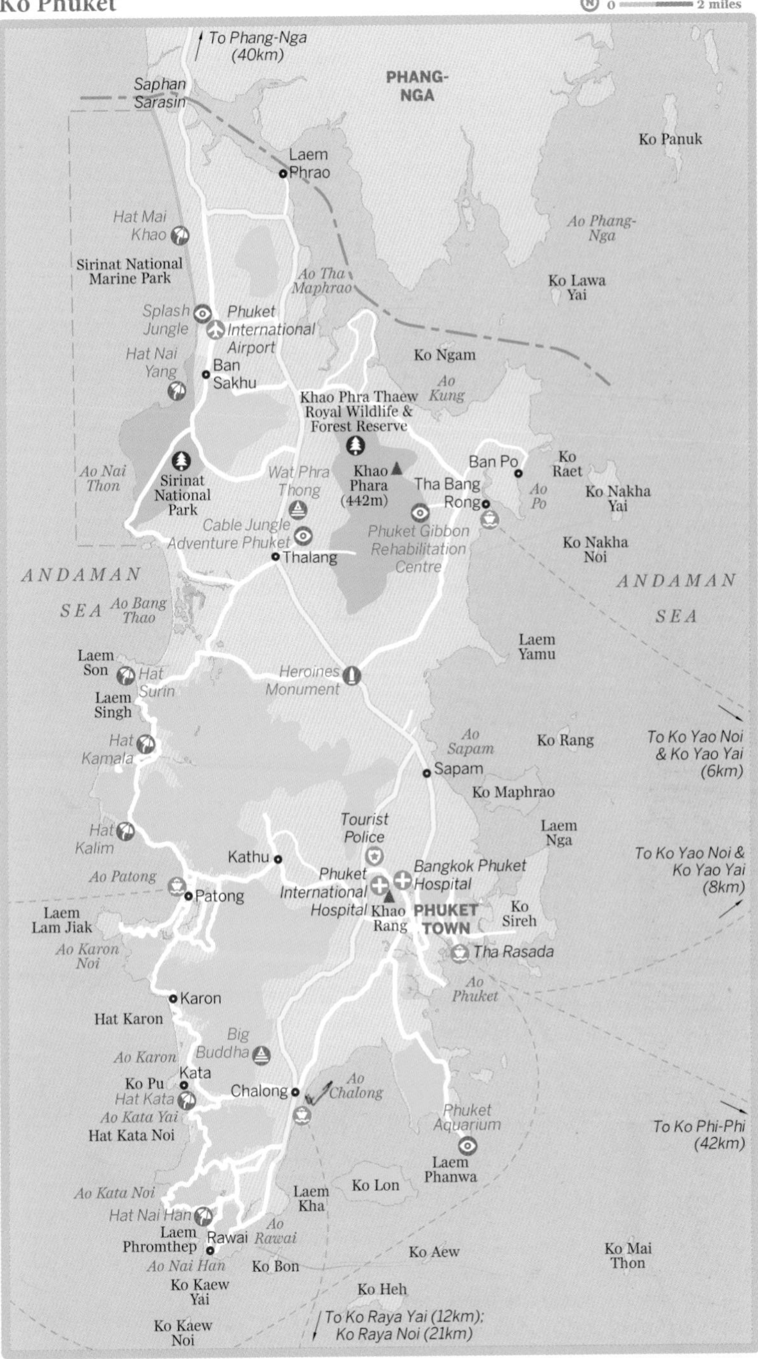

0 4 km
0 2 miles
To Phang-Nga (40km)
PHANG-NGA
Saphan Sarasin
Laem Phrao
Ko Panuk
Hat Mai Khao
Ao Phang-Nga
Sirinat National Marine Park
Ao Tha Maphrao
Ko Lawa Yai
Splash Jungle
Phuket International Airport
Hat Nai Yang
Ban Sakhu
Ko Ngam
Ao Kung
Khao Phra Thaew Royal Wildlife & Forest Reserve
Ban Po
Ko Raet
Ao Nai Thon
Sirinat National Park
Wat Phra Thong
Khao Phara (442m)
Tha Bang Rong
Ao Po
Ko Nakha Yai
Cable Jungle Adventure Phuket
Phuket Gibbon Rehabilitation Centre
Thalang
Ko Nakha Noi
ANDAMAN SEA
Ao Bang Thao
ANDAMAN SEA
Laem Yamu
Laem Son
Hat Surin
Heroines Monument
Laem Singh
Hat Kamala
Ao Sapam
Ko Rang
To Ko Yao Noi & Ko Yao Yai (6km)
Sapam
Ko Maphrao
Tourist Police
Laem Nga
Hat Kalim
Kathu
To Ko Yao Noi & Ko Yao Yai (8km)
Bangkok Phuket Hospital
Ao Patong
Phuket International Hospital
Patong
Laem Lam Jiak
Khao Rang
PHUKET TOWN
Ko Sireh
Ao Karon Noi
Tha Rasada
Ao Phuket
Karon
Hat Karon
Big Buddha
Ao Karon
Kata
Ko Pu
Chalong
Ao Chalong
Hat Kata
Ao Kata Yai
Phuket Aquarium
To Ko Phi-Phi (42km)
Hat Kata Noi
Laem Phanwa
Ao Kata Noi
Laem Kha
Ko Lon
Hat Nai Han
Ao Rawai
Laem Phromthep
Rawai
Ko Aew
Ko Mai Thon
Ao Nai Han
Ko Bon
Ko Kaew Yai
Ko Heh
Ko Kaew Noi
To Ko Raya Yai (12km); Ko Raya Noi (21km)

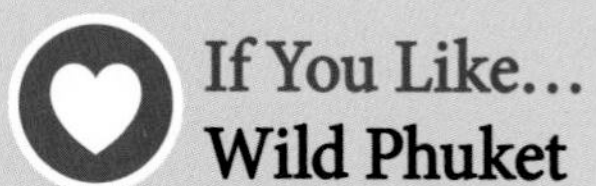

If You Like... Wild Phuket

If you like the natural-side of Phuket, check out these animal and forest attractions.

1 **PHUKET AQUARIUM**
(Map p291; ☎0 7639 1126; www.phuketaquarium.org; Laem Phanwa; adult/child 100/50B; ⏰8.30am-4.30pm) Located on a scenic cape, Phuket Aquarium displays a varied collection of tropical fish and other marine life. Experience it with a stroll along the walk-through tunnel. Afterwards head to the waterfront seafood restaurants, a great place to hang out and watch the pleasure skiffs and painted fishing boats.

2 **PHUKET GIBBON REHABILITATION CENTRE**
(Map p291; ☎0 7626 0492; www.gibbonproject.org; donations encouraged; ⏰9am-4pm) In the royal forest reserve, this small wildlife centre adopts and rehabilitates gibbons that have been kept in captivity.

3 **CABLE JUNGLE ADVENTURE PHUKET**
(Map p291; ☎08 1977 4904; 232/17 Moo 8, Th Bansuanneramit; per person 1950B; ⏰9am-6pm) Tucked into the hills is this maze of eight ziplines linking cliffs to ancient trees. Closed-toe shoes are a must.

Surfing

Phuket is an undercover surf destination. The best waves arrive between June and September, when annual competitions are held in Hat Kata and Hat Kalim.

PHUKET SURF
(☎08 7889 7308, 08 1684 8902; www.phuketsurf.com) On Hat Kata Yai's southern cove; offers surf lessons starting at 1500B for a half-day, as well as board rentals for 100/300B per hour/day.

PHUKET SURFING
(☎0 7628 4183; www.phuketsurfing.com) Just in front of Phuket Surf and sharing a roof with Nautilus dive, it rents boards by the hour for 100B to 150B.

KITEBOARDING

One of the world's fastest growing sports is also one of Phuket's coming fads. The three best spots are Hat Nai Yang, Karon (in the low season) and Rawai (ideal conditions for beginners in the high season).

KITE BOARDING ASIA Kiteboarding
(☎08 1591 4594; www.kiteboardingasia.com; lessons from 4000B) Its main office is on Hat Nai Yang, but it has a kiosk on the south end of Hat Karon that's open in the low season.

Courses

MOM TRI'S BOATHOUSE Cooking
(☎0 7633 0015; www.boathousephuket.com; 2/2 Th Kata (Patak West), Hat Kata; per person one day/weekend 2200/3500B) Offers a fantastic weekend Thai cooking class with its renowned chef, Rattana.

BLUE ELEPHANT RESTAURANT & COOKERY SCHOOL Cooking
(☎0 7635 4355; www.blueelephant.com; 96 Th Krabi, Phuket Town; half-day classes 2800B) Phuket's newest cookery school is in the stunning restored 1903 Sino-Portuguese style Phra Phitak Chyn Pracha Mansion. There are a variety of options from short group lessons to five-day private training (78,000B). Morning classes take in a market visit.

Tours

AMAZING BIKE TOURS Cycling
(☎0 7628 3436; www.amazingbiketoursthailand.asia; 32/4 Moo 9, Th Chaofa, Chalong; day trips from 1600B) Phuket's best new adventure outfitter leads small groups on half-day bicycle tours through the Khao Phra Thaew Royal Wildlife & Forest Reserve, and it offers terrific day trips around Ko

Yao Noi and the gorgeous beaches and waterfalls of Thai Muang in nearby Phang-Nga Province.

Information

Dangers & Annoyances

During the May to October monsoon, large waves and fierce undertows can make it too dangerous to swim.

Renting a motorcycle or motorbike can be a high-risk proposition. Thousands of people are injured or killed every year on Phuket's highways.

There have been recent late-night motorbike muggings and stabbings on the road leading from Patong to Hat Karon, and on the road between Kata and the Rawai–Hat Nai Han area. There have been a few recent random sexual assaults on women, as well.

Medical Services

Bangkok Phuket Hospital (Map p291; ☎0 7625 4425; www.phukethospital.com; Th Yongyok Uthit) Reputedly the favourite with locals.

Phuket International Hospital (Map p291; ☎0 7624 9400; www.phuketinternationalhospital.com; Th Chalermprakiat) International doctors rate this hospital as the best on the island.

Tourist Information

Tourism Authority of Thailand (☎0 7621 2213; www.tat.or.th; 73-75 Th Phuket, Phuket Town; 8.30am-4.30pm)

Getting There & Away

Air

Phuket International Airport (☎0 7632 7230) is 30km northwest of Phuket Town; it takes around 45 minutes to an hour to reach the southern beaches from here.

Some regional airline carriers include the following:

Air Asia (www.airasia.com) In addition to several daily flights to Bangkok (around 1480B), it also flies direct to Hong Kong (5000B), Chiang Mai (1600B), Singapore (1400B), Bali (2730B) and other destinations.

Bangkok Airways (☎0 7622 5033; www.bangkokair.com; 58/2-3 Th Yaowarat) Has daily flights to Ko Samui (2380B) and Bangkok (1725B).

Nok Air (www.nokair.com) Links Phuket with Bangkok.

THAI (☎0 7621 1195; www.thaiairways.com; 78/1 Th Ranong, Phuket Town) Operates around seven daily flights to Bangkok (from around 3000B) with connections to/from several other cities in Thailand, as well as international destinations.

Several other international airlines fly to Phuket and have offices in Phuket Town including the following:

Dragonair (☎0 7621 5734; Th Phang-Nga, Phuket Town)

Korean Airlines (☎0 7621 6675; 1/8-9 Th Thungkha, Phuket Town)

Phuket's Moo•ay Tai Explosion *ADAM SKOLNICK*

Over the past few years, spurred in no small part by the increasing global presence and popularity of Mixed Martial Arts, several *moo•ay tai* (also spelled *muay thai;* Thai boxing) gyms catering to international male and female athletes have sprouted off the beach in Phuket.

The whole thing started with Pricha 'Tuk' Chokkuea and his gym, **Rawai Muay Thai** (☎08 1476 9377; www.rawaimuaythai.com; 43/42 Moo 7, Th Sai Yuan). The best new gym is Avison's **Promthep Muay Thai Camp** (☎08 5786 2414; www.promthepmuaythai.com; 91 Moo 6, Soi Yanui).

Detour: Big Buddha

Set on a hilltop just northwest of Chalong circle and visible from almost half of the island, the Big Buddha (พระใหญ่; Map p291) has the best view on Phuket. Once you're up here, pay your respects at the golden shrine, then step up to Big Buddha's glorious plateau where you can peer into Kata's bay, glimpse the shimmering Karon strand and, on the other side, survey the serene Chalong harbour where the channel islands look like pebbles.

Malaysia Airlines (☎0 7621 6675; 1/8-9 Th Thungkha, Phuket Town)

Silk Air (☎0 7621 3891; www.silkair.com; 183/103 Th Phang-Nga, Phuket Town)

Ferry & Speedboat

Tha Rasada, north of Phuket Town, is the main pier for boats to Ko Phi Phi with connections to Krabi and Ko Lanta. For quicker service to Krabi and Ao Nang via the Ko Yao Islands, boats leave from Tha Bang Rong north of Tha Rasada.

Minivan

Travel agencies all around Phuket Island sell tickets (which include the ferry fare) for air-conditioned minivans down to Ko Samui and Ko Pha-Ngan. Air-conditioned minivan services to Krabi, Surat Thani and several other locations are also available.

Phuket Town

เมืองภูเก็ต

POP 94,325

Long before tourist T-shirts or flip-flops, Phuket was an island of rubber trees, tin mines and cash-hungry merchants. Wander down streets clogged with Sino-Portuguese architecture housing arty coffeeshops, galleries, wonderful inexpensive restaurants and hip little guest houses; peek down alleyways to find Chinese Taoist shrines shrouded in incense smoke.

Sights

SINO-PORTUGUESE ARCHITECTURE Heritage Architecture

Stroll along the streets of Thalang, Dibuk, Yaowarat, Ranong, Phang-Nga, Rasada and Krabi for a glimpse of some of the best architecture on offer. Soi Romanee off Th Thalang is the most ambient area of town. The most magnificent buildings are the **Standard Chartered Bank** (Th Phang-Nga), Thailand's oldest foreign bank; the **THAI office** (Th Ranong); and the **old post office building**, which now houses the **Phuket Philatelic Museum** (Th Montri; admission free; ⏰9.30am-5.30pm). The best-restored residential properties are found along Th Dibuk and Th Thalang.

SHRINE OF THE SERENE LIGHT Shrine

(ศาลเจ้าแสงธรรม; Saan Jao Sang Tham; ⏰8.30am-noon & 1.30-5.30pm) A handful of Chinese temples inject some added colour into the area, but the Shrine of the Serene Light, tucked away at the end of a 50m alley near the Bangkok Bank of Commerce on Th Phang-Nga, is a cut above the rest.

PHUKET THAIHUA MUSEUM Museum

(พิพิธภัณฑ์ภูเก็ตไทยหัว; 28 Th Krabi; admission 200B; ⏰9am-5pm) This flashy new museum, set in an old Sino-Portuguese home, is filled with photos and exhibits on Phuket's history. The last room is covered in photos of local dishes – and if this makes you hungry, info on where to find the food stalls is listed on the wall.

Sleeping

SINO HOUSE Hotel $$

(☎0 7623 2494; www.sinohousephuket.com; 1 Th Montri; r 2000-2500B; ❄@) Shanghai style meets *Mad Men* chic at this impressive old town offering. The rooms are

PAUL KENNEDY/LONELY PLANET IMAGES ©

Don't Miss Vegetarian Festival

Loud popping sounds like machine-gun fire fill the streets, the air is nearly opaque with grey-brown smoke and men and women traipse along blocked-off city roads, their cheeks pierced with skewers and knives or, more surprisingly, lamps and tree branches; some of the flock have blood streaming down their fronts or open lashes across their backs. No, this isn't a war zone, this is the Vegetarian Festival, one of Phuket's most important festivals, centred in Phuket Town.

The festival, which takes place during the first nine days of the ninth lunar month of the Chinese calendar (usually late September or October) celebrates the beginning of 'Taoist Lent', when devout Chinese abstain from eating meat. But more obvious to the outsider are the daily processions winding their way through town with floats of ornately dressed children and *gà·teu·i* (ladyboys), near armies of flag-bearing colour-coordinated young people and, most noticeably, men and women engaged in outrageous acts of self-mortification.

Those participating as mediums bring the nine deities to earth by entering into a trance state, piercing their cheeks with an impressive variety of objects, sawing their tongues or flagellating themselves with spiky metal balls. Surreal and overwhelming hardly describes it.

The TAT office in Phuket prints a helpful schedule of events for the Vegetarian Festival each year.

massive with mod furnishings, fantastic handmade ceramic basins and quarter-moon shower tubs in the bathrooms. There's an on-site **Raintree Spa** and long-term rates (18,000B per month) are available.

Eating

There's good food in Phuket Town, and meals here cost a lot less than those at the beach.

KA JOK SEE Thai, International $$$
(☎0 7621 7903; kajoksee@hotmail.com; 26 Th Takua Pa; dishes 180-480B; ⏰dinner Tue-Sun) Dripping old Phuket charm and creaking under the weight of the owner's fabulous trinket collection, this atmospheric little eatery offers great food, top-notch music and – if you're lucky – some sensationally camp cabaret.

CHINA INN Thai Fusion $$
(Th Thalang; dishes 80-250B) The organics movement meets Phuket cuisine at this turn-of-the-century shophouse. There's red curry with crab, a host of veggie options, homemade yoghurt and fruit smoothies with organic honey. There's also a gallery here with textiles, carvings and clothes from Myanmar (Burma) and Laos.

UPTOWN RESTAURANT Thai $
(Th Tilok Uthit; dishes 30-60B; ⏰10am-9pm) This classic, breezy Chinese-style cafe may not look fancy, but look around and you'll notice mounted photos of Thai celebrities who have stopped by to slurp the spectacular noodles.

COOK Italian, Thai $
(☎0 7625 8375; 101 Th Phang-Nga; dishes 60-120B) The Thai owner-chef used to cook Italian at a megaresort, so when he opened this ludicrously inexpensive old town cafe he fused the two cultures. Order the sensational green curry pizza with chicken, or the pork curry coconut-milk pizza, and fall in love.

WILAI Thai $
(14 Th Thalang; dishes from 65B; ⏰breakfast & lunch) Wilai serves Phuket soul food. It does Phuketian *pàt tai* with some kick to it, and a fantastic *mèe sua* (noodles sautéed with egg, greens, prawns, chunks of sea bass and squid). Wash it down with fresh chrysanthemum juice.

Drinking & Entertainment

This is where you can party like a local. Bars buzz until late, patronised almost exclusively by Thais and local expats.

TIMBER HUT Club
(☎0 7621 1839; 118/1 Th Yaowarat; admission free; ⏰6pm-2am) Thai and expat locals have been filling this old clubhouse every night for nearly 20 years. They gather at long wooden tables on two floors, converge around thick timber columns, swill whiskey, and sway to live bands that swing from hard rock to funk to hip-hop with aplomb.

BO(OK)HEMIAN Cafe
(☎0 7625 2854; 61 Th Thalang; ⏰9am-10pm; 📶) Every town should have a coffee house this cool. The split-level open design feels both warm and leading edge. It has wi-fi, used books for sale, gourmet coffee and tea, and damn good chocolate cake.

Getting There & Around

To/From the Airport

Despite what airport taxi touts would like you to believe, a bright orange **government airport bus** (www.airportbusphuket.com; tickets 85B) runs between the airport and Phuket Town via the Heroines Monument about every hour between 6am and 7pm. There's also a minibus service at the airport that will take you into Phuket Town for 150B per person. Patong, Kata and Karon beaches cost 180B if there are enough passengers. Metered taxis should cost no more than 550B (including airport tax) to anywhere around the island.

Bus

You'll find the **bus terminal** (☎0 7621 1977) just to the east of the town centre, within walking distance of the many hotels.

Car

There are cheap car-rental agencies on Th Rasada near **Pure Car Rent** (☎0 7621 1002; www.purecarrent.com; 75 Th Rasada), which is a good choice.

Sŏrng·tăa·ou & Túk-túk

Large bus-sized *sŏrng·tăa·ou* run regularly from Th Ranong near the day market to the various Phuket beaches (25B to 40B per person). These run from around 7am to 5pm; outside these times you have to charter a túk-túk to the beaches, which will set you back 500B to Patong, Karon and Kata, 340B to 400B for Rawai and 600B to Kamala. You'll have to bargain.

Rawai ราไวย์

Now this is a place to live, which is exactly why Phuket's rapidly developing south coast is teeming with retirees, Thai and expat entrepreneurs, and a service sector that, for the most part, moved here from somewhere else.

Sights & Activities

Hat Nai Han, with its crescent of white sand backed by causarinas, bobbing yachts, seafront temple Wat Nai Han and monsoon-season surf break, is the best beach in the area, but there are also smaller, hidden beaches that are just as beautiful.

Sleeping

All the lodging in lovely Hat Nai Han is reached via a skinny, rutted paved road that begins from the Phuket Yacht Club parking lot (yes, you can drive past the guard) – or charter a long-tail from Rawai for 500B.

ROYAL PHUKET YACHT CLUB Hotel **$$$**

(**☎0 7638 0200; www.royalphuket yachtclub.com; 23/3 Moo 1, Th Viset, Hat Nai Han; r from 6800B; ❄@☒**) Still a destination for many a transcontinental yachty, there's an air of old-world elegance here, especially in its fabulous lobby-bar spinning with ceiling fans. Rooms feature large terraces – and stunning bay views – and there's every creature comfort you could imagine somewhere on-site.

Eating & Drinking

There are a dozen tasty seafood grills roasting fresh catch along the roadside near Hat Rawai.

RUM JUNGLE Restaurant **$$$**

(**☎0 7638 8153; 69/8 Th Sai Yuan; meals 300-500B; ⏰dinner, closed Sun**) The best restaurant in the area and one of the best in all of Phuket is family run and spearheaded by a terrific Aussie chef. The New Zealand lamb shank is divine, as are the steamed clams and the pasta sauces are all made from scratch.

Hat Kata หาดกะตะ

Kata attracts a lively crowd with its shopping and busy beach without the seedy hustle endemic to Patong up the coast. While you might not find a secluded strip of sand, you will find plenty to do and plenty of easy-going folks to clink beers with.

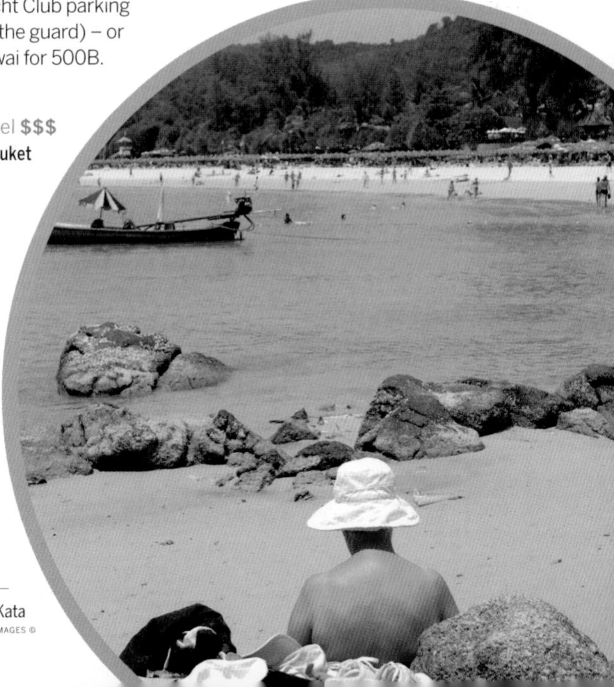

Hat Kata

AUSTIN BUSH/LONELY PLANET IMAGES ©

Sights & Activities

If you're looking for an alternative to the St Tropez–esque south Kata crush, make a left turn (west) just before the main road rises up and heads towards Karon, continue past the cluster of Thai-food joints and you'll find a gorgeous stretch of Kata beach in the secluded, rocky north end (ie Hat Kata Yai) where long-tails bob in the tide.

Sleeping

MOM TRI'S VILLA ROYALE Hotel $$$
(**0 7633 3568; www.villaroyalephuket.com; ste incl breakfast from 12,500B;**) Tucked away in a secluded Kata Noi location with the grandest of views, Villa Royale is a supremely romantic place with fabulous food. Unwind in beautiful rooms straight out of the pages of *Architectural Digest* and guiltless pleasures include the attached spa and a saltwater pool – if you prefer a tamer version of the real thing – which is just steps away.

SAWASDEE VILLAGE Hotel $$$
(**0 7633 0979; www.phuketsawasdee.com; 38 Th Ked Kwan; bungalows 6500-8500B;**) This is a boutique resort with a lush, opulent but compact footprint built in classic Thai style. Ornate, peaked-roof bungalows have wood floors, beamed ceilings and doors open onto a thick tropical landscape laced with *koi* (carp) canals and gushing with waterfalls.

SUGAR PALM RESORT Hotel $$
(**0 7628 4404; www.sugarpalmphuket.com; 20/10 Th Kata; r incl breakfast 3700-5200B;**) It's a 'chic chill-out world' at the Sugar Palm, as this Miami-meets-Thailand-style resort claims. Rooms, decorated in urban whites, blacks and lavender, are exceptional value and sublimely comfy, and all surround a black-bottomed, U-shaped pool. It's a block to the beach in the heart of Kata's lively shopping and restaurant strip.

Eating

There's some surprisingly classy food in Kata, though you'll be paying for it. For cheaper eats, head to Th Thai Na and to the cluster of affordable, casual seafood restaurants on Th Kata (Patak West) near the shore.

BOATHOUSE WINE & GRILL Mediterranean $$$
(**0 7633 0015; www.boathousephuket.com; 2/2 Th Kata (Patak West); mains 450-950B; breakfast, lunch & dinner**) The perfect place to wow a fussy date, the Boathouse is the pick of the bunch for most local foodies. The atmosphere can be a little stuffy – this

Papaya salad
JAB265407/DREAMSTIME ©

Hat Kata (p297)

PUWANAI/DREAMSTIME©

is the closest Phuket gets to old-school dining – but the Mediterranean fusion food is fabulous, the wine list expansive and the sea views sublime.

CAPANNINA Italian $$

(☎0 7628 4318; capannina@fastmail.fm; 30/9 Moo 2, Th Kata; mains 200-700B) Everything here – from the pastas to the sauces – are made fresh and you can taste it. The ravioli and gnocchi are memorable, and the risotto comes highly recommended. It has great pizzas, calzones and veal Milanese, too.

OASIS Fusion $$$

(☎0 7633 3423; Th Kotanod; meals 350-600B) Two restaurants in one, the top shelf is an Asian fusion tapas bar blessed with live jazz. The lower level is a candlelit fine-dining patio restaurant where you can sample fresh barracuda fillet with a sun-dried herb crust while you watch the oblong paper lanterns swing in the trees.

THAI KITCHEN Thai $

(Th Thai Na; meals 80B; ⏲breakfast, lunch & dinner) Good rule of thumb: if a humble, roadside cafe is packed with Thai people, you can be certain that the food will rock. The green curry (warning: your nose will run) and glass-noodle dishes are superb. It's just down the road from, ahem, 'Pussy Bar'.

Drinking

Kata's nightlife tends to be pretty mellow.

SKA BAR Bar

(⏲till late) At Kata's southernmost cove, tucked into the rocks and seemingly intertwined with the trunk of a grand old banyan tree, is our choice for oceanside sundowners. The Thai bartenders add to Ska's funky Rasta vibe, and the canopy dangles with buoys, paper lanterns and the flags of 10 countries.

RATRI JAZZTAURANT Bar

(☎0 7633 3538; Kata Hill; ⏲6pm-midnight; dishes 145-345B) Hang out on the hillside terrace, listen to live jazz, watch the sun go down and enjoy delicious Thai food. Now *this* is a vacation.

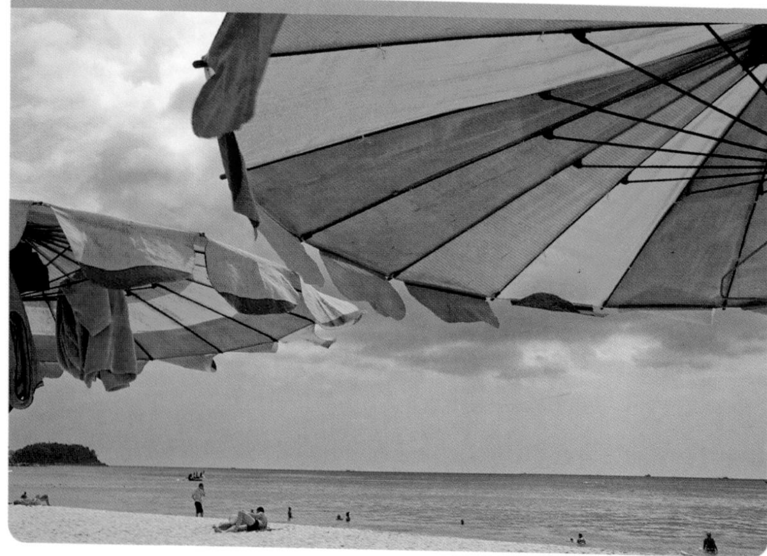

GLENN VAN DER KNIJFF/LONELY PLANET IMAGES ©

Hat Karon

หาดกะรน

Karon is like Patong and Kata's love child: it's chilled-out, a touch glamorous and a tad cheesy with some sleazy corners. There are two megaresorts and package tourists aplenty here, but there's still more sand space per capita than either Patong or Kata. The further north you go the more chic and beautiful the beach gets, culminating at the northernmost edge, accessible from a rutted road that extends past the vendors and food stalls, where the water is like turquoise glass.

Sleeping

IN ON THE BEACH Hotel $$

(☎0 7639 8220; www.karon-inonthebeach.com; 695-697 Moo 1, Th Patak; r from 3500B; ❄@📶🏊) This is a sweet, tasteful inn on Karon Park. The location is sublime, and the rooms – think marble floors, wi-fi, air-con, ceiling fans, horseshoe-shaped pool – and come with sea views. With substantial low-season discounts, this is the perfect surf lair.

Eating & Drinking

There are a few cheap Thai and seafood places off the roundabout (including a number of beachside seafood houses under one louvred roof 100m north of it) and a similar group on the main road near the southern end of Hat Karon.

PAD THAI SHOP Thai $

(Th Patak East; dishes 40B; ⏰breakfast, lunch & dinner) On the busy main road behind Karon, just north of the tacky Ping Pong Bar, is this glorified food stand where you can find rich and savoury chicken stew (worthy of rave reviews in its own right) and the best *pàt tai* on planet earth. Spicy and sweet, packed with prawns, tofu, egg and peanuts, and wrapped in a fresh banana leaf, you will be grateful. It closes at around 7pm.

NAKANNOI Bar

(☎08 7898 5450; Karon Plaza; ⏰5pm-1am) It's a boho arthouse hideaway with original canvasses on the walls, found-art decor (including antique motorcycles and bicycles), a concrete island bar and a permanent bandstand, where the owner jams with his mates after 8pm almost every night.

Hat Patong

Patong is a free for all. Anything, from a Starbucks 'venti latte' to a, ahem, companion for the evening is available for the right price. And while that's true about dozens of other, phonier, destinations, Patong doesn't try to hide what it is.

Of course, that doesn't mean you're going to like it. But when you arrive you'll take one look at the wide, white-sand beach and its magnificent crescent bay, and you'll understand how all this started.

Diving and spa options abound, as well as upscale dining, street-side fish grills, camp cabaret, Thai boxing, dusty antique shops and one of Asia's coolest shopping malls.

Sleeping

BURASARI Hotel **$$$**
(☎0 7629 2929; www.burasari.com; 18/110 Th Ruamchai; r 2700-9300B; ❄📶🏊) It's a lovely maze of swimming pools and waterfalls, etched columns, cushion-strewn lounges and bars. Rooms are more simple but chic with flat screen TVs, queen-sized beds and bamboo accents. The **Naughty Radish** cafe here serves outrageous customisable salads (from 180B) and the best smoothies (120B) on Phuket.

BAIPHO, BAITHONG & SALA DEE Guest House **$$**
(☎0 7629 2074, 0 7629 2738; www.baipho.com, www.baithong.com, www.saladee.com; 205/12-13 & 205/14-15 Th Rat Uthit 200 Pee; r 1800-3300B; ❄📶) These three arty guest houses are all on the same little soi under the same friendly and organised management. The dimly lit, nest-like rooms are all unique so ask to see a few if possible. The **Lounge**, downstairs at Baithong, serves cocktails and very good Italian and Thai food as well as gourmet snacks. Guests can use the pool at the unsightly Montana Grand Phuket next door.

Eating

Patong has stacks of restaurants and the trick is to steer around the watered-down Thai and poorly executed Western food clogging most main drags. The most glamorous restaurants are in a little huddle above the cliffs on the northern edge of town.

Bargain seafood and noodle stalls pop up across town at night – try the lanes on and around Th Bangla, or venture over to

Gay Pride In Phuket

Although there are big gay-pride celebrations in Bangkok and Pattaya, the **Phuket Gay Pride Festival** is considered by many to be the best in Thailand, maybe even southeast Asia. It usually happens between February and April but whenever it blooms, the whole island – but Patong specifically – is packed with (mostly male) revellers from all over the world.

The main events of the four-day weekend party are a huge beach volleyball tournament and, of course, the Grand Parade, featuring floats, cheering crowds and beautiful costumes in the streets of Patong. In recent years, the festival has also included social-responsibility campaigns against child prostitution and substance abuse, and for HIV awareness.

For updates on future festivals or for more information about the scene in general, go to www.gaypatong.com.

the **Patong Food Park** (Th Rat Uthit; 4pm-midnight) once the sun drops.

LIM'S Thai **$$$**
(0 7634 4834; www.lim-thailand.com; 28 Th Phrabaramee, Soi 7; meals 300-600B; 6pm-midnight) Lim's is 500m uphill from the coast road to Kamala. It's a modern, moulded-concrete dining room and lounge serving upscale Thai cuisine. When celebrities land in Phuket, most spend at least one evening here.

MENGRAI SEAFOOD Seafood **$$**
(Soi Tun; meals 120-300B) Located down a sweaty, dark soi off Th Bangla is a wonderful food court serving fresh, local food. The stalls towards the end of the soi serve daily curries that local expats swear by.

CHICKEN RICE BRILEY Hai **$**
(Patong Food Park, Th Rat Uthit; meals 35-45B; breakfast & lunch) The only diner in the Patong Food Park to offer sustenance when the sun shines.

Drinking

Th Bangla is Patong's beer and bar-girl mecca and features a number of spectacular, go-go extravaganzas, where you can expect the usual mix of gyrating Thai girls and often red-faced Western men. That said, the atmosphere is more carnival than carnage and you'll find plenty of Western women pushing their way through the throng to the bar.

TWO BLACK SHEEP Pub
(0895 921 735; www.twoblacksheep.net; 172 Th Rat Uthit; 11am-2am) Owned by a fun Aussie couple (he's a musician, she's a chef), this old-school pub is a great find. It has good grub and live music nightly. From 8pm to 10pm there's an acoustic set, then Chilli Jam, the house band, gets up and rocks till the last call. And it bans bar girls, which keeps everything at a PG level.

LA GRITTA Bar
(0 7634 0106; www.amari.com; 2 Th Meun-ngern; 10.30am-11.30pm) A spectacular, modern restaurant that doesn't fit in with the ageing bones of this once-great property, but who cares? With tiered booths, massive yet muted light boxes and a deck that is just centimetres above the boulder-strewn shore, there is no better place for a sunset cocktail.

MONTE'S Bar
(Th Phisit Karani; 11am-midnight) Now this, my friends, is a tropical pub. There's a thatched roof, a natural-wood bar, dozens of orchids and a flat screen for ball games. The barflies swarm on Fridays for Monte's famous Belgian-style mussels, and on the weekends he fires up the grill.

Entertainment

Cabaret and Thai boxing are something of a speciality here.

PHUKET SIMON CABARET Cabaret
(0 7634 2011; www.phuket-simoncabaret.com; Th Sirirach; admission 700-800B; performances nightly 7.30pm & 9.30pm) About 300m south of town, this cabaret offers entertaining transvestite shows. The 600-seat theatre is grand, the costumes are gorgeous and the ladyboys (*gà·teu·i*) are convincing. The house is often full – book ahead.

SOUND PHUKET Club
(0 7636 6163; www.soundphuket.com; Jung Ceylon complex, Unit 2303, 193 Th Rat Uthit; admission varies; 10pm-4am) When internationally renowned DJs come to Phuket these days, they are usually gigging amid the rounded, futuristic environs of Patong's hottest (and least sleazy) nightclub. If top-shelf DJs are on the decks, expect to pay up to 300B entry fee.

Hat Kamala หาดกมลา

A chilled-out hybrid of Hat Karon and Hat Surin, calm but fun Kamala tends to lure a mixture of longer-term lower-key partying guests, a regular crop of Scandinavian families and young couples. The bay is magnificent, turquoise and serene with shore breakers that lull you to sleep. The entire beach is backed with lush rolling hills, which one can only hope are left alone...forever.

Sights & Activities

Local beach boffins will tell you that **Laem Singh**, just north of Kamala, is one of the best capes on the island. Walled in by cliffs, there is no road access so you have to park your vehicle on the headland and clamber down a narrow path, or you could charter a long-tail (1000B) from Hat Kamala. It gets crowded.

PHUKET FANTASEA Theatre

(**0 7638 5000; www.phuket-fantasea.com; admission with/without dinner 1900/1500B; 6-11.30pm Fri-Wed**) This is a US$60 million 'cultural theme park' located just east of Hat Kamala. Despite the billing, there aren't any rides, but there is a show that takes the colour and pageantry of Thai dance and combines this with state-of-the-art light-and-sound techniques that rival anything found in Las Vegas (think 30 elephants). Kids especially will be captivated by the spectacle, but it is over-the-top cheesy, and cameras are forbidden.

Sleeping & Eating

LAYALINA HOTEL Hotel **$$$**

(**0 7638 5942; www.layalinahotel.com; r incl breakfast 5500-7700B;**) Nab one of the split-level suites with very private rooftop terraces at this small boutique hotel for romantic sunset views over white sand and blue sea. The pool is ridiculously small – but that turquoise ocean *is* only steps away.

ROCKFISH Fusion **$$**

(**0 7627 9732; www.rockfishrestaurant.com; 33/6 Th Kamala Beach; dishes 150-1000B; breakfast, lunch & dinner**) Perched above the river mouth and the bobbing long-tails, with beach, bay and mountain views, is Kamala's best dining room. It rolls out gems such as braised duck breast with kale, and prosciutto-wrapped scallops.

Hat Surin หาดสุรินทร์

With a wide, blonde beach, water that blends from pale turquoise in the shallows to a deep blue on the horizon and two lush, boulder-strewn headlands, Surin could easily attract tourists on looks alone. Ah, but there are stunning galleries,

Hat Surin

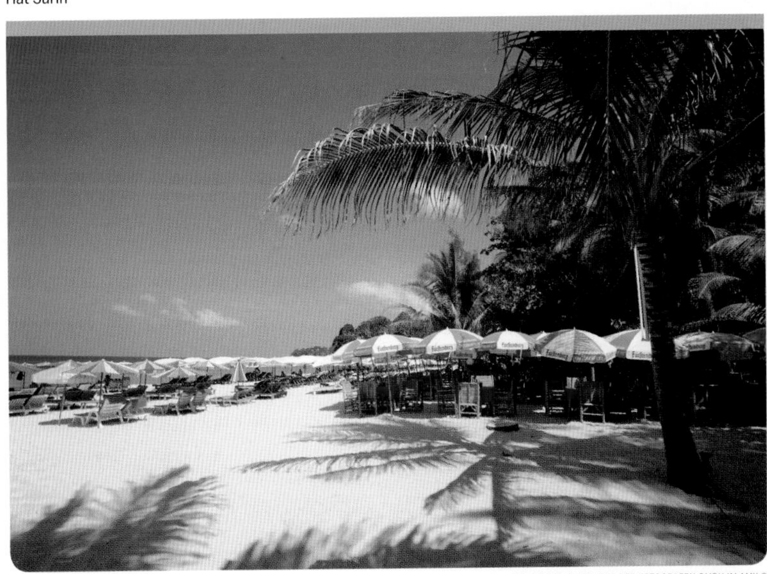

five-star spa resorts and wonderful beach-front dining options, too.

Sleeping

Hat Surin is home to some of Phuket's classiest resorts, but there's little available for people on small budgets.

TWIN PALMS Resort $$$
(0 7631 6500; www.twinpalms-phuket.com; r 6100-38,800B;) This is the Audrey Hepburn of Phuket's hotels – it's classic yet completely contemporary. There's a pervasive feeling of space with minimalist, artsy swimming pools everywhere that are fringed by delicate white frangipani. It's a few minutes' walk to the beach. Expats from all over Phuket can be found eating the island's most popular **brunch** (open noon to 2pm; buffet 1300B) here on Sundays

BENYADA LODGE Hotel $$
(0 7627 1261; www.benyadalodge-phuket.com; r 2800-3500B;) Chic, modern rooms – with black louvred closets, terracotta-tiled bathrooms and silk, pastel-coloured throw pillows scattered in the lounging corner – are a great bargain for this area. Take in the sunset and have a dip in the pool at the rooftop bar or it's only a few minutes' walk to the beach.

Eating

For cheap seafood, your first stop should be the numerous, fun and delicious seafront dining rooms.

TASTE Fusion $$
(08 7886 6401; tapas 160-225B) The best of a new breed of urban-meets-surf eateries along the beach. Dine indoors or alfresco on meal-sized salads, perfectly cooked fillet mignon or a variety of Thai-Mediterranean starters and mains.

Left: Long-tail boats, Ao Bang Thao; **Below:** Elephant, Ao Bang Thao
(LEFT) AUSTIN BUSH/LONELY PLANET IMAGES ©; (BELOW) AUSTIN BUSH/LONELY PLANET IMAGES ©

Ao Bang Thao

Almost as large and even more beautiful than Patong Bay, the stunning, 8km white-sand sweep of Ao Bang Thao has several personalities. The southern half is home to a sprinkling of three-star bungalow resorts. Further inland you'll find an old fishing village laced with canals along with a number of upstart villa subdivisions.

The Hideaway Day Spa here has an excellent reputation. It offers traditional Thai massage, sauna and mud body wraps in a tranquil wooded setting at the edge of a lagoon. Treatments start at 1500B.

Sleeping

ANDAMAN BANGTAO BAY RESORT Hotel $$$
(0 7627 0246; www.andamanbangtaobayresort.com; bungalows 3900-5900B;) Every bungalow has a sea view and there's a summer-camp vibe at this pleasant little resort. The design is very Thai, with woodcarvings on the walls and coconuts hanging from the eaves of the roofs, but for this price we expected a little more luxury.

Eating

Many of Phuket's finest eateries are found just outside Laguna's main gate, and there are even more at the seafood-oriented beach cafes south of the Banyan Tree Phuket.

TATONKA International $$$
(0 7632 4349; Th Srisoonthorn; dishes 250-300B; dinner Thu-Tue) This is the home of 'globetrotter cuisine', which owner-chef Harold Schwarz developed by taking fresh local products and combining them with

Europe, Colorado and Hawaii cooking techniques.

SIAM SUPPER CLUB International **$$$**
(**0 7627 0936; Hat Bang Thao; dishes 180-450B)** One of the hippest spots on Phuket where the 'infamous' come to sip cocktails, listen to jazz and eat an excellent meal. The menu is predominantly Western with gourmet pizzas, seafood cioppino and hearty mains such as veal tenderloin with wild mushrooms on truffle mash.

Sirinat National Park อุทยานแห่งชาติสิรินาถ

Comprising the beaches of Nai Thon, Nai Yang and Mai Khao, as well as the former Nai Yang National Park and Mai Khao wildlife reserve, **Sirinat National Park** (**0 7632 8226; www.dnp.go.th; admission 200B; 8am-5pm)** encompasses 22 sq km of coastal land, plus 68 sq km of sea.

The whole area is a 15-minute or less drive from Phuket International Airport, which makes it particularly convenient for a first stop.

Sleeping & Eating

Hat Nai Thon

If you're after a lovely arc of fine golden sand, away from the buzz of Phuket busy-ness, Hat Nai Thon is it. Swimming is quite good here except at the height of the monsoon, and there is some coral near the headlands at either end of the bay.

NAITHONBURI Hotel **$$$**
(**0 7620 5500; www.naithonburi.com; Moo 4, Th Hat Nai Thon; r 3500-4500B)** A mellow megaresort if ever there was one. Yes, it has 222 rooms, but it rarely feels too crowded. Rooms are spacious with terracotta tile floors, Thai silks on the bed and private balconies. The enormous pool is lined with lounges and daybeds. Its **Chao Lay Bistro** (mains from 180B) is as swank as Nai Thon gets.

Hat Nai Yang & Hat Mai Khao

Hat Nai Yang's bay is sheltered by a reef that slopes 20m below the surface – which makes for good snorkelling in the dry season and fantastic surfing in the monsoon season.

About 5km north of Hat Nai Yang is Hat Mai Khao, Phuket's longest beach. Sea turtles lay their eggs here between November and February. Take care when swimming, as there's a strong year-round undertow.

ANANTARA PHUKET Hotel **$$$**
(**0 7633 6100; www.phuket.anantara.com; 888 Moo 3, Tumbon Mai Khao; villas from 35,000B;** @) Phuket's newest all-villa property opens onto a serene lotus-filled lagoon that extends to the beach. It also offers the **Bua Luang**

Buddha statues, Tham Seua (p316)
PAUL KENNEDY/LONELY PLANET IMAGES ©

Spa and the hotel's **Sea Fire Salt Restaurant** is worth a romantic splurge even if you're not staying here.

SALA RESORT & SPA Hotel **$$$**
(☎0 7633 8888; www.salaphuket.com; 333 Moo 3, Tambon Maikhao; r from 11,550B, villas from 15,750B; ❄@🛜≋) This uberstylish, boutique property is a blend of Sino-Portuguese and art-deco influences with mod flair. It's the kind of place that makes everyone feel like a celebrity. It also offers spa services.

NAI YANG BEACH RESORT Hotel **$$**
(☎0 7632 8300; www.naiyangbeachresort.com; 65/23-24 Th Hat Nai Yang; r from 3600B; ❄@🛜≋👪) This workhorse of a midranger is as clean as it is busy and dominates causarina-lined Hat Nai Yang. The lowest-end rooms are fan cooled, while higher-end ones sport modern Thai style and are quite chic.

KRABI PROVINCE

Krabi Town กระบี่

POP 27,500

Krabi Town is majestically situated among impossibly angular limestone karsts jutting from the mangroves but mid-city you're more likely to be awe-struck by the sheer volume of guest houses and travel agencies packed into this compact, quirky little town. Western restaurants are ubiquitous, as are gift shops that all sell the same ol' trinkets. Krabi Town is a necessary transit link to Railay and Ko Phi-Phi.

Sleeping

Krabi has an exceptional and ever-improving guest house scene but go to nearby Ao Nang if you crave luxury.

PAK-UP HOSTEL Hostel **$**
(Map p308; ☎0 5611 955; www.pakuphostel.com; 87 Th Utarakit; dm 180-200B, d 600B; ❄🛜) This snazzy hostel features several uber-hip 10-bed dorms with big wooden bunks built into the wall, each equipped with personal lockers. Massive, modern shared bathrooms have cold-water stalls as well as a few hot-water rain showers.

CHAN CHA LAY Guest House **$**
(Map p308; ☎0 7562 0952; www.chanchalay.com; 55 Th Utarakit; r 400-700B, r without bathroom 250B; ❄) The rooms here with en suite and decorated in gorgeous Mediterranean blues with polished-concrete semi-outdoor bathrooms, are Krabi's most stylish and comfortable.

Eating & Drinking

NIGHT MARKET Thai **$**
(Map p308; Th Khong Kha; meals 20-50B) The most popular and pleasant place for an evening meal is near the Khong Kha pier. Menus are in English but the food is authentic: try papaya salad, fried noodles, *đôm yam gûng* (prawn and lemon grass soup) and sweet milky Thai desserts.

Getting There & Away

Air

Most domestic carriers offer flights between Bangkok and Krabi International Airport (one way around 4400B, 1¼ hours). Bangkok Air (www.bangkokair.com) has a daily service to Ko Samui for around 3800B.

Boat

Boats to Ko Phi-Phi and Ko Lanta leave from the passenger pier at Khlong Chilat, about 4km southwest of Krabi. Travel agencies will arrange free transfers when you buy a boat ticket from them.

The largest boat operator is PP Family Co (☎0 7561 2463; www.phiphifamily.com; Th Khong Kha), which has a ticket office right beside the pier in town. In high season there are boats to Ko Phi-Phi (300B, 1½ hours) at 9am, 10.30am, 1.30pm and 3pm, while in low season the schedule is reduced to two boats per day.

From November to May, there is only one daily boat to Ko Lanta (350B, two hours) leaving Krabi at 11.30am.

Krabi

Krabi

Sleeping
- 1 Chan Cha Ley C3
- 2 Pak-up Hostel C2

Eating
- 3 Night Market C2

Transport
- 4 PP Family Co D3
- 5 Sŏrng·tăa·ou to Ao Nang & Hat Noppharat Thara B2
- 6 Sŏrng·tăa·ou to Ao Nang & Hat Noppharat Thara A2

If you want to get to Railay, long-tail boats leave from Krabi's Khong Kha pier to Hat Rai Leh East (150B, 45 minutes) from 7.45am to 6pm.

Sŏrng·tăa·ou run between the two piers for 50B or a taxi costs 300B to 400B.

Bus

The **Krabi bus terminal** (**☎0 7561 1804; cnr Th Utarakit & Hwy 4)** is in nearby Talat Kao, about 4km north of Krabi. Air-conditioned government buses leave for Bangkok (720B, 12 hours) at 7am, 4pm and 5.30pm. There's a very plush 24-seat VIP bus to Bangkok (1100B) departing at 5.30pm daily.

From Bangkok's southern bus terminal, buses leave at 7.30am and between 7pm and 8pm. Regular, air-conditioned government buses from Talat Kao also service Phuket (145B, 3½ hours), Surat Thani (140B, 2½ hours) and Trang (90B, two hours).

Sŏrng·tăa·ou

Sŏrng·tăa·ou run from the bus station to central Krabi and on to Hat Noppharat Thara (40B) and Ao Nang (60B). There are services from 6am to 6.30pm.

Ao Nang อ่าวนาง

POP 12,400

Granted, you're not breaking ground, but there's still plenty to like about Ao Nang, a beach town that's unabashedly devoted to tourism.

Sleeping

SOMKIET BURI RESORT Hotel $$
(**☎0 7563 7320; www.somkietburi.com; r 3000-6200B;** ❄📶🏊) This place just might inspire you to slip into a yoga pose. The lush jungle grounds are filled with ferns and orchids, while lagoons, streams and mean-

dering wood walkways guide you to the 26 large and creatively designed rooms.

Eating

SOI SUNSET Seafood $$
(☎0 7569 5260; Soi Sunset; dishes 60-400B; ⏰lunch & dinner) At the western end of the beach is this narrow pedestrian-only alley housing several romantic seafood restaurants with gorgeous views of an island-dotted ocean. One of the best (and most popular) is Krua Ao Nang at the end of the strip.

Drinking & Entertainment

There's no shortage of bars in Ao Nang.

LAST CAFÉ Cafe, Bar
(⏰11am-7pm) At the far southern end of Hat Ao Nang is this barefoot beach cafe, with cold beer and cool breezes.

Getting There & Around

Bus, Car & Minivan

Sŏrng·tăa·ou run to/from Krabi (50B, 20 minutes) starting at the Krabi bus terminal (add 10B to the fare) via Th Maharat, the Khong Kha pier in Krabi and on to Hat Noppharat Thara and Ao Nang. From Ao Nang to Hat Noppharat Thara it's 20B.

Airport buses to and from Ao Nang cost 80B to 100B and leave throughout the day. Private taxis from the airport cost about 800B.

Minibuses go to destinations all over the south including Phuket (350B to 400B, three to four hours) and Ko Lanta (400B, two hours)

Dozens of places along the strip rent out small motorcycles for 150B to 200B. Budget Car Hire charges around 1600B.

Boat

Boats to Railay's Hat Rai Leh West are run by Ao Nang Long-tail Boat Service (☎0 7569 5313; www.aonangboatco-op.com) and rates are 80B per person from 7.30am to 6pm or 150B per person from 6pm to 6am.

Ferries and speedboats leave from the nearby pier at Hat Noppharat Thara to Ko Phi-Phi, Ko Lanta, Phuket and the Ko Yao Islands.

Railay ไร่เล

Krabi's fairytale limestone crags come to a dramatic climax at Railay (also spelled Rai Leh), the ultimate jungle gym for rock- climbing fanatics. This quiet slice of paradise fills in the sandy gaps between each craggy flourish, and although it's just around the bend from chaotic tourist hustle in Ao Nang, the atmosphere here is nothing short of laid-back, Rasta-Thai haven.

Activities

Rock Climbing

With nearly 500 bolted rock-climbing routes, ranging from beginner to challenging advanced climbs, all with unparalleled cliff-top vistas, it's no surprise that Railay is among the top climbing spots in the world. The newest buzz is deep-water soloing, where climbers free-climb ledges over deep water – if you fall you will most likely just get wet, so even daring beginners can give this a try.

The going rate for climbing courses is 800B to 1000B for a half-day and 1500B to 2000B for a full day. Three-day courses (6000B) will involve lead climbing, where you clip into bolts on the rock face as you ascend. Experienced climbers can rent gear sets from any of the climbing schools for 800/1300B for a half-/full day – the standard set consists of a 60m rope, two climbing harnesses and climbing shoes.

HIGHLAND ROCK CLIMBING Rock Climbing
(☎08 0693 0374; chaow_9@yahoo.com; Hat Rai Leh East) If you're bunking on the mountain, this is the man to climb with.

HOT ROCK Rock Climbing
(☎0 7562 1771; www.railayadventure.com; Hat Rai Leh West) Hot Rock has a very good

reputation and is owned by one of the granddaddies of Railay climbing.

Diving & Snorkelling

Several **dive** operations in Railay run trips out to Ko Poda and other dive sites. Full-day, multi-island **snorkelling** trips to Ko Poda, Chicken Island and beyond can also be arranged through any of the resorts for about 1800B (maximum six people) or you can charter a long-tail (half-/full day 1700/2200B) from Hat Railay West.

Flame Tree Restaurant (Hat Rai Leh West) rents out **sea kayaks** for 200B per hour or 800B per day.

Sleeping & Eating

Hat Railay West

RAILAY BAY RESORT & SPA Hotel $$$
(☎0 7562 2570-2; www.railaybayresort.com; bungalows 3700-17,800B; ❄@≋) Elegant bungalows with big windows, white walls and rustic-chic timber terraces run right across the peninsula to Hat Railay East via gorgeously planted grounds. Bungalows on the east side are older, with dark-tinted windows, and are the least expensive.

SAND SEA RESORT Hotel $$
(☎0 7562 2608; www.krabisandsea.com; bungalows 1950-5950B; ❄@≋) The lowest-priced resort on this beach offers everything from ageing fan-only bungalows to newly remodelled cottages with every amenity.

Hat Rai Leh East

SUNRISE TROPICAL RESORT Hotel $$
(☎0 7562 2599; www.sunrisetropical.com; bungalows incl breakfast 2500-5750B; ❄@≋) Bungalows here rival the better ones on Hat Railay West but are priced for Hat Rai Leh East – so we think this is one of the best deals in Railay.

ANYAVEE Hotel $$
(☎0 7581 9437; www.anyavee.com; bungalows 2800-7000B; ❄@≋) A quirky resort but one with more style than most on this beach. Bungalows here have lots of windows, making them bright but not private.

Railay Highlands

RAILAY PHUTAWAN RESORT Hotel $$
(☎08 4060 0550, 0 7581 9478; www.phuritvalleyresort.com; bungalows 1140-1940B, r 1640B; @❄) The best options here are the super-spacious polished cement bungalows highlighted with creamy yellow walls, big rain shower bathrooms and all the trimmings of a high-end resort.

RAILAY CABANA Guest House $
(☎0 7562 1733, 08 4057 7167; bungalows 350-600B) Superbly located high in the hills in a bowl of karst cliffs, this is your hippie tropical mountain hideaway. Simple, clean thatched-bamboo bungalows are surrounded by mango, mangosteen, banana and guava groves. The only sounds are birds chirping and children laughing.

Hat Ton Sai หาดต้นไทร

COUNTRYSIDE RESORT Hotel $
(☎08 5473 9648; www.countryside-resort.com; cabins 850B; ❄@) This is a UK–owned property with attractive solar-powered cabins. There are high ceilings, lace curtains and ceiling fans. Top-row nests have insane karst views, and you'll love Ewok-faced Ollie, the property mascot.

Drinking

There's a bunch of places on the beaches where you can unwind and get nicely inebriated.

CHILLOUT BAR Bar $
(Hat Ton Sai) Right on the beach and with several levels of decks this is where the bigger name Thai and international bands play when they're in town. At other times, it's the ideal place to lounge with a beer.

Getting There & Around

Long-tail boats to Railay run from Khong Kha pier in Krabi and from the seafronts of Ao Nang and Ao Nam Mao. Boats between Krabi and Hat Rai Leh East leave every 1½ hours from 7.45am to 6pm when they have six to 10 passengers (150B, 45 minutes). Chartering the whole boat costs 1500B.

Boats to Hat Rai Leh West or Hat Ton Sai from Ao Nang cost 80B (15 minutes) from 7.30am to 6pm or 150B at other times; boats don't leave until six to eight people show up.

From October to May the *Ao Nang Princess* runs from Hat Noppharat Thara National Park headquarters to Ko Phi-Phi with a stop at Hat Rai Leh West. The fare to Ko Phi-Phi from Railay is 350B.

Ko Phi-Phi Don เกาะพีพีดอน

With its flashy, curvy, blonde beaches and bodacious jungles it's no wonder that Phi-Phi has become the darling of the Andaman Coast. And, like any good starlet, this island can party hard all night and still look like a million bucks the next morning.

Diving

Crystal-clear Andaman water and abundant marine life make the perfect recipe for top-notch scuba. An open-water certification course costs around 12,900B, while the standard two-dive trips cost from 3200B. Trips out to Hin Daeng/Hin Muang will set you back 5500B.

ADVENTURE CLUB Diving
(☎08 1970 0314; www.phi-phi-adventures.com) Our favourite diving operation on the island runs an excellent assortment of educational, ecofocused diving, hiking and snorkelling tours.

BLUE VIEW DIVERS Diving
(☎0 7581 9395; www.blueviewdivers.com) Focuses on community involvement and beach clean-ups (its latest effort cleared up 700 tonnes of rubbish) and is the only shop to offer dives from a long-tail boat.

Snorkelling

A popular snorkelling destination is **Ko Mai Phai** (Bamboo Island), 5km north of Ko Phi-Phi Don. Snorkelling trips cost between 600B and 2400B, depending on whether you travel by long-tail or motorboat.

Rock Climbing

Yes, there are good limestone cliffs to climb on Ko Phi-Phi Don, and the views

Ao Lo Dalam, Ko Phi-Phi Don

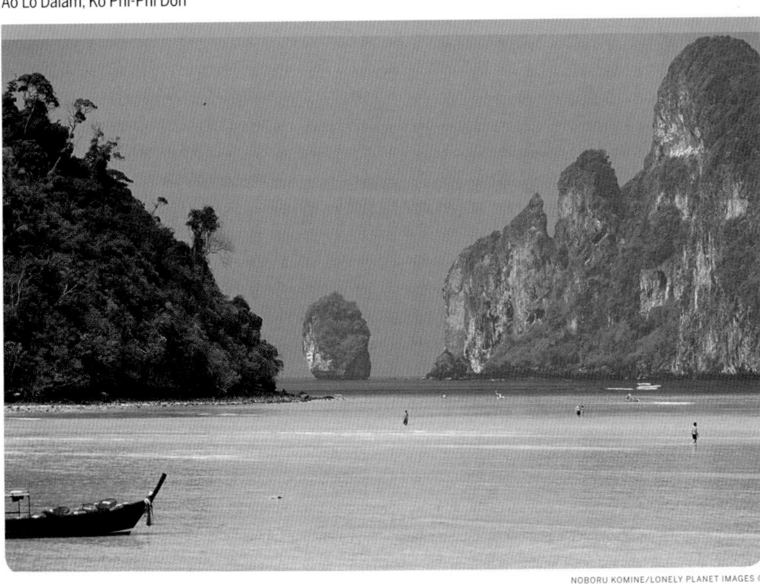

are spectacular. **Spider Monkey** (☎0 7581 9384; www.spidermonkeyclimbing.com) is run by Soley, one of the most impressive climbers on Phi-Phi. One of the bigger outfits around is **Cat's Climbing Shop** (☎08 1787 5101; www.catclimbingshop.com) in the tourist village.

Sleeping

Finding accommodation on this ever-popular island has never been easy and you can expect serious room shortages at peak holiday times. Masses of touts meet incoming boats and, while often annoying, can make your life easier.

Be sure you lock the door while you sleep and close all the windows when you go out. Break-ins can be a problem.

Ton Sai Village

The flat, hourglass-shaped land between Ao Ton Sai and Ao Lo Dalam is crowded with loads of lodging options.

MAMA BEACH RESIDENCE Hotel **$$**

(☎08 8443 1363, 0 7560 1365; www.mama-beach.com; r 2500-3800B;) Popular with French travellers, this is an uncommonly chic block-style hotel right on the best part of Ao Ton Sai beach. Mod-con–equipped rooms have large white tiled floors, sea-view terraces with relaxing wood deck furniture, and bathrooms with stone sinks and showers bordered with loose seashells. Seaside yoga classes (1¼ hours, 400B) are offered several nights a week at 6pm.

WHITE Guest House **$$**

(☎0 7560 1300; www.whitephiphi.com; r 1500-1800B;) Geared towards the 'flashpacker' crowd, the White has two comfy and surprisingly quiet locations in Tonsai Village – the better being the White 2 that has a few rooftop suites with patios. Squeaky clean rooms, decked out with TVs and safes, are very white (of course) with hip touches such as black-and-white tiled hot-water bathrooms.

Hat Hin Khom

This area has a few small white-sand beaches in rocky coves that are relatively quiet. It's about a 15-minute jungle walk from both Hat Yao and the Ao Ton Sai bustle.

VIKING NATURES RESORT Hotel **$$**

(☎08 3649 9492; www.vikingnaturesresort.com; bungalows 1000-6500B;) OK, it's funky (in all senses of the word), but the wood, thatch and bamboo bungalows here are dreamily creative and stylish with lots of driftwood, shell mobiles and hammock-decked lounging spaces with outrageous views of Ko Phi-Phi Leh. All bungalows have mosquito nets

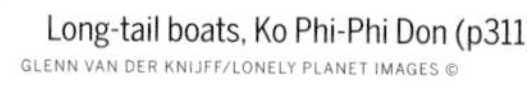

Long-tail boats, Ko Phi-Phi Don (p311)

and balconies, but the cheaper rooms don't have their own bathrooms.

Hat Ya

You can either walk here in about 30 minutes from Ton Sai via Hat Him Khom or take a long-tail (100B to 150B) from Ton Sai pier. This long stretch of pure-white beach is perfect for swimming and well worth the walk, but don't expect to have it to yourself – it's popular with families and sporty types playing volleyball.

PHI-PHI HILL RESORT Guest House **$$**
(**☎0 7561 8203; www.phiphihill.com; bungalows 700-2000B;** ❄ @) High up in a very quiet plantation, this simple resort spans the island's southern bluff so you can watch the sun rise on one side and set on the other. The best deals are the big, clean wooden fan-cooled, cold-water bungalows on the sunset side. It closes from May to October.

Hat Phak Nam

This a gorgeous white-sand beach is nestled on the same bay as a small fishing hamlet. To get here, either charter a long-tail from Ao Ton Sai for around 500B (150B by shared taxi boat upon your return), or make the very sweaty one-hour hike over the viewpoint.

RELAX BEACH RESORT Hotel **$$**
(**☎08 1083 0194, 08 9475 6536; www.phiphirelaxresort.com; bungalows 1400-4400B;** ❄ @ ≈) There are 47 unpretentious but pretty Thai-style bungalows with wood floors, two-tiered terraces with lounging cushions and mosaic bathrooms in the newest nests. All are rimmed by lush jungle – there's a good restaurant and breezy bar, and it's worked by incredibly charming staff who greet and treat you like family.

Ao Lo Bakao

The fine stretch of palm-backed sand ringed by dramatic hills, is one of Phi-Phi's most lovely, with offshore views over aqua bliss to Bamboo and Mosquito Islands. Phi-Phi Island Village arranges transfers for guests but on your own a charter from Ao Ton Sai will cost 800B.

PHI-PHI ISLAND VILLAGE Hotel **$$$**
(**☎0 7636 3700; www.ppisland.com; bungalows 7200-21,500B;** ❄ 📶 ≈) This place really is a village unto itself: its whopping 100 bungalows take up much of the beachfront with palms swaying between them. Facilities vary from the family friendly and casual to romantic dining experiences and pampering spa treatments.

Eating

Most of the resorts, hotels and bungalows around the island have their own restaurants. Ao Ton Sai is home to some reasonably priced restaurants but don't expect haute cuisine.

LOCAL FOOD MARKET Thai **$**
(**Ao Ton Sai; ⊙breakfast, lunch & dinner**) The cheapest and most authentic eats are at the market. A handful of local stalls huddle on the narrowest sliver of the isthmus and serve up scrumptious *pàt tai,* fried rice, *sôm·đam* (spicy green papaya salad) and smoked cat fish.

PAPAYA Thai **$**
(**☎08 7280 1719; Ton Sai Village; dishes 80-300B**) The food here is cheap, tasty and spicy. You'll get some real-deal Thai food served in heaping portions. It has basil and chilli, all the curries and *đôm yam,* too.

Drinking & Entertainment

A rowdy nightlife saturates Phi-Phi.

SUNFLOWER BAR Bar
(**Ao Lo Dalam**) Poetically ramshackle, this driftwood gem is still the chillest bar in Phi-Phi. Destroyed in the 2004 tsunami, the owner rebuilt it with reclaimed wood. The long-tail booths are named for the four loved ones he lost in the flood.

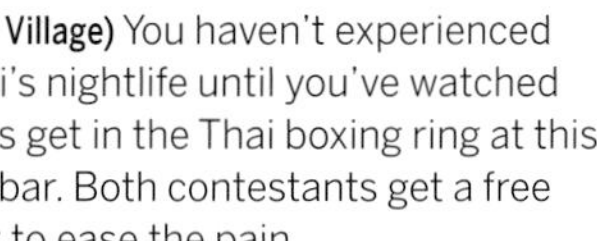

REGGAE BAR Bar

(Tourist Village) You haven't experienced Phi-Phi's nightlife until you've watched tourists get in the Thai boxing ring at this rowdy bar. Both contestants get a free bucket to ease the pain.

SLINKY BAR Club

(Ao Lo Dalam) This was the beach dance floor of the moment when we visited. Expect the standard fire show, buckets of candy juice and throngs of folks mingling, flirting and flailing to throbbing bass on the sand.

Getting There & Away

Boats depart from Krabi for Ko Phi-Phi (300B, 1½ hours) at 9am and 3.30pm, and from Ao Nang (350B, 1½ hours), there's one boat at 3.30pm each day. From Phuket, boats leave at 9am, 2.30pm and 3pm and return from Ko Phi-Phi at 9am, 1.30pm and 3pm (400B, 1¾ to two hours). Boats to Ko Lanta, leave Phi-Phi at 11.30am and 2pm and return from Ko Lanta at 8am and 1pm (300B, 1½ hours). For Railay (350B, 1¼ hours), take the Ao Nang–bound ferry.

Getting Around

There are no roads on Ko Phi-Phi Don so transport on the island is mostly by foot, although long-tail boats can be chartered at Ao Ton Sai for short hops around Ko Phi-Phi Don and Ko Phi-Phi Leh.

Ko Lanta เกาะลันตา

POP 20,000

Long and thin, and covered in bleach-blond tresses, Ko Lanta is Krabi's sexy beach babe. The largest of the 50-plus islands in the local archipelago, this relaxing paradise effortlessly caters to all budget types with its west-coast parade of peach sand – each beach better than the next. The northern beaches are busy but fun and things get more and more mellow as you head southbound.

Ko Lanta is relatively flat compared to the karst formations of its neighbours, so the island can be easily explored by motorbike.

Sights

KO LANTA MARINE NATIONAL PARK National Park

(อุทยานแห่งชาติเกาะลันตา; adult/child 400/200B) Established in 1990, this marine national park protects 15 islands in the Ko Lanta group, including the southern tip of Ko Lanta Yai. The **national park headquarters** is at Laem Tanod, on the southern tip of Ko Lanta Yai, reached by a steep and corrugated 7km dirt track from Hat Nui. There are some basic hiking trails and a **scenic lighthouse**, and you can hire long-tails here for island tours during the low season.

Activities

Diving & Snorkelling

Some of Thailand's top spots are within arm's reach of Ko Lanta. The best diving can be found at the undersea pinnacles called **Hin Muang** and **Hin Daeng**, about 45 minutes away. Hin Daeng is considered by many to be Thailand's second-best dive site after Richelieu Rock, near the Burmese border (p285).

Trips out to Hin Daeng/Hin Muang cost around 5000B to 6000B, while trips to Ko Haa tend to be around 3500B to 4500B.

Numerous tour agencies in the main tourist areas can organise snorkelling trips out to Ko Rok Nok, Ko Phi-Phi and other nearby islands.

SCUBAFISH Diving

(☎0 7566 5095; www.scuba-fish.com) One of the best dive operations on the island is located at Baan Laanta Resort on Ao Kantiang; there's also a small second office at the Narima resort.

Sleeping

Some resorts close down for the May-to-October low season, others drop their rates by 50% or more.

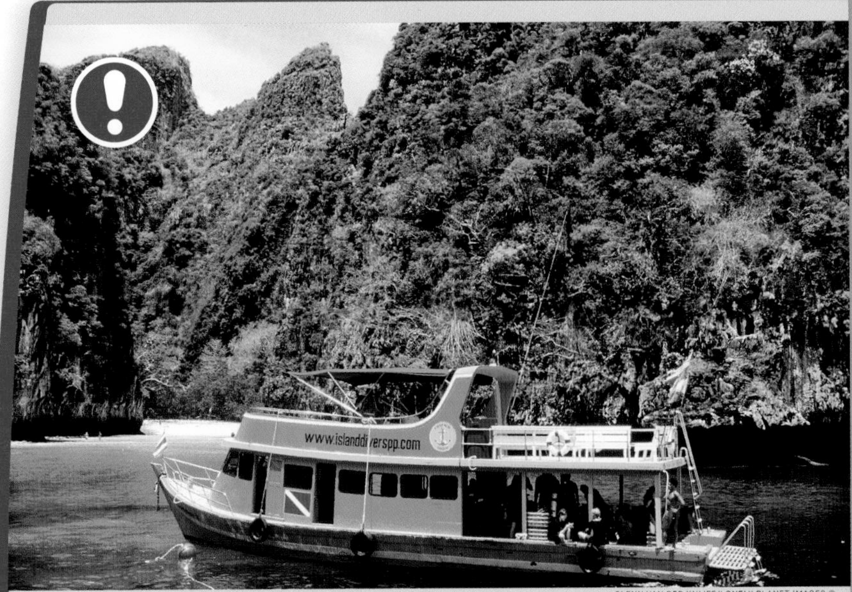

GLENN VAN DER KNIJFF/LONELY PLANET IMAGES ©

Don't Miss Ko Phi-Phi Leh

Rugged Ko Phi-Phi Leh (เกาะพีพีเล) is the smaller of the two Phi-Phi islands and is protected on all sides by soaring cliffs. Coral reefs crawling with marine life lie beneath the crystal-clear waters and are hugely popular with day-tripping snorkellers. Two gorgeous lagoons await in the island's interior – **Pilah** on the east coast and **Ao Maya** on the west coast. In 1999 Ao Maya was controversially used as the setting for the filming of *The Beach,* based on the popular novel by Alex Garland.

At the northeastern tip of the island, **Viking Cave** (Tham Phaya Naak) is a big collection point for swifts' nests. Nimble collectors scamper up bamboo scaffolding to gather the nests. Before ascending, they pray and make offerings of tobacco, incense and liquor to the cavern spirits. This cave gets its misleading moniker from 400-year-old graffiti left by Chinese fishermen.

There are no hotels on Phi-Phi Leh and most people come here on one of the ludicrously popular day trips out of Phi-Phi Don. Tours last about half a day and include snorkelling stops at various points around the island, with detours to Viking Cave and Ao Maya. Long-tail trips cost 800B; by motorboat you'll pay around 2400B. Expect to pay a 400B national-park day-use fee upon landing.

It is possible to camp on Phi-Phi Leh through **Maya Bay Camping** (☎08 6944 1623; www.mayabaycamping.com; per person 2100B). It offers action-packed overnight trips that include kayaking, snorkelling, lunch, dinner, and sleeping bags under the stars.

Hat Khlong Dao

This is an outstanding 2km stretch of white sand with no rocks, which makes it perfect for swimming. Unfortunately garbage does accumulate when the tides shift.

COSTA LANTA Hotel **$$$**
(☎0 7566 8168; www.costalanta.com; r from 6200B; ❄@令≋) Here are incredibly Zen abodes nestled in a coconut-palm garden laced with tidal canals at the north end of Hat Khlong Dao. Everything from the

Detour: Tham Khao Maikaeo

Monsoon rains pounding away at limestone cracks and crevices for millions of years have created this complex of forest caverns and tunnels. There are chambers as large as cathedrals, dripping with stalactites and stalagmites, and tiny passages that you have to squeeze through on hands and knees. There's even a subterranean pool you can take a chilly swim in. Sensible shoes are essential and getting totally covered in mud is almost guaranteed.

Tham Khao Maikaeo (ถ้ำเขาไม้แก้ว) is reached via a guided trek through the jungle. A local family runs treks to the caves (with torches) for around 200B. The best way to get here is by rented motorcycle, or most resorts can arrange transport.

Close by, but reached by a separate track from the dirt road leading to the marine national park headquarters, **Tham Seua** (Tiger Cave) also has interesting tunnels to explore; elephant treks run up here from Hat Nui.

floors to the walls and the washbasins are polished concrete and the barn doors of each cabana open on two sides to maximise air flow.

Hat Khlong Khong

This is thatched-roof, Rasta-bar bliss with plenty of beach volleyball games, moon parties and the occasional well-advertised mushroom shake (imbibe at own risk). Still, it's all pretty low-key and all ages are present. The beach goes on forever in either direction.

BEE BEE BUNGALOWS Guest House $

(08 1537 9932; www.beebeebungalows.com; bungalows 400-800B;) One of the best budget spots on the island, Bee Bee's super-friendly staff care for a dozen creative bamboo cabins – every one is unique and a few are up on stilts in the trees. The on-site restaurant has a library of tattered paperbacks to keep you busy while you wait for your delicious Thai staples.

Ao Kantiang

A superb sweep of sand backed by mountains is also its own self-contained little village complete with minimarts, internet cafes, motorbike rental and restaurants.

PHRA NANG LANTA Hotel $$$

(0 7566 5025; lanta@vacation village.co.th; studios 6000B;) The gorgeous Mexican-style adobe concrete studios are huge and straight off the pages of an architectural mag. Interiors are decorated with clean lines, hardwoods and whites accented with bright colours.

KANTIANG BAY VIEW RESORT Hotel $$

(0 7566 5049; www.kantiangbay.net; bungalows 500-2000B;) Choose between the cheap, rickety, not-exactly-spotless wood-and-bamboo bungalows or the more expensive, candy-coloured tiled rooms with minifridge. The bamboo-clad restaurant serves decent, *fa ràng* (Westerner)–friendly Thai dishes.

Ao Khlong Jaak

The splendid beach here is named after the inland waterfall.

ANDALANTA RESORT Hotel $$$

(0 7566 5018; www.andalanta.com; bungalows 2600-6900B;) You'll find beach-style, modern air-conditioned bungalows (some with a loft) and simple fan-cooled ones; all face the sea. The garden i s a delight, and there's an ambient restaurant and the waterfall is just a 30- to 40-minute walk away.

Ao Mai Pai

LA LAANTA Hotel **$$$**

(☎0 7566 5066; www.lalaanta.com; bungalows 2800-6200B;) This is barefoot elegance at it's finest. Owned and operated by a young, hip, English-speaking Thai-Vietnamese couple, this is the grooviest spot on the entire island.

Eating

Don't miss the seafood restaurants along the northern edge of Ban Sala Dan. With tables on verandahs over the water, they offer fresh seafood sold by weight (which includes cooking costs).

BEAUTIFUL RESTAURANT Seafood **$$**

(☎0 7569 7062; Ban Ko Lanta; mains 100-200B) This is the best of the old town's seafood houses. Tables are scattered on four piers that extend into the sea. The fish is fresh and exquisitely prepared.

LANTA SEAFOOD Seafood **$$**

(☎0 7566 8411; Ban Sala Dan) The best option of the seafood-by-weight options. Order the *Ƅlah tôrt kà mîn* – its white snapper rubbed with fresh, hand-ground turmeric and garlic, then deep fried.

Getting There & Away

Boat

There is one passenger ferry connecting Krabi's Khlong Chilat pier with Ko Lanta, which departs from Ko Lanta at 8am (400B, two hours) and returns from Krabi at 11am.

Boats between Ko Lanta and Ko Phi-Phi run year-round, although service can peter out in the low season if there are too few passengers. Ferries usually leave Ko Lanta at 8am and 1pm (300B, 1½ hours); in the opposite direction boats leave Ko Phi-Phi at 11.30am and 2pm.

Minivan

Daily minivans to Krabi airport (280B, 1½ hours) and Krabi Town (250B, 1½ hours) leave hourly between 7am and 3.30pm. From Krabi, minivans depart hourly from 8am till 4pm. Minivans to Phuket (350B, four hours) leave Ko Lanta every two hours or so, but are more frequent in the high season.

Getting Around

Most resorts send vehicles to meet the ferries – which means a free ride *to* your resort. Motorcycles (250B per day) can be rented all over the island. Unfortunately, very few places provide helmets and none provide insurance, so take extra care on the bumpy roads.

Thailand In Focus

Shadow puppet performance

Thailand Today

> *Thais continue to experience stable and improving standards of living. Modernisation marches on.*

belief systems
(% of population)

95 Buddhist

5 Muslim

1 Christian

if Thailand were 100 people

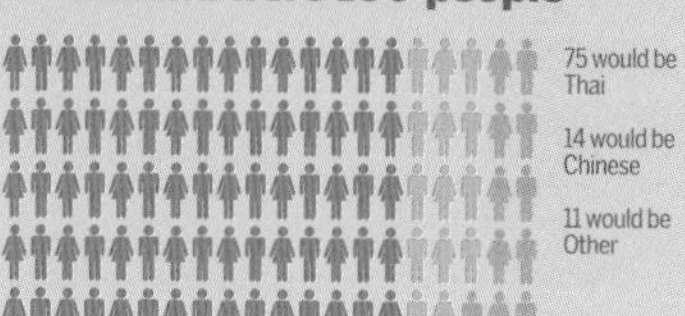

75 would be Thai

14 would be Chinese

11 would be Other

population per sq km

Thailand

USA

UK

≈ 32 people

Pedestrian overpass, Bangkok (p51)

Political Stability?

After a five-year period of political instability initiated by the 2006 coup d'état, Thailand reached a political plateau with the 2011 general election. Ousted prime minister Thaksin Shinawatra's politically allied party, Puea Thai, won a clear majority of parliamentary seats, and his sister Yingluck Shinawatra, a political novice, was elected prime minister. She is Thailand's first female prime minister and this was the fifth straight electoral win for a Thaksin-backed political party. There was no resistance from opposition groups or the military.

In Prime Minister Yingluck's first days in office she set about fulfilling campaign promises, such as raising the national minimum wage to 300B per hour (a 30% increase), extending symbolic olive branches to the monarchy and the military, and pledging to work towards national reconciliation. Her appointments for the important cabinet-level positions of security and defence sidestepped hardliners in favour of two candidates who were

TONY BURNS/LONELY PLANET IMAGES ©

believed to straddle the political/military divide.

During the height of the crisis, the Western press was intrigued by the apparent class divide that defined the two political sides: the proletariat (pro-Thaksin) Red Shirts and the aristocratic (anti-Thaksin) Yellow Shirts. In the middle of the extremes were the uncolour coded Thais who had sympathies with both sides. They might have agreed with the Red Shirts on the grounds of restoring democracy and are disapproving of the military's and the court's meddling in politics, but they were sceptical of the Red Shirts' unquestioning loyalty to Thaksin.

The Ageing King

Thais don't often discuss the topic openly, but many are worried about their beloved monarch, Bhumibol Adulyadej. Now in his mid-80s, he is the world's longest-serving king and is respected, and virtually worshipped, by his subjects. But as the king's health has declined, his role in society has diminished. He has been hospitalised for nearly two years and his public appearances are rare.

In King Bhumibol's more active years, he was viewed as a stabilising force in times of political crisis. But he has not exercised that role during the most recent political troubles, which are partly due to the impending power vacuum that will result after his passing and the power-consolidating efforts of then–prime minister Thaksin. Beginning in 2006, the anti-Thaksin faction adopted the colour yellow, which is the colour associated with the king's birthday, to signal their allegiance with the political interests of the monarchy.

The heir apparent, his son the Crown Prince Vajiralongkorn, has assumed many of the royal duties his father previously performed.

Teflon Economy

From an economic perspective, you'd never know that Thailand is so politically divided. The former Asian tiger economy has moved into the new millennium as a Teflon economy: misfortune doesn't seem to stick. Outside forces – the global recession, a weakening US dollar – have had some negative effects on the economy. From 2008 to 2009, manufacturing and exports, which constitute about half of GDP, took a dip but rebounded a year later with a growth rate that rivalled the boom times of the mid-1990s. With or without democracy, investors remain confident in the country, and tourism continues to grow despite the bloody Bangkok clashes in 2010. High growth is expected for 2011, meaning that unemployment remains relatively low and that Thais continue to experience stable and improving standards of living. Modernisation marches on.

History

Birthday celebrations for King Bhumibol Adulyadej, Bangkok

TOM COCKREM/LONELY PLANET IMA

Thai history has all the dramatic elements to inspire the imagination: palace intrigue, wars waged with spears and elephants, popular protest movements and a penchant for 'smooth-as-silk' coups.

From the Beginning

Though there is evidence of prehistoric peoples, most scholars start the story of Thai nationhood at the arrival of the 'Tai' people during the first millennium AD. The Tai people migrated from southern China and spoke Tai-Kadai, a family of tonal languages said to be the most significant ethno-linguistic group in southeast Asia. The language group branched off into Laos (the Lao people) and Myanmar (the Shan). Most of these

4000–2500 BC

Prehistoric inhabitants of northeastern Thailand develop agriculture and tool-making.

new arrivals were farmers and hunters who lived in loosely organised villages, usually near a river source, with no central government or organised military.

The indigenous Mon people are often recognised as assembling an early confederation (often referred to as Mon Dvaravati) in central and northeastern Thailand from the 6th to 9th centuries. Little is known about this period, but scholars believe that the Mon Dvaravati had a centre in Nakhon Pathom, outside of Bangkok, with outposts in parts of northern Thailand.

The ancient superpower of the region was the Khmer empire, based in Angkor (in present-day Cambodia), which expanded across the western frontier into present-day northeastern and central Thailand starting in the 11th century. Sukhothai and Phimai were regional administrative centres connected by roads with way-station temples that made travel easier and were a visible symbol of imperial power. The Khmer monuments started out as Hindu but were later converted into Buddhist temples after the regime converted. Though their power would eventually decline, the Khmer imparted to the evolving Thai nation an artistic, bureaucratic and even monarchical legacy.

Thai history is usually told from the perspective of the central region, where the current capital is. But the southern region has a separate historical narrative that didn't merge with the centre until the modern era. Between the 8th and 13th centuries, southern Thailand was controlled by the maritime empire of Srivijaya, based in southern Sumatra (Indonesia), and controlled trade between the Straits of Malacca.

The Rise of Thai Kingdoms

While the regional empires were declining in the 12th to 16th centuries, Tai peoples in the hinterlands established new states that would eventually unite the country.

Lanna Kingdom

In the northern region, the Lanna kingdom, founded by King Mengrai, built Chiang Mai (meaning 'new city') in 1292 and proceeded to unify the northern communities into one cultural identity. For a time Chiang Mai was something of a religious centre for the region. However, Lanna was plagued by dynastic intrigues, fell to the Burmese in 1556 and was later eclipsed by Sukhothai and Ayuthaya as the progenitor of the modern Thai state.

Sukhothai Kingdom

Then just a frontier town on the westernmost edge of the ailing Khmer empire, Sukhothai expelled the distant power in the mid-13th century and crowned the local chief as the first king. But it was his son Ramkhamhaeng who led the city-state

6th–11th centuries
The Mon Dvaravati thrive in central Thailand.

10th century
Tai peoples arrive in Thailand.

1283
Early Thai script is invented by King Ramkhamhaeng of Sukhothai.

to become a regional power with dependencies in modern-day Laos and southern Thailand. The city-state's local dialect (known as Siamese Tai) became the language of the ruling elite and the king is credited for inventing an early version of the script used today. Sukhothai replaced Chiang Mai as a centre of Theravada Buddhism on mainland Southeast Asia. The monuments that were built and created many surviving monuments that helped define a distinctive architectural style. After his death, however, Ramkhamhaeng's empire disintegrated. In 1378 Sukhothai became a tributary of Ayuthaya.

The Best... Historical Sights

1 Sukhothai (p205)

2 Ayuthaya (p102)

3 Phimai (p125)

4 Phanom Rung (p128)

Ayuthaya Kingdom

Close to the Gulf of Thailand, the city-state of Ayuthaya grew rich and powerful from the international sea trade. The legendary founder was King U Thong, one of 36 kings and five dynasties that steered Ayuthaya through a 416-year lifespan.

Ayuthaya presided over an age of commerce in southeast Asia. Its main exports were rice and forest products, and many commercial and diplomatic foreign missions set up headquarters outside the royal city.

Ayuthaya adopted Khmer court customs, honorific language and ideas of kingship. The monarch styled himself as a Khmer *devaraja* (divine king) instead of the Sukhothai ideal of *dhammaraja* (righteous king). Ayuthaya paid tribute to the Chinese emperor, who rewarded this ritualistic submission with generous gifts and commercial privileges.

Ayuthaya's reign was constantly under threat from the expansionist Burmese. The city was occupied in 1569 but later liberated by King Naresuan. In 1767 Burmese troops successfully sacked the capital and dispersed the Thai leadership into the hinterlands. The destruction of Ayuthaya remains a vivid historical event in the nation, and the tales of court life are as evocative as the stories of King Arthur.

The Bangkok Era

The Revival

With Ayuthaya in ruins and the dynasty destroyed, a general named Taksin filled the power vacuum and established a new capital in 1768 in Thonburi, across the river from modern-day Bangkok. King Taksin was deposed and executed in 1782 by subordinate generals. One of the leaders of the coup, Chao Phraya Chakri, was crowned King Yot Fa (Rama I), the founder of the current Chakri dynasty. He moved the capital across the river to the Ko Ratanakosin district of present-day Bangkok.

1351
The legendary kingdom of Ayuthaya is founded.

1767
Ayuthaya falls at the hands of the Burmese.

1768–82
King Taksin rules from the new capital of Thonburi.

The new kingdom was viewed as a revival of Ayuthaya and its leaders attempted to replicate the former kingdom's laws, government practices and cultural achievements. They also built a powerful military that avenged Burmese aggression, kicking them out of Chiang Mai and charging into Laos and Cambodia. The Bangkok rulers continued courting Chinese commercial trade and cultural exchange.

The Best... Landmarks of the Bangkok Era

1 Wat Arun (p65)

2 Wat Phra Kaew & Grand Palace (p74)

3 Dusit Palace Park (p71)

The Reform Era

The Siamese elite had long admired China, but by the 1800s the West dominated international trade and geopolitics.

King Mongkut (Rama IV), often credited for modernising the kingdom, spent 27 years prior to assuming the crown as a monk in the Thammayut sect, a reform movement he founded to restore scholarship to the faith. During his reign the country was integrated into the prevailing market system that broke up royal monopolies and granted more rights to foreign powers.

Mongkut's son, King Chulalongkorn (Rama V) took greater steps in replacing the old political order. He abolished slavery and introduced the creation of a salaried bureaucracy, a police force and a standing army. His reforms brought uniformity to the legal code, law courts and revenue offices. Schools were established along European models. Universal conscription and poll taxes made all men the king's men. Many of the king's advisors were British, who ushered in a remodelling of the old Ayuthaya-based system.

Distant subregions were brought under central command and railways were built to link them to population centres. Pressured by French and British colonies on all sides, the modern boundaries of Siam came into shape, partly from ceding territory.

Successive kings continued to adopt European procedures and models to better survive in the new world order.

Democracy vs Dictator

The 1932 Revolution

During a period of growing independence movements in the region, a group of foreign-educated military officers and bureaucrats led a successful (and bloodless) coup against absolute monarchy in 1932. But democracy did not (and still doesn't) have a smooth road ahead.

The pro-democracy party soon splintered and, by 1938, General Phibul Songkhram, one of the original democracy supporters, seized control of the country as Japanese

1782

King Taksin dies; Chakri dynasty is founded; and Bangkok becomes the new capital.

1868–1910

King Chulalongkorn (Rama V) reigns; it's a time of modernisation and European imperialism. Left: Rama V's Bang Pa In Palace (p110)

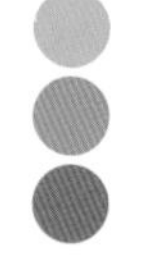

aggression during WWII changed the regional political landscape. Phibul (pronounced 'pee-boon') was staunchly anti-royalist, strongly nationalistic and pro-Japanese, allowing that country to occupy Thailand as a base for assaults on British colonies in southeast Asia. In the post-WWII era, Phibul positioned Thailand as an ally of the US with staunch anti-communist policies.

Name Changes

The country known today as Thailand has had several monikers:

- The Khmers are credited for naming this area 'Siam'.
- In 1939 the name of the country was changed from Siam (Prathet Syam) to Thailand (Prathet Thai).

The Cold War

During the Cold War and the US conflict in Vietnam, the military leaders of Thailand gained legitimacy and economic support from the US in exchange for the use of military installations in Thailand.

By the 1970s a new era of political consciousness bubbled up from the universities, marking a period of cultural turmoil. In 1973 more than half a million people – intellectuals, students, peasants and workers – demonstrated in Bangkok and in major provincial towns, demanding a constitution from the military government. The bloody dispersal of the Bangkok demonstration on 14 October led to the collapse of the regime and the creation of an elected constitutional government. This lasted only three years until another protest movement was brutally squashed and the military returned in the name of civil order.

By the 1980s the so-called political soldier General Prem Tinsulanonda forged a period of political and economic stability that led to the 1988 election of a civilian government. Prem is still involved in politics today as the president of the palace's privy council, a powerful position that joins the interests of the monarchy with the military.

The Business Era

The new civilian government was composed of former business executives, many of whom represented provincial commercial interests instead of Bangkok-based military officials, signalling a shift in the country's political dynamics. Though the country was doing well economically, the government was accused of corruption and vote-buying and the military moved to protect its privileged position with a 1991 coup.

Elected leadership was restored shortly after the coup and the Democrat Party, with the support of business and the urban middle class, dominated the parliament. The 1997 Asian currency crisis derailed the surging economy and the government was criticised for its ineffective response. That same year, the parliament passed the watershed 'people's constitution' that enshrined human rights, freedom of

1932
A bloodless revolution ends absolute monarchy.

1939
The country's English name is officially changed from Siam to Thailand.

1941
Japanese forces enter Thailand.

expression and granted more power to a civil society to counter corruption. (The 1997 constitution was thrown out during the 2006 coup.)

By the turn of the millennium, the economy had recovered and business interests had succeeded the military as the dominant force in politics. The telecommunications billionaire and former police officer Thaksin Shinawatra ushered in the era of the elected CEO. He was a capitalist with a populist message and garnered support from the rural and urban poor, and the working class. From 2001 to 2005 Thaksin and his Thai Rak Thai party transformed national politics into one-party rule.

The Ongoing Crisis

Though Thaksin enjoyed massive popular support, his regime was viewed by urban intellectuals as a kleptocracy, with the most egregious example of corruption being the tax-free sale of his family's Shin Corporation stock to the Singaporean government in 2006, a windfall of 73 billion baht (US$1.88 billion) that was engineered by special legislation. This enraged the upper and middle classes and led to street protests in Bangkok. Meanwhile behind the scenes, Thaksin had been working to replace key military figures with his loyalists, strategic moves that would realign the military's

Monsoon rains, Bangkok

1946
King Bhumibol Adulyadej (Rama IX) accedes; Thailand joins the UN.

1957
A successful coup by Sarit Thanarat starts a period of military rule that lasts until 1973.

1968
Thailand is a founding member state of the Association of southeast Asian Nations.

More than Fashion

Through the contentious political battles resulting from the 2006 coup, the warring factions have adopted coloured T-shirts to identify themselves. Thaksin opponents wear yellow, the colour traditionally associated with the monarchy. Thaksin supporters wear red, which has been dubbed the colour of democracy. Those who support the monarchy but not a political side have recently adopted pink as the new yellow.

long-standing allegiance to the Bangkok aristocracy.

On 19 September 2006 the military staged a bloodless coup, the first in 15 years, which brought an end to the country's longest stretch of democratic rule. The military dissolved the constitution that had sought to ensure a civil government and introduced a new constitution that limited the resurgence of one-party rule by interests unsympathetic to the military and the elites.

Since the coup, political stability has yet to be achieved. Reinstatement of elections restored Thaksin's political friends to power, a victory that was unacceptable to Bangkok's aristocracy who, with the implicit support of the military, staged huge protests that closed down Bangkok's two airports for a week in 2008.

See Thailand Today (p320) for the next instalment of Thailand's ongoing political drama.

The Modern Monarchy

The country's last absolute monarch was King Prajadhipok (Rama VII) who accepted the 1932 constitution, abdicated the throne and went into exile. By 1935 the new democratic government had reinstated the monarchy, appointing the abdicating king's 10-year-old nephew, Ananda Mahidol (Rama VIII), who was living in Europe at the time. In 1946, after the king came of age, he was shot dead under mysterious circumstances. His younger brother was crowned King Bhumibol (Rama IX) and remains monarch today.

At the beginning of his reign King Bhumibol was primarily a figurehead promoted by various factions to appeal to the public's imagination of national unity. The military dictator, General Sarit, who controlled the government from 1958 to 1963, supported the expansion of the king's role as a symbol of modern Thailand. The attractive royal couple, King Bhumibol and Queen Sirikit, made state visits abroad, met Elvis and were portrayed in photographs in much the same way as the US president John F Kennedy and his wife: young and fashionable models of the post-war generation.

Through rural development projects the king became regarded as the champion of the poor. The Royal Project Foundation was created in 1969 and is credited for helping to eradicate opium cultivation among the northern hill tribes. During the violence

1973
Civilian demonstrators overthrow the military dictatorship; a democratic government is installed.

1997
The Asian economic crisis hits; 'people's constitution' is passed in parliament.

2004
A Boxing Day tsunami kills 5000 people and damages tourism and fishing on the Andaman Coast. Right: Memorial plaques for the tsunami victims

of the 1970s protest movements, the king came to be regarded as a mediating voice in tumultuous times and called for the resignation of the military leaders. He also gave his consent to the reinstatement of military rule three years later, a symbolic gesture that helped ensure civil order. During another political crisis in 1992, the king summoned the leaders of the warring factions to the palace in an effort to quell street protests. His annual birthday speech (5 December) is often regarded as something akin to the US State of the Union address and indicates palace sentiments towards rival factions.

The king is in his 80s now and his health has been failing while the country's political future remains uncertain. Since the late 1950s the palace and the military have been closely aligned, a relationship that is currently cemented by General Prem Tinsulanonda, a retired military commander, former prime minister and current high-ranking palace advisor who is believed to have instigated the 2006 coup. In previous political confrontations, the king has appeared to be above the bickering, but the palace's role in ousting the popular prime minister and the ensuing street protests between anti-Thaksin groups, who wear the royal colours and proclaim to be protecting the king, and the pro-Thaksin groups, who see themselves as the inheritors of the 1932 revolution, indicates a destabilisation of the monarch as a unifying figure. Though King Bhumibol has carved out a unique niche for the postmodern monarch, it is uncertain whether this role will survive the current political crisis and be inherited by his son, Crown Prince Vachiralongkorn.

The Best... Historic Museums

1 Bangkok National Museum (p65)

2 Chiang Mai City Arts & Cultural Centre (p145)

3 Hilltribe Museum & Education Center (p191)

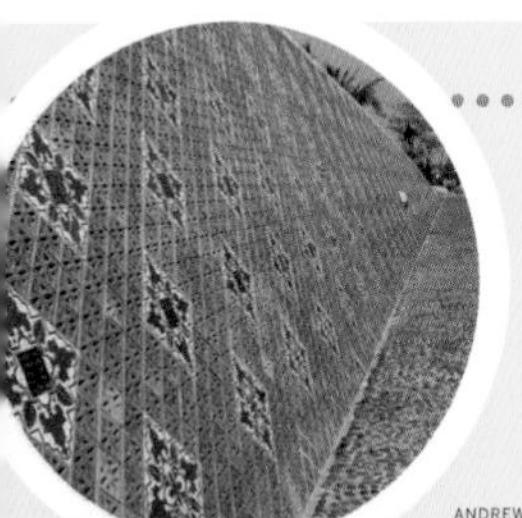

ANDREW BAIN/LONELY PLANET IMAGES ©

2006
Prime Minister Thaksin Shinawatra is ousted by a military coup.

2011
Yingluck Shinawatra becomes the first female prime minister; destructive floods hit the country.

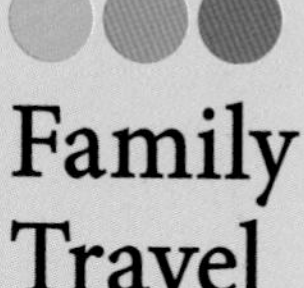

Family Travel

Thai students, Bangkok

RAY LASKOWITZ/LONELY PLANET IMAGES

Thais are so family focused that even grumpy taxi drivers want to pinch your baby's cheeks and play a game of peekaboo (called já ăir). On crowded buses, adults will stand so that children can sit, and hotel and restaurant staff willingly set aside chores to become a child's playmate.

Sights & Activities

Children will especially enjoy the beaches, as most are in gentle bays good for beginner swimmers. For more experienced swimmers, some of the Gulf and Andaman islands have near-shore reefs for snorkelling and fish-spotting.

Crocodile farms, monkey shows and tiger zoos abound in Thailand, but conditions are often below Western standards. There is a new generation of ecotour projects – in Ayuthaya, Chiang Mai and Lampang – that focus on humane conditions and animal conservation. The mahout-training schools and elephant sanctuaries are excellent places to see the revered pachyderm in a dignified setting. Older children will enjoy jungle-trekking tours that often include elephant rides and bamboo rafting. Many of the beach resorts, such as Phuket and Ko Chang, also have wildlife encounters, waterfall spotting and organised water sports.

In urban areas, kids might feel cooped up, in which case a hotel with a small garden or swimming pool will provide necessary play space. Playgrounds are not widespread or well maintained, though every city has an exercise park where runners and families go in the early evening. Though Bangkok is lean on green, it is still great fun for little ones in awe of construction sites and mass transit and for older ones obsessed with shopping malls.

If you're worried about long-distance journeys with a fussy passenger, opt for the train. Kids can walk around the carriage and visit the friendly locals; they are assigned the lower sleeping berths which have views of the stations, trotting dogs and dust-kicking motorcycles.

The Best... Kid-Friendly Beaches

1 Ko Samui: Bo Phut (p253) and Choeng Mon (p253)

2 Ko Lanta (p314)

3 Hua Hin (p244)

4 Ko Samet (p116)

Kid-Friendly Eats

In general, Thai children don't start eating spicy food until primary school; before then they seemingly survive on *kôw nĕe·o* (sticky rice) and junk food. Other child-friendly meals include chicken in all of its nonspicy permutations – *gài yâhng* (grilled chicken), *gài tôrt* (fried chicken) and *gài pàt mét má·môo·ang* (chicken stir-fried with cashews). Some kids will even branch out to *kôw pàt* (fried rice), though the strong odour of *nám blah* (fish sauce) might be a deal breaker. Helpful restaurant staff will enthusiastically recommend *kài jee·o* (Thai-style omelette), which can be made in a jiffy.

If all else fails, tropical fruits and fruit juices are ubiquitous and delectable and will keep the kids hydrated. Of course, most tourist centres also have Western restaurants catering to homesick eaters of any age.

Need to Know

- **Changing Facilities** Non-existent.
- **Cots** By special request at midrange and top-end hotels.
- **Health** Drink a lot of water; wash hands regularly; warn children against playing with animals.
- **Highchairs** Sometimes available in resort areas.
- **Nappies** (diapers) Minimarkets and 7-Elevens carry small sizes; Tesco Lotus or Tops Market for size 3 or larger.
- **Strollers** Bring a compact umbrella stroller.
- **Transport** Car seats and seat belts are not widely available on public or hired transport.

Culture & Customs

Street poster of King Bhumibol Adulyadej, Bangkok (p51)

RICHARD NEBESKY/LONELY PLANET IMAGES

It is easy to love Thailand: the pace of life is unhurried and the people are friendly and kind-hearted. A smile is a universal key in most social situations, a cheerful disposition will be met in kind, and friendships are spontaneous creations requiring little more than curiosity and humour. Though Thais don't expect foreigners to know much about their country, they are delighted and grateful if they do.

The Monarchy

Thailand's most striking cultural quirk is the deep reverence for the reigning monarch, King Bhumibol Adulyadej (boo-mee-pone a-dun-ya-det). Pictures of the king are enshrined in nearly every household and business. Life-size billboards of the monarchy line Th Ratchadamnoen Klang, Bangkok's royal avenue. His image, which is printed on money and stamps, is regarded as sacred, and criticising the king or the monarchy is a prosecutable offence.

The monarch's relationship to the people is intertwined with the religion; it is deeply spiritual and personal. Though not a universal belief, many view the king as a god, or at least as a father figure (his birthday is recognised as national Father's Day) and as a protector of the good of the country. In times of political crisis, Thais have often looked to this figurehead for guidance. However, the most recent political upheaval (starting with the 2006 coup) indicates a general unease regarding the ailing monarch and the succession of Crown Prince Vachiralongkorn.

The National Psyche

In most social situations, establishing harmony is often a priority and Thais take personal pride in making others feel at ease.

Sà·nùk

Thais place a high value on having *sà·nùk* (fun). It is the underlying measure of a worthwhile activity and the reason why the country ranks so highly as a tourist destination. Thais are always up for a party, be it of their own invention or an import. Case in point: Thais celebrate three new years – the eve of the resetting of the international calendar, the Chinese lunar New Year and Songkran (the southeast Asian Buddhist new year).

This doesn't mean that Thais are adverse to work. On the contrary, most offices are typically open six, sometimes seven, days a week, and professionals from poor farming families are expected to have side jobs to provide extra income to their parents. But every chore has a social aspect to it that lightens the mood and keeps it from being too 'serious' (a grave insult). Thais labour best as a group to avoid loneliness and ensure an element of playfulness. The backbreaking work of rice farming, the tedium of long-distance bus driving, the dangers of a construction site: Thais often mix their work tasks with socialising. The famous Thai smile comes from a genuine desire to enjoy life.

Thais in the tourism industry extend this attitude towards their guests and will often describe foreign visitors as needing a rest after a year of hard work. This cultural mindset reflects the agricultural calendar in which a farmer works from dawn to dusk during the rice-planting and harvesting season then rests until the next year's rains. That rest period involves a lot of hanging out, going to festivals and funerals (which are more party than pity) and loading up family and friends into the back of a pick-up truck for a *têe·o* (trip). Thais have been practising the art of a good time for a long time.

Beloved Monarchs

Looking back through history, there have been other monarchs who have crossed into national-hero status, including King Chulalongkorn (Rama V; 1868–1910), whose picture often decorates residences and amulets. He travelled to Europe, built fine Victorian-style palaces and is greatly revered, especially in Bangkok and by Thais who have travelled abroad.

Status

Though Thai culture is famously nonconfrontational and fun-loving, it isn't a social free-for-all. Thais are very conscious of status and the implicit rights and responsibilities that go along with one's station in life. Buddhism plays a large part in defining the social strata, with the heads of the family, religion and monarchy sitting at the top of various tiers. A good indicator of status is the depth of the *wâi* (the traditional prayer-like greeting motion). In most cases the fingertips will touch between the lips and nose but will migrate above the crown of the head when greeting or showing gratitude to a monk.

Gauging where you, as a foreigner, fit into this system is a convenient ice-breaker. Thais will often ask a laundry list of questions: where are you from, how old are you, are you married, do you have children? They are sizing you up in the social strata. In most cases, you'll get the best of both worlds: Thais will care for you as if you are a child and

honour you as if you are a *pôo yài* (literally 'big person', or elder). When sharing a meal, don't be surprised if a Thai host puts the tastiest piece of fish on your plate.

Thais regard each other as part of an extended family and will use familial prefixes such as *pêe* (elder sibling) and *nórng* (younger sibling) when addressing friends as well as blood relations. This convention is often translated into English by bilingual Thais, leading foreigners to think that their Thai friends have large immediate families. Thais might also use *ɓăh* (aunt) or *lung* (uncle) to refer to an older person. Rarely do foreigners get embraced in this grand family reunion; *fa·ràng* is the catch-all term for foreigner. It is mostly descriptive but can sometimes express cultural frustrations.

Saving Face

Interconnected with status is the concept of 'saving face', a common consideration in Asian cultures. In a nutshell, 'face' means that you strive for social harmony by avoiding firm or confrontational opinions and avoiding displays of anger. Thais regard outbursts of emotion and discourteous social interactions as shameful, whereas Westerners might shrug them off as minor embarrassments or a necessary by-product in achieving fairness.

Social Conventions & Etiquette

Thais are generally tolerant of most social faux pas as they assume that foreign visitors know very little about their culture. Their graciousness should be returned with a concerted effort of respect.

Greetings

The traditional Thai greeting is with a prayer-like palms-together gesture known as a *wâi*. If someone shows you a *wâi*, you should return the gesture, unless the greeting comes from a child or a service person. A *wâi* can also express gratitude or an apology.

Children wearing traditional tribal dress during Loi Krathong festivities, Chiang Mai
FELIX HUG/LONELY PLANET IMAGES ©

Dos & Don'ts

- Stand for the royal and national anthems.
- Don't show anger or frustration.
- Remove shoes before entering homes or temples; step over the threshold.
- Keep your feet off furniture.
- In temples, sit in the mermaid position (with your feet tucked behind you).
- If invited to someone's house, bring a gift of fruit or drinks.
- Pass and receive things with your right hand.
- Use your spoon like a fork and fork like a knife.

Foreigners are continually baffled by when and how to use the *wâi* and such cultural confusion makes great conversation fodder: Thais are usually delighted to have the opportunity to explain.

The all-purpose greeting is a cheery *'sà·wàt·dee kráp'* if you're male or *'sà·wàt·dee kâ'* if you're female. A smile usually accompanies this and goes a long way to diffuse any nervousness or shyness that a Thai might have when interacting with a foreigner. Also, Thais are great connoisseurs of beauty and a smile improves one's countenance.

Visiting Temples

When visiting a temple, it is very important to dress modestly (covered to the elbows and the ankles) and to take your shoes off when you enter any building that contains a Buddha image. Buddha images are sacred objects, so don't pose in front of them for pictures and definitely do not clamber on them. When visiting a religious building, act like a worshipper by finding a discreet place to sit in the 'mermaid' position (with your feet tucked behind you so that they point away from the Buddha images). Also take the time to observe the worshippers' prayer rituals and feel free to attempt them yourself to honour the sacred space. Temples are maintained from the donations received and contributions from visitors are appreciated.

Touching

In the more traditional parts of the country, it is not proper for members of the opposite sex to touch one another, either as lovers or as friends. Hand-holding is not acceptable behaviour outside of Bangkok. But same-sex touching is quite common and is typically a sign of friendship, not sexual attraction. Older Thai men might grab a younger man's thigh in the same way that buddies slap each other on the back. Thai women are especially affectionate with female friends, often sitting close to one another or linking arms. Women should not touch monks or their belongings; they should not sit next to them on public transport or accidentally brush against them on the street.

Religion

Reclining Buddha, Wat Pho (p69), Bangkok

Religion is a fundamental component of Thai society and culture, and colourful examples of daily worship can be found on nearly every corner. Walk the streets early in the morning and you'll see the solemn progression of the Buddhist monks engaged in bin·da·bàht, the daily house-to-house alms food-gathering. Small household shrines decorate the humblest abodes and protective amulets, ranging from discreet to overt, are common pieces of jewellery.

Buddhism

Approximately 95% of Thai people are Theravada Buddhists. This form of Buddhism is often called the Southern School because it travelled from the Indian subcontinent to Southeast Asia. Mahayana, the other branch of Buddhism, followed a northern migration through Nepal, Tibet, China and the rest of East Asia. The two forms differ in doctrine, canonical texts and monastic practices.

Religious Principles

Buddhism was born in India in the 6th century. A prince named Siddhartha Gautama left his life of privilege, seeking religious fulfilment. According to the Hindu practices of the time, he became an ascetic and subjected himself to many years of severe austerity before he realised that this was not the way to reach the end of suffering. He became known as Buddha, 'the enlightened' or 'the awakened', and spoke of four noble truths that had the power to liberate any human being who could realise them.

The four noble truths deal with the nature and origin of suffering and the path to the cessation of suffering. Loosely explained this includes *dukkha* (all forms of existence are subject to suffering, disease, imperfection), *samudaya* (the origin of suffering is desire), *nirodha* (cessation of suffering is the giving up of desire) and *magga* (the path to cessation of suffering is the eightfold path).

The eightfold path is often described as the middle path: a route between extreme asceticism and indulgence. Following the path will lead to *nibbana* ('nirvana' in Sanskrit), which literally means the 'blowing out' or extinction of all grasping and thus of all suffering. Effectively, *nibbana* is also an end to the cycle of rebirths (both moment-to-moment and life-to-life) that is existence.

Houses of the Holy

Many dwellings in Thailand have a 'spirit house' for the property's *prá poom* (guardian spirits). Based on pre-Buddhist animistic beliefs, guardian spirits live in rivers, trees and other natural features and need to be honoured (and placated) – like a respected but sometimes troublesome family member. Elaborate doll's-house-like structures, where the spirits can 'live' comfortably separated from human affairs, are consecrated by a Brahman priest and receive daily offerings of rice, fruit, flowers and water.

Religious Practice

In reality, most Thai Buddhists aim for rebirth in a 'better' existence rather than the supramundane goal of *nibbana*. By feeding monks, giving donations to temples and worshipping regularly at the local temple they hope to improve their lot, acquiring enough merit (*bun* in Thai) to prevent rebirths (or at least reduce their number). The concept of rebirth is almost universally accepted in Thailand, even by non-Buddhists.

Thai Buddhists look to the Triple Gems for guidance in their faith: the Buddha, the *dhamma* and the *sangha*. The Buddha, in a myriad of sculptural forms, is usually the centrepiece of devotional activity inside a temple and many of the most famous Thai Buddha images have supernatural tales associated with them. The *dhamma* is chanted morning and evening in every temple and taught to every Thai citizen in primary school. There are two *sangha* sects in Thailand: the Mahanikai and Thammayut. The former places more emphasis on scholarship, while the latter prefers proficiency in meditation.

Hinduism & Animism

There are many enduring legacies of Hinduism and animism in Thai culture and in the practice of Thai Buddhism today. Hinduism was the religious parent of Buddhism, imparting lasting components of mythology, cosmology and symbolism. Thais recognise the contributions of Hinduism and treat its deities with reverence. Bangkok is especially rich in Hindu shrines, where Thai Buddhists worship devoutly. Many of the royally associated ceremonies stem from Brahmanism.

Spirit worship and Buddhism have comingled to the point that it is difficult to filter the two. Monks often perform obviously animistic rituals, and Thais believe that making merit (Buddhist religious rituals) benefits deceased relatives. In fact, many of the religious rituals of Thai Buddhists, apart from meditation, appear to be deeply rooted in the spirit world. Household shrines and spirit houses are erected to shelter and placate the guardian spirits of the land. Trees are wrapped in sacred cloth to

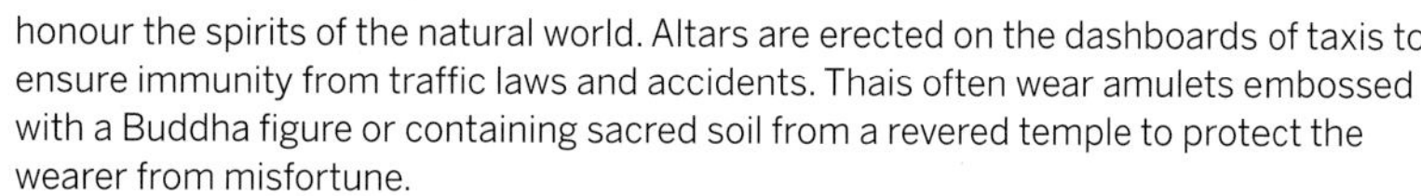

honour the spirits of the natural world. Altars are erected on the dashboards of taxis to ensure immunity from traffic laws and accidents. Thais often wear amulets embossed with a Buddha figure or containing sacred soil from a revered temple to protect the wearer from misfortune.

Monks & Monasteries

Every Thai male is expected to become a monk (*prá* or *prá pík·sù* in Thai) for a short period in his life, optimally between the time he finishes school and the time he starts a career or marries. A family earns great merit when one of its sons 'takes robe and bowl' and many young men enter the monastery to make merit for a deceased patriarch or matriarch. Traditionally, Buddhist Lent (*pan·săh*), which begins in July and coincides with the three-month period of the rainy season, is when most temporary monks enter the monastery. Nowadays, however, men may spend as little as a week there.

Historically the temple provided a necessary social safety net for families in need. The monastery was a de facto orphanage, caring for and educating children whose parents couldn't provide for them, and a retirement home for older rural men. Though these charitable roles are not as sought after today, the temples still give refuge and sanctuary to all living creatures. This might mean that they help feed families in need, adopt orphaned or injured animals and give shelter to overnight travellers (usually impoverished Thai university students).

Although Thai monks take a vow of poverty, it is not unusual to see them using mobile (cell) phones, smoking or shopping at the market. The degree to which monastic orders are adhered to varies by individual and temple; because monkhood is somewhat compulsory, not every participant is guided by deep religious convictions.

Buddhist monks

In Thai Buddhism, women who seek a monastic life are given a minor role in the temple that is not equal to full monkhood. A Buddhist nun is known as *mâa chee* (mother priest) and lives as an *atthasila* (following eight precepts of Buddhism's code of ethics as opposed to the five for lay people and 227 for ordained monks) nun, a position traditionally occupied by women who had no other place in society. Thai nuns shave their heads, wear white robes and take care of temple chores. Generally speaking, *mâa chee* aren't considered as prestigious as monks and don't have a function in the laypeople's merit-making rituals.

The Best... Buddhist Festivals

1 Ork Phansaa (p44)

2 Khao Phansaa (p43)

3 Songkran (p43)

Temple Visits

Thai Buddhism has no particular sabbath day when the faithful are supposed to congregate at the temple. Instead, Thai Buddhists visit whenever they feel like it, most often on *wan prá* (holy days), which occur every seventh or eighth day, depending on phases of the moon.

A temple visit is usually a social affair involving groups of friends, families or office workers. Thais will also make special pilgrimages to famous temples in other regions as sightseeing and merit-making outings. For the older generation this is the time to show off their most beautiful Thai silk dresses, which follow a standard pattern style of a tailored shirt and ankle-length skirt. The younger generation regards these dresses as old-fashioned but the act of merit-making remains timeless.

Most merit-makers visit the *wí·hăhn* (the central sanctuary), which houses the primary Buddha figure. Worshippers will offer lotus buds (a symbol of enlightenment) or flower garlands, light three joss sticks and raise their hands to their forehead in a prayerlike gesture.

Other merit-making activities include offering food to the temple *sangha* (community), meditating (individually or in groups), listening to monks chanting *suttas* (Buddhist discourse) and attending a *têht* or *dhamma* (teachings) talk by the abbot or some other respected teacher.

Thai Buddhists will also visit the temple to consult with monks in order to pick an auspicious time to get married, start a business or perform child-naming rituals. Funeral rites are also held at the temple.

See p335 for tips on temple etiquette.

Islam & Other Religions

Although Thailand is predominantly Buddhist, the minority religions often practise alongside one another. The green-hued onion domes of a mosque mark a neighbourhood as Muslim, while large, rounded doorways flanked by red paper lanterns mark the location of a *săhn jôw,* a Chinese temple dedicated to the worship of Buddhist, Taoist and Confucian deities.

About 4.6% of the population are followers of Islam. The remainder are Christian, including missionary-converted hill tribes and Vietnamese immigrants, as well as Confucians, Taoists, Mahayana Buddhists and Hindus.

The majority of Muslims in Thailand live in the southern provinces, though there are pockets in Bangkok and central and northern Thailand. In the southernmost provinces the Muslims are ethnic Malays, while northern Thailand's Muslims are Yunnanese descendants. The form of Islam found in southern Thailand is mixed with elements of Malay culture and animism, creating a more culturally relaxed religion

than that of Arab nations. Thai Muslim women function in the society as actively as their Buddhist sisters: working outside the home, getting a mainstream education and being equal partners with their spouses. There is a degree of separation of the sexes in the classrooms and at the mosques. Headscarves are prevalent but not mandatory: sometimes a visitor only realises that someone is is a Muslim when they decline an offering of pork at the dinner table.

Devout Thai Muslims often encounter spiritual incompatibilities with their identities as Thai citizens, which is largely defined by the Buddhist majority. The popular view of the Thai monarch as a god, or at least godlike, is heresy for a monotheistic religion like Islam, though many Thai Muslims respect and even love the king and do not voice open criticism of his veneration. Muslims also avoid alcohol and gambling (in varying degrees) – two pursuits that define much of rural life for Buddhist Thais. In this way, religious precepts keep the two cultures distinct and slightly distrustful of each other.

The Deep South

The southernmost provinces of Yala, Pattani and Narathiwat contain the country's largest Muslim majority and have long been geographically isolated and culturally alien to the mainstream society. Historically, parts of these provinces were independent sultanates that were conquered by the Bangkok-based kings. During the ultranationalist era in the 1940s, this region responded with separatist resistance, later becoming a sanctuary for communist and insurgent activities in the 1980s. Violence flared again in the early 2000s and has persisted, with no end in sight; most observers classify the conflict as an ethno-nationalist struggle.

Thai Cuisine

Garlic and rice fields, Mae Hong Son Province (p216)

AUSTIN BUSH/LONELY PLANET IMAGES ©

Thai food – one of the country's most famous exports – balances spicy, sweet, sour and salty flavours in complex and zesty combinations. Ingredients are fresh, flavours are assertive and the sting of the beloved chilli triggers an adrenaline rush.

Rice

In the morning Thais rise with two fundamental smells: rice being cooked and the burning joss sticks offered to household shrines. The start of the new day means another opportunity to eat rice, which is synonymous with eating. (The Thai word 'to eat' is *gin kôw*, literally 'to eat rice'.)

Rice can be steamed, fried, boiled in a soup, formed into noodles or made into a dessert. In its steamed form it is eaten with a spoon and, in the case of *kôw něe·o* (sticky rice), eaten with the fingers. It appears at the breakfast, lunch and dinner table and is even sought out as a late-night snack. The classic morning meal is a watery rice soup (either *jóhk* or *kôw đôm*) that is the ultimate comfort food, the equivalent of oatmeal on a cold winter day. The next meal of the day will probably be a stir-fry or curry, typically served over rice, bought from a street stall or shopfront canteen and

quickly gobbled down. In provincial towns, everyone heads out to the night market to see and be seen and to eat more rice, usually in the form of a stir-fry.

Noodles

When rice just won't do there is another, albeit rice-derivative, alternative: *gŏo·ay đěe·o* (rice noodles). Day or night, city or village, *gŏo·ay đěe·o* is the original Thai fast-food served by itinerant vendors or from humble shopfronts. It is a ubiquitous and highly adaptive dish that demonstrates Thais' penchant for micro-managing flavours. You choose the kind of noodle, the kind of meat and you flavour it yourself with a little fish sauce, sugar, vinegar and chillies; don't shy away from the sugar, it works wonders.

There are three basic kinds of rice noodles – *sên yài* (wide), *sên lék* (thin) and *sên mèe* (thinner than thin) – as well as *bà·mèe,* which is a curly noodle made from wheat flour and egg. Most of these only appear in noodle soups but a few are used in various stir-fries, such as *pàt tai* (thin rice noodles stir-fried with dried or fresh shrimp, tofu and egg).

Head to the morning market for a bowl of *kà·nŏm jeen* (rice noodles doused in a thin curry). Spicy, fishy, salty, soupy, this dish is all the flavours rolled into one and piled high with strange pickled and fresh vegetables that will make you feel as if you've grazed on the savannah and swum through the swamp. *Kà·nŏm jeen* is usually served at rickety wooden tables shared with working-class ladies dressed in polyester market clothes.

Tips on Tipples

- Thai beers, such as Singha (pronounced 'sing'), are hoppy lagers and often mixed with ice to keep them cool and palatable.
- Fruit shakes are refreshing on a hot day and are served with a pinch of salt to help regulate body temperature.
- Sweet iced coffee and tea are popular street stall drinks.
- Thais get their drink on with rice whisky mixed with ice, soda water and a splash of Coke.

Curries

The overseas celebrity of Thai cuisine, curry (*gaang*) enjoys an entirely different position on home turf. It is a humble dish that is usually eaten for breakfast or lunch. At roadside stands, especially in southern Thailand, big metal pots contain various curry concoctions of radioactive colours. When you ask vendors what they have, they'll lift the lids and name the type of meat in each: *gaang gài* (curry with chicken), *gaang Ƀlah* (shorthand for sour fish curry). In Bangkok, street-side vendors and small shops will display their curry-in-a-hurry in buffet-style trays. In either case, you point to one and it will be ladled over rice. Use a spoon to scoop it up and push the lime leaves to the side (they aren't edible).

All curries start with a basic paste that includes ground coriander seed, cumin seed, garlic, lemongrass, kaffir lime, galangal, shrimp paste and chillies (either dried or fresh). Thai cooks used to make these from scratch but these days they go to the market and buy it in bulk. The curry paste recipe varies from region to region: *gaang mát·sà·màn* (Muslim curry) uses star anise, considered a Thai-Muslim spice. Most visitors know their curries by their colour, mainly red (from dried red chillies) and green (from fresh green chillies). Green curry is a classic central-Thai dish.

A true Thai curry will be a fairly thin soup containing curry paste, some meat and aubergines (eggplant); depending on the type of curry, it may or may not have coconut milk. A garnish of basil leaves might be added at the end of cooking. The four flavours (salty, sweet, spicy and sour) should be at play but, to cater to foreigners, some curries will be excessively sweet and thick from too much sugar and coconut milk.

Regional Cuisines

Over the past 20 years there has been so much migration within Thailand that many of the once region-specific dishes have been adopted throughout the country as part of its national cuisine.

Northern Thai

True to its Lanna character, northern Thai cuisine is more laid-back, the flavours are mellow and the influences have migrated over mountains from Myanmar (Burma) and China. The curry and noodle dishes are hearty for chilly mornings. Thanks to the travelling Chinese caravans and settlers, northern cuisine is enamoured with pork, which features in almost every dish including *sâi òo·a* (local-style sausages), *kâap mŏo* (fried crackling snacks) and the popular street food *mŏo bîng* (grilled pork skewers). The Burmese influence has imparted the use of turmeric and ginger (though some could argue that northern Burmese was influenced by Chinese) into the curry pastes used in *gaang hang·lair* (rich pork stew). Northern flavours favour sour notes. Pickled vegetables are loaded on top of the signature noodle dishes of *kôw soy* (wheat-and-egg noodles with a thick coconut red curry) and *kà·nŏm jeen nám ngée·o* (rice noodles

Thai curries

served with thin curry broth made with pork and tomatoes); shallots and lime wedges are common seasoning garnishes.

Northern Thailand shares Isan's love of *kôw nĕe·o*, which is often served in rounded wicker baskets and accompanies such standard dishes as *nám prík òrng* (a chilli paste made with ground pork and tomato).

Southern Thai

Along the narrow Malay peninsula of southern Thailand, a whole different flavour constellation awaits. Southern Thai food draws from the traditions of seafaring traders, many of whom were Muslims from India, or ethnic Malays, who are now referred to as Thai-Muslims. Indian-style flat bread (known as roti) often competes with rice as a curry companion or is drizzled with sugar and sweetened condensed milk as a market dessert. Turmeric imparts its telltale yellow hue to *kôw mòk gài* (chicken biryani) and southern-style fried chicken. The curries here are flamboyant, with dry-roasted spice bases prepared in the Indian fashion and lots of locally produced coconut milk. Shaved, milked, strained and fresh, the coconut is a kitchen mainstay. Coconuts were once the cash crop of the now-famous island getaways, and the favoured son or daughter inherited the interior land where the plantations thrived. The coastal land was less desirable and fell into the hands of the humble fishermen, a paradigm overturned by tourism. Seafood is plentiful and fresh in southern cuisine. Plump squids are grilled and served on a stick with an accompanying sweet-and-spicy sauce. Whole fish are often stuffed with lemongrass and limes and barbecued over a coconut-husk fire.

The Best... Street-Vendor Meals

1 *kôw pàt* – fried rice.

2 *gŏo·ay đĕe·o pàt kêe mow* – stir-fried noodles with basil, lots of chillies and a choice of meat (usually chicken).

3 *pàt gá·prow* – freshly sliced chillies, holy basil and a choice of chicken or pork stir-fry served over rice.

4 *pàt pàk ká·náh* – stir-fried Chinese kale, often matched with *mŏo gròrp* (crispy fried pork).

5 *ƀah·tôrng·gŏh* – Chinese-style doughnuts served in the morning.

Northeastern Thai

Northeastern labourers, housekeepers and taxi drivers never leave home without their triumvirate dishes: *sôm·đam* (green papaya salad), *kôw nĕe·o* and *gài yâhng* (grilled chicken).

In the morning, the barbecue carnage begins with large, open-coal grills loaded up with marinated chicken, sending up big plumes of smoke that waft across the city as free advertising. Alongside the grill is a large mortar and pestle in which the *sôm·đam* is prepared. In go strips of green papaya, sugar, chillies, fish sauce, green beans, tomatoes, dried shrimps and a few special requests: peanuts to make it *sôm·đam Thai*; or field crabs and *ƀlah ráh* (fermented fish sauce) to make it *sôm·đam Lao* (referring to the ethnic Lao who live in northeastern Thailand).

The vendor pounds the ingredients together with the pestle to make a musical 'pow-pow-pow' sound that is sometimes used as an onomatopoetic nickname. Isan girls are often told that they'll make good wives if they are adept at handling the pestle when making *sôm·đam* – the obvious sexual connotations are intended.

Arts & Architecture

Mural, Wat Phra Kaew (p74), Bangkok

Thais have a refined sense of beauty that is reflected in their rich and varied artistic traditions, from Buddhist sculpture to temple architecture. Monarchs were the country's great artistic patrons; their funeral monuments were ornate temple stupas, and handicrafts were developed specifically for royal use. Today religious artwork continues to dominate the artistic imagination but has been adapted to the modern context with museum multimedia installations and contemporary canvas works.

Religious Art

Although most Thais go to temples for religious reasons, tourists go for artistic appreciation. Temples are the country's artistic repositories where you'll find ornate murals depicting Hindu-Buddhist mythology and Buddha sculptures, which define Thailand's most famous contribution to the world of religious art.

Always instructional in intent, temple murals often show depictions of the *jataka* (stories of the Buddha's life) and the Thai version of the Hindu epic *Ramayana*. Reading the murals requires both knowledge of these religious tales and an understanding of the murals' spatial relationship and chronology. Most murals are divided into scenes, in which the main theme is depicted in the centre with resulting events taking place above and below the central action. Usually in the

corner of a dramatic episode between the story's leading characters are independent scenes of Thai village life: women carrying bamboo baskets, men fishing, or a happy communal get-together. All of these simple village folk wear the ubiquitous Thai smile.

Early temple murals were made from natural pigments, a temperamental medium that didn't survive the elements. The study and application of mural painting has been kept alive and today's practitioners often use improved techniques and paints that hold much longer than before.

Alongside the vivid murals in the sacred temple spaces are revered Buddha images that trace Thailand's sculptural evolution. The country is most famous for its graceful and serene Buddhas that emerged during the Sukhothai era.

Artistic Periods

The development of Thai religious art and architecture is broken into different periods or schools defined by the patronage of the ruling capital. The best examples of a period's characteristics are seen in the depiction of the Buddha's facial features, the top flourish on the head, the dress and the position of the feet in meditation.

Another signature of the artistic periods is the size and shape of the temples' *chedi* (stupas) – telltale characteristics are shown in the pedestal and the central bell before it begins to taper into the uppermost tower.

Contemporary Art

Adapting traditional themes and aesthetics to the secular canvas began around the turn of the 20th century, as Western influence surged in the region. In general, Thai painting favours abstraction over realism and continues to preserve the one-dimensional perspective of traditional mural paintings. There are two major trends in Thai art: the updating of religious themes and the tongue-in-cheek social commentary.

Italian artist Corrado Feroci is often credited as the father of modern Thai art. He was first invited to Thailand by Rama VI in 1924 and built Bangkok's Democracy Monument, among other European-style statues. Feroci founded the country's first fine arts institute in 1933, a school that eventually developed into Silpakorn University, Thailand's premier training ground for artists. In gratitude, the Thai government made Feroci a Thai citizen, with the Thai name Silpa Bhirasri.

The Modern Buddha

In the 1970s Thai artists began to tackle the modernisation of Buddhist themes through abstract expressionism. Leading works in this genre include the mystical pen-and-ink drawings of Thawan Duchanee. Receiving more exposure overseas, Montien Boonma used the ingredients of Buddhist merit-making, such as gold leaf, bells and candle wax, to create abstract temple spaces within museum galleries.

Protest & Satire

In Thailand's quickly industrialising society, many artists watched as the rice fields became factories, the forests became asphalt and the spoils went to the politically connected. During the student activist days of the 1970s the Art for Life Movement was the banner under which creative discontents – including musicians, intellectuals and painters – rallied against the military dictatorship and embraced certain aspects of communism and workers' rights. Sompote Upa-In and Chang Saetang are two important artists from that period.

An anti-authority attitude continues today. Manit Sriwanichpoom is best known for his Pink Man on Tour series, in which he depicted artist Sompong Thawee in a pink suit and with a pink shopping cart amid Thailand's most iconic attractions, suggesting that Thailand's culture and natural spaces were for sale. He's since

Thailand's Artistic Periods

PERIOD	TEMPLE & *CHEDI* STYLES	BUDDHA STYLES	EXAMPLES
Dvaravati period (7th-11th centuries)	rectangular-based *chedi* with stepped tiers	Indian-influenced with a thick torso, large hair curls, arched eyebrows to represent a flying bird, protruding eyes, thick lips and a flat nose	Phra Pathom Chedi, Nakhon Pathom; Lopburi Museum, Lopburi; Wat Chama Thawi, Lamphun
Srivijaya Period (7th-13th centuries)	Mahayana-Buddhist-style temples; Javanese-style *chedi* with elaborate arches	Indian influenced: heavily ornamented, humanlike features and slightly twisted at the waist	Wat Phra Boromathat, Chaiya; Wat Phra Mahathat Woramahawihaan and National Museum, Nakhon Si Thammarat
Khmer period (9th-11th centuries)	Hindu-Buddhist temples; corn-cob-shaped *prang*	Buddha meditating under a canopy of the seven-headed *naga* and atop a lotus pedestal	Phimai, Nakhon Ratchasima; Phanom Rung, Surin
Chiang Saen-Lanna period (11th-13th centuries)	Teak temples; square-based *chedi* topped by gilded umbrella; also octagonal-base *chedi*	Burmese influences with plump figure, round, smiling face and footpads facing upwards in meditation pose.	Wat Phra Singh, Chiang Mai; Chiang Saen National Museum
Sukhothai period (13th-15th centuries)	Khmer-inspired temples; slim-spired *chedi* topped by a lotus bud	Graceful poses, often depicted 'walking', no anatomical human detail	Sukhothai Historical Park, Sukhothai
Ayuthaya period (14th-18th centuries)	Classical Thai temple with three-tiered roof and gable flourishes; bell-shaped *chedi* with tapering spire	Ayuthaya-era king, wearing a gem-studded crown and royal regalia	Ayuthaya Historical Park, Ayuthaya
Bangkok-Ratanakosin period (19th century)	Colourful and gilded temple with Western-Thai styles; mosaic-covered *chedi*	Reviving Ayuthaya style	Wat Phra Kaew, Wat Pho and Wat Arun, Bangkok

followed up this series with other socially evocative photographs poking fun at ideas of patriotism and nationalism.

Finding a Home for Art

In this hierarchical society, artistic innovation is often stifled by the older generation that holds prestige and power. In the 1990s there was a push to move art out of the dead zones of the museums and into the public spaces beyond the reach of the cultural authoritarians. An artist and art organiser, Navin Rawanchaikul, started his 'in-the-streets' collaborations in his home town of Chiang Mai and then moved his

big ideas to Bangkok, where he filled the city's taxi cabs with art installations, a show that literally went on the road. His other works have had a way with words, such as the mixed-media piece *We Are the Children of Rice (Wine)* in 2002 and his rage against the commercialisation of museums in his epic painting entitled *Super (M)art Bangkok Survivors* (2004), which depicts famous artists, curators and decision-makers in a crowded Paolo Veronese setting. The piece was inspired by the struggles the Thai art community had in getting the new contemporary Bangkok art museum to open without it becoming a shopping mall in disguise.

Pop Fun

True to the Thai nature, some art is just fun. The works of Thaweesak Srithongdee are pure pop. He paints flamboyantly cartoonish human figures woven with elements of traditional Thai handicrafts or imagery. In a similar vein, Jirapat Tasanasomboon depicts traditional Thai figures in comic-book-style fights or in sensual embraces with Western icons. In *Hanuman is Upset!* the monkey king chews up the geometric lines of Mondrian's famous gridlike painting.

Sculpture

Although lacking in commercial attention, Thai sculpture is often considered to be the strongest of the contemporary arts: not surprising considering the country's relationship with Buddha figures. Moving into nonreligious arenas, Khien Yimsiri is the modern master creating elegant human and mythical forms out of bronze. Kamin Lertchaiprasert explores the subject of spirituality and daily life in his sculptural installations, which often include a small army of papier-mâché figures. His exhibit *Ngern Nang* (Sitting Money) included a series of figures made of discarded paper bills from the national bank and embellished with poetic instructions on life and love.

Thai dancers

Theatre & Dance

Traditional Thai theatre consists of dance-dramas, in which stories are acted out by masked or costumed actors. There is a variety of classical forms, sharing cultural influences from Chinese operas, stylised Indian dancing and Khmer court performances. Traditional theatre was reserved for royal or religious events but, with the modernisation of the monarchy, the once-cloistered art forms have lost their patrons and gone into decline.

Traditional Thai dance, on the other hand, has survived quite well in the modern era and is still widely taught in schools and universities. The dances involve precise and synchronised hand and foot motions that are pieced together to tell a story.

Handicrafts

Thailand's handicrafts live on for the tourist markets, and some have been updated by chic Bangkok designers.

- **Ceramics** The best-known ceramics are the greenish Thai-style celadon and central Thailand's *ben·jà·rong* (five colour), an adaptation of a Chinese style.
- **Lacquerware** Northern Thailand is known for this handicraft inherited from Burma.
- **Textiles** The northeast is famous for *mát·mèe* cloth – a thick cotton or silk fabric woven from tie-dyed threads. Each hill tribe has a tradition of embroidery; Chiang Mai and Chiang Rai are popular handicraft centres.

Kŏhn & Lí·gair

Kŏhn is a masked dance-drama depicting scenes from the *Ramakian* (the Thai version of India's *Ramayana*). The central story revolves around Prince Rama's search for his beloved Princess Sita, who has been abducted by the evil 10-headed demon Ravana and taken to the island of Lanka.

Most often performed at Buddhist festivals by troupes of travelling performers, *lí·gair* is a gaudy, raucous theatrical art form thought to have descended from drama rituals brought to southern Thailand by Arab and Malay traders. It contains a colourful mixture of folk and classical music, outrageous costumes, melodrama, slapstick comedy, sexual innuendo and up-to-date commentary.

Classical & Folk Dance

Inherited from the Khmer, classical dance was a holy offering performed by the earthly version of *apsara* (heavenly maidens blessed with beauty and skilled in dance, who are depicted in graceful positions in temple murals and bas reliefs). But traditional dancing enjoyed its own expressions in the villages and defined each region. In some cases the dances describe the rice-planting season, while others tell tales of flirtations. During local festivals and street parades, especially in the northeast, troupes of dancers, ranging from elementary-school age to college age, will be swathed in traditional costumes, ornate headdresses and white-powder make-up to perform synchronised steps accompanied by a marching band.

Puppet Theatre

Puppet theatre (*lá·kon lék*) was once a popular court entertainment. Stories were drawn from Thai tales, particularly *Phra Aphaimani*, and occasionally from the *Ramakian*.

The puppets were 1m-high marionettes made of paper and wire, dressed in elaborate costumes modelled on those of the *kŏhn* and were manipulated by two to three puppetmasters to imitate the dance movements that depicted the great battles.

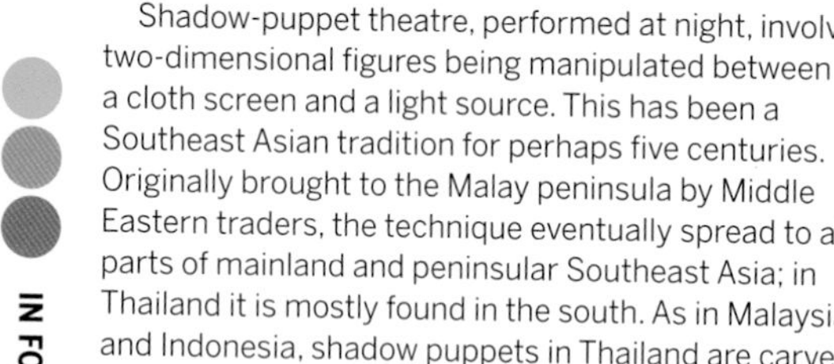

Shadow-puppet theatre, performed at night, involves two-dimensional figures being manipulated between a cloth screen and a light source. This has been a Southeast Asian tradition for perhaps five centuries. Originally brought to the Malay peninsula by Middle Eastern traders, the technique eventually spread to all parts of mainland and peninsular Southeast Asia; in Thailand it is mostly found in the south. As in Malaysia and Indonesia, shadow puppets in Thailand are carved from dried buffalo or cow hides (*năng*).

Like their Malay-Indonesian counterparts, Thai shadow puppets represent an array of characters from classical and folk drama, principally the *Ramakian* and *Phra Aphaimani*. A single puppetmaster manipulates the cut-outs, which are bound to the ends of buffalo-horn handles. Shadow puppets still occasionally appear at temple festivals in the south. Performances are also held periodically for tour groups or visiting dignitaries from Bangkok.

The Best... Traditional Theatre & Dance in Bangkok

1 Chalermkrung Royal Theatre (p85)

2 Aksra Theatre (p85)

3 National Theatre (p85)

Music

Classical Thai music features a dazzling array of textures and subtleties, hair-raising tempos and pastoral melodies. The classical orchestra is called the *ɓèe pâht* and can include as few as five players or more than 20. Among the more common instruments is the *ɓèe*, a woodwind instrument that has a reed mouthpiece; it is heard prominently at Thai-boxing matches. The *rá·nâht èhk*, a bamboo-keyed percussion instrument resembling the xylophone, carries the main melodies. The slender *sor*, a bowed instrument with a coconut-shell soundbox, is sometimes played solo by street buskers.

If you take a cab in Bangkok, you're likely to hear Thailand's version of country music: *lôok tûng* (literally 'children of the fields'). Lost love, tragic early death and the plight of the hard-working farmers are popular themes sung plaintively over a melancholy accompaniment. More upbeat is *mŏr lam*, a folk tradition from the rural northeast that has been electrified with a fast-paced beat.

Step into a shopping mall or a Thai disco and you'll hear the bouncy tunes of Thai pop (also dubbed 'T-pop'), a favourite with teens. The ageing hippies from the protest era of the 1970s and 1980s pioneered *pleng pêu·a chee·wít* (songs for life), which feature in the increasingly hard-to-find Thai country bars. The 1990s gave birth to an alternative pop scene – known as 'indie'. The band Modern Dog is the genre's surviving pioneer.

Traditional Residential Architecture

Traditional Thai homes were adapted to the weather, the family and artistic sensibilities. These antique specimens were humble dwellings consisting of a single-room wooden house raised on stilts. More elaborate homes, for the village chief or minor royalty for instance, might link a series of single rooms by elevated walkways. Since many Thai villages were built near rivers, the elevation provided protection from flooding during the annual monsoon. During the dry season the space beneath the house was used as a hideaway from the heat of the day, an outdoor kitchen or as a barn for farm animals. Later this all-purpose space would shelter bicycles and motorcycles. Once plentiful in Thai forests, teak was always the material of choice for wooden structures and its use typically indicates that a house is at least 50 years old.

Rooflines in central, northern and southern Thailand are steeply pitched and often decorated at the corners or along the gables with motifs related to the *naga*, a mythical water serpent long believed to be a spiritual protector of Tai cultures throughout Asia.

In Thailand's southern provinces it's not unusual to come upon houses of Malay design, using high masonry pediments or foundations rather than wooden stilts. Residents of the south also sometimes use bamboo and palm thatch, which are more plentiful than wood. In the north, the homes of community leaders were often decorated with an ornate horn-shaped motif called *galare*, a decorative element that has become shorthand for old Lanna architecture. Roofs of tile or thatch tend to be less steeply pitched, and rounded gables – (a feature inherited from Myanmar (Burma) – can also be found further north.

The Best... Old-Fashioned Thai Houses

1 Jim Thompson House, Bangkok (p87)

2 Baan Sao Nak, Lampang (p187)

3 Suan Phakkad Palace Museum, Bangkok (p65)

Temple Architecture

The most striking examples of Thailand's architectural heritage are the Buddhist temples (wát), which dazzle in the tropical sun with wild colours and soaring rooflines.

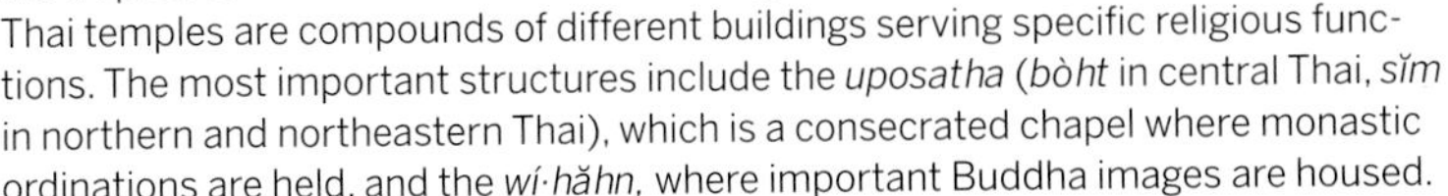

Thai temples are compounds of different buildings serving specific religious functions. The most important structures include the *uposatha* (*bòht* in central Thai, *sĭm* in northern and northeastern Thai), which is a consecrated chapel where monastic ordinations are held, and the *wí·hăhn*, where important Buddha images are housed.

Another classic component of temple architecture is the presence of one or more *chedi* (stupas), a solid mountain-shaped monument that pays tribute to the enduring stability of Buddhism. *Chedi* come in myriad styles, from simple inverted bowl-shaped designs imported from Sri Lanka to the more elaborate octagonal shapes found in northern Thailand. Many are believed to contain relics (often pieces of bone) belonging to the historical Buddha. Some *chedi* also house the ashes of important kings and royalty. In northern and northeastern Thailand such stupas are known as *tâht*. A variation of the stupa inherited from the Angkor kingdom is the corn-cob-shaped *prang*, a feature in the ancient Thai temples of Sukhothai and Ayuthaya. Dotting the grounds of most temples are smaller, squarish *chedi* that contain the ashes of deceased worshippers.

Other structures typically found in temple compounds include one or more *săh·lah* (often spelt 'sala'; open-sided shelters) that are used for community meetings and *dhamma* (Buddhist philosophy) lectures; a number of *gù·đì* (monastic quarters); a *hŏr đrai* (Tripitaka library), where Buddhist scriptures are stored; plus various ancillary buildings, such as schools and clinics.

Contemporary Architecture

Thais began mixing traditional architecture with European forms in the late 19th and early 20th centuries, as exemplified by Bangkok's Vimanmek Teak Mansion and certain buildings of the Grand Palace.

The port cities of Thailand, including Bangkok and Phuket, acquired fine examples of Sino-Portuguese architecture – buildings of stuccoed brick decorated with an ornate facade – a style that followed the sea traders during the colonial era. In Bangkok this style is often referred to as 'old Bangkok' or Ratanakosin.

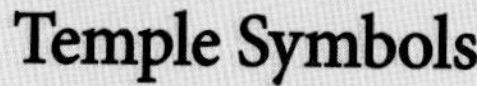

Temple Symbols

The architectural symbolism of Thai temples relies heavily on Hindu-Buddhist iconography.

Naga, the mythical serpent that guarded Buddha during meditation, appears on handrails at temple entrances. A silhouette of the birdlike *chôr fáh* adorns the tip of the roof. Three-tiered roofs represent the triple gems of Buddhism: the Buddha, the *dhamma* and the *sangha* (the Buddhist community).

The lotus, a reminder of religious perfection, decorates temple gates and posts, veranda columns and spires of Sukhothai-era *chedi* and often form the pedestal for images of the meditating Buddha. Lotus buds are used solely for merit-making, not for secular decoration.

Buildings of mixed heritage in the north and northeast exhibit French and English influences, while those in the south typically show Portuguese influence. Shophouses *(hôrng tăa·ou)* throughout the country, whether 100 years or 100 days old, share the basic Chinese shophouse design, in which the ground floor is reserved for trading purposes while the upper floors contain offices or residences.

Modernism & Beyond

In the 1960s and 1970s the trend in modern Thai architecture, inspired by the European Bauhaus movement, shifted towards a stark functionalism: the average building looked like a giant egg carton turned on its side. When Thai architects began experimenting with form over function during the building boom of the mid-1980s, the result was high-tech designs such as ML Sumet Jumsai's famous Robot Building on Th Sathon Tai in Bangkok. Rangsan Torsuwan, a graduate of the Massachusetts Institute of Technology (MIT), introduced the neoclassic (or neo-Thai) style. A traditional-building specialist, Pinyo Suwankiri designs temples, government buildings and shrines for hospitals and universities in Thailand. His work is ubiquitous and the blueprint for an institutional aesthetic of architecture.

In the new millennium, shopping centres and hotels have reinterpreted the traditional Thai house through an industrial modernist perspective. Geometric cubes are defined by steel beams and glass curtains.

Environment

Mountains, Chiang Rai Province (p190)

AUSTIN BUSH/LONELY PLANET IMAGES ©

Thailand clings to a southern spur of the Himalayas in the north, cradles fertile river plains at its core and tapers between two warm, shallow seas fringed by coral reefs. Its shape is often likened to an elephant's head, with the Malay peninsula representing the trunk. Spanning 1650km and 16 latitudinal degrees from north to south, Thailand has the most diverse climate of any country in mainland southeast Asia.

Northern Thailand

Northern Thailand is fused to Myanmar (Burma), Laos and southern China through the southeast-trending extension of the Himalayan mountain range known as the Dawna-Tenasserim. The tallest peak is Doi Inthanon (measured heights vary from 2565m to 2576m), which is topped by a mixed forest of hill evergreen and swamp species, including a thick carpet of moss. Monsoon forests comprise the lower elevations and are made up of deciduous trees, which are green and lush during the rainy season but dusty and leafless during the dry season. Teak is one of the most highly valued monsoon forest trees but it now exists only in limited quantities and is illegal to harvest.

The cool mountains of northern Thailand are considered to be some of the most accessible and rewarding birding destinations in Asia and are populated by montane species and migrants with clear Himalayan affinities, such as flycatchers and thrushes.

Central Thailand

In the central region the topography mellows into a flat rice basket, fed by rivers that are as revered as the national monarchy. Thailand's most exalted river is the Chao Phraya, which is formed by the northern tributaries of the Ping, Wang, Yom and Nan – a lineage as notable as any aristocrat's. The river delta spends most of the year in cultivation, changing with the seasons from fields of emerald-green rice shoots to golden harvests. This region has been heavily sculpted by civilisation: roads, fields, cities and towns have transformed the landscape into a working core.

In the western frontier, bumping into the mountainous border with Myanmar (Burma) is a complex of forest preserves that cover 4.4 million acres – the largest protected area in southeast Asia and a largely undisturbed habitat for endangered elephants and tigers. These parks have little in the way of tourist infrastructure or commercial development.

Environmental Trivia

- Thailand is equivalent in area to the size of France.
- Bangkok sits at about N14° latitude, level with Madras, Manila, Guatemala and Khartoum.
- The Mekong rivals the Amazon River in terms of biodiversity.
- Thailand is home to six types of venomous snakes, including the pit viper and the king cobra.
- Thailand's limestone formations are a soft sedimentary rock created by shells and coral from an ancient sea bed 250 to 300 million years ago.

Northeastern Thailand

The landscape of Thailand's northeastern region is occupied by the arid Khorat Plateau rising some 300m above the central plain. This is a hardscrabble land where the rains are meagre, the soil is anaemic and the red dust stains as stubbornly as the betel nut chewed by the ageing grandmothers. The dominant forest is dry dipterocarp, which consists of deciduous trees that shed their leaves in the dry season to conserve water. The region's largest forest preserve is Khao Yai National Park, which, together with nearby parks, has been recognised as a Unesco World Heritage Site. The park is mainly arid forest, a favourite of hornbills and over 300 other bird species. There is a small population of wild elephants in the park but development around the perimeter has impacted important wildlife corridors.

Mekong River

Defining the contours of Thailand's border with Laos is the Mekong River, southeast Asia's artery. The Mekong is a workhorse, having been dammed for hydroelectric power, and a mythmaker, featuring in local people's folktales and festivals. The river winds in and out of the steep mountain ranges to the northeastern plateau where it swells and contracts according to seasonal rainfall. In the dry season, riverside farmers plant vegetables in the muddy floodplain, harvesting the crop before the river reclaims its territory.

As the former Indochinese countries have become more open and accessible, scientists have begun to document the regions of the Mekong River and have identified it as having an impressive biodiversity. As many as 1000 previously unidentified species of flora and fauna have been discovered in the last decade in the Mekong region (which includes Vietnam, Laos and Cambodia).

Southern Thailand

The kingdom's eastern rivers dump their waters and sediment into the Gulf of Thailand, a shallow basin off the neighbouring South China Sea. In the joint of the fishhook-shaped gulf is Bangkok, surrounded by a thick industrial zone that has erased or polluted much of the natural environment. The extremities of the gulf, both to the east and to the south, are more characteristic of coastal environments: mangrove swamps form the transition between land and sea and act as the ocean's nursery, spawning and nurturing fish, bird and amphibian species. Thailand is home to nearly 75 species of these salt-tolerant trees that were once regarded as wastelands and vulnerable to coastal development.

The long slender 'trunk' of land that runs between the Gulf of Thailand and the Andaman Sea is often referred to as the Malay peninsula. This region is Thailand's most tropical: rainfall is plentiful, cultivating thick rainforests that stay green year-round. Malayan flora and fauna predominate and a scenic range of limestone mountains meanders from land to sea.

On the west coast, the Andaman Sea is an outcropping of the larger Indian Ocean and home to astonishing coral reefs that feed and shelter thousands of varieties of fish and act as breakwaters against tidal surges. Many of the coral-fringed islands are designated as marine national parks, limiting – to some degree – coastal development and boat traffic. The 2010 global coral bleaching phenomenon (in which El Niño weather conditions contributed to warmer sea temperatures) killed or damaged significant portions of Thailand's reefs.

Mekong River

National Parks & Protected Areas

With 15% of the kingdom's land and sea designated as park or sanctuary, Thailand has one of the highest percentages of protected areas of any Asian nation. There are over 100 national parks, plus over 1000 'nonhunting areas', wildlife sanctuaries, forest reserves, botanical gardens and arboretums.

Thailand began its conservation efforts in 1960 with the creation of a national system of wildlife sanctuaries under the Wild Animals Reservation and Protection Act, followed by the National Parks Act of 1961. Khao Yai National Park was the first wild area to receive this new status.

Despite promises, official designation as a national park or sanctuary does not guarantee protection from development or poaching. Local farmers, hunters and moneyed interests often circumvent conservation efforts. Enforcement of environmental regulations lacks political will and proper funding. Foreign visitors are often confused by Ko Chang, Ko Samet and Ko Phi-Phi's protected status despite their development as beach resorts. In some cases private ownership of land pre-dated the islands' protected status, while in other cases rules are bent for powerful people.

The Best... National Parks

1 Khao Yai National Park (p126)

2 Khao Sok National Park (p284)

3 Doi Inthanon National Park (p169)

4 Similan Islands Marine National Park (p288)

5 Ao Phang-Nga Marine National Park (p288)

Survival Guide

Buddhist monks

DOMINIC BONUCCELLI/LONELYPLANET IMAGES ©

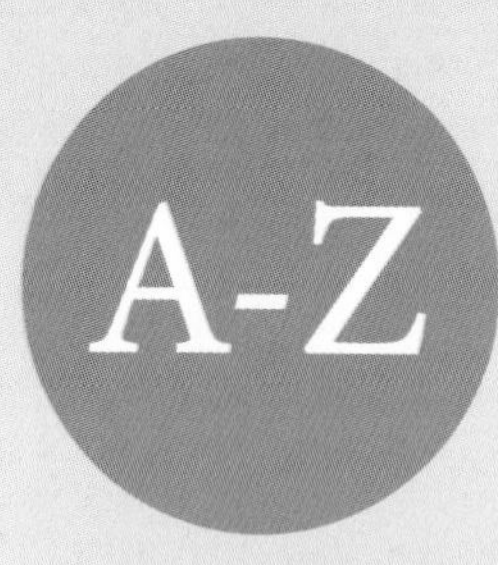

A-Z Directory

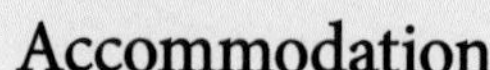

Accommodation

Thailand offers a wide variety of accommodation from cheap and basic to pricey and luxurious. Accommodation rates listed in this book are high-season prices. Icons are included to indicate internet access, wi-fi, swimming pools or air-con availability. If there isn't an air-con icon, assume that there's only a fan.

A two-tiered pricing system has been used in this book to determine budget category (budget, midrange, top end). In big cities and beach resorts, rates under 1000B are budget, under 3000B are midrange, with top end over 3000B. For small towns, rates under 600B are budget, under 1500B are midrange and top end over 1500B.

HOTELS

In provincial capitals and small towns, the only options are often older Thai-Chinese hotels, once the standard in all of Thailand. Most cater to Thai guests and English is usually limited.

In recent years, there has been a push to fill the budget gap for ageing backpackers or young affluent travellers who want the ambience of a guest house with the comforts of a hotel. Now in major tourist towns, 'flashpacker' hotels have dressed up the utilitarian options of the past with stylish decor and more creature comforts.

International chain hotels can be found in Bangkok, Chiang Mai, Phuket and other high-end beach resorts. Many of these upscale resorts incorporate traditional Thai architecture with modern minimalism.

Most top-end hotels and some midrange hotels add a 7% government tax (VAT) and an additional 10% service charge. The additional charges are often referred to as 'plus plus'. A buffet breakfast will often be included in the room rate. If the hotel offers Western breakfast, it is usually referred to as 'ABF', meaning 'American breakfast'.

Midrange and chain hotels, especially in major tourist destinations, can be booked in advance and some offer internet discounts through their websites or online agents. They also accept most credit cards, but only a few deluxe places accept American Express.

Business Hours

The following are standard hours for different types of businesses in Thailand. Reviews in this book list only variations from these standards. All government offices and banks are closed on public holidays.

Banks 9.30am to 3.30pm Monday to Friday; ATMs accessible 24 hours.

Bars 6pm to midnight (officially); closing times vary due to local enforcement of curfew laws; bars close during elections and certain religious public holidays.

Practicalities

- *Bangkok Post* and the *Nation* English-language news daily.
- There are more than 400 AM and FM radio stations; short-wave radios can pick up BBC, VOA, Radio Australia, Deutsche Welle and Radio France International.
- Six VHF TV networks carry Thai programming, plus TrueVision cable with international programming.
- The main video format is PAL.
- Thailand uses 220V AC electricity; power outlets most commonly feature two-prong round or flat sockets.
- Thailand follows the international metric system. Gold and silver are weighed in *bàat* (15g).

Book Your Stay Online

For more accommodation reviews by Lonely Planet authors, check out hotels.lonelyplanet.com/Thailand. You'll find independent reviews, as well as recommendations on the best places to stay. Best of all, you can book online.

Clubs (discos) 8pm to 2am; closing times vary due to local enforcement of curfew laws; clubs close during elections and certain religious public holidays.

Government offices 8.30am to 4.30pm Monday to Friday; some close for lunch (noon to 1pm), while others are open Saturday (9am to 3pm).

Live-music venues 6pm to 1am; closing times vary due to local enforcement of curfew laws; clubs close during elections and certain religious public holidays.

Restaurants 10am to 10pm; some shops specialise in morning meals and close by 3pm.

Stores Local stores: 10am to 6pm daily; department stores 10am to 8pm daily. In some small towns, local stores close on Sunday.

Customs Regulations

The **customs department** (www.customs.go.th) maintains a helpful website with specific information about customs regulations. The following items can be brought into the country duty free:

- a reasonable amount of personal effects (clothing and toiletries)
- professional instruments
- 200 cigarettes
- 1L of wine or spirits

Thailand prohibits the import of the following items:

- firearms and ammunition (unless registered in advance with the police department)
- illegal drugs
- pornographic media

When leaving Thailand, you must obtain an export licence for any antiques reproductions or newly cast Buddha images (except personal amulets). Submit two front-view photos of the object(s), a photocopy of your passport, along with the purchase receipt and the object(s) in question, to the **Department of Fine Arts** (☎ 0 2628 5032). Allow four days for the application and inspection process to be completed.

Climate

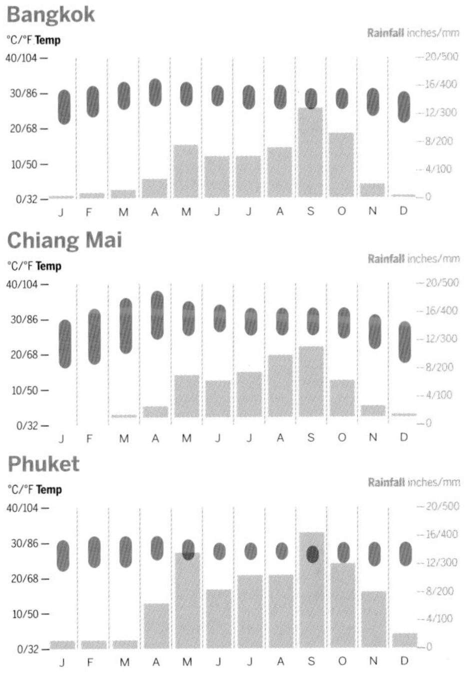

Bangkok

°C/°F Temp | Rainfall inches/mm

40/104 – 30/86 – 20/68 – 10/50 – 0/32 | 20/500 – 16/400 – 12/300 – 8/200 – 4/100 – 0

J F M A M J J A S O N D

Chiang Mai

°C/°F Temp | Rainfall inches/mm

40/104 – 30/86 – 20/68 – 10/50 – 0/32 | 20/500 – 16/400 – 12/300 – 8/200 – 4/100 – 0

J F M A M J J A S O N D

Phuket

°C/°F Temp | Rainfall inches/mm

40/104 – 30/86 – 20/68 – 10/50 – 0/32 | 20/500 – 16/400 – 12/300 – 8/200 – 4/100 – 0

J F M A M J J A S O N D

Electricity

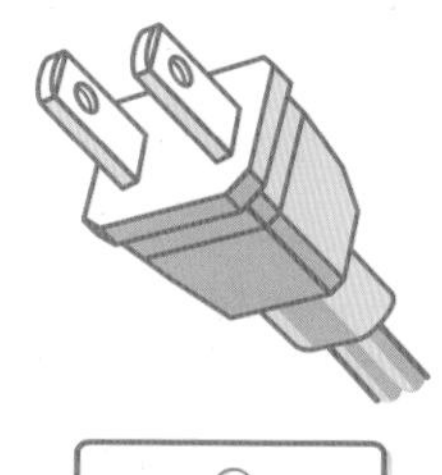

220V/50Hz

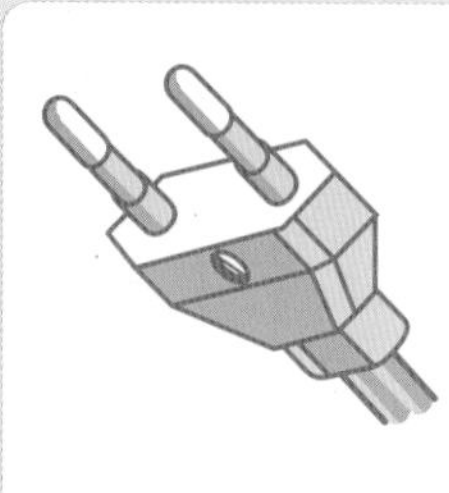

220V/50Hz

Embassies & Consulates

Foreign embassies are located in Bangkok; some nations also have consulates in Chiang Mai.

Australia (Map p84; ☎ 0 2344 6300; www.thailand.embassy.gov.au; 37 Th Sathon Tai, Bangkok)

Canada Bangkok (☎ 0 2636 0540; www.thailand.gc.ca; 15th fl, Abdulrahim Bldg, 990 Th Phra Ram IV); Chiang Mai Consulate (☎ 0 5385-0147; 151 Superhighway, Tambon Tahsala)

China Bangkok (☎ 0 2245 7044; www.chinaembassy.or.th; 57 Th Ratchadaphisek); Chiang Mai Consulate (☎ 0 5327 6125; 111 Th Chang Lor, Tambon Haiya)

Denmark (Map p84; ☎ 0 2343 1100; www.ambbangkok.um.dk; 10 Soi 1, Th Sathon Tai; Bangkok) Consulates in Phuket and Pattaya.

France (☎ 0 2657 5100; www.ambafrance-th.org; 35 Soi 36, Th Charoen Krung); Bangkok Visa & Culture Services (Map p84; ☎ 0 2627 2150; 29 Th Sathon Tai); Chiang Mai Consulate (☎ 0 5328 1466; 138 Th Charoen Prathet) Consulates also in Phuket & Surat Thani.

Germany (Map p84; ☎ 0 2287 9000; www.bangkok.diplo.de; 9 Th Sathon Tai, Bangkok)

India (Map p80; ☎ 0 2258 0300-6; indianembassy.in.th; 46 Soi Prasanmit/Soi 23, Th Sukhumvit); Bangkok Visa Application Centre (☎ 02 6652 9681; www.ivac-th.com; Glass Haus Bldg, 15th fl, suite 1503, Th Sukhumvit); Chiang Mai Consulate (☎ 0 5324 3066; 33/1 Th Thung Hotel, Wat Gate)

Ireland (Map p84; ☎ 0 2677 7500; www.irelandinthailand.com; 28th fl, Q House, Th Sathon Tai, Bangkok) Consulate only; the nearest Irish embassy is in Kuala Lumpur.

Israel (Map p80; ☎ 0 2204 9200; bangkok.mfa.gov.il; Ocean Tower 2, 25th fl, 25 Soi 19, Th Sukhumvit, Bangkok)

Japan Bangkok (Map p84; ☎ 0 2207 8500; www.th.emb-japan.go.jp; 177 Th Withayu/Wireless Rd); Chiang Mai Consulate (☎ 0 5320 3367; 104-107 Airport Business Park, Th Mahidon)

Netherlands (Map p72; ☎ 0 2309 5200; www.netherlandsembassy.in.th; 15 Soi Tonson, Th Ploenchit, Bangkok)

New Zealand (Map p72; ☎ 0 2254 2530; www.nzembassy.com; 14th fl, M Thai Tower, All Seasons Pl, 87 Th Withayu, Bangkok)

Philippines (Map p80; ☎ 0 2259 0139; www.philembassy-bangkok.net; 760 Th Sukhumvit, Bangkok)

Russia (Map p76; ☎ 0 2234 9824 www.thailand.mid.ru; 78 Soi Sap, Th Surawong) Consulates in Pattaya and Phuket.

Singapore (Map p76; ☎ 0 2286 2111; www.mfa.gov.sg/bangkok; 129 Th Sathon Tai, Bangkok)

South Africa (Map p84; ☎ 0 2659 2900; www.saembbangkok.com; 12A fl, M Thai Tower, All Seasons Place, 87 Th Withayu)

Spain (Map p80; ☎ 0 2661 8284; es.embassyinformation.com; 23 fl, Lake Ratchada Office Complex, 193 Th Ratchadaphisek)

Switzerland (Map p72; ☎ 0 2674 6900; www.eda.admin.ch/bangkok; 35 Th Withayu)

UK Bangkok (Map p72; ☎ 0 2305 8333; ukinthailand.fco.gov.uk; 14 Th Withayu/Wireless Rd); Chiang Mai Consulate (☎ 0 5326 3015; British Council, 198 Th Bamrungrat) Consulate also in Pattaya.

US Bangkok (Map p72; ☎ 0 2205 4049; http://bangkok.usembassy.gov; 95 Th Withayu); Chiang Mai Consulate (☎ 0 5310 7777; 387 Th Wichayanon)

Gay & Lesbian Travellers

Thai culture is relatively tolerant of both male and female homosexuality. There is a fairly prominent gay and lesbian scene in Bangkok, Pattaya and Phuket. With regard to dress or mannerism, lesbians and gays are generally accepted without comment. However, public displays of affection – whether heterosexual or homosexual – are frowned upon. **Utopia** (www.utopia-asia.com) posts lots of Thailand information for gay and lesbian visitors and publishes a guidebook to the kingdom for homosexuals.

Health

Dr Trish Batchelor

The majority of major cities and popular tourist areas are well developed with adequate and sometimes excellent medical care.

Travellers tend to worry about contracting exotic infectious diseases when visiting the tropics, but such infections are far less common than problems with pre-existing medical conditions such as heart disease, and accidental injury (especially as a result of traffic accidents).

The following advice is a general guide and does not replace the advice of a doctor trained in travel medicine.

BEFORE YOU GO

Pack medications in clearly labelled original containers and obtain a signed and dated letter from your physician describing your medical conditions, medications and syringes or needles.

If you take any regular medication bring double your needs in case of loss or theft. In Thailand you can buy many medications over the counter without a doctor's prescription, but it can be difficult to find the exact medication you are taking.

INSURANCE

Even if you're fit and healthy, don't travel without health insurance – accidents *do* happen. You may require extra cover for adventure activities such as rock climbing or diving, as well as scooter/motorcycle riding. If your health insurance doesn't cover you for medical expenses abroad, ensure you get specific travel insurance. Most hospitals require an upfront guarantee of payment (from yourself or your insurer) prior to admission. Inquire before your trip about payment of medical charges and retain all documentation (medical reports, invoices etc) for claim purposes.

VACCINATIONS

Specialised travel-medicine clinics are your best source of information on which vaccinations you should consider taking. Ideally you should visit a doctor six to eight weeks before departure, but it is never too late. Ask your doctor for an International Certificate of Vaccination (otherwise known as the yellow booklet), which will list all the vaccinations you've received. The **Centers for Disease Control** (CDC; www.cdc.gov) has a traveller's health section that contains recommendations for vaccinations. The only vaccine required by international regulations is yellow fever.

MEDICAL CHECKLIST

Recommended items for a personal medical kit include:

- antifungal cream, eg Clotrimazole
- antibacterial cream, eg Muciprocin
- antibiotic for skin infections, eg Amoxicillin/Clavulanate or Cephalexin
- antibiotics for bacterial diarrhoea, eg Norfloxacin, Ciprofloxacin or Azithromycin; for giardiasis or amoebic dysentery take Tinidazole
- antihistamine – eg Cetrizine for daytime and Promethazine for night
- antiseptic, eg Betadine
- antispasmodic for stomach cramps, eg Buscopan
- contraceptives
- decongestant

- DEET-based insect repellent
- oral rehydration solution for diarrhoea (eg Gastrolyte), diarrhoea 'stopper' (eg Loperamide) and antinausea medication (eg Prochlorperazine)
- first-aid items such as scissors, Elastoplasts, bandages, gauze, thermometer (but not one with mercury), sterile needles and syringes (with a doctor's letter), safety pins and tweezers
- hand gel (alcohol based) or alcohol-based hand wipes
- ibuprofen or another anti-inflammatory
- indigestion medication, eg Quick Eze or Mylanta
- laxative, eg Coloxyl
- migraine medicine – for migraine suffers
- paracetamol
- Permethrin to impregnate clothing and mosquito nets if at high risk
- steroid cream for allergic/itchy rashes, eg 1% to 2% hydrocortisone
- sunscreen, hat and sunglasses
- throat lozenges
- thrush (vaginal yeast infection) treatment, eg Clotrimazole pessaries or Diflucan tablet
- Ural or equivalent if you are prone to urine infections

IN THAILAND

AVAILABILITY & COST OF HEALTH CARE

Bangkok is considered the nearest centre of medical excellence for many countries in Southeast Asia. Private hospitals are more expensive than other medical facilities but offer a superior standard of care and English-speaking staff. Such facilities are listed throughout this book. The cost of health care is relatively cheap in Thailand compared to most Western countries.

Self-treatment may be appropriate if your problem is minor (eg traveller's diarrhoea), you are carrying the appropriate medication and you are unable to attend a recommended clinic or hospital.

Buying medication over the counter is not recommended, because fake medications and poorly stored or out-of-date drugs are common.

INFECTIOUS DISEASES

DENGUE FEVER

This mosquito-borne disease is increasingly problematic throughout Southeast Asia, especially in the cities. As there is no vaccine it can only be prevented by avoiding mosquito bites. The mosquito that carries dengue is a daytime biter, so use insect-avoidance measures at all times. Symptoms include high fever, severe headache (especially behind the eyes), nausea and body aches (dengue was previously known as 'breakbone fever'). Some people develop a rash (which can be very itchy) and experience diarrhoea. The southern islands of Thailand are particularly high-risk areas. There is no specific treatment, just rest and paracetamol – do not take aspirin or ibuprofen as they increase the risk of haemorrhaging. See a doctor to be diagnosed and monitored.

HIV

HIV is now one of the most common causes of death in people under the age of 50 in Thailand. Always practice safe

Further Resources

- **International Travel & Health** (www.who.int/ith) Health guide published by the World Health Organization (WHO).
- **Centers for Disease Control & Prevention** (www.cdc.gov) Country-specific advice.
- **Healthy Travel: Asia & India** Lonely Planet's guide includes pre-trip planning, emergency first aid, and immunisation and disease information.
- **Traveller's Health: How to Stay Healthy Abroad** (by Dr Richard Dawood) Considered the 'health bible' for international holidays.
- **Travelling Well** (by Dr Deborah Mills) Health guidebook and website (www.travellingwell.com.au).
- **Healthy Living in Thailand** (published by the Thai Red Cross) Recommended for long-term travellers.

sex, avoid getting tattoos or using unclean syringes.

MALARIA

There is an enormous amount of misinformation concerning malaria. Malaria is caused by a parasite transmitted by the bite of an infected mosquito. The most important symptom of malaria is fever, but general symptoms such as headache, diarrhoea, cough or chills may also occur – the same symptoms as many other infections. A diagnosis can only be made by taking a blood sample.

Most parts of Thailand visited by tourists, particularly city and resort areas, have minimal to no risk of malaria, and the risk of side effects from taking antimalarial tablets is likely to outweigh the risk of getting the disease itself. If you are travelling to high-risk rural areas (unlikely for most visitors), seek medical advice on the right medication and dosage for you.

Travellers are advised to prevent mosquito bites by taking these steps:

- use a DEET-containing insect repellent on exposed skin; natural repellents such as citronella can be effective, but must be repeatedly applied
- sleep under a mosquito net, ideally impregnated with Permethrin
- choose accommodation with screens and fans
- impregnate clothing with Permethrin in high-risk areas
- wear long sleeves and trousers in light colours
- use mosquito coils
- spray your room with insect repellent before going out for your evening meal

RABIES

This uniformly fatal disease is spread by the bite or lick of an infected animal – most commonly a dog or monkey. You should seek medical advice immediately after any animal bite and commence post-exposure treatment. Having a pre-travel vaccination means the post-bite treatment is greatly simplified.

TYPHOID

This serious bacterial infection is spread through food and water. It gives a high and slowly progressive fever, severe headache, and may be accompanied by a dry cough and stomach pain. It is diagnosed by blood tests and treated with antibiotics. Vaccination is recommended for all travellers spending more than a week in Thailand, or travelling outside of the major cities. Be aware that vaccination is not 100% effective so you must still be careful with what you eat and drink.

TRAVELLER'S DIARRHOEA

Traveller's diarrhoea is by far the most common problem affecting travellers – up to 50% of people will suffer from some form of it within two weeks of starting their trip. In over 80% of cases, traveller's diarrhoea is caused by a bacteria (there are numerous potential culprits), and responds promptly to treatment with antibiotics.

Here we define traveller's diarrhoea as the passage of more than three watery bowel movements within 24 hours, plus at least one other symptom such as vomiting, fever, cramps, nausea or feeling generally unwell.

Treatment consists of staying well hydrated; rehydration solutions such as Gastrolyte are the best for this. Antibiotics such as Norfloxacin, Ciprofloxacin or Azithromycin will kill the bacteria quickly.

Giardia lamblia is a parasite that is relatively common in travellers. Symptoms include nausea, bloating, excess gas, fatigue and intermittent diarrhoea. 'Eggy' burps are often attributed solely to giardiasis. The treatment of choice is Tinidazole, with Metronidazole being a second-line option.

ENVIRONMENTAL HAZARDS

FOOD

Eating in restaurants is the biggest risk factor for contracting traveller's diarrhoea. Ways to avoid it include eating only freshly cooked food, and avoiding food that has been sitting around in buffets.

HEAT

Many parts of Thailand are hot and humid throughout the year. For most people it takes at least two weeks to adapt to the hot climate. Prevent swelling of the feet and ankles as well as muscle cramps caused by excessive sweating by avoiding dehydration and excessive activity in the hot hours of the day.

Heat stroke is a serious medical emergency and requires immediate medical treatment. Symptoms come on suddenly and include weakness, nausea, a hot dry body with a body temperature of over 41°C, dizziness, confusion, loss of coordination, fits and eventually collapse and loss of consciousness.

INSECT BITES & STINGS

Bedbugs live in the cracks of furniture and walls and then migrate to the bed at night to feed on you. You can treat the itch with an antihistamine.

Leeches are found in humid rainforest areas. They do not transmit any disease but their bites are often intensely itchy for weeks afterwards and can easily become infected. Apply an iodine-based antiseptic to any leech bite to help prevent infection.

SKIN PROBLEMS

Prickly heat is a common skin rash in the tropics, caused by sweat being trapped under the skin. Treat it by taking cool showers and using powders.

Cuts and scratches become easily infected in humid climates. Immediately wash all wounds in clean water and apply antiseptic. If you develop signs of infection, see a doctor. Coral cuts can easily become infected.

SUNBURN

Even on a cloudy day sunburn can occur rapidly. Use a strong sunscreen (at least factor 30), making sure to re-apply after a swim, and always wear a wide-brimmed hat and sunglasses outdoors.

TRAVELLING WITH CHILDREN

Thailand is relatively safe for children from a health point of view. It is wise to consult a doctor who specialises in travel medicine prior to travel to ensure your child is appropriately prepared. A medical kit designed specifically for children includes paracetamol or Tylenol syrup for fevers, an antihistamine, itch cream, first-aid supplies, nappy-rash treatment, sunscreen and insect repellent.

WOMEN'S HEALTH

Pregnant women should receive specialised advice before travelling. The ideal time to travel is in the second trimester (16 and 28 weeks), when pregnancy-related risks are at their lowest. Avoid rural travel in areas with poor transportation and medical facilities. Most of all, ensure travel insurance covers all pregnancy-related possibilities, including premature labour.

In Thailand's urban areas, supplies of sanitary products are readily available. Your personal birth-control option may not be available so bring adequate supplies. Heat, humidity and antibiotics can all contribute to thrush. Treatment of thrush is with antifungal creams and pessaries such as Clotrimazole. A practical alternative is one tablet of fluconazole (Diflucan). Urinary-tract infections can be precipitated by dehydration or long bus journeys without toilet stops; bring suitable antibiotics.

Jellyfish Stings

Box jellyfish stings range from minor to deadly. A good rule of thumb, however, is to presume a box jelly is dangerous until proven otherwise.

There are many other jellyfish in Thailand that cause irritating stings but no serious effects. The only way to prevent these stings is to wear protective clothing, which provides a barrier between human skin and the jellyfish.

Thanks to Dr Peter Fenner for the inform4ation in this boxed text.

Holidays

Government offices and banks close on the following days.

1 January New Year's Day

February (date varies) Makha Bucha Day, Buddhist holy day

6 April Chakri Day, commemorating the founder of the Chakri dynasty, Rama I

13–14 April Songkran Festival, traditional Thai New Year and water festival

5 May Coronation Day, commemorating the 1946 coronation of HM the King and HM the Queen

1 May Labour Day

May/June (date varies) Visakha Bucha, Buddhist holy day

July (date varies) Asarnha Bucha, Buddhist holy day

12 August Queen's Birthday

23 October Chulalongkorn Day

October/November (date varies) Ork Phansaa, the end of Buddhist 'lent'

5 December King's Birthday

10 December Constitution Day

31 December New Year's Eve

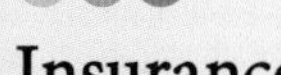

Insurance

A travel-insurance policy to cover theft, loss and medical problems is a good idea. Policies offer differing medical-expense options. There is a wide variety of policies available, so check the small print. Be sure that the policy covers ambulances or an emergency flight home.

Some policies specifically exclude 'dangerous activities', which can include scuba diving, motorcycling or even trekking. A locally acquired motorcycle licence is not valid under some policies.

Worldwide travel insurance is available at www.lonelyplanet.com/travel_services. You can buy, extend and claim online anytime – even if you're already on the road.

Internet Access

You'll find plenty of internet cafes just about everywhere. The going rate is anywhere from 40B to 120B an hour, depending on how much competition there is. Connections tend to be pretty fast and the machines are usually well maintained. Wireless access (wi-fi) is usually available in most hotels and guest houses though staff aren't adept at fixing downed services. Wi-fi signal strength deteriorates in the upper floors of a multistorey building so check to see if your floor has a nearby router.

Legal Matters

In general, Thai police don't hassle foreigners, especially tourists. One major exception is drugs, which most Thai police view as either a social scourge against which it's their duty to enforce the letter of the law, or an opportunity to make untaxed income via bribes.

If you are arrested for any offence, the police will allow you the opportunity to make a phone call to your embassy or consulate in Thailand, if you have one, or to a friend or relative if not. There's a whole set of legal codes governing the length of time and manner in which you can be detained before being charged or put on trial, but a lot of discretion is left to the police. In the case of foreigners, the police are more likely to bend these codes in your favour. However, as with police worldwide, if you don't show respect you will make matters worse.

Thai law does not presume an indicted detainee to be either 'guilty' or 'innocent' but rather a 'suspect', whose guilt or innocence will be decided in court. Trials are usually speedy.

The **tourist police** (☎ 1155) can be very helpful in cases of arrest. Although they typically have no jurisdiction over the kinds of cases handled by regular cops, they may be able to help with translations or with contacting your embassy. You can call the hotline number 24 hours a day to lodge complaints or to request assistance with regards to personal safety.

Money

The basic unit of Thai currency is the baht. There are 100 satang in one baht; coins include 25-satang and 50-satang pieces and baht in 1B, 2B, 5B and 10B coins. Older coins have Thai numerals only, while newer coins have Thai and Arabic numerals. The 2B coin is similar in size to the 1B coin but it is gold in colour.

Paper currency is issued in the following denominations: 20B (green), 50B (blue), 100B (red), 500B (purple) and 1000B (beige).

ATMS & CREDIT/ DEBIT CARDS

Debit and ATM cards issued by a bank in your own country can be used at ATMs around Thailand to withdraw cash (in Thai baht only) directly from your account back home. ATMs are widespread throughout the country and can be relied on for the bulk of your spending cash.

Thai ATMs now charge a 150B foreign-transaction fee on top of whatever currency conversion and out-of-network fees your home bank charges.

Credit cards as well as debit cards can be used for purchases at some shops, hotels and restaurants. The most commonly accepted cards are Visa and MasterCard. American Express is typically only accepted at high-end hotels and restaurants.

To report a lost or stolen credit/debit card, call the following hotlines in Bangkok:

American Express (☎ 0 2273 5544)

MasterCard (☎ 001 800 11887 0663)

Visa (☎ 001 800 441 3485)

CHANGING MONEY

Banks or the rarer private moneychangers offer the best foreign-exchange rates. When buying baht, US dollars are the most accepted currency, followed by British pounds and euros. Most banks charge a commission and duty for each travellers cheque cashed.

FOREIGN EXCHANGE

As of 2008, visitors must declare if they are arriving or departing with an excess of US$20,000. There are also certain monetary requirements for foreigners entering Thailand; demonstration of adequate funds varies per visa type but typically does not exceed a traveller's estimated trip budget. Rarely will you be asked to produce such financial evidence, but be aware that such laws do exist. The **Ministry of Foreign Affairs** (www.mfa.go.th) can provide more detailed information.

It's legal to open a foreign-currency account at any commercial bank in Thailand. As long as the funds originate from out of the country, there aren't any restrictions on maintenance or withdrawal.

TIPPING

Tipping is not generally expected in Thailand. The exception is loose change from a large restaurant bill; if a meal costs 488B and you pay with a 500B note, some Thais will leave the 12B change. It's not so much a tip as a way of saying 'I'm not so money grubbing as to grab every last baht'.

At many hotel restaurants or other upmarket eateries, a 10% service charge will be added to your bill. When this is the case, tipping is not expected. Bangkok has adopted some standards of tipping, especially in restaurants frequented by foreigners.

Safe Travel

Although Thailand is not a dangerous country to visit, it is smart to exercise caution, especially when it comes to dealing with strangers (both Thai and foreigners) and travelling alone.

ASSAULT

Assault of travellers is rare in Thailand, but it does happen. Causing a Thai to 'lose face' (feel public embarrassment or humiliation) can sometimes elicit an inexplicably strong and violent reaction. Oftentimes alcohol is the number one contributor to bad choices and worse outcomes.

DRUGGINGS & DRUG POSSESSION

It is illegal to buy, sell or possess opium, heroin, amphetamines, hallucinogenic mushrooms and marijuana in Thailand. Belying Thailand's anything-goes atmosphere are severe punishments for possession and trafficking that are not relaxed for foreigners. Possession of drugs can result in at least one year of prison time. Drug smuggling – defined as attempting to cross a border with drugs in your possession – carries considerably higher penalties, including execution.

SCAMS

Thais can be so friendly and laid-back that some visitors are lulled into a false sense of security, making them vulnerable to scams of all kinds. Bangkok is especially good at long-involved frauds that dupe travellers into thinking that they've made a friend and are getting a bargain on highly valuable gem stones (which are actually pretty, sparkling glass).

Follow TAT's number-one suggestion to tourists: *Disregard all offers of free shopping or sightseeing help from strangers*. These invariably take a commission from your purchases. See the boxed text, p86, for more information.

THEFT & FRAUD

Exercise diligence when it comes to your personal belongings. Ensure that your room is securely locked and carry your most important effects (passport, money, credit cards) on your person. Take care when leaving valuables in hotel safes.

Follow the same practice when you're travelling. A locked bag will not prevent theft on a long-haul bus.

When using a credit card, don't let vendors take your credit card out of your sight to run it through the machine. Unscrupulous merchants have been known to rub off three or four or more receipts with one purchase.

To avoid losing all of your travel money in an instant, use a credit card that is not directly linked to your bank account back home so that the operator doesn't have access to immediate funds.

Contact the **tourist police** (☎1155) if you have any problems with consumer fraud.

TOUTS & COMMISSIONS

Touting is a longtime tradition in Asia, and while Thailand doesn't have as many touts as, say, India, it has its share. In Bangkok, túk-túk drivers, hotel employees and bar girls often take new arrivals on city tours; these almost always end up in high-pressure sales situations at silk, jewellery or handicraft shops.

Touts also steer customers to certain guest houses that pay a commission. Travel agencies are notorious for talking newly arrived tourists into staying at badly located, overpriced hotels.

Some travel agencies often masquerade as TAT, the government-funded tourist information office. Be aware that the official TAT offices do not make hotel or transport bookings.

When making transport arrangements, talk to several travel agencies to look for the best price, as the commission percentage varies greatly between agents.

Telephone

The telephone country code for Thailand is ☎66 and is used when calling the country from abroad. All Thai telephone numbers are preceded by a '0' if you're dialling domestically (the '0' is omitted when calling from overseas). After the initial '0', the next three numbers represent the provincial area code. If the initial '0' is followed by an '8', then you're dialling a mobile phone.

INTERNATIONAL CALLS

If you want to call an international number from a telephone in Thailand, you must first dial an international access code plus the country code followed by the subscriber number.

In Thailand, there are various international access codes charging different rates per minute. The standard direct-dial prefix is ☎001; it is operated by **CAT** (www.cthai.com) and is considered to have the best sound quality; it connects to the largest number of countries but is also the most expensive. The next best is ☎007, a prefix operated by TOT with reliable quality and slightly cheaper rates. Economy rates are available with ☎007, ☎008 and ☎009; all of which use Voice over Internet Protocol (VoIP), with varying but adequate sound quality.

The following are some common international country codes: ☎61 Australia, ☎44 UK and ☎1 US.

Many expats use **DeeDial** (www.deedial.com), a direct-dial service that requires a prepaid account managed through the internet. The cheapest service they offer is the 'ring-back' feature, which circumvents local charges on your phone.

There are also a variety of international phonecards available through CAT offering promotional rates less than 1B per minute.

PHONES

The easiest phone option in Thailand is to acquire a mobile phone equipped with a local SIM card.

Thailand is on the GSM network and mobile phone providers include AIS, DTAC and True Move.

You have two hand-phone options: you can buy a mobile phone in Thailand at one of the urban shopping malls or phone stores near the markets in provincial towns. Or you can use an imported phone that isn't SIM-locked (and one that supports the GSM network). SIM cards and refill cards (usually sold in 300B to

500B denominations) can be bought from 7-Elevens throughout the country.

There are various promotions but rates typically hover at around 1B to 2B per minute anywhere in Thailand and between 5B and 9B for international calls. SMS is usually 3B per message, making it the cheapest 'talk' option.

Mobile Broadband

Thailand's telecommunications companies and state-owned agencies have been wrangling over the 3G (mobile broadband platform) for so many years that the new-generation technology has since been surpassed by 4G. Thailand is the only Asean country not to have the service despite a huge number of smartphone users. In 2010 and 2011, contracts to operate the services were awarded and then suspended by the courts, approval to import equipment has been delayed and now it looks like 2012 might be the year of 3G, maybe.

Time

Thailand's time zone is seven hours ahead of GMT/UTC (London). At government offices and local cinemas, times are often expressed according to the 24-hour clock, e.g. 11pm is written '23.00'.

Toilets

Increasingly, the Asian-style squat toilet is less of the norm in Thailand. There are still specimens in rural places, provincial bus stations, older homes and modest restaurants, but the Western-style toilet is becoming more prevalent and appears wherever foreign tourists can be found.

If you encounter a squat, here's what you should know. You should straddle the two footpads and face the door. To flush, use the plastic bowl to scoop water out of the adjacent basin and pour into the toilet bowl. Some places supply a small pack of toilet paper at the entrance (5B), otherwise bring your own stash or wipe the old-fashioned way with water.

Even in places where sit-down toilets are installed, the septic system may not be designed to take toilet paper. In such cases there will be a waste basket where you're supposed to place used toilet paper and feminine hygiene products. Some modern toilets also come with a small spray hose – Thailand's version of the bidet.

Tourist Information

The government-operated tourist information and promotion service, **Tourism Authority of Thailand** (TAT; www.tourismthailand.org), was founded in 1960 and produces excellent pamphlets on sightseeing, accommodation and transport. Check the destination chapters for the TAT office in the towns you're planning to visit.

The following are a few of TAT's overseas information offices; check TAT's website for contact information in Hong Kong, Taipei, Seoul, Tokyo, Osaka, Fukuoka, Stockholm and Rome.

Australia (☎ 02 9247 7549; www.thailand.net.au; Level 2, 75 Pitt St, Sydney, NSW 2000)

France (☎ 01 53 53 47 00; 90 Ave des Champs Élysées, 75008 Paris)

Germany (☎ 069 138 1390; www.thailandtourismus.de; Bethmannstrasse 58, D-60311, Frankfurt/Main)

Malaysia (☎ 603 216 23480; www.thaitourism.com.my; Suite 22.01, Level 22, Menara Lion, 165 Jalan Ampang, Kuala Lumpur, 50450)

Singapore (☎ 65 6235 7901; c/o Royal Thai Embassy, 370 Orchard Rd, 238870)

UK (☎ 020 7925 2511; www.tourismthailand.co.uk; 3rd fl, Brook House, 98-99 Jermyn St, London SW1Y 6EE)

USA (☎ 323 461 9814; 1st fl, 611 North Larchmont Blvd, Los Angeles, CA 90004)

Travellers with Disabilities

Thailand presents one large, ongoing obstacle course for the mobility impaired. With its high curbs, uneven footpaths and nonstop traffic, Bangkok can be particularly difficult. Many streets must be crossed via pedestrian bridges flanked with steep stairways, while buses and boats don't stop long enough even for the fully abled. Rarely are there any ramps or other access points for wheelchairs.

A number of more expensive top-end hotels make consistent design efforts to provide disabled access to their properties. Other deluxe hotels with high employee-to-guest ratios are usually good about accommodating the mobility impaired by providing staff help where building design fails. For the rest, you're pretty much left to your own resources.

Counter to the prevailing trends, **Worldwide Dive & Sail** (www.worldwidediveandsail.com) offers live-aboard diving programs for the deaf and hard of hearing.

Some organisations and publications that offer tips on international travel include the following.

Accessible Journeys (www.disabilitytravel.com)

Mobility International USA (www.miusa.org)

Society for Accessible Travel & Hospitality (www.sath.org)

Visas

The **Ministry of Foreign Affairs** (www.mfa.go.th) oversees immigration and visas issues. Check the website or the nearest Thai embassy or consulate for application procedures and costs.

Thailand's Immigration Offices

The following are two common immigration offices where visa extensions and other formalities can be addressed. Remember to dress in your Sunday best when doing official business in Thailand and do all visa business yourself (don't hire a third party). For all types of visa extensions, bring along two passport-sized photos and one copy each of the photo and visa pages of your passport.

- **Bangkok immigration office** (Map p84; ☎0 2287 3101; Soi Suan Phlu, Th Sathon Tai; ⏲9am-noon & 1-4.30pm Mon-Fri, 9am-noon Sat)
- **Chiang Mai immigration office** (Map p146; ☎0 5320 1755-6; Th Mahidon; ⏲8.30am-4.30pm Mon-Fri)

TOURIST VISAS & EXEMPTIONS

The Thai government allows tourist-visa exemptions for 41 different nationalities, including those from Australia, New Zealand, the USA and most of Europe, to enter the country without a prearranged visa.

For those arriving in the kingdom by air, a 30-day visa is issued without a fee. For those arriving via a land border, the arrival visa is 15 days.

Without proof of an onward ticket and sufficient funds for one's projected stay, any visitor can be denied entry, but in practice this is a formality that is rarely checked.

VISA EXTENSIONS & RENEWALS

If you decide you want to stay longer than the allotted time, you can extend your visa by applying at any immigration office in Thailand. The usual fee for a visa extension is 1900B. Those issued with a standard stay of 15 or 30 days can extend their stay for seven to 10 days (depending on the immigration office) if the extension is handled before the visa expires. The 60-day tourist visa can be extended by up to 30 days at the discretion of Thai immigration authorities.

Another visa-renewal option is to cross a land border. A new 15-day visa will be issued upon your return and some short-term visitors make a day trip out of the 'visa run'. See the destination chapters for land border information and border formalities.

If you overstay your visa, the usual penalty is a fine of 500B per day, with a 20,000B limit. Fines can be paid at the airport or in advance at an immigration office. If you've overstayed only one day, you don't have to pay. Children under 14 travelling with a parent do not have to pay the penalty

Women Travellers

Women face relatively few problems in Thailand. With the great amount of respect afforded to women, an equal measure should be returned.

Thai women, especially the younger generation, are showing more skin than in the recent past. That means almost everyone is now dressing like a bar girl and you can wear spaghetti strap tops and navel-bearing shirts (if only they were still trendy) without offending Thais' modesty streak. But to be on the safe side, cover up if you're going deep into rural communities.

Attacks and rapes are not common in Thailand, but incidents do occur, especially when an attacker observes a vulnerable target: a drunk or solo woman. If you return home from a bar alone, be sure to have your wits about you. Avoid accepting rides from strangers late at night or travelling around in isolated areas by yourself – common sense stuff that might escape your notice in a new environment filled with hospitable people.

Transport

Getting There & Away

Flights, tours and rail tickets can be booked online at www.lonelyplanet.com/bookings.

ENTERING THE COUNTRY

Entry procedures for Thailand, by air or by land, are straightforward: you'll have to show your passport (see p369 for information about visa requirements); and you'll need to present completed arrival and departure cards. Blank arrival and departure cards are usually distributed on the incoming flight or, if arriving by land, can be picked up at the immigration counter.

You do not have to fill in a customs form on arrival unless you have imported goods to declare. In that case, you can get the proper form from Thai customs officials at your point of entry. See p359 for Thai customs information about minimum funds requirements.

AIR

AIRPORTS

Bangkok is Thailand's primary international and domestic gateway. There are also smaller airports throughout the country serving domestic and sometimes inter-regional routes.

Suvarnabhumi International Airport (BKK; ☎ 0 2132 1888) Receives nearly all international flights and most domestic flights. It is located in Samut Prakan, 30km east of Bangkok and 110km from Pattaya. The airport name is pronounced *sù·wan·ná·poom.*

Don Muang Airport (DMK; ☎ 0 2535 1111) Bangkok's second airport is still used for domestic flights operated by Nok Air and Orient Thai (formerly One-Two-Go). Be aware of this when booking connecting flights on these airlines.

Phuket International Airport (HKT; ☎ 0 7632 7230) International Asian destinations include Hong Kong, Singapore and Bali on Air Asia. Direct charter flights from Europe are also available.

Chiang Mai International Airport (CNX; **www.chiangmaiairportonline.com**) International Asian destinations include Kuala Lumpur, Taipei and Singapore.

TICKETS

In some cases – when travelling to neighbouring countries or to domestic destinations –

it is still convenient to use a travel agent in Thailand. The amount of commission an agent will charge often varies so shop around to gauge the discrepancy in prices. Paying by credit card generally offers protection, because most card issuers provide refunds if you can prove you didn't get what you paid for. Agents who accept only cash should hand over the tickets straightaway and not tell you to 'come back tomorrow'. After you've made a booking or paid your deposit, call the airline and confirm that the booking was made.

Air fares during the high season (December to March) can be expensive.

Getting Around

AIR

Hopping around the country by air continues to be affordable. Most routes originate from Bangkok, but Chiang Mai, Ko Samui and Phuket all have a few routes to other Thai towns.

BOAT

The true Thai river transport is the *reu·a hăhng yow* (long-tail boat), so-called because the propeller is mounted at the end of a long drive shaft extending from the engine.

Between the mainland and islands in the Gulf of Thailand or the Andaman Sea, the standard craft is a wooden boat, 8m to 10m long, with an inboard engine, a wheelhouse and a simple roof to shelter passengers and cargo. Faster, more expensive hovercraft or jetfoils are available in tourist areas.

BUS & MINIVAN

The bus network in Thailand is prolific and reliable, and is a great way to see the countryside and sit among the locals. The Thai government subsidises the Transport Company *(bò·rí·sàt kŏn sòng)*, usually abbreviated to Baw Khaw Saw (BKS).

By far the most reliable bus companies in Thailand are the ones that operate out of the government-run BKS stations. In some cases the companies are entirely state owned, in others they are private concessions.

Increasingly though, minivans are the middle-class option. Minivans are run by private companies and because their vehicles are smaller they can depart from the market (instead of the out-of-town bus stations) and will deliver guests directly to their hotel. Just don't sit in the front so you don't see the driver's daredevil techniques!

RESERVATIONS

You can book air-con BKS buses at any BKS terminal. Privately run buses can be booked through most hotels or any travel agency, but it's best to book directly through a bus office to be sure that you get what you pay for.

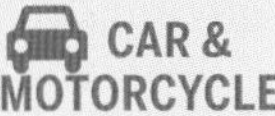

CAR & MOTORCYCLE

DRIVING LICENCE

Short-term visitors who wish to drive vehicles (including motorcycles) in Thailand need an International Driving Permit.

FUEL & SPARE PARTS

Modern petrol (gasoline) stations are in plentiful supply all over Thailand wherever there are paved roads. In more-remote, off-road areas *ben·sin/nám·man rót yon* (petrol containing benzene) is usually available at small roadside or village stands. All fuel in Thailand is unleaded, and diesel is used by trucks and some passenger cars. In 2007, Thailand introduced several alternative fuels, including gasohol (a blend of petrol and ethanol that comes in different octane levels, either 91% or 95%) and compressed natural gas, used by taxis with bifuel capabilities.

HIRE & PURCHASE

Cars, 4WDs and vans can be rented in most major cities and airports from local companies as well as international chains. Local companies tend to have cheaper rates than the international chains, but their fleets of cars tend to be older and not as well maintained. Check the tyre treads and general upkeep of the vehicle before committing.

Motorcycles can be rented in major towns, and in smaller tourist centres from guest houses and mum-and-dad businesses. Renting a motorcycle in Thailand is relatively easy and a great way to independently tour the countryside. For daily rentals, most businesses will ask that you leave your passport as a deposit. Before renting a motorcycle, check the vehicle's condition and ask for a helmet (which is required by law).

Many tourists are injured riding motorcycles in Thailand

Săhm·lór & Túk-túk

Săhm·lór are three-wheeled pedicabs that are typically found in small towns where traffic is light and old-fashioned ways persist.

The modern era's version of the human-powered săhm·lór is the motorised túk-túk. They're small utility vehicles, powered by screaming engines (usually LPG-powered) and a lot of flash and sparkle.

With either form of transport the fare must be established by bargaining before departure. In tourist centres, túk-túk drivers often grossly overcharge foreigners, so have a sense of how much the fare should be before soliciting a ride. Hotel staff are helpful in providing reasonable fare suggestions.

because they don't know how to handle the vehicle and are unfamiliar with road rules and conditions. Drive slowly, especially when roads are slick, to avoid damage to yourself and to the vehicle, and be sure to have adequate health insurance. If you've never driven a motorcycle before, stick to the smaller 100cc step-through bikes with automatic clutches. Remember to distribute weight as evenly as possible across the frame of the bike to improve handling.

INSURANCE

Thailand requires a minimum of liability insurance for all registered vehicles on the road. The better hire companies include comprehensive coverage for their vehicles. Always verify that a vehicle is insured for liability before signing a rental contract; you should also ask to see the dated insurance documents. If you have an accident while driving an uninsured vehicle, you're in for some major hassles.

ROAD RULES & HAZARDS

Thais drive on the left-hand side of the road (most of the time!). Other than that, just about anything goes, in spite of road signs and speed limits.

The main rule to be aware of is that right of way goes to the bigger vehicle; this is not what it says in the Thai traffic law, but it's the reality. Maximum speed limits are 50km/h on urban roads and 80km/h to 100km/h on most highways – but on any given stretch of highway you'll see various vehicles travelling as slowly as 30km/h and as fast as 150km/h.

Indicators are often used to warn passing drivers about oncoming traffic. A flashing left indicator means it's OK to pass, while a right indicator means that someone's approaching from the other direction. Horns are used to tell other vehicles that the driver plans to pass. When drivers flash their lights, they're telling you not to pass.

LOCAL TRANSPORT

CITY BUS & SŎRNG·TĂA·OU

Bangkok has the largest city-bus system in the country, while Udon Thani and a few other provincial capitals have some city bus services. The etiquette for riding public buses is to wait at a bus stop and hail the vehicle by waving your hand palm-side downward. You typically pay the fare once you've taken a seat or, in some cases, when you disembark.

Elsewhere, public transport is provided by *sŏrng·tăa·ou* (a small pick-up truck outfitted with two facing rows of benches for passengers). They sometimes operate on fixed routes, just like buses, but they may also run a share-taxi service where they pick up passengers going in the same general direction. You can usually hail a *sŏrng·tăa·ou* anywhere along its route and pay the fare when you disembark.

MASS TRANSIT

Bangkok is the only city in Thailand to have an above-ground and underground light-rail public transport system. Known as the Skytrain and the Metro, respectively, both systems have helped to alleviate the capital's notorious traffic jams.

MOTORCYCLE TAXI

Many cities in Thailand have *mor·đeu·sai ráp jâhng* (100cc to 125cc motorcycles) that can be hired, with a driver, for short distances. If you're empty-handed or travelling with a small bag, they can't

Road Distances (Km)

	Aranya Prathet	Ayuthaya	Bangkok	Chiang Mai	Chiang Rai	Chumphon	Hat Yai	Hua Hin	Khon Kaen	Mae Hong Son	Mae Sai	Mukdahan	Nakhon Ratchasima	Nakhon Sawan	Nong Khai	Phitsanulok	Phuket	Sungai Kolok	Surat Thani	Tak	Trat
Ayuthaya	246																				
Bangkok	275	79																			
Chiang Mai	844	607	685																		
Chiang Rai	1014	777	775	191																	
Chumphon	727	531	452	1138	1308																
Hat Yai	1268	1072	993	1679	1849	555															
Hua Hin	458	262	183	869	1039	269	810														
Khon Kaen	432	397	440	604	774	902	1443	633													
Mae Hong Son	1013	767	800	225	406	1298	1839	1029	829												
Mae Sai	1082	845	746	259	68	1376	1917	1107	842	474											
Mukdahan	601	524	680	917	1087	1029	1570	760	313	1142	1155										
Nakhon Ratchasima	239	204	257	744	914	709	1250	440	193	969	982	320									
Nan	816	609	663	323	208	1139	1603	886	558	514	263	1000	760								
Nong Khai	598	563	516	720	890	1068	1609	799	166	945	958	347	359	1755							
Phitsanulok	535	298	420	309	479	829	1370	560	295	578	547	608	435	728	411						
Phuket	1125	929	862	1536	1706	412	474	667	1300	1696	1774	1427	1107	276	1466	1227					
Sungai Kolok	1555	1359	1210	1966	2136	842	287	1097	1730	2126	2204	1857	1357	1462	1896	1657	761				
Surat Thani	927	731	635	1338	1508	214	401	469	1102	1498	1576	1229	909	1288	1268	1029	286	791			
Tak	581	335	435	280	460	866	1407	597	441	432	528	754	544	354	557	146	1264	1694	1066		
Trat	285	392	313	999	1169	765	1306	496	717	1397	1237	886	524	996	883	690	1163	1593	965	727	
Ubon Ratchathani	444	367	620	881	1051	872	1413	603	277	1106	1119	157	163	1091	443	572	1270	1700	1072	707	729

be beaten for transport in a pinch.

TAXI

Bangkok has the most formal system of metered taxis. In other cities, a taxi can be a private vehicle with negotiable rates. You can also travel between cities by taxi but you'll need to negotiate a price as few taxi drivers will run a meter for intercity travel.

TRAIN

Thailand's train system connects the four corners of the country and is most convenient as an alternative to buses for the long journey north to Chiang Mai or south to Surat Thani. The train is also ideal for short trips to Ayuthaya and Lopburi from Bangkok where traffic is a consideration.

The 4500km rail network is operated by the **State Railway of Thailand** (SRT; ☎1690; www.railway.co.th) and covers four main lines: the northern, southern, northeastern and eastern lines. All long-distance trains originate from Bangkok's Hualamphong station.

CLASSES

The SRT operates passenger trains in three classes – 1st, 2nd and 3rd – but each class varies considerably depending on whether you're on an ordinary, rapid or express train.

COSTS

Fares are determined on a base price with surcharges added for distance, class and train type (special express, express, rapid, ordinary). Extra charges are added if the carriage has air-con and for sleeping berths (either upper or lower).

RESERVATIONS

Advance bookings can be made from one to 60 days before your intended date of departure. You can make bookings in person from any train station. Train tickets can also be purchased at travel agencies, which usually add a service charge to the ticket price. If you are planning long-distance train travel from outside the country, you should email the **State Railway of Thailand** (passenger-ser@railway.co.th) at least two weeks before your journey. You will receive an email confirming the booking. Pick up and pay for tickets an hour before leaving at the scheduled departure train station.

It is advisable to make advanced bookings for long-distance sleeper trains between Bangkok and Chiang Mai or from Bangkok to Surat Thani, especially around Songkran in April and peak tourist-season months of December and January.

For short-distance trips you should purchase your ticket at least a day in advance for seats (rather than sleepers).

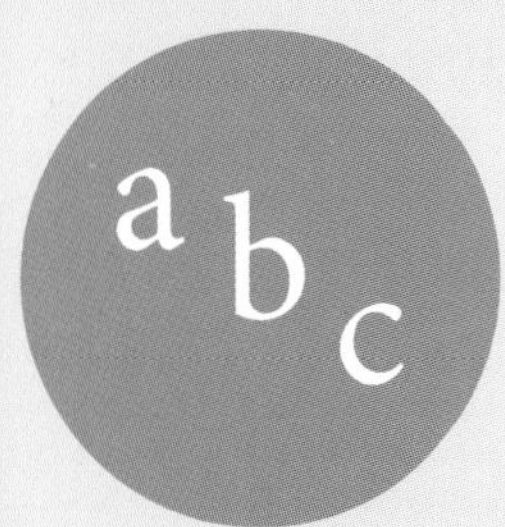

Language

There are different ways of writing Thai in the Roman alphabet – we have chosen one method below. The hyphens indicate syllable breaks within words, and some syllables are further divided with a dot to help you pronounce them. Thai is a tonal language – the accent marks on vowels represent these low, mid, falling, high and rising tones.

Note that after every sentence, men add the polite particle *káp*, and women *ká*.

To enhance your trip with a phrasebook, visit **lonelyplanet.com**. Lonely Planet iPhone phrasebooks are available through the Apple App store.

BASICS

Hello.
สวัสดี — sà-wàt-dee

How are you?
สบายดีไหม — sà-bai dee măi

I'm fine.
สบายดีครับ/ค่า — sà·bai dee kráp/kâ (m/f)

Excuse me.
ขออภัย — kŏr à-pai

Yes./No.
ใช่/ไม่ — châi/mâi

Thank you.
ขอบคุณ — kòrp kun

You're welcome.
ยินดี — yin dee

Do you speak English?
คุณพูดภาษาอังกฤษได้ไหม — kun pôot pah-săh ang-grìt dâi măi

I don't understand.
ผม/ดิฉันไม่เข้าใจ — pŏm/dì-chăn mâi kôw jai (m/f)

How much is this?
เท่าไร — tôw-rai

Can you lower the price?
ลดราคาได้ไหม — lót rah-kah dâi măi

ACCOMMODATION

Where's a hotel?
โรงแรมอยู่ที่ไหน — rohng raam yòo têe năi

Do you have a single/double room?
มีห้องเดี่ยว/เตียงคู่ไหม — mee hôrng dèe·o/đee·ang kôo măi

EATING & DRINKING

I'd like (the menu), please.
ขอ (รายการอาหาร) หน่อย — kŏr (rai gahn ah-hăhn) nòy

What would you recommend?
คุณแนะนำอะไรบ้าง — kun náa-nam à-rai bâhng

That was delicious.
อร่อยมาก — à-ròy mâhk

Cheers!
ไชโย — chai-yoh

Please bring the bill/check.
ขอบิลหน่อย — kŏr bin nòy

I don't eat ...
ผม/ดิฉันไม่กิน ... — pŏm/dì-chăn mâi gin . . . (m/f)

eggs	ไข่	kài
fish	ปลา	Ƀlah
nuts	ถั่ว	tòo·a
red meat	เนื้อแดง	néu·a daang

EMERGENCIES

I'm ill.
ผม/ดิฉันป่วย — pŏm/dì-chăn Ƀòo·ay (m/f)

Help!
ช่วยด้วย — chôo·ay dôo·ay

Call a doctor!
เรียกหมอหน่อย — rêe·ak mŏr nòy

Call the police!
เรียกตำรวจหน่อย — rêe·ak đam·ròo·at nòy

Where are the toilets?
ห้องน้ำอยู่ที่ไหน — hôrng nám yòo têe năi

DIRECTIONS

Where's (a market/restaurant)?
(ตลาด/ร้านอาหาร) อยู่ที่ไหน — (đà-làht/ráhn ah-hăhn) yòo têe năi

What's the address?
ที่อยู่คืออะไร — têe yòo keu à-rai

Could you please write it down?
เขียนลงให้ได้ไหม — kĕe·an long hâi dâi măi

Can you show me (on the map)?
ให้ดู (ในแผนที่) ได้ไหม — hâi doo (nai păan têe) dâi măi

Behind the Scenes

Our Readers

Many thanks to the travellers who used the last edition and wrote to us with helpful hints, useful advice and interesting anecdotes:

Martin Bogsrud, Inbal Frankenstein, Toby Frankenstein, Rowan Gibbons, David Hargreaves, Michael Hershman, Robin Jones, Rosalind Kuan, John Tomalin

Author Thanks

CHINA WILLIAMS

Thanks to Nong who was a wonderful second mother to Felix and a good 'wife' to me; Lisa on Ko Chang; Chris and Gae in Hua Hin; and Ted and Mark in Pattaya. Felix sends his love to Kan, Goong and Pa too. More thanks to Mason, Jane, Joe, Kong and Ruengsang. And to my husband who survived so long without us. Final shout-out to the co-authors and the LP crew.

Acknowledgments

Climate map data adapted from Peel MC, Finlayson BL & McMahon TA (2007) 'Updated World Map of the Köppen-Geiger Climate Classification', *Hydrology and Earth System Sciences*, 11, 163344.

Cover photographs: Front: Long-tail boats, Krabi Province, Nicholas Pitt; Back: Floating market, Bangkok, Greg Elms, Lonely Planet Images. Many of the images in this guide are available for licensing from Lonely Planet Images: www.lonelyplanetimages.com.

This Book

This guidebook was commissioned in Lonely Planet's Melbourne office, and produced by the following:

Commissioning Editors Shawn Low, Ilaria Walker
Coordinating Editor Gabrielle Innes
Coordinating Cartographer Jacqueline Nguyen
Coordinating Layout Designer Wendy Wright
Managing Editors Bruce Evans, Anna Metcalfe
Managing Cartographer David Connolly, Adrian Persoglia
Managing Layout Designer Jane Hart
Assisting Editors Janice Bird, Dianne Schallmeiner
Assisting Cartographer Alex Leung
Assisting Layout Designers Yvonne Bischofberger, Virginia Moreno
Cover Research Naomi Parker
Internal Image Research Rebecca Skinner
Language Content Annelies Mertens
Thanks to Ryan Evans, Joshua Geoghegan, Chris Girdler Laura Jane, Yvonne Kirk, Trent Paton, Peter Shields, Laura Stansfeld, Gerard Walker

SEND US YOUR FEEDBACK

We love to hear from travellers – your comments keep us on our toes and help make our books better. Our well-travelled team reads every word on what you loved or loathed about this book. Although we cannot reply individually to postal submissions, we always guarantee that your feedback goes straight to the appropriate authors, in time for the next edition. Each person who sends us information is thanked in the next edition, and the most useful submissions are rewarded with a free book.

Visit **lonelyplanet.com/contact** to submit your updates and suggestions or to ask for help. Our award-winning website also features inspirational travel stories, news and discussions.

Note: We may edit, reproduce and incorporate your comments in Lonely Planet products such as guidebooks, websites and digital products, so let us know if you don't want your comments reproduced or your name acknowledged. For a copy of our privacy policy visit lonelyplanet.com/privacy.

NOTES

NOTES

Index

D

E

F

G

H

I

J

K

000 Map pages

L

M

N

O

P

Q

R

S

000 Map pages

T

U

V

W

Y

Z

How to Use This Book

These symbols will help you find the listings you want:

- Sights
- Beaches
- Activities
- Courses
- Tours
- Festivals & Events
- Sleeping
- Eating
- Drinking
- Entertainment
- Shopping
- Information/ Transport

These symbols give you the vital information for each listing:

- Telephone Numbers
- Opening Hours
- Parking
- Nonsmoking
- Air-Conditioning
- Internet Access
- Wi-Fi Access
- Swimming Pool
- Vegetarian Selection
- English-Language Menu
- Family-Friendly
- Pet-Friendly
- Bus
- Ferry
- Metro
- Subway
- London Tube
- Tram
- Train

Reviews are organised by author preference.

Look out for these icons:

FREE No payment required

A green or sustainable option

Our authors have nominated these places as demonstrating a strong commitment to sustainability – for example by supporting local communities and producers, operating in an environmentally friendly way, or supporting conservation projects.

Map Legend

Sights
- Beach
- Buddhist
- Castle
- Christian
- Hindu
- Islamic
- Jewish
- Monument
- Museum/Gallery
- Ruin
- Winery/Vineyard
- Zoo
- Other Sight

Activities, Courses & Tours
- Diving/Snorkelling
- Canoeing/Kayaking
- Skiing
- Surfing
- Swimming/Pool
- Walking
- Windsurfing
- Other Activity/ Course/Tour

Sleeping
- Sleeping
- Camping

Eating
- Eating

Drinking
- Drinking
- Cafe

Entertainment
- Entertainment

Shopping
- Shopping

Information
- Bank
- Embassy/ Consulate
- Hospital/Medical
- Internet
- Police
- Post Office
- Telephone
- Toilet
- Tourist Information
- Other Information

Transport
- Airport
- Border Crossing
- Bus
- Cable Car/ Funicular
- Cycling
- Ferry
- Metro
- Monorail
- Parking
- Petrol Station
- Taxi
- Train/Railway
- Tram
- Other Transport

Routes
- Tollway
- Freeway
- Primary
- Secondary
- Tertiary
- Lane
- Unsealed Road
- Plaza/Mall
- Steps
- Tunnel
- Pedestrian Overpass
- Walking Tour
- Walking Tour Detour
- Path

Geographic
- Hut/Shelter
- Lighthouse
- Lookout
- Mountain/Volcano
- Oasis
- Park
- Pass
- Picnic Area
- Waterfall

Population
- Capital (National)
- Capital (State/Province)
- City/Large Town
- Town/Village

Boundaries
- International
- State/Province
- Disputed
- Regional/Suburb
- Marine Park
- Cliff
- Wall

Hydrography
- River/Creek
- Intermittent River
- Swamp/Mangrove
- Reef
- Canal
- Water
- Dry/Salt/ Intermittent Lake
- Glacier

Areas
- Beach/Desert
- Cemetery (Christian)
- Cemetery (Other)
- Park/Forest
- Sportsground
- Sight (Building)
- Top Sight (Building)

CELESTE BRASH

Phuket & the Andaman Coast Celeste first arrived in Thailand as a student of Thai language, history and culture at Chiang Mai University. She's come back to the country many times since and has done the gamut from wild nights on Ko Phang-Ngan to weeks of silence at Wat Suanmok. Her award-winning travel stories have appeared in *Travelers' Tales* books and she's been published in a slew of newspapers and magazines from the *LA Times* to *Islands* magazine. Celeste has lost count of how many Lonely Planet guides she's contributed to but her heart is irrevocably stuck on Southeast Asia, and Thailand is her first love. When not dragging her husband and two children to exotic places, she and her family live in Portland, Oregon. Find her on the web at www.celestebrash.com.

Read more about Celeste at:
lonelyplanet.com/members/celestebrash

AUSTIN BUSH

Bangkok, Northern Thailand, Deep South Austin came to Thailand in 1998 on a language scholarship at Chiang Mai University. The lure of city life and a need for employment and spicy food eventually led Austin to Bangkok. And city life, employment and spicy food have managed to keep him there since. But escaping Bangkok, particularly for the mountains of northern Thailand, is one of his favourite things about contributing to this particular guide. A native of Oregon and a freelance writer and photographer who often focuses on food, samples of Austin's work can be seen at www.austinbushphotography.com.

ALAN MURPHY

Chiang Mai Province Alan discovered Southeast Asia sometime in the mid-1990s when he travelled extensively around the region. Since then he has returned to live and work as a volunteer in Chiang Mai, advocating for the rights of migrant workers around the Mekong region. Among other journalistic endeavours, Alan has written and updated guidebooks for Lonely Planet since 1999, and loves the opportunity to get under the skin of a new destination. This was his first time working on the *Thailand* guide and he was very happy to be assigned Chiang Mai – a city with a real heart and a fantastic diversity of people. It seems more like home every time he returns.

BRANDON PRESSER

Ko Samui & the Lower Gulf Growing up in a land where bear hugs are taken literally, this wanderlust-y Canadian always craved swaying palms and golden sand. A trek across Southeast Asia as a teenager was the clincher — he was hooked, returning year after year to scuba dive, suntan, and savour spoonfuls of spicy sôm·đam (spicy papaya salad). After leaving his job at the Louvre, Brandon picked up his pen and rucksack, and became a full-time freelance travel writer. He's since contributed to over 20 Lonely Planet titles from *Iceland* to *Thailand* and many 'lands' in between.

Our Story

A beat-up old car, a few dollars in the pocket and a sense of adventure. In 1972 that's all Tony and Maureen Wheeler needed for the trip of a lifetime – across Europe and Asia overland to Australia. It took several months, and at the end – broke but inspired – they sat at their kitchen table writing and stapling together their first travel guide, *Across Asia on the Cheap*. Within a week they'd sold 1500 copies. Lonely Planet was born.

Today, Lonely Planet has offices in Melbourne, London and Oakland, with more than 600 staff and writers. We share Tony's belief that 'a great guidebook should do three things: inform, educate and amuse'.

Our Writers

CHINA WILLIAMS

Coordinating Author, Hua Hin & Eastern Seaboard China first came to Thailand to teach English in Surin way back in 1997, a few months prior to the country's currency crisis. Since then she has shuttled across the Pacific to work on various Thailand guidebooks. This is her third trip with her son, who is now four years old. Be assured that all the beaches in the Upper Gulf and Eastern Seaboard have been kid-tested and mother-approved, including the wholesome bits of prostitute-city Pattaya. China lives in Catonsville, Maryland (USA), with her husband, Matt, and son, Felix.

MARK BEALES

Central Thailand After receiving a scholarship to study journalism, Mark worked as a reporter for 13 years. In 2004 he swapped the chilly shores of England for the sunnier coasts of Thailand. As well as being a freelance writer, Mark has worked as a teacher and TV presenter. Highlights on this trip included waking up to a giant hornbill attempting to prise open the door of his tree-top cabin and meeting an impossibly cute one-day-old elephant in Ayuthaya. When Mark isn't on the road, he teaches English at an international school in Rayong. For more on Mark's work, visit www.markbeales.com.

Read more about Mark at:
lonelyplanet.com/members/markbeales

TIM BEWER

Northeastern Thailand While growing up, Tim didn't travel much except for the obligatory pilgrimage to Disney World and an annual summer week at the lake. He's spent most of his adult life making up for this, and he has since visited more than 70 countries, including most of those in Southeast Asia. After university he worked as a legislative assistant before quitting to backpack around West Africa. It was during this trip that he decided to become a freelance travel writer and photographer, and he's been at it ever since. When he isn't shouldering a backpack somewhere he lives in Khon Kaen, Thailand, where he jointly runs the Isan Explorer (www.isanexplorer.com) tour company.

Read more about Tim at:
lonelyplanet.com/members/timbewer

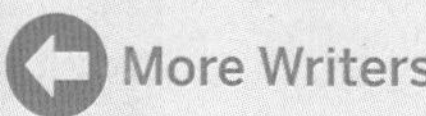
More Writers

Published by Lonely Planet Publications Pty Ltd
ABN 36 005 607 983
2nd edition – April 2012
ISBN 978 1 74220 114 6

10 9 8 7 6 5 4 3 2 1
Printed in China